IRIS UNIVERSITY REVIEW

A JOURNAL OF IRISH STUDIES

Editor
Emilie Pine

Associate Editor
Lucy Collins

Books Editor
Paul Delaney

SPECIAL ISSUE
Golden Jubilee: Irish Studies Now

Volume 50 Number 1   **Spring/Summer 2020**

Subscription rates for 2020

Two issues per year, published in May and November

		Tier	UK	EUR	RoW	N. America
Institutions	Print & Online	1	£62.00	£70.00	£74.00	$122.00
		2	£79.00	£87.00	£91.00	$151.00
		3	£97.00	£105.00	£109.00	$180.00
		4	£117.00	£125.00	£129.00	$214.00
		5	£133.00	£141.00	£145.00	$240.00
	Online	1	£52.00	£52.00	£52.00	$85.00
		2	£66.00	£66.00	£66.00	$109.00
		3	£81.00	£81.00	£81.00	$134.00
		4	£100.00	£100.00	£100.00	$165.00
		5	£112.00	£112.00	£112.00	$185.00
	Additional print volumes		£55.00	£63.00	£67.00	$112.00
	Single issues		£43.00	£48.00	£50.00	$83.00
Individuals	Print		£32.50	£40.00	£44.50	$75.00
	Online		£32.50	£32.50	£32.50	$54.50
	Print & Online		£41.50	£49.00	£53.50	$89.50
	Back issues/single copies		£18.00	£22.00	£24.50	$41.00

How to order

Subscriptions can be accepted for complete volumes only. Print prices include packing and airmail for subscribers outside the UK. Volumes back to the year 2000 are included in online prices. Print back volumes will be charged at the current volume subscription rate.

All orders must be accompanied by the correct payment. You can pay by cheque in Pounds Sterling or US Dollars, bank transfer, Direct Debit or Credit/Debit Card. The individual rate applies only when a subscription is paid for with a personal cheque, credit card or credit/debit card. Please make your cheques payable to Edinburgh University Press Ltd. Sterling cheques must be drawn on a UK bank account.

Orders for subscriptions and back issues can be placed by telephone, on +44(0)131 650 4196, by fax on +44(0)131 662 3286, using your Visa or Mastercard credit cards, or by email on journals@eup.ed.ac.uk. Alternatively, you can use the online order form at www.euppublishing.com/iur/page/subscribe.

Requests for sample copies, subscription enquiries, and changes of address should be sent to Journals Department, Edinburgh University Press Ltd, The Tun – Holyrood Road, 12(2f) Jackson's Entry, Edinburgh EH8 8PJ, UK; email: journals@eup.ed.ac.uk

IASIL MEMBERSHIP

Subscription to the journal comes with membership of the International Association for the Study of Irish Literatures (IASIL). Details of IASIL membership can be found at www.iasil.org

Advertising Advertisements are welcomed and rates are available on request. Advertisers should send their enquiries to Journals Marketing (email: JournalMarketing@eup.ed.ac.uk).

Contents

Abstracts

Matthew Kennedy, Some Things are Worth Losing to Become./? Trans Masculinity | Queer Autoethnography | Where theory and the Body Collide

This essay seeks to interrogate what it means to become a legible man as someone who held space as a multiplicity of identities before realising and negotiating my trans manhood. It raises the question of how we as trans people account for the shifting nature of our subjectivity, our embodiment and, indeed, our bodies. This essay locates this dialogue on the site of my body where I have placed many tattoos, which both speak to and inform my understanding of myself as a trans man in Ireland. Queer theory functions as a focal tool within this essay as I question family, home, transition, sexuality, and temporality through a queer autoethnographic reading of the tattoos on my body. This essay pays homage to the intersecting traditions within queer theory and auto-ethnography. It honours the necessity for the indefinable, for alternative knowledge production and representations, for the space we need in order to become, to allow for the uncertainty of our becoming.

Deirdre Flynn, On Being Precarious

In this essay, I reflect on my experience of part-time, fixed term, zero-hour, short-term, and unpaid contracts in academia. Precarious contracts are one of the biggest challenges facing our industry as neo-liberal values rule our institutions, impacting our teaching, research, and quality of life.

Emma Creedon, Disability, Identity, and Early Twentieth-Century Irish Drama

This essay assesses the role of physical disability in early twentieth-century Irish dramatic literature. In particular, by focusing on such plays as W.B. Yeats's *On Baile's Strand* (1903) and the character of Johnny Boyle

Irish University Review 50.1 (2020): v–xi
DOI: 10.3366/iur.2020.0423
© Edinburgh University Press
www.euppublishing.com/iur

in Sean O'Casey's *Juno and the Paycock* (1924), it critiques the tradition of identifying characters with disabilities solely by their physical impairment and exploiting disability as metaphor; physical disability has been historically employed as a synecdoche for a thwarted morality, or blindness as an allegory for prophecy. However, scholarly criticisms of the Social Model of Disability have demonstrated how disability can be reappropriated to reconceptualize notions of bodily normalcy. Furthermore, this essay suggests that the convention of "cripping up", an industry term describing the practice of an able-bodied actor playing a character with a physical disability, contributes to the marginalization of those with physical disability in Irish culture. The result is the potential degradation of the disabled body, a stylized performance evoking vaudevillian conventions; performance thus engenders belief in stereotype.

Michael Pierse, Ireland's Working-class Literature: Neglected Themes, Amphibian Academics, and the Challenges Ahead

Irish working-class history, culture, and literature are attracting increasing academic interest. With the publication of *A History of Irish Working-Class Writing* (2017), Declan Kiberd could write that its focus on 'an astonishing range of writing – from work-songs and political rhymes to poetry and government reports, from novels and plays to biographies by or about working people', would 'set many of the terms of cultural debate in the decade to come'. This essay asks a number of timely questions in that regard: What is the likely shape of that future debate, in terms of class and culture in Ireland, and what are the lacunae that will guide research and publishing priorities for those who engage with it in academia and the arts? What has been achieved in terms of the recent scholarly inquiry into working-class writing and what are that inquiry's blindspots and limitations? The international contexts, historical breadth, categorical limitations, and institutional and societal challenges are all surveyed in this necessarily short sketch of some of the major issues.

Lisa Fitzpatrick, Contemporary Feminist Protest in Ireland: #MeToo in Irish Theatre

This essay draws upon the work of Judith Butler, Sara Ahmed, and Germaine Greer to consider the #MeToo movement and its reflection in the work of the author's students and the scandal at Dublin's Gate Theatre. Taking competing conceptions of freedom as they are materialised in this activism as it starting point, the essay questions intergenerational feminist ideas about the nature of freedom and its relationship to fear and to harassment. The essay returns to the feminist principle that 'the personal is the political' to reflect on women's lived experiences of threat and harassment, and young women's resistance to their objectification.

Anne Mulhall, The Ends of Irish Studies? On Whiteness, Academia, and Activism

This essay reflects on the meaning of 'the political' in relation to academic work, in particular Irish Studies and literary scholarship. Speaking from the standpoint of my involvements as an ally-activist in grassroots migrant justice organising and my work as an academic, the essay explores the intersections, conflicts, and contradictions at play at the intersections between academia and activism, the literary and the political, representation and self-representation, with a particular focus on the work of BAME writers, including writers and activists in the asylum seeker movement.

Chiamaka Enyi-Amadi and Emma Penney, Are We Doing Diversity Justice? A Critical Exchange

This critical exchange is based on a conversation between the authors which took place during the *Irish University Review* Roundtable Discussion: Displacing the Canon (2019 IASIL Conference, Trinity College Dublin). As authors we give first-hand accounts of our experience writing, editing, and teaching in Ireland, attempting to draw out concerns we have for the future of Irish literature and Irish Studies that specifically relate to race. The conversation here suggests that race directly impacts what we consider valuable in our literary culture. We both insist on decentring universalism as a governing literary critical concept and insist on the urgent application of critical race analysis to the construction of literary value systems in Ireland.

Cóilín Parsons, Oceans Apart: Amitav Ghosh, John Millington Synge, and Weak Comparison

This article compares John Millington Synge's *The Aran Islands* (1907) and Amitav Ghosh's *In An Antique Land* (1992), travelogues, histories, and anthropological investigations of maritime societies. Both books tell of a world marked by syncretism and synthesis, and deep and unbroken time, and their narratives are fractured, fragmented, temporally promiscuous, and logically paratactical. In comparing these two books, the article asks what it means, and what it could yield, to read together two accounts of oceanic lives from opposite ends of the twentieth century and from distinct continents and oceans? What emerges is the outline of a 'speculative practice of weak comparison' that allows us to extend how we understand the contexts of an object of study called 'Irish' literature. By rethinking the scale of Irish literature, the article concludes, we necessarily decentre Ireland, and find opportunities to disaggregate Irish literature and its Irishness, setting a new agenda for comparative studies of Ireland that range widely in space and time.

Patricia Kennon, Reflecting Realities in Twenty-First-Century Irish Children's and Young Adult Literature

This article explores the evolution of Irish youth literature over the last four decades and these texts' engagement with cultural, political, and social transformations in Irish society. The adult desire to protect young people's 'innocence' from topics and experiences deemed dark or deviant tended to dominate late twentieth-century Irish youth literature. However, the turn of the millennium witnessed a growing capacity and willingness for Irish children's and young-adult authors to problematize hegemonic power systems, address social injustices, and present unsentimental, empowering narratives of youth agency. Post-Celtic Tiger youth writing by Irish women has advocated for the complexity of Irish girlhoods while Irish Gothic literature for teenagers has disrupted complacent narratives of Irish society in its anatomy of systemic violence, trauma, and adolescent girls' embodiment. Although queer identities and sexualities have been increasingly recognised and represented, Irish youth literature has yet to confront histories and practices of White privilege in past and present Irish culture and to inclusively represent the diverse, intersectional realities, identities, and experiences of twenty-first-century Irish youth.

Margaret Kelleher, Irish Culture(s): Hyphenated, Bilingual, or Plurilingual?

This article begins with a review of the usage of the term 'Anglo-Irish' (including the background to the establishment of the Chair of Anglo-Irish Literature and Drama in UCD in 1966), and examines the critical fortunes of an alternative term, 'Hiberno-English'. In the light of both contemporary creative practice and historical antecedents, it explores the possibilities extended by reconceptualising Irish literature and culture as bilingual (even plurilingual): not only as a 'backward look' but also as a means of securing more hospitable and open fora for cultural creativity in our present.

Éilís Ní Dhuibhne Almqvist, Reflections on Memoir as a New Genre

The article opens with a brief overview of memoir writing in Ireland, with special reference to early twentieth-century regional memoirs in the Irish language. The validity of the view that memoirs are much more numerous now than in the past is assessed. Various categories of memoir are described, as is the relationship between fiction, auto-biography, and memoir. Finally, the author recounts her own experience of writing a memoir after many decades of writing fiction. She comments on the relationship of fiction and memoir in her own writing experience, and on differences between the genres as regards process, publication, and reaction.

Eric Falci, Rethinking Form (Yet Again) in Contemporary Irish Poetry

This essay provides a reconsideration of the centrality of form in discussions of Irish poetry and suggests ways of revivifying those discussions by moving away from the tired dyad of mainstream lyric and experimental (or alternative or innovative) poetry. Moving through examinations of Paul Muldoon, Medbh McGuckian, Ciaran Carson, Sinéad Morrissey, Maurice Scully, and Catherine Walsh, this essay aims to pivot the conversation about Irish poetry so that more attention might be paid to the concrete textures and practices of contemporary poets such that we are better able to see and describe the implications and ramifications of their work.

Marie-Louise Coolahan, New Technologies of Research and Digital Interpretation for Early Modern Irish Studies

This article outlines the vastly expanded ecosystem of digital projects and resources of use to researchers of early modern Ireland. It traces the evolution of objectives and practice from the earliest goal of making texts visible and accessible, through to the creation of resources that added value to digitised texts and, most recently, the aggregation of resources by making them interoperable (able to speak to each other), as well as enabling users to extract and manipulate data themselves. The tumult of sixteenth- and seventeenth-century Ireland – reiterated cycles of warfare, colonial encroachment and resistance, religious reformation, plural ethnicities – means that such research has to be interdisciplinary, drawing in not only historicist and literary approaches but also language specialists, palaeographers, archaeologists, and geographers. Digital modes of representation have opened up this interdisciplinarity, which remains to be fully exploited by researchers. The creation of resources for the study of early modern Ireland should itself be considered an act of research-in-practice. The article concludes by considering the challenges of sustainability, open access, discoverability, and autodidactism.

Lucy Collins, Hidden Collections: The Value of Literary Archives

Archives play an important role in preserving literary history, but they also have the potential to change that history, by making the papers of Irish writers, editors, and publishers available, as well as by documenting larger literary and social moments. By facilitating the preservation and arrangement of these materials, archivists support new ways of interpreting and communicating historical and artistic processes to a wide audience. Archives are themselves interesting subjects of study, helping us to understand how national traditions and intellectual priorities evolve. This essay explores the value of Irish literary archives to the contemporary scholar, and considers some of the factors that shape a writer's legacy.

Dianne Hall and Ronan McDonald, Irish Studies in Australasia

This article gives an overview, and brief history, of Irish studies in Australia and New Zealand, within an academic context and beyond. It surveys major publications and formal initiatives, but also accounts for why Irish studies has been less vibrant in Australian than other Anglophone countries in the Irish diaspora. The Irish in Australia have a distinct history. Yet, in recent years and in popular understanding, they have also sometimes been absorbed into 'white' or Anglo-Celtic Australia. This makes their claims to distinctiveness less pressing in a society seeking to come to terms with its migrant and dispossessed indigenous populations.

Andrew Fitzsimons, The English Language Issue: Irish Studies in Japan

This essay seeks to give an overview of Irish Studies in Japan. I outline the institutional context and climate within which Irish Studies scholars operate in Japan, present a brief account of the history and achievements of, and specific challenges faced by, IASIL Japan, and finally, look very briefly at the problems posed in Japan by the primacy of an English-language, Anglo-American paradigm in academic discourse.

Ondřej Pilný, Irish Studies in Continental Europe

This essay seeks to give an overview of the study of Ireland and its culture in continental Europe from the late eighteenth century up to the present day. It discusses the early interest in Ossianic poetry, Celtic philology, and travel writing, together with the internationalist standing of modernist writers such as Joyce and Beckett as the roots of how and under which rubric Irish culture has been received by the general public and studied at universities, and then proceeds to examine the current state of Irish Studies and its prospects on the European continent.

Beatriz Kopschitz Bastos, Irish Studies in South America

This essay seeks to give an overview of the Irish presence, the institutional context, and the singular nature of Irish Studies in South America, historically and today. It presents an insight into some of the major advances and the principal themes of Irish Studies in this non-Anglophone environment: translation; performance; film studies; migration and diaspora studies; comparative studies; teaching. It thus considers the contribution of this particular field – Irish Studies in South America – in the wider context of transnational and comparative cultural analysis.

Notes on Contributors

JOHN BRANNIGAN is Professor of English and Head of the School of English, Drama and Film in University College Dublin. He is the author of several books, including *Archipelagic Modernism: Literature in the Irish and British Isles, 1890–1970* (Edinburgh UP, 2015) and *Race in Modern Irish Literature and Culture* (Edinburgh UP, 2009). He was editor of the *Irish University Review* from 2010 to 2016.

LUCY COLLINS is Associate Professor of English at University College Dublin. Books include *Poetry by Women in Ireland: A Critical Anthology 1870–1970* (2012) and a monograph, *Contemporary Irish Women Poets: Memory and Estrangement* (2015), both from Liverpool University Press. She has published widely on contemporary poets from Ireland, Britain, and America, and is co-founder of the Irish Poetry Reading Archive, a national digital repository.

MARIE-LOUISE COOLAHAN is a Professor of English at the National University of Ireland Galway. She is the author of *Women, Writing, and Language in Early Modern Ireland* (2010), multiple book chapters, and articles in journals including *The Seventeenth Century, Critical Quarterly,* and *Early Modern Women*. She has co-edited *Katherine Philips: Form, Reception, and Literary Contexts* (with Gillian Wright, 2018). Most recently, she has edited a special issue of the *Journal of Medieval and Early Modern Studies*: 'The Cultural Dynamics of Reception'. She is Principal Investigator of the ERC-funded project, *RECIRC: The Reception and Circulation of Early Modern Women's Writing, 1550–1700* (recirc. nuigalway.ie).

EMMA CREEDON is an Irish Research Council Government of Ireland Postdoctoral Fellow based at the Moore Institute at the National University of Ireland, Galway. She is currently working on a project entitled 'Performing Physical Disability: Challenging Representations of the Body in Modern and Contemporary Irish Drama'. She is the author of *Sam Shepard and the Aesthetics of Performance* (Palgrave Macmillan, 2015), the co-editor of *The Theatre and Films of Mark O'Rowe* (Carysfort Press, 2015), and her research has also been published

Irish University Review 50.1 (2020): xii–xviii
DOI: 10.3366/iur.2020.0424
© Edinburgh University Press
www.euppublishing.com/iur

in *Journal of Contemporary Drama in English* and *Word and Text: A Journal of Literary Studies and Linguistics.*

CHIAMAKA ENYI-AMADI is a writer, editor, performer, and arts facilitator. She chaired the panel at 'Are We Doing Diversity Justice', along with co-organiser Dr Emma Penny for IASIL 2019 Conference. Her work is published in *Poetry International* 125, *Poetry Ireland Review* 129, RTÉ Poetry Programme, Smithereens Press, *The Bohemyth, The Irish Times, The Art of the Glimpse: 100 Irish Short Stories* (Head of Zeus 2020, edited by Sinéad Gleeson) and *Writing Home: The 'New Irish' Poets* (Dedalus Press, 2019, co-edited by Chiamaka Enyi-Amadi & Pat Boran). She was the 2019 recipient of the Poetry Ireland Access Cúirt Bursary. She blogs on WordPress and tweets @AmadiEnyi.

ERIC FALCI is Professor of English at the University of California, Berkeley. He is the author of *Continuity and Change in Irish Poetry, 1966–2010* (2012) and the *Cambridge Introduction to British Poetry, 1945–2010* (2015), as well as a number of essays on twentieth and twenty-first-century Irish and British poetry. Along with Paige Reynolds, he is the co-editor of *Irish Literature in Transition, 1980–2020,* to be published in 2020 by Cambridge University Press.

LISA FITZPATRICK is Senior Lecturer in Drama at University of Ulster, and course director for the MA in Contemporary Performance Practice. She completed her PhD at University of Toronto. Her work is mainly concerned with gender, violence, and conflict, and her monograph *Rape on the Contemporary Stage* investigates the representation of sexual violence in contemporary British and Irish theatre. She is currently working with Kabosh Theatre Company on sexual violence and conflict. She co-convenes the Feminist Working Group for IFTR, and is a founding member of the Irish Society for Theatre Research.

ANDREW FITZSIMONS is a Professor in the Department of English Language and Cultures at Gakushuin University, Tokyo. His publications include *The Sea of Disappointment: Thomas Kinsella's Pursuit of the Real* (UCD Press, 2008); *Thomas Kinsella: Prose Occasions 1951–2006,* ed. (Carcanet, 2009); *What the Sky Arranges* (Isobar Press, 2013); *A Fire in the Head* (Isobar Press, 2014); and *The Sunken Keep* (Isobar Press, 2017), a translation of Giuseppe Ungaretti's *Il Porto Sepolto.*

DEIRDRE FLYNN is a lecturer in twenty-first-century literature at Mary Immaculate College, University of Limerick. She has worked in UCD, NUI Galway, and UL. Her research interests include World

Literature, Literary Urban Studies, Postmodernism, Haruki Murakami, Irish Studies, Theatre, and Feminism. She has written, directed, and acted for theatre and worked as a journalist for over seven years. She is currently preparing a monograph on Haruki Murakami and has published two co-edited collections on Irish Literature (Palgrave). From 2015–2017 she was the Chair of Sibéal, the gender and feminist network.

ANNE FOGARTY is Professor of James Joyce Studies at University College Dublin, Director of the Dublin James Joyce Sumer School, and co-editor with Luca Crispi of the *Dublin James Joyce Journal*. She has co-edited, with Timothy Martin, *Joyce on the Threshold* (2005), with Morris Beja, *Bloomsday 100: Essays on "Ulysses"* (2009), and with Fran O'Rourke, *Voices on Joyce* (2015). She has published widely on aspects of twentieth and twenty-first century Irish writing, particularly on women authors. She is currently working on a new edition of *Dubliners* for Penguin; a collection of essays, co-edited with Marisol Morales Ladrón, on Deirdre Madden is forthcoming from Manchester University Press.

DIANNE HALL is Associate Professor of History at Victoria University, Melbourne. She has been one of the editors of *Australasian Journal of Irish Studies* and a member of the committee of the Irish Studies Association of Australia and New Zealand since 2006. Her research interests are in the history of gender, violence, and religion in early modern Ireland and in the history of the Irish in Australia. She has published articles on these topics in *Gender and History, Irish Historical Studies, Journal of Religious History,* and *History Australia*. Her most recent monograph with Elizabeth Malcolm is *A New History of the Irish in Australia* (NewSouth Publishing, 2018).

MAURICE HARMON, Emeritus Professor of Anglo-Irish Literature and Drama at University College Dublin, academic and poet, founder editor of the Irish University Review. He has published studies of prose writers from William Carleton to Mary Lavin and Seán O'Faoláin and of poets from Patrick Kavanagh and Austin Clarke to Thomas Kinsella and Seamus Heaney. His *Selected Essays*, 2006, provides readings of Irish writers over three centuries. In 2008 Irish Academic Press published his study of Thomas Kinsella as poet and translator, *Thomas Kinsella: Designing for the Exact Needs*. Dr Harmon's reputation as poet has grown with the publication of *Hoops of Holiness*, 2016, his sixth collection.

MARGARET KELLEHER is Professor and Chair of Anglo-Irish Literature and Drama at University College Dublin. Recent publications include *The Maamtrasna Murders: Language, Life and Death in*

Nineteenth-Century Ireland, published by University College Dublin Press and awarded the Michael J. Durkan Prize for Books on Language and Culture by the American Conference of Irish Studies in 2019. She is Chair of the Irish Film Institute and UCD academic lead for the Museum of Literature Ireland (MoLI), a collaboration between UCD and the National Library of Ireland, open to the public at Newman House, St Stephen's Green.

MATTHEW KENNEDY is a poet, activist, and novice boxer from Cork. He has been involved in queer activism pertaining to trans liberation, trans healthcare, and reproductive justice for the past five years and is dedicated to anti-capitalist grassroots action. His undergraduate degree is in History and English from University College Cork, his MA degree is in Gender Studies, and his current PhD is within University College Dublin in the School of Social Policy, Social Work, and Social Justice. His masters thesis involved a queer autoethnographic exploration of his own trans masculinity and catalysed his PhD in Transnormativity and the Everyday Lifeworlds of Young Trans Individuals in Ireland. He is a recipient of the Irish Research Council Employment-Based Scholarship and his employment partner is BeLonG To Youth Services, Ireland's National LGBTI+ youth service where he acts as the NGO's Policy and Research officer.

PATRICIA KENNON is a lecturer in children's and young adult literature and culture in the School of Education, Maynooth University, Ireland. She is the president of the Irish Society for the Study of Children's Literature, a former editor in chief and features editor of *Inis: the Children's Books Ireland* magazine, and a former president of iBbY Ireland, the Irish national section of the International Board on Books for Young People. Her research interests include young-adult science fiction, gender and sexualities in youth literature and popular culture, and intercultural education.

BEATRIZ KOPSCHITZ BASTOS is a faculty member in the Post-graduate Programme in English at the Federal University of Santa Catarina, production director of *Cia Ludens*, a Brazilian theatre company dedicated to Irish theatre, and an executive member of IASIL. Her publications, as editor or co-editor, include: *Ilha do Desterro 58 – Contemporary Irish Theatre* (2010); the bilingual series *Ireland on Film: Screenplays and Critical Contexts* (2011-present); *Coleção Brian Friel* (Hedra, 2013); *Cole ção Tom Murphy* (Iluminuras, 2019); *Vidas irlandesas: o cinema de Alan Gilsenan em contexto* (Insular, 2019); *Ilha do Desterro 73.2 – The Irish Theatrical Diaspora* (2020); and *Contemporary Irish Documentary Theatre* (Bloomsbury, 2020).

RONAN McDONALD holds the Gerry Higgins Chair of Irish Studies at the University of Melbourne. He is President of the Irish Studies Association of Australia and New Zealand. He has research interests in Irish literature, the history of criticism, and the value of the humanities. His books include *Tragedy and Irish Literature* (2002), *The Cambridge Introduction to Samuel Beckett* (2007), and *The Death of the Critic* (2008). Recent edited collections include *The Values of Literary Studies: Critical Institutions, Scholarly Agendas* (Cambridge University Press, 2015) and *Flann O'Brien and Modernism* (2014). His monograph on *Irish Revival, Modernism and the Making of Literary Value* is forthcoming with Cambridge UP. He is the series editor for *Cambridge Themes in Irish Literature and Culture*.

KATIE MISHLER is a Government of Ireland Enterprise Partnership Postdoctoral Fellow at University College Dublin and Museum of Literature Ireland. Her current project combines archival research, the digital humanities, and Irish gothic theory to map nineteenth-century Dublin gothic writing. She researches and publishes on urban gothic writing, the female gothic, New Woman fiction, Joyce, and literary and cultural representations of pregnancy and abortion. She is the Editorial Fellow at the *Irish University Review* and the research assistant at the *Spenser Review*.

ANNE MULHALL is a lecturer in the School of English, Drama, Film, and Creative Writing in UCD. She is co-director with Aideen Quilty of UCD Centre for Gender, Feminism & Sexualities (CGFS). She has published extensively on feminist and queer studies, critical migration studies, and contemporary Irish literature and culture.

CHRISTOPHER MURRAY is Emeritus Professor of English, Drama and Film at University College Dublin and is a former editor of *Irish University Review*. Among his books are *Twentieth-Century Irish Drama: Mirror up to Nation* (1997), *Seán O'Casey: Writer at Work, A Biography* (2004), and *The Theatre of Brian Friel: Tradition and Modernity* (2014). In addition he has edited *Samuel Beckett: 100 Years, Centenary Essays* (2006), *Brian Friel : Essays, Diaries, Interviews 1964–1999* (1999) and *'Alive in Time': The Enduring Drama of Tom Murphy, New Essays* (2010), and has published widely on Irish drama and theatre history.

ÉILÍS NÍ DHUIBHNE ALMQVIST was born in Dublin in 1954. I She is a fiction writer, literary critic, folklore scholar, and lecturer in Creative Writing. She writes in both Irish and English, and has written almost thirty books, and won several awards for her work, including the Irish PEN Award 2015 for an Outstanding Contribution to Irish Literature.

Her latest books are *Selected Stories* (Dalkey Archive 2017) and a memoir, *Twelve Thousand Days* (Blackstaff Press 2018). She is a member of Aosdána, and she is president of The Folklore of Ireland Society.

CÓILÍN PARSONS is Associate Professor of English at Georgetown University, where he teaches modernism, Irish literature, and post-colonial literature and theory. He is the author of *The Ordnance Survey and Modern Irish Literature* (Oxford 2016), and co-editor of *Science Technology, and Irish Modernism* (Syracuse, 2016) and *Relocations: Reading Culture in South Africa* (Cape Town, 2105).

EMMA PENNEY is a Roger McHugh scholar at the UCD School of English, Drama, and Film. Her PhD thesis, entitled 'Class Acts: Working-Class Feminism and the Women's Movement in Ireland', explores the distinctive feminist activism of working-class women's groups in Ireland throughout the 1980s. Her thesis carries out the first analysis of the literary archive of these groups, which had been previously uncollected, offering new critical frameworks on the impact of social-class on creative form, and challenging traditional literary value-systems. Emma is committed to bringing the method-ologies of working-class studies, a growing international field, to bear on Irish Studies scholarship where there has been a significant absence of class analysis. She is also the cofounder of the UCD Decolonial Platform where she works with staff and students on decolonising curricula and research culture.

MICHAEL PIERSE is Senior Lecturer in Irish Literature at Queen's University Belfast. His research mainly explores the writing and cultural production of Irish working-class life. Over recent years, this work has expanded into new multi-disciplinary contexts, including the study of festivals and theatre-as-research practices. Michael has also been working recently on representations of race and marginalised identities generally in Ireland. He is author of *Writing Ireland's Working-Class: Dublin After O'Casey* (Palgrave: 2011) and editor of the recent collections, *A History of Irish Working-Class Writing* (Cambridge University Press, 2017) and *Rethinking the Irish Diaspora: After The Gathering* (Palgrave, 2018; co-edited with Dr Johanne Devlin Trew).

ONDŘEJ PILNÝ is a Professor of English and American Literature and the Director of the Centre for Irish Studies at Charles University, Prague. He is the author of *The Grotesque in Contemporary Anglophone Drama* (2016) and *Irony and Identity in Modern Irish Drama* (2006), and editor of an annotated volume of J.M. Synge's works in Czech translation, six collections of essays, and five journal issues on subjects ranging from

Irish literature and theatre to cultural relations between Ireland and Europe, Anglophone drama and theatre, cultural memory, and structuralist theory. His translations into Czech include works by J.M. Synge, Flann O'Brien, Samuel Beckett, Brian Friel, Martin McDonagh, Enda Walsh, and Mark O'Rowe. He is the current Chairperson of IASIL and a former Vice-President of EFACIS (2013–2019).

ANTHONY ROCHE, Professor Emeritus in the School of English, Drama and Film at University College Dublin. He has published six books and numerous articles and chapters on Irish drama and theatre from the late nineteenth century to the present. His *Best Loved Bernard Shaw* will be published in Spring 2021 by the O'Brien Press. He was editor of the *Irish University Review* from 1998 to 2002 and more recently served as Chair of the *IUR* Management Board. In 2007 he hosted the Triennial IASIL Conference at UCD and in July 2020 will deliver one of the plenary lectures at the University of Lodz in Poland. In 2019 he was a judge for *The Irish Times* Irish Theatre Awards.

Emilie Pine

Criticism, Diversity, Openness: Irish Studies Now

[Editor's Note: I write this as I work from home in Dublin on 18 March 2020. Last night the Irish Taoiseach gave a national address, beginning: 'This is a Saint Patrick's Day like no other. A day that none of us will forget. Today's children will tell their own children and grandchildren about the national holiday in 2020 that had no parades or parties, but instead saw everyone staying at home to protect each other. In years to come, let them say of us, when things were at their worst, we were at our best.' I have no foresight about what the days and weeks and months to come will bring. There are moments when what I do – writing and editing – feels irrelevant, as the world around us changes and shifts, when health seems the only priority. But even today, with news of crisis and death around the world, as I look at this jubilee issue I believe that we have to celebrate, that it remains important to take stock of where we have come from, where we are, and what we have achieved.

In marking fifty years of Irish studies in the *Irish University Review*, we celebrate the value of emotional and intellectual investment in the world around us, from people to poetry, from landscape to language, from society to story. I hope that an issue such as this, though it can cure no physical ill or compensate for the great losses many have incurred, may help us in some small way to know who we are, and to navigate the way ahead.]

***

A few years ago, in a side room at a conference, I gave a talk on publication strategies to a group of PhD students. I offered an overview of journal publishing from the editor's side of the desk, explained what a journal expects, and answered questions (yes, house style matters; yes, peer review is anonymous; no, you can't send the same article to multiple journals simultaneously). One student asked if you should only send work to a journal that has published on that author or topic before. It seemed a simple question, but like all the best questions it prompted a complicated answer. I said that while I would obviously not advise sending work on twenty-first-century writing to a journal on eighteenth-century literature, at the same time, innovation does not happen if we all create more of the same.

Irish University Review 50.1 (2020): 1–5
DOI: 10.3366/iur.2020.0425
© Edinburgh University Press
www.euppublishing.com/iur

To my mind, none of the essays in this issue represents 'more of the same', and if there is a single reason for this, it is that all of the authors are writing as themselves. I do not say this lightly. Even in 2020, it is still a courageous act to write oneself into the critical discussion. That courage is manifest throughout these pages, in essays that demonstrate the intellectual reward of acknowledging the self. In 'Some Things Are Worth Losing to Become', Matthew Kennedy profoundly connects to his body as a way of theorising belonging and identity formation. Kennedy shows us the impact of culture on the self, demonstrating the affective and intellectual potential of culture to change minds and bodies, and to help us to be our true selves. Negotiating who we are in a complex cultural and political context can be difficult for all of us, and perhaps never more so than in the supposedly safe space of the classroom. In her essay in response to #MeToo, Lisa Fitzpatrick re-evaluates how the personal and the political overlap, led by her teaching practice and the needs of a new generation of students marked by both vulnerability and resilience. The personal is a way into the critical, and in her essay on memoir as a new genre, Éilís Ní Dhuibhne Almqvist writes about the need to find a form to express grief and, like Kennedy, shows how personal experience can enrich how we understand genres of writing.

Our emotions are often engaged by the texts and subjects that we study, and so emotional resilience is a topic increasingly relevant for both our discourses and our teaching. But it should not be a required skill for going to work. As Deirdre Flynn demonstrates, however, in 'On Being Precarious', the field of Irish Studies is now defined, as is so much of the higher education and arts sectors, by deeply unfair employment practices resulting in great personal hardship. Precarity is corrosive for the individual trying to survive it. But it is also a kind of slow violence against the discipline. Without job security for those entering the field, the dangerous questions will not get asked, coercive certainties will not be challenged, and discrimination will not be con-fronted. Flynn's essay is outstandingly brave. And it is a clarion call for those of us with tenure to take action.

Irish studies has no founding charter, no list of commandments, or global constitution. It emerges from the interests of individuals and groups, and it will always reflect the times, in terms of what it includes, and also what it excludes. Exclusion is a difficult word, because it implies a conscious decision to prohibit entry into a field. But we would not be honest in our reflections if we did not admit that Irish Studies has been marked by exclusion. Emma Creedon writes powerfully of the ways that Irish theatre has stereotyped and excluded the disabled body; her essay is also an implicit critique of those of us who have written about theatre without paying adequate attention to these bodies. Likewise, Michael Pierse questions why working-class Irish writing still suffers from critical neglect and calls for greater attention to class diversity in Irish literature. Diversity is an ever-shifting category. In 'Are we doing diversity justice?', Chiamaka Enyi-Amadi and Emma Penney shine a light on how non-white writers only find themselves included in the canon if they address 'relevant' subjects like migration. In the same vein, Anne Mulhall lays bare the power hierarchies within Irish Studies, the challenge for artists and writers outside of the academy to be heard, and the potential for activism within academia. Reading these contributions, it is hard to avoid the realisation that the tacit rules of inclusion may appear to create diversity, but can sometimes maintain exclusionary practices of othering.

Exclusion has always been with us and the *IUR*, as Katie Mishler shows in her analysis of the journal's record on gender, time period, and geographic origin, is not immune to this historic problem. On gender, though the journal's representation of women has improved over the past five decades to the point where we have gender parity of female/male critics, the journal is still far from gender parity of subject. In the 2010s, only 29% of articles focussed on women writers (we want to read essays on these women; we want to publish them; send them in). Analysis of the time periods covered by the journal also shows that when we say 'Irish literature' it is predominantly *modern* Irish literature that is being addressed. It has long been the ambition of the journal's editors to see more work on pre-1900 writers appear in the journal, and that quest continues (we want to read essays on these periods; we want to publish them; send them in). Finally, the majority of the essays published in this journal originate in Ireland, the US, and the UK. This bias is partly due to the wonderful journals published on Irish studies in other parts of the world, nevertheless we would love to see more exchange (we want to read essays from everywhere; we want to publish them; send them in). Irish studies means different things in different contexts. With that in mind, I invite you to read essays on Irish studies internationally by Dianne Hall and Ronan McDonald (Australia and New Zealand), Andrew Fitzsimons (Japan), Ondřej Pilný (Continental Europe), and Beatriz Kopschitz Bastos (South America).

Though it is important to reflect on where we could go, there are many reasons for celebrating where we are – from the impact of actively encouraging submissions on women's writing (reflected in the fifty-fifty gender balance in the 2019 general issue) to the generative impact of seeing Irish literatures through new lenses. Children's literature has only been critically appreciated in recent decades, and Patricia Kennon illustrates the value of diversifying the genres we consider as 'literary', particularly given the role of this genre in representing young people to themselves. In 'New Technologies of Research' Marie-Louise Coolahan discusses the positive role that digital approaches have to play in investigating early modern Irish studies, in a creative juxtaposition of new and old. Likewise, Lucy Collins argues that literary archives allow for more than preservation, enabling new areas for exploration and changing perceptions. Comparative work across temporal and geographic spaces can also bring new meanings to the surface, as Cóilín Parsons argues in his case for 'weak comparison' between writers of very different contexts. Equally, Margaret Kelleher writes on bilingualism as a multifaceted genre of Irish writing, arguing that paying attention to bilingualism is not only important in terms of understanding the scope of writing in the Irish tradition, but encourages us as critics to do more comparative work – 'transcending the English/Irish binary' – a conceptual shift mirroring that from inclusion to openness. All of these essays are marked by the 'formal restlessness' that Eric Falci identifies in contemporary Irish poetry; his essay is a salutary reminder of the necessity of looking again at the 'rules' of literature and the value of 'open-ended attention'.

As we celebrate the Golden Jubilee of the *Irish University Review,* we honour the vision of all its contributors, now and then – and we honour its editors. In his reflection on founding the *Irish University Review* in 1970, Maurice Harmon states that his primary purpose was 'to create a space ... in which to be heard and read'. Harmon was motivated to found the journal because 'up to this point, if you thought of doing something on one of the minor dramatists ... [or] writing about emerging poets in the late 1950s and 1960s ... there was virtually no chance of being published'. The founding principles of the *IUR*, then, have always been to open up the space of its pages to variety and particularity, depth and complexity. To quote the journal's second editor, Christopher Murray, 'The role of a journal such as this is to stimulate thought about art, its nature, and its relationships to society, politics and philosophy. It should supply a bridge between the creative writer and the intelligent public.' In his essay, Anthony Roche pays tribute to the ways the *IUR* has built this bridge, becoming over the decades not just an outlet for, but central to, Irish literary studies. Roche also pays tribute to how 'meaningful' it was for him when he was invited to become editor. John Brannigan echoes this sentiment: 'editing the *Irish University Review* ... was one of the best and most rewarding experiences of my academic life.' Part of that reward comes, as Brannigan puts it, from the privilege of seeing 'the shape of current trends and practices in your field and sometimes ... help[ing] to influence new directions or convergences.' In her reflections on editing the *IUR*, Anne Fogarty notes the importance of the journal as a venue for emerging work, 'the principal means by which we test out work in progress and convey new approaches to others in our field'. It is part of the 'sustaining work of editors', as Fogarty puts it, to ensure this work reaches a readership.

Since 2017, it has been my great privilege, and responsibility, to take on the role of editor, having begun my association with the journal as assistant editor in 2008. Reading the essays by former editors in this issue I am struck by the continuities of the role – from the desire to widen the intellectual discussion, to the practical task of getting each issue to press (the housework of academic publishing). Reading their reflections on commissioning, reviewing, and proofreading, I am reminded that tradition and innovation are always closely intertwined. Most of all, I am struck by the editors' multiple investments – of time, of thought, and of care – in this ongoing and monumental project. It is my great honour to be able to thank Maurice, Chris, Tony, Anne, and John in the pages of the journal they have made, to pay tribute to their leadership and mentorship, and to celebrate their enduring legacies.

An editor does not produce a journal alone, it takes a village! The journal is incredibly fortunate in its brilliant editorial team – Lucy Collins, Paul Delaney, and Katie Mishler – and in the many individuals whose work contributes to the production of the journal through the Management, Editorial, and Advisory Boards, and at Edinburgh University Press. All of us are grateful that the School of English, Drama, and Film at University College Dublin has, since the beginning, provided a home for the journal. Finally, the journal has been extremely lucky in its formative and enduring affiliation to the International Association for the Study of Irish Literatures.

Mapping the contours of the *Irish University Review* is partly achieved by naming, cataloguing, and counting: under the guidance of its six editors, over the past fifty years, the journal has published fifty volumes, including forty special issues, and represented the work of more than 1120 creative and academic contributors in over 800 articles and literary pieces. That is quite a legacy. But the journal is much more than even those significant numbers can convey. The *Irish University Review* publishes the best work in the field, work that helps us towards deeper knowledge of the literary traditions, writers, and canons that we know and love. Since its inception, the journal's work has also been, however, to challenge that canon and to open up the categories of knowledge, so that we can all see ourselves and our values – as writers, readers, and students – reflected in some ways in these pages. As Maurice Harmon said in a 1976 editorial, we strive for 'successive acts of definition and scrutiny'. That statement seems both an accurate reflection of what the *IUR* has achieved since 1970, and a mission statement for the next fifty years.

Maurice Harmon

In the Beginning (1970–1986)

I am delighted that Emilie Pine has decided to mark the fifty years of growth and change in the *Irish University Review: A Journal of Irish Studies*. Initially the journal grew out of the stirring of interest in the field of Irish studies in the late 1950s and early 1960s mainly in Ireland and America. But scholars in the field were isolated. To improve this situation two young historians, Emmet Larkin and Lawrence J. McCaffney, with the support of John V. Kelleher, a Harvard English professor, founded the American Committee for Irish Studies, to offset this isolation and to bring people together through conferences and organised discussion. In the early 1960s I came back to Ireland from a spell in America to work alongside Roger McHugh at University College Dublin. For years McHugh had been building up a course of lectures on Anglo-Irish literature, outlining its parameters, defining what could be included under the term Anglo-Irish, and working out its origins, associations, and development. In America at the same time John V. Kelleher was defining and presenting a similar perspective. McHugh and Kelleher recognised what the other was doing. When Kelleher gave a course of lectures at University College Dublin, he brought intellectual rigour into the discussion and showed what could be done when the work was subjected to exacting scrutiny. I was fortunate in that I attended lectures and seminars by both men, both at UCD and at Harvard.

In his lectures McHugh emphasised the role of identification and responsibility, arguing that writers might identify with specific locations or specific issues and see it as their responsibility to reflect it, to show its strengths and weaknesses. Their primary task was to illuminate the world they knew, to show its particular strengths and weaknesses. Gradually what would emerge would be a more layered understanding of Irish society in all its variety, richness, and complexity, a world demonstrably different from English society and its preoccupations and affinities as reflected in the literature. It was becoming quite clear when reading histories of English literature that the attempt to fit Irish literature into that canon lead to confusion and contradictions.

Irish University Review 50.1 (2020): 6–9
DOI: 10.3366/iur.2020.0426
© Edinburgh University Press
www.euppublishing.com/iur

While most Irish writers of the nineteenth century could be fitted into the English canon without too much difficulty the same could not be said about poets like Thomas Davis, James Clarence Mangan, and Samuel Ferguson or novelists such as Maria Edgeworth, William Carleton, or Joseph Sheridan Le Fanu. Then there are the various scholars who edited and translated into English material from the Gaelic past in both poetry and prose, be that material from medieval Irish literature and Old Irish or later Irish, and those nineteenth-century antiquarians and folklorists who paved the way for such as W.B. Yeats with his evocation of the fairy world and his affinity with Irish mythology. Moreover, no history of English literature could easily accommodate Yeats's heroes, such as Cuchulain or Deirdre of the Sorrows. Successive writers like Douglas Hyde, Lady Gregory, and J.M. Synge and, indeed, other dramatists encouraged by the Abbey Theatre to abandon the hated stage Irishman and to focus instead on expressing 'the deeper thoughts and emotions of Ireland', helped to bring depth, colour, and distinction to the literature and the national identity. Even the Abbey's stage sets revealed different areas of Irish life, while actors could speak in the idiom of different regions. What was needed was a forum for discussion of the particularities of these literatures.

Why did I establish the journal in 1970? I was fortunate in that in the late 1960s I had been appointed editor of the *University Review,* a general journal, not noted for the quality of its material or its regularity, giving voice to interests of the Graduates of the National University of Ireland. In 1967 when I did a special interdisciplinary issue on Fenians and Fenianism to coincide with the centenary of the rising in 1867, I began to see what might be done and set about transforming it into a journal with limited but specific purposes; the sub-title, *a Journal of Irish Studies,* indicated where the newly titled *Irish University Review* intended to function. The basic aim was to provide material which would be of interest to scholars worldwide working in the field of Irish studies and also to provide publication opportunities for them. Prior to its arrival, if you wanted to publish something on W.B. Yeats or James Joyce, for example, there were several outlets available to you but if you wanted to publish something on one of the minor or lesser-known writers it was much more difficult to be published. That was the challenge, to create a space for yourself in which to be heard and read. Up to this point, if you thought of doing something on one of the minor dramatists such as T.C. Murray, Lennox Robinson, or Padraic Colum, there was little chance of being published. If you thought, as I did, of writing about emerging poets in the late 1950s and 1960s, poets like Thomas Kinsella, John Montague, and Richard Murphy, there was virtually no chance of being published, even though they were clearly a new generation of writers with a distinctive sensibility, marked by unique circumstances that needed to be defined.

Starting a new journal was not easy, nor was it easy to fund it. It takes a long time, years, to get a journal going, to ensure that it comes out regularly (a major point for me). For a long time it was a one-man operation. It was clear enough that a journal has to have a central voice and someone in charge of the many different activities the editor has to be involved with, from the selection of material to be published and the copyediting to the quality of the paper, the type of print, the selection and design for the cover. All of these concerns, these details, must cohere to help establish a journal in the world and make what I will call an impression. The first issue of the *Irish University Review* in 1970 was important in setting the style and standards, but the first is also the easiest to do. The editor relies on his contacts in the scholarly world, and so invites some of them – the best he/she can find – to contribute. But the editor then quickly finds that journals consume material. So he/she plans ahead, getting the bones of two or perhaps three issues together. In the early issues the *Irish University Review* included short literary works, new poetry, short stories, even one-act plays. This was a way, or at least a means, of attracting younger writers and of broadening the scope of the journal, which began to gain a reputation out of trial and inevitable error. It soon became a source of pride, however, as it kept going, twice yearly, fighting for high standards, and could demonstrate that University College Dublin had at last established a major publication dedicated to Irish studies and to scholarship.

Then there was the eternal question of funding. Printers have to be paid, there are running expenses, the costs of sending out review copies and the postage to subscribers. Building up a subscription list, indeed, was crucial to the success of *Irish University Review*. This was a chore, but very worthwhile. The hunt for advertisers was another chore, but important for survival. I had good support from my executive board, however, especially from Patrick Lynch (Economics), who had contacts in the Educational Building Society so that a small stipend was available twice a year; support too from John O'Meara (Classics), who knew College politics well enough to identify pitfalls and perhaps to advise on securing secretarial help, which I did. This too was an important milestone. In general, while friends and colleagues wished me well and admired what I was doing, there was no question of asking them for financial assistance. One must be prepared for this reality, the loneliness of the long-distance editor. Or so it was in the beginning. I think it is a lot easier on the financial and management fronts now. Then there is the securing of an efficient, reliable publisher. I did that with Seamus Cashman and his Wolfhound Press. Later we had Kevin Brophy of Brophy Books, and then Colour Books. All were vital in ensuring the timetabling, delivery, and quality of the journal at prices we could afford. I have to add too that with the establishment of the International Association of Anglo-Irish Literature in 1970 and its willingness to make *Irish University Review* in part its official organ by submitting an annual bibliography bulletin to the autumn issue (edited at first by the incomparable 'Paul' Pollard of Trinity College Dublin), the members contracted to take the journal at a reduced rate. Later on the Japan branch of the International Association for the Study of Anglo-Irish Literature, the title to be modified around 1990 to get rid of the term 'Anglo-Irish' for 'Irish Literatures', likewise agreed to take a subscription for its members. This support on two fronts was very important to the survival of the journal and is greatly appreciated.

In 1974 when I did a Special Issue, the first of the special issues, on Austin Clarke, I also realised what could be done. I wanted each special issue to be a milestone in the study of a writer, to mark a scholarly stage in the study of his or her work and to include a bibliography of criticism about the work. After Clarke, Special Issues included Sean O'Faolain (1976), Richard Murphy (1977), Mary Lavin (1979), and many more, such as Eavan Boland, Brian Coffey, Brian Friel, Benedict Kiely, and so on, as the other editors who came later will discuss in this Jubilee issue. All had a good standard of scholarship, a biographical element, and a bibliography of primary and secondary material. After a few years of my editorship, two colleagues, Dr J.C.C. Mays and Jonathan Williams, came to my assistance on the board and they were very welcome, one for his scholarly presence, the other for his practical knowledge of editing and publishing. I enjoyed their support and companionship.

Remembering now the years when I began preparing materials that would become the first issue in 1970 of the *Irish University Review, A Journal of Irish Studies*, and the subsequent sixteen years that followed as its editor, have been challenging. I thank the current editor, Emilie Pine, for the invitation to contribute to this Golden Jubilee issue, and wish her and her assistant editor, Lucy Collins, and their team every success as they continue to extend the position of *Irish University Review* as the leading journal of its kind.

Christopher Murray

Murphy, Deevy, Stuart: Literature and Society (1987–1997)

To my mind, there are three types of special issue published by the *IUR*: the commemorative, the celebratory, and the thematic. The commemorative is revisionism in the mode of new historicism, such as 'Spenser in Ireland (1596–1996)'. The celebratory may take two forms, on authors established or authors identified as deserving greater recognition. It could also take the form of a *Festschrift*. The thematic focuses on a critical or theoretical topic, such as 'Contexts of Irish Writing' (1991). Selection has never been systematic, however, and the editor was always free to choose an author or topic for a special issue for the executive to discuss. By the time I became editor, in late 1986, thirteen special issues had been published, four of them already out of print: on Austin Clarke (1974), Brian Coffey (1975), Richard Murphy (1977), and Samuel Beckett (1984). The date of the last-mentioned was an astute move by Maurice Harmon two years before Beckett's eightieth birthday flooded the market. It is a scarce item today.

In my own case, I tried for a special issue every year, occasionally calling upon a guest editor. The first for me as editor was the Tom Murphy issue in 1987. I had by that time been associated with the journal for about twelve years, and in 1980 had guest edited a commemorative issue to mark the centenary of Seán O'Casey. That was fun. I chose as subtitle *Roots and Branches* to signify space for influence on and influence by O'Casey. The idea worked well for the contributors I carefully chose, but looking back I'm not sure that commissioning topics is necessarily a good thing. With the Murphy issue I thought my introduction on the 'rough and holy theatre of Thomas Murphy' would open up his world and style, leaving the contributors to their own devices. That probably worked better.

The big difference I experienced between this and the O'Casey issue, however, was that now I was dealing with a living author, indeed living nearby in Dublin. I had come to know Murphy reasonably well since the late 1970s, a difficult time for him, after *The Sanctuary Lamp* (1975)

Irish University Review 50.1 (2020): 10–16
DOI: 10.3366/iur.2020.0427
© Edinburgh University Press
www.euppublishing.com/iur

caused the kind of controversy that does no author any good. But a few years later he announced that he was working on a 'noir' play suggested by all the films he had been watching late at night. This was *The Blue Macushla*, staged at the Abbey in 1980, a fascinating piece with the perfectly cast but in this instance disappointing Donal McCann in the leading role of manager of a seedy Dublin nightclub, with a chanteuse (Deirdre Donnelly) called Roscommon and a lot of mobsters in the background. It was part parable part parody of the political situation, the corruption as Murphy saw in Ireland's tolerance of IRA violence. It didn't quite work under Jim Sheridan's direction. Murphy believed in it and rewrote it several times for other productions elsewhere but in the end, as he told me, he felt he had to let it go. He would sometimes have a fondness for a play as for a wayward child. About *The Gigli Concert*, however, he had no doubt ever. He knew he had a theme (the Faustian pact) as comment on contemporary Ireland, its unacknowledged sense of a collapsing identity and a failure to be honest. It was over this play I had most contact with him, by letter and by occasional meetings in his apartment along the Appian Way, Ranelagh. As directed by Patrick Mason at the Abbey its huge success, in spite of its enormous length (three and a half hours playing time), established Murphy among the greats at last. Moving to Galway after this to work with Druid, Murphy created two more major successes, *Conversations on a Homecoming* and *Bailegangaire*.

I decided to build the *IUR* special issue mainly around these three plays. My contributors were brilliant: Fintan O'Toole, Vivian Mercier, Riana O'Dwyer, Colm Tóibín, Ger Fitzgibbon, Tony Roche, Patrick Mason (in interview), Harry White, Gerry Stembridge, and others, many of them on an upward curve in their careers, all enthusiastic and committed. At the last minute I got the psychoanalyst Ivor Brown to contribute 'The Madness of Genius', a fine flourish to end with. I dedicated the issue to Siobhán McKenna, who had died while I was preparing it. She and Murphy were close friends. Her final role was in *Bailegangaire* with the Druid Theatre in 1985.

Murphy's subsequent career solidified his reputation as one of the best playwrights to grace the Irish theatre in the twentieth century. Brian Friel, in a rare programme note for the Abbey, said: 'The most distinctive, the most restless, the most obsessive imagination at work in the Irish theatre today is Tom Murphy's.'[1] That this note should have been written for *The Blue Macushla* is perhaps ironic, and yet, taking Friel's capacity to see beneath the surface, perhaps a key to appreciating that neglected play. On 5 September 2017, on behalf of the Arts Council of Ireland, President Michael D. Higgins bestowed on him the title *Saoi* of *Aosdána*, the Irish artists association's highest honour, formerly held by Beckett and Friel. He died in Dublin on 15 May 2018.

*

The special issue commemorating Teresa Deevy (1894–1963) was published in 1995. I'm not sure how Tom Murphy and Teresa Deevy would have got on. Not well, I fear, as they would have been polar opposites, and yet Murphy's *Alice Trilogy* (2005) is not far in empathy from the way Deevy understood the Alices of this world. 1995 marked the Silver Jubilee issue of the *IUR* and the choice of Deevy as subject was a happy one. The centenary of her birth had occurred in the preceding year, when a revival of her best-known work, *Katie Roche*, went up on the Abbey's Peacock stage, directed by Judy Friel in a tight, bold production. One could sense something in the theatrical air, some stirring in the fight to have women's voices heard more often within the Irish theatre. Marina Carr had just joined the scene, determined to speak out in anger and frustration over some of the same situations that formed the core of Deevy's work. The revival of interest in Deevy in the 1990s was born out of this coincidence of revolt and the representation of women in Irish theatre. It can even be claimed that the publication of this special issue of the *IUR* furthered the enormous increase in research and publication about Deevy which continues to the present day.[2]

Katie Roche, the iconic Deevy play, had premiered at the old Abbey Theatre on 16 March 1936, while Yeats was still general manager. Directed by Hugh Hunt, and with scene design by Tanya Moiseiwitsch, it was very well cast from the stock company, with Eileen Crowe as Katie, her husband in real life F.J. McCormick as Stanislaus, the man Katie foolishly marries, Ria Mooney as Amelia, Stanislaus's sister and kind friend to Katie, Arthur Shields as the young Michael whom she favours, and Michael J. Dolan as Reuben, the travelling man who beats Katie in a key scene and declares he is her father. Minor roles were taken by Cyril Cusack, May Craig, and Barry Fitzgerald. That was about as good as it got at the Abbey in its glory days. It was enough to make Deevy's reputation. Her play travelled to New York on tour with the Abbey players the following year. The revival on the main stage in the new Abbey, nine years after it opened its doors in 1966, was ably directed by a young Joe Dowling, future artistic director of the Abbey and the Guthrie in Minneapolis. He cast Jeananne Crowley in the lead role, and she was superb. Fortunately for me, Crowley agreed to launch the special issue at UCD, in the company of Deevy's relations, including Deevy's nephew, Jack Deevy, who had provided me with a copy of the script of *Wife to James Whelan* for inclusion in this special issue. Crowley was of the view that '[a]lthough the play [*Teresa Deevy*] is still relevant today, it was particularly so when it was written. ... The life force was being crushed in Irish women in the 1930s, culminating with de Valera's Constitution in 1937.'[3]

The neglect of Deevy by the old Abbey after the 1930s is something of an enigma. One factor was the attitude of Ernest Blythe, the general manager who succeeded Yeats in 1941 and who disliked her work, rejecting the new scripts she submitted. Yet Deevy had in 1932 won the Abbey Theatre Management's playwriting contest for her *Temporal Powers*, a three-act play, directed by Lennox Robinson and found by the judges to be 'strikingly original, powerful and dramatic.'[4] Joseph Holloway, the diarist, admired her early work but had interesting doubts about *Katie Roche*: 'A play of goings and comings and short pistol-shot sentences and strange delays – a puzzling play... I wonder how future audiences will take the piece.'[5]

To provide an answer would be the aim of the *IUR* special issue, the full title of which was *Teresa Deevy and Irish Women Playwrights*. I had Maureen Waters on Lady Gregory's '*Grania*: A Feminist Voice' setting the stage for the quasi-feminist emphasis in Deevy's own work, while Anthony Roche explored *Katie Roche* by bookending her play with Synge's *The Shadow of the Glen* (1904) and Carr's *The Mai* (1994). The common theme he isolates is 'a breaching of boundaries which the respectable husbands are anxious to keep in place.'[6] Cathy Leeney argued that Deevy's plays 'comprise a forceful and coherent body of work which may be said to ... describe a search for identity and a future. The terms of this search are psychologically authentic and complex. They are hemmed in by the crushing orthodoxies of postcolonial Ireland in that decade [the 1930s] and especially by the implications for women of those orthodoxies.'[7] This point was also emphasised by Martina Ann O'Doherty in her introduction to the Deevy play she had re-discovered, *Wife to James Whelan* (1956). Judy Friel, who directed the 1994 revival of *Katie Roche*, addressed issues in Deevy's biography and her choice, as a single woman who was deaf, of the theatre as her profession. Finally, Eibhear Walshe discussed Deevy's gender warfare in a wider context: 'the rebellious heroines ... are chastised into submission by physical violence, in each case by a father or husband. Each woman yearns for a destiny and a fate beyond the limited modes available.'[8]

This special issue made an impact. The Irish-American diaspora has adopted Deevy's work in the twenty-first century, by both staging and publishing the plays. Such scholar-practitioners as Charlotte Headrick and Eileen Kearney have been to the fore in this field, and their anthology *Irish Women Dramatists: 1908–2001* (Syracuse University Press, 2014) included *The King of Spain's Daughter*. For his part Jonathan Bank initiated The Teresa Deevy Project in 2010 at the Mint Theater, New York, of which he is artistic director, specifically 'to bring this neglected writer the attention she deserves.'[9] American premieres followed. To date he has directed the three full-length plays to good reviews, *Wife to James Whelan*, *Temporal Powers*, and *Katie Roche*, together with the *Suitcase under the Bed* (2017), a selection of four 'lost' one-acts.[10] In addition, Bank has published two volumes of Deevy's plays, including unstaged one-acts, appropriately titled *Teresa Deevy Reclaimed*.[11]

In Dublin, meantime, the Abbey took up the Deevy challenge once again after the 'Waking the Feminists' campaign got under way in late 2016. As a result, *Katie Roche* received a studied, researched revival on the Abbey's main stage in August 2017, and the new Directors Graham McLaren and Neil Murray issued a press release announcing: 'The Abbey Theatre is committed to elevating the work of women in Irish theatre. *Katie Roche* is a brilliant play from the Irish canon. Welcoming Teresa's [*sic*] work back to our stage is just one way we hope to correct the issues of gender inequality that we see in our own society today.'[12] It's a start.

*

The final special issue I wish to comment on was my last. It was thematic, the topic being 'Literature, Criticism and Theory'. In a foreword to my Tom Murphy issue I wrote: 'The role of a journal such as this is to stimulate thought about art, its nature, and its relationships to society, politics and philosophy. It should supply a bridge between the creative writer and the intelligent public.'[13] As time went on I tried to ensure that the special issues were academic but also of general interest. To that end I did specials on John Montague and Brian Moore, and was delighted when my colleagues Brian Donnelly, Terry Dolan, Peter Denman (Maynooth), Anthony Roche, and Anne Fogarty offered to guest-edit issues on attractive topics. For my swansong in 1997 I took a chance and went for something abstract. The idea behind this issue was firstly 'to illustrate the diversity of critical approaches currently available in Anglo-Irish studies (the term, while undoubtedly troublesome, must be endured).' I wouldn't say that now. The term is obsolete. Secondly, to offer 'some sort of progress report on Irish studies [that's better!] today and on the approaches found useful, from stylistics to feminist theory, from new historicism to post-colonial theory.'[14]

The cover, designed by Kevin Brophy, provided one clue to the theme. It shows the novelist and poet Francis Stuart receiving the same prestigious award that Tom Murphy was later to receive, that of *Saoi* of *Aosdána* from the President of Ireland (then Mary Robinson) on behalf of the Arts Council of Ireland. Stuart, now deceased, was a controversial figure because during World War Two he travelled to Berlin where allegedly he made radio broadcasts in support of the Reich. Stuart always denied this. However, my introduction quoted an assertion from an *Irish Times* journalist who begged to differ with him: 'To have volunteered to serve that enemy of civilization and of art is not just a mistake on a par with life's other little blunders. It is a cosmic error from which no full escape is possible.' And so a controversy erupted over Stuart's impending state recognition. Within that controversy a particular topic raised was the freedom of the artist to express himself/herself. Ciarán Benson, chair of the Arts Council at this time, used the occasion of a book launch (of *Krino*) to defend artistic freedom. I asked Ciarán if he would allow me to publish his statement in the *IUR*. And he did that.[15] He found himself in the company of two other contributors who, avoiding the controversy, wrote theoretically on Stuart as fiction writer.

At the launch of our special issue at Belfield (the UCD campus) on 8 May 1997, the speaker was Terence Brown, a literary critic of great eminence. To my relief he gave a detailed and very positive response to the issue, containing articles by Luke Gibbons on 'Hysteria and the Literary Revival', Shaun Richards on 'Brian Friel and Postcolonial Criticism', and Conor Mac Carthy on 'Ideology and Geography in Dermot Bolger's *The Journey Home*', among others. Brown puzzled, however, over the graphic picture on the front cover with three details on the back including Mrs Robinson's wristwatch, wondering if 'time' or history was the point (when in fact it was Stuart's obeisance to national authority). Stuart took a libel action against the *Irish Times* related to another article published on 22 October 1997 which contradicted a claim made by Stuart that he had never written or expressed an anti-Semitic statement. This was a different matter. In June 1999 the libel case went to the High Court but when it was called Stuart's defence counsel announced it had been settled and, a statement having been read out by the counsel for the *Irish Times* expressing withdrawal and regret, as well as an agreement to pay costs, the prosecuting counsel said the only order required from the court was to strike out the action. Mr Justice Kelly made the order on consent. The business was done. And so to bed.

NOTES

1. Brian Friel, *Essays, Diaries, Interviews 1964–1999*, ed. by Christopher Murray (London: Faber and Faber, 1999), pp.89–91 (p.89).
2. It is not possible to list all references here, but see Cathy Leeney, *Irish Women Playwrights 1900–1939: Gender and Violence on Stage* (New York: Peter Lang, 2010), pp.161–92 and p.230 n.13 for guidance.
3. Katie Donovan, 'What Katie did first', *Irish Times* 9 April 1994, 'Weekend', p.4.
4. *Joseph Holloway's Irish Theatre Volume Two: 1932–1937*, ed. by Robert Hogan and Michael J. O'Neill (Dixon, CA: Proscenium Press, 1969), p.12. She shared the prize with Paul Vincent Carroll.
5. *Joseph Holloway's Irish Theatre Volume Two: 1932–1937*, p.52.
6. Anthony Roche, 'Woman on the Threshold: J.M. Synge's *The Shadow of the Glen*, Teresa Deevy's *Katie Roche*, and Marina Carr's *The Mai*', *Irish University Review* 25.1 (1995), 143–62 (p.145).

7. Cathy Leeney, 'Themes of Ritual and Myth in Three Plays by Teresa Deevy', *Irish University Review* 25.1 (1995), 88–116 (p.88).

8. Eibhear Walshe, 'Lost Dominions: European Catholicism and Irish Nationalism in the Plays of Teresa Deevy', *Irish University Review* 25.1 (1995), 133–42 (p.133).

9. 'The Teresa Deevy Project', *Teresa Deevy Reclaimed*, Volume One, ed. by Jonathan Bank, Christopher Morash, and John P. Harrington (New York: Mint Theater Company, 2011), p.vii.

10. Only one of these one-acts had been staged before this, namely *The King of Spain's Daughter* (Abbey, 1935), the others being *Strange Birth*, *In the Cellar of My Friend*, and *Holiday House*. I am grateful to Charlotte Headrick (Oregon State University) for the update on these performances at the Mint. Ten one-acts are included in *Teresa Deevy Reclaimed*, Volume Two, ed. by Jonathan Bank, Christopher Morash, and John P. Harrington (New York: Mint Theater, 2017).

11. *Teresa Deevy Reclaimed*, ed. by Jonathan Bank, John P. Harrington, Christopher Morash (New York: Mint Theater, 2011, 2017).

12. 'Katie Roche Research Pack', available at: https://3kkb1z11gox47nppd3tlqcmq-wpengine.netdna-ssl.com/wp-content/uploads/2017/10/KATIE-ROCHE_RESEARCH-PACK-2017.pdf Viewed 01/03/2019.

13. Christopher Murray, 'Foreword', *Irish University Review* 17.1 (1987), vii.

14. Christopher Murray, 'Introduction: Stirring the Pot Withershins', *Irish University Review* 27.1 (1997), 1–6 (p.5).

15. Ciarán Benson, 'The Artist and Society: *Krino 1986–1996*', *Irish University Review* 27.1 (1997), 69–73.

Anthony Roche

A Work in Progress (1998–2002)

I am going to try to convey a sense of the path I followed to becoming *IUR* editor by looking at the first three decades of the journal's history through an autobiographical lens. I think such an approach will best convey how central the *Irish University Review* has been to my professional life and to the development of the subject which I still persist in calling Anglo-Irish Literature. The journal was founded in 1970, which was my first full year as a student of English at Trinity College, Dublin. During my four years there, I developed a special love of, and interest in, the literature of my own country (in English). In tutorials, I remember working on J.M. Synge with Brendan Kennelly and on James Joyce and Seán O'Faoláin with David Norris (which is where Maurice Harmon first enters the picture). Brendan championed Frank O'Connor, whose stories I enjoyed but found rather too sentimental. David preferred Seán O'Faoláin as more astringent (as did I, at the time) and agreed that I could write a tutorial essay on his short stories. It was at this point (1972) I came across a full-length critical monograph on Seán O'Faoláin written by Maurice Harmon. The book was outstanding, not just on technical aspects of the short stories but on the facets of Irish society and history that they illuminated. The reason for this soon became apparent; though he had done his postgraduate work in the US, Maurice Harmon was Irish and by 1972 had returned to Ireland and was teaching Anglo-Irish Literature in the English Department at University College Dublin. It was extremely rare when I was an undergraduate student to find a writer on Anglo-Irish Literature who was not American. I also learned that Maurice had founded and was editing a journal called the *Irish University Review*, though I did not take that discovery further at the time.

During the late 1970s and early 1980s, I was a graduate student at the University of California at Santa Barbara, where I was awarded an MA and a PhD for a thesis on Synge supervised by my mentor, Vivian Mercier. During the 1970s, Vivian contributed two articles to Special Issues of the *Irish University Review*: 'Mortal Anguish, Mortal Pride: Austin Clarke's Religious Lyrics' in a Special Issue on Clarke

Irish University Review 50.1 (2020): 17–22
DOI: 10.3366/iur.2020.0428
© Edinburgh University Press
www.euppublishing.com/iur

(Spring 1974) and 'The Professionalism of Seán O'Faoláin' in a Special Issue on O'Faoláin (Spring 1976). I read the latter cover to cover and was particularly delighted to come upon an article by Eilís Dillon entitled 'Sean O'Faoláin and the Young Writer'. Eilís and Vivian had married in 1974. She had accompanied him to his professorial post in Santa Barbara, where she continued to write her hugely successful historical novels. Here was an Irish female contributor to the *IUR* (they were still rare enough in 1976 and usually American or Canadian) and a practicing professional writer rather than an academic. Maurice Harmon had also cajoled O'Faoláin himself into contributing the first essay in the Special Issue, appropriately entitled 'A Portrait of the Artist as an Old Man'. I had less connection with the Austin Clarke Special Issue but read Vivian's essay and a number of others. What I remember most vividly was the black bordered announcement at the end of the editorial: 'When this issue was in press, we learned with deep regret of Austin Clarke's death on 19 March 1974 at his home in Templeogue'.

During the summer of 1981, while back in Ireland, I made renewed contact with David Norris and asked to give a panel paper at the forthcoming Centenary Symposium on James Joyce, which was scheduled to take place in Dublin the following year. David was as good as his word. He was involved in organising the Joyce event but was not directly responsible for the academic programme: that was in the hands of Maurice Harmon (the Joyce Centenary Symposium was that rarest and most welcome of things, a joint UCD-TCD collaboration). David had, he said, recommended me to Maurice in the highest possible terms. A few days later Maurice Harmon phoned in what was our first meeting (albeit over the phone – those were the days before e-mail) and invited me to be on a *Portrait* panel at the Dublin Symposium. But Maurice went further. Did I, he asked, know anything about Thomas Kilroy? To which I replied: how could anyone called Roche not be familiar with the author of *The Death and Resurrection of Mister Roche*? Maurice then said that in that same summer of 1982 he was organising a Triennial Conference of the International Association for the Study of Anglo-Irish Literature (IASAIL, as it then was) at UCD and invited me to give a panel paper on Thomas Kilroy.

Over the next few years Maurice and I stayed in touch. He commissioned a first book review from me for the *Irish University Review*: it was on Synge, my PhD subject, and was the lead review in *IUR* 13.2 (Autumn, 1983). The books I reviewed were Nicholas Grene's edition of Synge's *The Well of the Saints* and Toni O'Brien Johnson's *Synge: The Medieval and the Grotesque*. Maurice also said he was planning a Special Issue of the *IUR* on contemporary Irish drama and invited me to contribute: I readily agreed. This is the point at which Christopher Murray enters the narrative. In 1986 I learned that Chris had taken over from Maurice as editor of the *IUR* (after an incredible seventeen years). I soon met up with Chris (for the very first time) to discuss my contribution to what had now become a Special Issue on the contemporary Irish playwright Tom Murphy. In 1985, when I met with Tom in Dublin, he very kindly gave me an advance script of his latest play, *Bailegangaire*, which was to be produced in Galway by Druid that December. After I had read it, I told him that in my view *Bailegangaire* was one of the greatest plays he had ever written and that a production, directed by Garry Hynes and with Siobhán McKenna playing Mommo, would be a huge theatrical success. Tom told me I was deluded (I reminded him of this exchange after the play opened to acclaim.). And so the Special Issue of the *IUR* on Tom Murphy (Spring, 1987)) was published with my 'Bailegangaire: Storytelling into Drama' in it. I managed to be back in Dublin for the launch of the Murphy issue in the Peacock Theatre, with the playwright himself in attendance.

In 1990 I was appointed to the (permanent) position of Lecturer in Anglo-Irish Literature and Drama in the Department of English (as it then was) in UCD. And so began a very happy twenty-six years teaching in that Department with great colleagues like the late Gus Martin, Declan Kiberd, Gerardine Meaney, Brian Donnelly, Chris Murray, John Barrett, and (later) Anne Fogarty, Frank McGuinness, and Emilie Pine. As for the *IUR*, it turned out that it hadn't gone away. In 1991 Chris Murray approached me and invited me to become a member of the Executive Board of the journal. Naturally, I accepted. As part of 'the deal', I got to guest-edit a Special Issue of the *IUR*. It didn't take long for me to settle on Eavan Boland as its focus. I had loved her poetry for a long time and was keenly aware of how she had extended the terrain of Irish poetry, shifting the setting and focus from the bog to the domestic interior, opening up the ground for other women poets. The issue was the result of my collaboration with a friend from Santa Barbara days, Jody Allen-Randolph, already well on her way to becoming the leading interpeter of Boland's poetry. The issue was hard work: it was going against the accepted grain of the (then) established order. In terms of our contributors it was anything but the case of 'round up the usual suspects'. Over and over Jody and I found we had to think outside of the (predominantly male) box. Boland was characteristically generous: agreeing to an interview and contributing an all-new, so-far-unpublished poetic sequence, 'Anna Liffey'.

In 1998 I was appointed Editor of the *Irish University Review* when Chris Murray stepped down after eleven years. I hope I have already said enough to indicate how meaningful this development was to me. I decided to start my run as editor with a Brian Friel Special Issue. Ever since I had seen a production of *Translations* at the Hampstead in London on my way back to Ireland in the summer of 1981, Friel had seemed to me the greatest of contemporary Irish playwrights, address-ing local issues in ways which seemed to cross borders and find equivalences in other cultures. I had devoted a chapter to him in my 1994 book on *Contemporary Irish Drama*; but there was clearly more to be said. I began with the contributions of two major Irish playwrights, Thomas Kilroy and Frank McGuinness. I also invited an essay from Richard Pine, not just because he was one of my oldest friends but because his book on Friel is the most profound study of the work I know. Without much hope, I asked Friel for an interview, but as was his practice he declined the invitation. He did, however, contribute new not-yet-published work to the issue, a scene from his version of Chekhov's *Uncle Vanya*.

There was one outstanding issue to be addressed in compiling the lineup of contributors to the Friel Special Issue. In 1992 a book of essays was published entitled *The Achievement of Brian Friel*, whose contributors were some of the most established names in Friel criticism. Almost all of the individual essays were of interest. But there was one huge problem when the collection was considered as a whole: all sixteen of the contrib-utions were by men. And this happened in the wake of the controversy over *The Field Day Anthology of Irish Literature* and its all-male editorial board the year before. I didn't manage a fifty-fifty ratio in the Friel issue. There were five women contributors out of a total of fifteen: Helen Lojek, Anna McMullan, Catriona Clutterbuck, Csilla Bertha, and José Lanters. Friel read these contributions with particular interest and forged professional relationships with those (and other women) who came to work on his plays in the coming years. I was particularly gratified to receive a five-page poem from Seamus Heaney entitled 'The Real Things' which dealt with putting on Shakespeare plays in a school full of Derry boys. One of them, Seamus Deane, launched the Brian Friel Special Issue at the Abbey Theatre in May of 1999. It was the year of Friel's seventieth birthday and the National Theatre was staging six of his plays. Seamus Heaney was there, but so too, amazingly, was Friel himself. I had received a phone call from him the week before asking what time events in the Abbey kicked off. I replied: 'Why do you want to know? You're not going to show up – you never do.' Brian quietly said: 'I thought I might come along.' At which point, I said: 'Brian, I was only taking a hand at you. I'd be delighted if you'd come. But if you do you must agree to show up at five and stay the entire time, you must sign autographs and you must have a photo taken with my wife, Katy, and our nine-month-old son, Merlin.' 'Oh, okay' came the reply from the other end of the phone. And I have photographs showing this most reticent of writers doing all of that. The whole experience of doing the Friel Special Issue meant a great deal to me and prompted all of my subsequent work on this wonderful playwright.

The Special Issue on Thomas Kilroy (Spring 2002) was similar in ways and some of the contributors were the same. But in ways it was also very different. Where Friel was the subject of monographs and critical essays, the hugely important contribution of Kilroy's groundbreaking plays of ideas had been severely underlooked in terms of criticism. Like the Boland issue, the Kilroy was a case of going against the grain, turning over the ground for what was essentially the first time. I was enormously helped in this task by the collaboration of Gerald Dawe, who co-edited the issue, and laid a welcome emphasis on including a goodly number of contributions from fellow creative writers and visual artists (including an extraordinary hawk-like sculpture of Kilroy on the cover by John Behan). In her recent fine book on Kilroy (*The Theatre of Thomas Kilroy: No Absolutes*), José Lanters makes important reference to a number of the essays in that Special Issue, those by Anne Fogarty and Anna McMullan in particular. The issue was launched at the Abbey in May of 2002 (with the playwright, his wife and daughter, and many of his family present) by Stephen Rea, co-founder of the Field Day Theatre Company and unforgettable in Kilroy's play of doubles, *Double Cross*.

Of the special issues of the *Irish University Review* I produced during my five year period as editor, I am shocked that none of them was on a woman author. Did I think I had fulfilled my obligation by producing the Boland Special Issue? It is now evident to me in retrospect, as it clearly was not at the time, that a commitment to women's writing was and should be ongoing rather than a token one-off event. If I was concentrating on playwrights, the extraordinary work of Marina Carr cried out for a Special Issue (it still does). I edited an issue on Contemporary Irish Fiction since I was well aware that, contrary to what most people believe, the Special Issues up to that point were not exclusively on single authors but also tackled themes and genres. This practice has increased in recent years but was there from the first days of the *IUR*. Maurice had edited Special Issues on Literary Dubliners, The Long Poem, and the National Library. Under Chris's editorship, the late Terry Dolan had guest-edited a Special Issue entitled 'The English of the Irish' (Spring 1990). I was conscious that at the time criticism of the contemporary Irish novel lagged behind that of poetry and drama, and so wished to give it a critical transfusion. That Special Issue had articles on the novels of Deirdre Madden, Éilís Ní Dhuibhne, and on Contemporary Irish Women's Fiction. But, I also reflect: could I not have managed a Special Issue on Edna O'Brien – and could the *IUR* not still? These reflections were prompted by current editor Emilie Pine's trenchant remarks at the launch in June 2018 of the Special Issue on Kate O'Brien, guest-edited by Paige Reynolds. On that occasion, Emilie said the percentage of women to male authors in the Special

Issues of the *IUR* across its fifty years was 14%. There's still a long way to go.

A too brief word on the general issues to close. In general, the *Irish University Review* runs the best of the many essays submitted to it, after they have been read and recommended by two specialist readers. That has been and remains the case. But there were a number of interventions I decided to make as editor in this regard. I particularly sought and encouraged articles by academics from around the world, since publications on Anglo-Irish Literature seemed to me overly dominated by Anglophone scholars from Ireland, England, the US, and Canada, Australia, and New Zealand. The annual IASIL conferences showed just how much good work was being done out there by scholars whose first language was not English. The other thing I did was to follow a lead from Chris Murray when he ran a talk he had attended by Helena Sheehan. Similarly, I decided to run a talk by Vic Merriman whose written version for the *IUR* he entitled 'Decolonisation Postponed: The Theatre of Tiger Trash' (Autumn, 1999). No article published in a general issue of the *IUR* has ever been more cited than this. One reason was that Vic's article was critical in a negative sense on the two writers discussed, Martin McDonagh and Marina Carr. This was virtually unheard of in critical writing on Anglo-Irish writers, where the implicit authorial stance on the work analysed was positive. Secondly, it was an early watermark in terms of the deployment of critical theory in the articles the *IUR* published. Chris Murray had edited a pioneering Special Issue on 'Literature, Criticism and Theory' in the Spring of 1997, but essays adopting this approach had been slow to filter through. Vic's postcolonial approach led him to conclude that the two play-wrights were perpetrating colonial sterotypes 'as a form of communal self-loathing'. I disagreed profoundly with the conclusions of 'The Theatre of Tiger Trash' but it was one of the most stimulating, thought-provoking critical pieces I had ever read and a timely reminder that we did not all have to be singing from the same hymn sheet.

I have retained a formal relationship with the *IUR* in the fifteen or so years since I stepped down as editor. Being invited to contribute to various Special Issues over the years has made me feel I might still have something to say. I stepped down as Chair of the journal's Managing Board in late 2018 after five years in that position; the journal is in very good hands and continues to be extremely fortunate in its choice of editors. I no longer have any formal links to the *IUR*, therefore, after thirty years. But as I hope my remarks here show it has always mattered to me and I will continue to read the issues and follow its ongoing progress with great interest. Let's face it, when it comes to this particular journal, I'm a lifer.

Anne Fogarty

Widening the Discussion (2003–2009)

Journals are a vital aspect of academic life and the principal means by which we test out work in progress and convey new approaches to others in our field. Yet they are routinely taken for granted, especially in the humanities, and count for dismayingly little in third-level systems measuring and rewarding impact and achievement. Admittedly, it is only when one actually takes on the task of general or guest editor that the concrete challenges of producing a literary journal are fully brought home. Like everyone else, I had been guilty of blithely overlooking the multiple roles played by editors as they elicit fresh work, structure and shape volumes for publication, network and consult with contributors, and ceaselessly sub-edit and proof-read. Like worker bees, the sustaining activity of editors, ironically, is only noticed when something goes wrong. Sadly, the typos are always your fault and yours alone. And the indispensable work of editors will likely only be really missed when it fails to happen at all.

I was editor of the *Irish University Review* from 2003 to 2009. But I had been inculcated into some of the behind-the-scenes administration of the journal long before that when I joined the editorial board in the mid-1990s, first by Professor Christopher Murray and then Professor Tony Roche, my predecessors as editors. Maurice Harmon, the *IUR's* only begetter, remained a *genius loci*, and was always to hand with kindly but apposite advice. Continuity and ongoing collaboration are striking aspects of the history of the *Irish University Review*; the baton of editor was duly passed on, but an abiding sense of responsibility marked, or maybe scarred, anyone who had once held the post.

The recent past frequently is a blur and retrospection can make it seem that things were more deterministic than was actually the case. How then to describe my seven years as editor of the journal I inherited in 2003? As the first woman editor of *IUR* and someone who has taught feminist theory and women's writing since the beginning of my teaching career in UCC in the mid-1980s, one of my main motivations was to redress some of the gender imbalance in the journal. Or at least

Irish University Review 50.1 (2020): 23–27
DOI: 10.3366/iur.2020.0429
© Edinburgh University Press
www.euppublishing.com/iur

that was my clarion call, principally to myself, at the time. Only two special issues had ever previously been devoted to a single woman writer, Mary Lavin and Eavan Boland, admittedly well-chosen subjects. Writing by women received sporadic attention in the articles regularly submitted to the journal. None of this was by design, more by sexist default and the painfully slow trickle-down effect of political movements. But, by and large, feminist scholarship had tended to by-pass the journal, even though Tony Roche had purposefully widened the scope of the texts covered and encouraged inclusiveness. Ruefully, it must be admitted, that broadening the remit of the journal has been the aim of each of the successive editors of *IUR* in turn. As with anthologies, journals are always recalibrating their fields of concern, but permanently dogged by gaps and omissions.

Indeed, editors are perennially torn between the wish to put their stamp on things and the need to attend to the many authors with whom they are dealing. Certainly, I know that I was forever divided between these two aspects of things: commissioning new content for the journal that would align it in my eyes more adequately with contemporary critical debates often took a back seat to the obligation to engage with and think through the essays that had been accepted and needed careful reworking prior to publication. Shaping and listening seemed to be regularly, although not always, at odds.

The annual special issues of the *IUR*, which were traditionally author-centred, serve in part as markers of change and measures of academic fashions and shifts of focus. Moreover, the excitement of seeing such volumes through to print was a highlight, particularly for the editor. Their publication punctuated each passing year, acting as a pleasingly tangible crescendo to a lot of invisible effort and hard slog. Unusually, the *IUR* celebrated their appearance with a launch, so that, often belatedly, there was a chance to meet up with the contributors and sometimes even the author in question and to take stock of what had been achieved. In 1996, to mark the quadri-centenary of *The Faerie Queene*, at the invitation of Chris Murray, I guest-edited 'Spenser in Ireland'. During my *IUR* tenure, I planned and oversaw special issues on Lady Gregory in 2004, Eiléan Ní Chuilleanáin in 2007 and, with Derek Hand, on Benedict Kiely in 2008. In addition, I worked with Margaret Kelleher on 'New Perspectives on the Irish Literary Revival' in 2003, with John Brannigan and Derek Hand on volumes centring on John McGahern and John Banville in 2005 and 2006, and with Peter Denman on 'Poems that Matter' in 2009.

From the 1980s onwards, Irish Studies was radically changed, indeed in some cases called into being as a serious area of academic inquiry, by politically charged critical debates and the advent of what is cursorily called 'theory' in English departments. Post-colonialism urged the interrogation of notions of seemingly watertight national literatures and fought for new ways of engaging politically with texts, especially those tainted by colonial values. When I did my BA in University College Cork in the late 1970s the study of English had centred squarely on the close reading of texts that were held deliberately apart from history. A sea-change in thinking in the 1980s meant that the socio-political contexts of literary works were suddenly paramount and explored in provocative and illuminating detail. Simultaneously, feminism made us aware of the narrowness and bias of the canon and the systematic neglect and devaluation of female authors. The publication of the first three volumes of the *Field Day Anthology* in 1990 rendered concrete how these fresh understandings upturned received ideas of an Irish literary canon and opened it up in startling ways. It was revolutionary to read Thomas Moore, Edmund Spenser, John Davies, and Edmund Burke, amongst many others, alongside each other, but discomfiting even infuriating to recognise that women's voices and a continuous female literary tradition had been disallowed.

The advent of Volumes IV and V of the *Field Day Anthology* devoted to Irish women's writing in 2003 fanned the flames of this debate about canonicity and the politics of the literary even further while showcasing seemingly innumerable seams of largely forgotten women authors. Above all, opinions clashed about what constituted the proper object for literary study and how marginalised, subaltern, or female voices could adequately be retrieved and analysed. Such debates however seem luxuriously *recherché* and beside the point given that feminism is the continuing blind spot in Irish cultural life if not in Irish Studies generally. Retrospectively, it must now be recognised that post-feminism wrongly presumed that the battle to feminise the canon and create equal spaces for women in the public sphere had been won. Many recent movements, it seems hardly necessary to add, such as #Waking the Feminists have vividly demonstrated the degree to which the silencing, slighting, and side-lining of women continues apace. Feminism is an abiding Irish fault-line and seems always to fall short of its own goals even on the part of its advocates. The retrieval, reinstatement, and recognition of female and subaltern voices in Ireland are ongoing endeavours and permanently unfinished business. Such voices have certainly not yet managed to change mainstream Irish cultural values or even become part of a recognizable and regularly invoked alternative canon.

Not surprisingly, the *IUR* special issues in which I was involved bear all this out, but they also show how the canon can be widened and interrogated in a piecemeal but incremental manner. The special issue on Spenser had been commissioned with the aim of widening the historical span of work considered by the *IUR* and, in a post-Field Day spirit, with the intention of scotching the notion of an 'Irish' text and recognising the hybrid British-Irish nature of literary heritage in the country. The contributors variably read *The Faerie Queene* as a text rooted simultaneously in the Elizabethan conquest of Ireland and also caught up in British sixteenth-century courtly politics. Crisply expert essays by Eiléan Ní Chuilleanáin and Patricia Coughlan, in particular, brought home the degree to which Spenser's epic has entirely different resonances when read against the backdrop of the late sixteenth-century North Munster landscape around Kilcolman or seen through the eyes of seventeenth-century Irish readers such as James Ware and Geoffrey Keating.

2004 was dominated by events to mark the centenary of Bloomsday and the founding of the Abbey theatre. Predictably, Augusta Gregory got little mentioned in the latter context and no effort was made by the Abbey Theatre to revive her plays or re-inspect her legacy. (Admittedly, Yeats's plays were just as studiously ignored). The *IUR* special issue hence plugged a pronounced gap and afforded a necessary opportunity to revisit the many facets of Gregory's output. Rescuing Gregory from the myth that calcified her as permanently aged, patrician, and *passé*, the essays humanised her, recognised her place in the ebb and flow of historical events, and placed a firm emphasis on her endeavours as active writer and arts practitioner. James Pethica illuminatingly traced not just parallels between her plays and those of Synge but also showed how an underground rivalry with the latter spurred and moulded her artistic ambitions. Paige Reynolds' painstaking archival research, by contrast, revealed that Gregory, contrary to current views of her, became a celebrity in the course of the first Abbey tour of the States in 1911 due to her handling of public confrontations, while Lucy McDiarmid in discussing Gregory's relations with Yeats and Wilfred Scawen Blunt persuasively argued that she used her connections with powerful men not to efface herself further but to insert herself into public affairs. Anthony Roche provocatively inscribed her as a predecessor by tracing her influence on Samuel Beckett and Martin McDonagh, while Cathy Leeney equally daringly contended, citing Wittgenstein's adage, if a lion could talk we would not understand him, that we need to view Gregory's play *Grania* outside the contexts of the Revival and its penchant for Celtic myth as a consequential feminist New Woman play that innovatively depicts the impediments to female desire and male same-sex impulses.

The special issue on Eiléan Ní Chuilleanáin afforded the welcome occasion to plumb the work of a contemporary poet that, though held in high regard and widely read, had been under-explored. Difficulty is often invoked as a prohibition conveniently barring further investigation of women authors. The contributors to this volume got past the cursory mantra of the enigmatic, often lazily used to sum up Ní Chuilleanáin's work, to identify the networks of spatial and architectural images that are regularly used as a finely wrought scaffolding in her poems. Above all, the volume crystallised the sense of Ní Chuilleanáin's importance as a philosophical poet and originator of deeply engaged, meditative lyrics. Jefferson Holdridge and Catriona Clutterbuck deftly uncovered the ways in which her work captures abiding interests in spirituality rendered not as orthodox vision but as oblique half-revelations, while Patricia Coughlan's rigorously perceptive examination points to Ní Chuilleanáin's expertise at inter-weaving reflections on life-experience and personal crises with carefully contrived patterns of antinomies and moral paradoxes.

If the special issues that I commissioned or edited succeeded in widening the discussion of contemporary Irish writing, which was still a relatively neglected field at the beginning of the twentieth century, and opening up perspectives on women authors and non-canonical texts such as the novels and short stories of Benedict Kiely, the general issues I worked on were less successful in meeting these goals, although this was not as apparent to me then as it is now. The canon of Irish literature remained obdurately in place in terms of the subject matter covered in these volumes with Joyce, Yeats, and Friel frequently represented. However, they did meet the objective of airing the work of female critics; with the exception of the Autumn/Winter 2004 issue, all of the volumes from 2003–9 achieved gender balance amongst the contributors. In particular, it is gratifying to note how many early career academics, now well-established critical authorities, were amongst this cohort, including Carol Taaffe, Lee M. Jenkins, Lisa Fitzpatrick, Paula Murphy, Pilar Villar Argáiz, Maria Johnston, Aintzane Legarreta Mentxaka, and Marisol Morales Ladrón.

The stock image of an editor is of a pernickety individual unduly worried about semi-colons or commas, fussily correcting texts, and reluctant to let them see the light of day for fear of lingering infelicities. While there may be an element of truth to this, it seems more apt to view editors as enabling project managers who work collaboratively with highly skilled and regularly changing international teams of writers. The labour of editing is largely invisible, but its results are manifold and long-lasting in terms of the work that is published after lengthy pro-cesses of revision and refinement and the intellectual cross-connections and bonds that are forged as a result. The pain of a wrongly placed comma or misquotation eventually recedes, but the friendships I gained as editor of the *IUR* remain a permanent enrichment.

John Brannigan

Shape, Balance, Innovation (2010–2016)

Editing the _Irish University Review_ for seven years was one of the best and most rewarding experiences of my academic life. When Chris Murray invited me to become journal editor, I felt an equal measure of honour and trepidation, and both for the same reason. I was already a member of the editorial board; I had published in the journal, guest edited a special issue on the work of John McGahern, and peer reviewed many submissions. I understood and revered the journal's long-standing reputation for quality and influence in the field of Irish Studies. I also understood the workload involved, which at that time included not just the usual tasks of a journal editor – screening submissions, commissioning peer reviewers, providing decisions and feedback to authors, copy-editing, proofing, and publishing journal issues – but also the tasks of a business manager. The journal was at that time, as had been the case since its foundation, published from University College Dublin, where we were fortunate to have the services of an administrative assistant, Kate Bateman, to assist with managing and collecting subscriptions and sales, distributing copies of the journal worldwide, managing bank accounts, and paying bills to cover designers, typesetters, and printers, among many other jobs. The journal was an international, peer-reviewed journal of the highest standing, with a global base of readers and subscribers, but it was published from a small portacabin office ('the hut', as Kate called it) in the grounds of the Belfield campus, dwarfed by shiny science buildings. The best decision I made when I agreed to become editor was to ask the journal's management board to appoint an Assistant Editor, to share the responsibilities for maintaining the journal's reputation and impact, to which the board duly and wisely responded by appointing Emilie Pine.

Over the course of 2009, and with the generous and judicious mentorship of my predecessor, Anne Fogarty, I gradually took on more responsibility for editing the journal, with the understanding that the first issue to appear on my watch would be the Spring 2010 special issue.

Irish University Review 50.1 (2020): 28–32
DOI: 10.3366/iur.2020.0430
© Edinburgh University Press
www.euppublishing.com/iur

This was a labour of love for all of us who worked on it, and who contributed to it, as it was a special issue devoted to the critical celebration of the work of Frank McGuinness, the internationally renowned and esteemed playwright and poet, who also happened to be our cherished colleague. It made eminent sense for the fortieth anniversary issue to be devoted to Frank's work, which has always been characterised by the same determined quest for excellence and originality as has been the mission of the *Irish University Review*.

Celebrating the fortieth anniversary of the journal in my first year as editor inevitably gave rise to much reflection about its history, purpose, and future. I was the first editor of the *Irish University Review* to have been born after the journal was founded. I mention this, trusting that it causes no embarrassment to my predecessors, to convey my acute sense of inheriting responsibility for an Irish Studies institution. At forty, one is led to believe, one has acquired a certain solidity and dependability. I remember Professor Terence Brown, on launching an *Irish University Review* special issue, commending the journal on the regularity and reliability of its two issues per year, always of steadfast quality. I began to notice also how frequently peer reviewers, in their comments to the editor, made reference to whether the essays they were assessing were a good fit for the *IUR*, whether they were appropriate for *IUR* style, whether they would be a departure from what *IUR* readers had come to expect. There was no mistaking that, at forty, the *IUR* was a mature benchmark of what counted for good scholarship in the field. Special issues were deemed to confer academic honour on their chosen subjects; getting published in the journal was also a matter of honour, an achievement hard won when six out of every seven essays submitted were not accepted for publication.

The authority and reverence afforded the *IUR* was testament to the vision, diligence, and wisdom of the journal's founder, Maurice Harmon, and previous editors, Chris Murray, Tony Roche, and Anne Fogarty, who had successively fought for and won its place in the Irish Studies community and in Irish academic publishing as a durable, quality publication. Dependability was only part of the story of the *IUR*'s reputation, which was also won through adaptation, creativity, and a good editor's nose for the innovation which might be blowing in the wind. I think here of the special issues of the journal which have had demonstrable impact on the shape of Irish literary studies, or essays which might have been rejected on grounds of relevance or convention but instead won scholars in our discipline around to new insights and ways of thinking. The mark of a good journal, indeed the mark of a good editor, is to get that balance right between maintaining the high standards expected of the best scholarly work in our discipline, and pushing the boundaries by gathering new work on underexplored or undercelebrated subjects. The difficulty of accomplishing this balance is that, in a journal which receives many more submissions than it has the capacity to publish, the editor's choices are largely shaped by the quality and range of submitted essays, the recommendations of peer reviewers, and the topics proposed or commissioned for special issues. During my tenure, I commissioned very few essays outside of the special issues, and then only to capture important work which had not yet found a voice in the critical record, or to address an imbalance in the range of authors or topics addressed.

One of the privileges of being the editor of a journal is to see the shape of current trends and practices in your field, to engage with the whole range of colleagues from emergent scholars to eminent professors, and, sometimes, to help to influence new directions or convergences. It is a role which is invested with much authority, but is totally dependent upon close and constant collaboration with authors, peer reviewers, the editorial team, board members, guest editors, copy-editors, typesetters, printers, cover designers, distributors, and, thankfully, also readers and subscribers. In my mind, what characterised my tenure as editor is an extraordinary sense of good fortune and goodwill. I was extraordinarily fortunate to work with as gifted and farsighted an Assistant Editor as Emilie Pine, who has a keen eye for good writing, and an intuitive sense of ideas that merited special issues. I was also extraordinarily fortunate to work with such talented guest editors on special issues. Ian Campbell Ross, Aileen Douglas, and Moyra Haslett were quick off the mark, building on the opportunity afforded by the brilliant work they had been doing in producing new editions of 'Early Irish Fiction' to put together a collection of essays on eighteenth-century Irish writing which expanded and challenged our canonical bias in Irish Studies towards twentieth-century texts. There were less travelled roads in twentieth-century Irish writing, too, however, as Lucy Collins demonstrated in the 2012 special issue which illuminated the hidden corners of poetry cultures in the mid-century period. A much needed blast of Queer theory and politics blew into the pages of the *IUR* with our bright orange special issue in 2013, edited by Anne Mulhall, whose pioneering influence was evident on every page. Cathy Leeney paid dual homage in the 2015 special issue to our colleague and former editor, Chris Murray, and to the field of twentieth-century Irish drama, which he has done so much to define. In the final special issue of my tenure, David Lloyd helped the *IUR* to find a home for experimental poetics, with such radically different voices from the mainstream of modern Irish poetry. In between, I indulged my own efforts to keep the red flag flying for the work of Brendan Behan.

If the special issues of the journal are the places where we, as an Irish Studies community, review and challenge our own perceptions of critical paradigms, focal points, canons, and innovations, a more organic sense of the current state of Irish literary and cultural studies was perhaps discernible from the general issues. Following the ebb and flow of literary critical fashion, it is possible to read the general issues for indications of prevailing authors, methods, or critical frameworks. One trend we noted, however, as the years went by, was that even when the gender of the authors of *IUR* submissions were fairly evenly balanced, there remained an alarming bias in the subjects addressed by those submissions towards male authors. Beckett, Banville, McGahern, Heaney, and Friel each drew their own steady stream of critical attention. Critical work on even the best known women writers came dropping slow. Similarly, submissions to the *IUR* tended to centre on one author; essays which addressed more conceptual aspects of the field were more rare. As a board, we discussed on several occasions the question as to whether such trends as we noted in our submissions were an indication of the state of Irish Studies, or the consequence of the journal having acquired associations with the institutionalisation of the discipline. Re-inventing the journal, now in its fiftieth year, as a home for emergent, innovative scholarship is an ongoing project for the editorial team.

To my mind, as is fitting of the leading journal in its field, the *IUR* is inseparable from the community of scholars it reflects and serves. It remains a source of marvel to me that, as academic life has come more and more under institutional pressure, and academics' time more and more subject to managerial control and 'performance management', so many colleagues from around the world gave their time and energy so willingly and generously to the unpaid labour of peer reviewing submissions. It remains marvellous also that so many authors, upon receiving bad news from me, and despite the intense scramble to publish that now defines early career building in academic life, took time to ask me to convey their gratitude to the reviewers for attending to their work so closely and constructively. In the academic contexts we find ourselves in, of a heavily commercialised and corporatized publishing world based on unpaid intellectual labour, and universities for whom publications are to be counted and not to be read, it is difficult to imagine for how long it will be possible to sustain the idea of a journal as embodying a community of scholars.

Institutional pressures of various kinds impacted on the journal during my time as editor. In the face of austerity cuts, UCD became no longer able to provide the administrative support it had given to the journal since its foundation. As we were going to press with our 2011 special issue, our printers went out of business. As more and more journals were being distributed electronically in corporate bundles, our institutional subscriber base was also declining. As a consequence, the Management Board of the journal took the decision, in consultation with our affiliated association, IASIL, to partner with an academic publisher, and since 2012 the journal has found a good home with Edinburgh University Press. The hut is now no more. Kate and I spent a dusty day clearing out the back issues, invoices, and receipts from the bowels of the Science block. Weekly visits to the bank were replaced with an annual royalty cheque. I did not miss the commercial aspects of journal management, and was able to concentrate instead on the intellectual challenges of editorship. At the heart of journal editing, and at the heart of the *IUR*, is the tireless pursuit of the fundamental mission of academic labour, which is to create and disseminate knowledge. At a time when even universities seem often to forget the value of such a mission, to have been involved in bringing the best new scholarship to publication was a privilege and an honour.

Katie Mishler

The *Irish University Review* in Numbers: Gender, Geography, and History

This survey presents an overview of the changing demographics of contributors to, as well as the changing focus of articles published within, the *Irish University Review*. As one of the leading journals of Irish studies, the publication history of the *Irish University Review* reflects wider trends and shifts within the field of Irish literary studies. The publication also has a longstanding history of presenting creative writing in the form of poetry and prose, and, as a result, creative writers have been counted as contributors (albeit without a specific subject focus in terms of gender or time period). Book reviews make an important contribution to the journal's promotion of the exchange of ideas, and additionally provide a fascinating history of the trends and shifts in Irish literary studies. However, for the purposes of this survey, which primarily seeks to uncover academic and literary contributions, reviews have been excluded.

When possible, this survey has identified the gender and geographic location of the contributor (the latter may or may not correspond to the contributor's nationality), as well as the gender and time period of the subject of the article. Although there may be contributors (or, indeed, subjects) who identify as trans, non-binary, or elsewhere on the spectrum of LGBTQI+, the presence of these gender identities and sexual orientations were notably absent from the available data. For this reason, the categories of male and female have been used to identify contributors and subjects. Additionally, it is impossible to account for the race and ethnic heritage of contributors or subjects based on the available data.

Overall, since the *Irish University Review* began publication in 1970, a total of 1120 contributors have published academic articles or creative writing pieces in the journal. Of this total, 758 men (68%) and 362 women (32%) have contributed to the *IUR*. Throughout the journal's history, over half (53%) of the contributors have been based on the island of Ireland. The remaining contributors tend to be from the

Irish University Review 50.1 (2020): 33–38
DOI: 10.3366/iur.2020.0431
© Edinburgh University Press
www.euppublishing.com/iur

United States (21%), Great Britain (13%), or Canada (8%). In terms of content, a total of 777 articles have been published, 613 of which have focused on a male subject (79%), whereas 164 (21%) have focused on a female writer. In terms of time period, nearly half (48%) of all published articles have been written about subjects active during the time frame of 1950–2000, whereas 31% have focused on 1900–1950, 10% on the 2000s, 7% on the nineteenth century, and 3% on other timeframes. Although these figures provide an overview of the publication's overall history, a more nuanced understanding of general shifts and trends is supplemented by a breakdown of these categories by decade. For example, as will be illustrated below, the attention paid to contemporary writing has grown significantly in recent years.

If we categorise these figures by decade, they clearly reflect general trends and shifts in both academia and the wider culture. In the 1970s, 131 contributors were men (86%) and 21 were women (14%). The majority of contributors were based on the island of Ireland (53%), followed by the United States (27%), Great Britain (9%), Canada (5%), and other regions (5%). In terms of subject, an overwhelming majority of articles (89 total, or 93%) focused on male writers, whereas the remaining articles (7 total, or 7%) were written about women writers. In terms of literary period, nearly half (49%) of subjects featured were active during 1900–1950, 32% during 1950–2000, and 13% during the nineteenth century, with the remaining 7% featuring other time periods. Notably, the first article to be contributed by a female academic in the publication's history was in 1972, whereas the first article to feature a female subject (Mary Lavin) was published in 1977.

The percentages from the 1980s show little change in terms of contributor demographics or content. Out of 182 contributors, 155 were men (85%) and 27 were women (15%). In terms of geographical location, 55% of contributors were based in Ireland, 23% in the United States, 11% in the UK, 6% in Canada, and 6% in other countries. Again, the twentieth century provides the predominant focus of articles, with 47% of articles focusing on figures from 1950–2000, 41% on 1900–1950, 10% on the 1800s, and 2% from other centuries.

The 1990s show some changes, particularly in terms of the gender of contributors and the gender of subjects, whereas most other categories remain largely unchanged. Out of 275 contributors, 199 were men (72%) and 76 were women (28%); geographically, 54% of contributors were located on the island of Ireland, 21% in the United States, 12% in the UK, 5% in Canada, and 9% in other areas. Of the featured subjects, 136 were male writers (80%) and 34 were female writers (20%), whereas 53% of subjects featured were from 1950–2000, 33% from 1900–1950, 6% from the 1800s, and 8% from other time periods (notably, 6% of these articles were about the sixteenth century).

The 2000s demonstrate the greatest change in demographics, particularly in terms of closing the gap between the gender of contributors. Out of 259 contributors, 153 (59%) were men and 106 (41%) were women. In terms of geographic breakdown, 52% were again based on the island of Ireland, 18% in Great Britain, 15% in the United States, 2% in Canada, and 13% in other countries, demonstrating some growth in contributors from outside the core Anglophone countries. Although there was a significant jump in the number of female contributors, the number of female subjects remained low: 73% of subjects were male, and 27% of subjects were female. In terms of time period, there was an increased focus on contemporary writing: 58% of articles focused on 1950–2000, 23% on 1900–1950, 15% on the 2000s, 2% on the nineteenth century, and 2% on other periods.

The 2010s saw the most significant shift. For the first time ever in the journal's publication history, slightly more women (132, or 52%) than men (120, or 48%) published work within the *Irish University Review*. This number is striking in comparison to the first decade of the journal. The geographic location stayed largely the same, as 53% of contributors were based in Ireland, 21% in the United States, 14% in Great Britain, 2% in Canada, and 9% in other diverse areas. In terms of subjects, 71% of articles focused on male writers, and 29% focused on female writers. There was again a greater representation of contemporary writing featured, with 35% of articles researching 1950–2000, 29% the 2000s, 20% the period of 1900–1950, and 10% on other periods.

Achieving gender equality in academia ensures that a diverse range of voices, approaches, and perspectives are given the opportunity to contribute to the state of the field. According to this study, the greatest change seen across the journal's publication history has been the increase of female contributors, growing from less than one-sixth (14%) in the 1970s to slightly over half (52%) in the 2010s. The shift towards gender parity corresponds to an increased cultural and critical awareness of feminist issues and women's rights, as well as increased education and publication opportunities for women. The diversification of scholars within Irish literary studies has subsequently led to a widening of critical frameworks to include feminist and queer theories, ultimately enriching the field. Unfortunately, it is beyond the scope of this study to acknowledge the breadth of contributions women have made to Irish literary studies both within and outside of the journal, particularly in terms of recovering female writers, questioning the canon, and pioneering scholarship on the relationship between gender, nation, and sexuality.

Although there has been some progress across decades, less than a third of scholarly articles published by the journal have focused on the work of female writers, suggesting that less critical work on female writers is being written, submitted, and accepted for publication. Given the ongoing efforts of feminist academics to promote the reading, teaching, publication, and critical review of Irish women's writing, there is hope that the number of articles on female writers will increase in the future. Additionally, future bibliographic studies of the history of Irish feminist criticism, the recovery of Irish women's writing, and the publication of Irish women writers are needed in order to shed more light on this subject.

The one demographic which remained relatively unchanged across decades is the geography of contributors. Outside of Ireland, the majority of contributors live and work in English-speaking countries with a history of Irish emigration (and which, subsequently, have been home to Irish studies centres and departments): the United States, Great Britain, and Canada. Although slightly over half of all contributors consistently have been living on the island of Ireland, the geographic range of contributors to this international journal reflects and promotes the global study of Irish writing.

One of the most interesting and potentially promising findings of the survey is the increased interest in contemporary writing. This interest in contemporary writing can partially be seen to have contributed to the increased interest in female writers. The production of new literature by new authors with new sensibilities and priorities presents opportunities for new forms of critical engagement, as well as the potential for reading and writing about more diverse work from a variety of perspectives, experiences, and identities. Ireland itself is seeing a shift in racial and ethnic demographics with increased immigration to the country, and an increased awareness of structural racism. This diversity and commitment to anti-racist action will hopefully be reflected in future Irish writing and criticism, which the *Irish University Review* promises to play an active role in shaping.

1970s

Contributors:

Men 131 (86%)
Women 21 (14%)

Subjects:

Men 89 (91%)
Women 7 (7%)

Literary Periods:

Pre-1800 10 (7%)
Nineteenth 19 (13%)
1900–1950 74 (4(%)
1950–2000 49 (32%)

Geographical Location:

Ireland 69 (53%)
USA 35 (27%)
Canada 7 (5%)
UK 12 (9%)
Rest of World 6 (5%)

1980s

Contributors:

Men 155 (85%)
Women 27 (15%)

Subjects:

Men 87 (94%)
Women 6 (6%)

Literary Periods:

Pre-1800 4 (2%)
Nineteenth 16 (10%)
1900–1950 68 (41%)
1950–2000 77 (47%)

Geographical Location:

Ireland 87 (55%)
USA 36 (23%)
Canada 9 (6%)
UK 17 (11%)
Rest of World 10 (6%)

1990s

Contributors:

Men 199 (72%)
Women 76 (28%)

Subjects:

Men 136 (80%)
Women 34 (20%)

Literary Periods:

Medieval 1 (.5%)
Sixteenth 12 (6%)
Eighteenth 3 (1.5%)
Nineteenth 11 (6%)
1900–1950 65 (33%)
1950–2000 104 (53%)

Geographical Location:

Ireland 129 (54%)
USA 49 (21%)
Canada 12 (5%)
UK 28 (12%)
Rest of World 21 (9%)

2000s

Contributors:		Subjects:		Literary Periods:		Geographical Location:	
Men	153 (59%)	Men	162 (73%)	Pre-1800	5 (2%)	Ireland	126 (52%)
Women	106 (41%)	Women	59 (27%)	Nineteenth	5 (2%)	USA	36 (15%)
				1900–1950	52 (23%)	Canada	6 (2%)
				1950–2000	134 (58%)	UK	43 (18%)
				2000s	35 (15%)	Rest of Europe	25 (10%)
						Rest of World	7 (3%)

2010s

Contributors:		Subjects:		Literary Periods:		Geographical Location:	
Men	120 (48%)	Men	139 (71%)	Pre-1600	6 (2.5%)	Ireland	118 (53%)
Women	132 (52%)	Women	58 (29%)	Seventeenth	6 (2.5%)	USA	47 (21%)
				Eighteenth	12 (5%)	Canada	4 (2%)
				Nineteenth	14 (6%)	UK	32 (14%)
				1900–1950	45 (20%)	Rest of Europe	17 (8)
				1950–2000	81 (35%)	Rest of World	3 (2%)
				2000s	66 (29%)		

Matt Kennedy

Some Things are Worth Losing to Become./?

Trans Masculinity | Queer Autoethnography | Where Theory and the Body Collide

***

'Will you go the whole way with this?' My mother, now sobbing hard into her second cappuccino in the Phoenix Park, referring to me getting phalloplasty surgery to medically construct a penis using what changes testosterone affords my genitals and a skin graft from my leg or arm. She doesn't know or ask the details, but I shake my head, lacking the words to explain how my embodiment was never in opposition to my genitals. I explain that the surgery is simply too dangerous and expensive at this point in time. 'But how will you be half and half? In-between? He/she? How will you be wanted or loved when you have no breasts but also no penis? How will you be?' We are both sobbing now.

***

I am writing from the in-between. In one month I will undergo a bilateral mastectomy, more commonly understood as top surgery, which is the removal of breast tissue and the reconstruction of a 'male' presenting chest frequently opted for by 'female to male' transgender people. I am writing, and changing, and writing, and theorising. I have been hurtling towards my own becoming, and at the same rapid pace I have been engaged in academic endeavours to account for my changing embodiment, shifting subjectivity, contested sexuality, and the anxiety that I will become that which I fear: a man. I have many

Irish University Review 50.1 (2020): 39–50
DOI: 10.3366/iur.2020.0432
© Edinburgh University Press
www.euppublishing.com/iur

questions surrounding these feelings; questions I may never have the answers to. One of these questions is that of my trans masculinity and its relation to my former identifications. Through theory I am engaged in an ongoing interrogation of what it means to become a legible man as someone who was born female and was a tomboy, a confused straight young woman, a lesbian, a stone butch, and a gender-non-conforming person before arriving, rooted, in trans masculinity.

Theory has always been the space where I can best account for my trans masculinity. Just as bell hooks saw theory as a location for healing,[1] I saw theory as a location to account for my becoming. Queer theory gave me an opportunity to engage in the liberatory practice described by hooks and presented me with a long lineage of theorists who saw me before I understood what I truly meant when I said 'I'.[2] As I discovered queer theory, I found an equally passionate engagement with auto-ethnography in my Gender Studies Masters. Autoethnography is an approach to research and writing that seeks to describe and system-atically analyse (*graphy*) personal experience (*auto*) in order to under-stand cultural experience (*ethno*);[3] queer autoethnographies allow for the creation of narratives which bring together the 'ideas, intentions, practices and affects of queer theory with the purposes and practice of autoethnography'.[4] The implementation of queer theory, fused with a prioritised queer identity as a significant theme within the autoethno-graphy, directs the academic reading of the text from queers 'doing' autoethnography towards an understanding of queer autoethnography. And so what follows is my version of such a queer autoethnography; a polyamorous relationship between my story, my queerness/transness, and my relationship and interpretation of theory. Queer theory acts as the foundational means to understanding the confessions of the 'I' within this article, and as a bridge between the narrative within the text and the real-life imitations of said experience.[5]

Moving beyond simply 'telling stories', autoethnography creates an academic space in which the researcher can critique and establish the possibility for change from *within* the 'politically and personally problematic worlds of everyday life'.[6] In this vein autoethnographies create new terrains of artistic research in which identities, embodiment, subjectivity, and an array of complex ideals are allowed to change and are opened up to interpretation, brick by brick deconstructing the ivory tower of the academy.[7] It is within this context that autoethnography and queerness intersect as methods and methodological approaches which seek to work against 'the fixity and firmness, certainty and closure, stability and rigid categorization of identities and experiences'.[8] It is this active engagement with the vulnerability of static identity that draws queer researchers, including myself, to autoethnography. Finally, autoethnography allows the researcher to engage with non-normative sources. My source is, so often, my body, in this case the tattoos on my body, which are personal referents to my queerness and transness. Tattoos are my method of taking back control over my body (a body which is often 'read' wrong); they are also deeply connected to theory, literature, cinema, and lived experiences. In this particular space, I want to account for my trans masculinity in theory, through a queer autoethnographic reading of my body as it is in this moment before it is changed utterly by surgery, as it has been changed utterly by tattoos and testosterone. The images on my body are an homage to the theories that both account for and inform my embodiment, sexuality, and subjectivity. They represent an opportunity for change, gender euphoria in the colour on my arms and the new hair on my face; by both I am changed utterly, undone.

THE ONLY TRANS IN THE VILLAGE
Nicole: *You don't seem like you're from around here.*
Brandon: *Where ... where do I seem like I'm from?*
Nicole: *Someplace ... beautiful.* (*Boys Don't Cry*, 1999[9])

Figure 1. Boys Don't Cry tattoo.

My 'BOYS DON'T CRY' tattoo is an explicit reference to the film (1991) directed by Kim Pierce, starring Hilary Swank as the late Brandon Teena; the tattoo creates in ink an homage to the cinematic account of

Teena's life leading up to his tragic murder. The tattoo encompasses more than a memorial of Brandon Teena's legacy in cinema, though – it is a reference to what Halberstam has called the 'Brandon archive': the cultural production of Brandon Teena's legacy as 'a resource, a productive narrative, a set of representations, a history, a memorial, and a time capsule'.[10] This tattoo makes my body a part of the 'Brandon Archive', serving as a reminder of my own rural trans masculinity, its vulnerability, its isolation. How different is Brandon Teena's Falls City, Nebraska from Ballinghassig, Co. Cork when both Brandon and I could've walked for miles through a landscape and never crossed paths with a body that would mirror our own?

Boys Don't Cry and the story of Brandon's life speak implicitly to the necessity to negate one's connection to a rural spatiality in order to consolidate a queer identity. I left bogland and green fields in favour of being a legible trans man in an urban centre. Queer metronormativity accounts for the migration of rural queers to urban centres in search of potentially greater acceptance for their queerness. The displacement of queer bodies from their rural place of origin to urban centres promotes a cultural ideal of tolerance away from the 'suspicion, persecution, and secrecy' of rural communities (Halberstam, p.37). I can empathise with the cultural figure of 'the only gay in the village', a phrase which constructs queer identity as antithetical to a rural attachment, but transness even more so has no place in the Irish countryside unless it is rendered invisible.

In Boys Don't Cry Brandon's masculinity and identity are only rendered unstable and warranting of punishment when he is subjected to the violence of inspection by the other rural men and discovered to be assigned female at birth (Halberstam, p.93). Up until this point he assimilates into the rural practices of masculinity – drinking and roughhousing; he is one of the boys. Lucas Crawford problematises the dichotomy of queer/urban versus homophobe/rural and makes the case for 'queer rural temporality', questioning Halberstam's framing of trans masculinity as fundamentally opposed to a rural existence.[11] However, there seems to be a lack of interrogation on Crawford's behalf as to what trans people risk when they make recognisable their queerness in the communities that knew them as their assigned sex at birth. There was never the opportunity for my masculinity to be recognised as legitimate in West Cork, where I was always understood as someone's daughter, where the biggest concern was always 'what will the neighbours think?' I was a trans man from Cork; the from is significant.

And in part maybe I internalised this narrative. Maybe despite my bravado, my swaggering trans masculinity as I bounded beneath the city lights, the isolation I had felt in rural West Cork remained, an isolation that drove me to leave and which means I cannot imagine returning. Brandon Teena did not subject himself to metronormativity, though it might have saved him; as Thomas Page McBee speculates, 'He could've moved to a city. Maybe he'd still be alive if he had'.[12] But, concludes, bravery kept Teena rooted, 'knowing that there's part of you that cannot be harmed'.[13] I understand why Brandon Teena did not leave the barren landscape of rural Nebraska; we should not need to migrate to urban centres to be legible, nor should our identities hinge on being stealthy in the areas that breathed life into us. My 'BOYS DON'T CRY' tattoo becomes, therefore, a complicated archive of emotion, a reminder of the violence trans bodies have endured, an ode to Brandon's memory: cinematic and cultural and a reference to rural trans masculinity, the desire to return eventually as the men we are to where we are from.

QUEER TEMPORALITY: U-HAULED BY THEORY

'Queer time for me is the dark nightclub, the perverse turn away from the narrative coherence of adolescence-early adulthood-marriage-reproduction-child rearing-retirement-death'.[14]

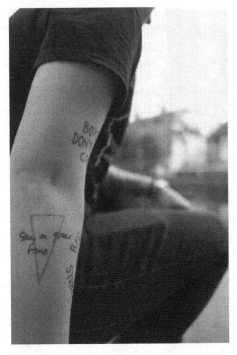

Figure 2. Stay on Queer Time tattoo.

In November 2017, during my Gender Studies Masters, I had the pleasure of attending a lecture by Jack Halberstam and he signed my copy of *In a Queer Time and Place: Transgender Bodies, Subcultural Lives*, writing: 'To Matt - Stay On Queer Time'. This is so utterly significant to me, my relationship to queer theory, temporality, and my body that I placed it forever on my arm in his handwriting. In relation to temporality and futurity, the notion of queer time as a juxtaposition to normative time is an idea that I was fascinated with since the moment I encountered it. Queer time, according to Halberstam, develops in 'opposition to the institutions of family, heterosexuality, and reproduction' (p.1) and represents not simply an alternative form of sexuality or gender but in fact an entirely altered way of life. Halberstam's theorisation of queer time is significantly positioned as an alternative to straight time, which can be understood best through Elizabeth Freeman's theorising of 'chrononormativity'[15] and Lee Edelman's 'reproductive futurity'.[16] Halberstam states that 'reproductive time and family time are, above all, heteronormative time/ space constructs' (p.10). Straight time is constructed as a methodological form of temporal organisation, which depends on reproduction, productivity, and the recreation of a normative population through normative sexuality and gender. Thus, straight time has intrinsic links to capitalism and the framing of worth and personhood on the basis of capital accumulation and production. Queer time emerges as the antithesis of the heteronormative organisation of time (Halberstam, p.4), which centres the politics of chrononormativity,[17] reproductive futurism, capitalist production, and normative gender and sexuality as the means of access to futurity.[18]

Queer time for me is an opportune displacement from the expectations placed upon me by heterosexual, cisgender society; it is a process of refusal of consumer and reproductive practices, subcultural production and tragic interiorities.[19] My transness places me in a time outside of time, a space where I can reconfigure my identity to be unrestricted by normative expectations of my body, my sexuality, my relationships, my academic endeavours, and any engagement with capitalism and systems of power. Halberstam's plea for me to 'Stay on Queer Time' functions on my body as a signifier of my disengagement from chronormativity but equally as a promise to destabilise the ways that 'straight time' confines bodies. In order to truly 'Stay on Queer Time' I need to recognise that which polices the orientation of my body into a regimented organisation of my life, efforts by systems of power and social cues to reorient my body back into normative time. Drawing from Sara Ahmed's *Queer Phenomenology*, 'the temporality of orientation reminds us that orientations are effects of what we tend toward, where the "toward" marks a space and time that is almost but not quite, available in the present'.[20] In order to be on 'straight time', one must not only 'tend' towards a cultural production of heterosexuality but equally turn one's back on all which society deems deviant or non-normative. To 'Stay on Queer Time' I must orient my body towards the queer, the trans, the unknown, the non-monogamous, anti-capitalist; I must recognise that queer time is not within the present for me to 'tend' to in the same way as 'straight time'; it may be that queer time is just beyond the horizon. This gives rise to José Esteban Muñoz's ideal of queerness as utopian.[21] By presenting queer time as an alternative to capitalist inscriptions of existence, queerness – and by extension transness – allows for a new space in which our existence is not policed by normativity and we can imagine an existence, a way of being, a sense of self that is an 'ideality that can be distilled from the past and used to imagine a future' (Muñoz, p.1).

EVEN STONE BUTCHES GET THE BLUES: WOMAN OR MAN?
Jess Goldberg: 'I'll send it to a place where they keep women's memories safe. Maybe someday, passing through this big city, you will stop and read it. Maybe you won't.' (Feinberg, p.6)

Figure 3. Stone Butch tattoo.

If *Boys Don't Cry* reveals to me a cinematic connection between my rural trans masculinity and that of Brandon Teena, *Stone Butch Blues* presents a literary manifestation of my contestation with my embodiment. When Leslie Feinberg was asked if *Stone Butch Blues* was real or a work of fiction, ze responded: 'Is it real? Oh, it's real all right. So real it bleeds. And yet it is a remembrance: Never underestimate the power of fiction, to tell the truth' (Feinberg, p.337). While it is impossible to know what aspects of the novel are fiction and which hold autobiographical influence, it is safe to assume that the main trajectory of the book is heavily influenced by Feinberg's own life. I adore this aspect of the novel where lived experience is moulded discretely into beautifully constructed fictional narratives. The novel's main plot follows Feinberg's own life in relation to the medical transition in which both Jess, the protagonist, and Feinberg hirself, halt HRT mid-process due to feelings of congestion in hir identity. This congestion is perfectly iterated as 'I don't feel like a man trapped in a woman's body. I just feel trapped' (Feinberg, p.171).

My first reading of *Stone Butch Blues* took place during the Christmas of 2017; I fluctuated between racked sobs and silent tears throughout the reading, feeling utterly seen by the words. The overlap and intersections in Jess's embodiment and my own were devastating, I could not put it down, I carried the book in my bag for months after, flicking through the pages whenever someone misgendered me, desperate to be understood, desperate to understand myself. The tattoo of the stone butch is a tribute to this text which, despite its vastness in accounting for what appears to be a very particular experience of trans identification, is incidentally incredibly reverential to my own experience and that of many trans masculine people. Since starting testosterone the text weighs even heavier when I carry it; when Jess begins taking testosterone and has top surgery, ze describes a newfound sense of gender euphoria, a sense of solace in hir skin for the first time: 'It had been so long since I'd been at home in my body' (Feinberg, p.184). And while Jess's gender euphoria comes at the cost of a loss of identification with lesbian culture and community, my gender euphoria in beginning HRT has had a profound effect on my embodiment. I am finally at home in my body, it no longer feels as though it is something I drag around with me. What leads to Jess's halting of HRT and zir presentation as a man is the complexity of passing:

> At first, everything was fun. The world stopped feeling like a gauntlet I had to run through. But very quickly I discovered that passing didn't just mean slipping below the surface, it meant being

buried alive. I was still me on the inside, trapped in there with all my wounds and fears. But I was no longer me on the outside (Feinberg, p.186).

Jess realises that hir 'passing' as a man is subsequently hir 'identities unbecoming'. While moving into the sphere of male masculinity may afford a sense of assimilation and safety, Jess still feels the effects of hir 'wounds and fears' (Feinberg, p.186). The masculinity that Jess is afforded in 'passing' is not one that denotes queerness or connection to a stone butch past but is in actuality the marker of a dismissed lesbian past. It signifies a 'moving up the ladder of social acceptability – importantly, not so much from female to male as from queer-looking butch to clean-cut straight young man'.[22]

I am now in a space of negotiating what it means to 'become a man'; as someone who was a queer-looking butch, after five months on testosterone I am more recognisable as a man, my voice breaking, my body producing hair at an accelerating rate, my genitals moving into the in-between, my breasts shrinking, hips diminishing, muscles hardening, veins visible. Sometimes I speak and I do not recognise the sound, occasionally caught off guard by my angular hairy body in the mirror. I pass now; I am a young man and I am afraid just as Jess was. I am afraid that my passing, my movement into a trans masculine embodiment, will cause me to lose touch with that which radicalised me and informed my identity, my lesbian past, my feminism, my stone butch identity melting as I become more accustomed to a body that finally feels like a home, allowing myself to be touched, to be seen. My male embodied stone butch tattoo is a reimagining of the protagonist within *Stone Butch Blues*, a trans masculine person who negotiates the complexity of passing, an art piece that functions as a reminder of my past and all the embodiments and subjectivities that have informed my understanding of the self to this moment.

'Trans bodies represent the art of becoming, the necessity of imagining, and the fleshly insistence of transivity':[23] to be trans is to exist in a constant state of remembering the versions of the self that existed before, contesting the version that holds the book now, still flicking through the pages, having carried it for months, I cry for different reasons upon re-encountering the text. I am faced with a divergence in mine and Jess's story yet I do not feel as though my new embodiment as a young queer man is in conflict with a past informed by a stone butch identity. I have learned through the theories of embodiment woven throughout *Stone Butch Blues* that there is a multiplicity to our lives as trans people. *Stone Butch Blues* as a novel is a depiction of the complexity of identity: butch, dyke, faggot, trans, queer, man, woman – Jess longs for answers to where hir body should reside. Does ze remain as a man losing hir queer identity but securing safety and a likeness for hir body, making a home out of hir body? Is there a way for trans people to have both? I will let you know when I find out.

./?

'Why so difficult, remembering the actual look of you? Without a photograph, without strain?'[24]

I chose to medically transition because everyone deserves the opportunity to build their body into a home, especially when the homes we come from feel hostile and unsafe to house our queerness. As a result of being trans, 'home is now a never-ending quest of my making', as Chase Joynt has written:

Yesterday I passed a trans woman stocking shelves in the aisle of the local drug store. We locked eyes. 'Home might be here', I thought.[25]

The title of this essay, 'Somethings are worth losing to become', references a final unseen tattoo with those words on a tombstone featuring the date I received my first testosterone shot. This tattoo is in relation to my feelings about my parents; getting the tattoo was a statement, all it was missing was a full stop; it had a sense of finality to it; I would lose them to become.

***

However, months pass, and we negotiate home and love and names, and we sit in the Phoenix Park and drink cold coffee. I smoke my father's cigarettes and I wonder should a question mark be placed at the end.

NOTES

Photography throughout this essay is by Stephen Moloney.

1. bell hooks, 'Theory as Liberatory Practice', *Yale Journal of Law and Feminism* 4.1 (1991), 1–12 (p.1).
2. See the work of Kate Bornstein, *Gender Outlaw: On Men, Women, and the Rest of Us* (London and New York: Routledge, 1994); Leslie Feinberg, *Stone Butch Blues: A Novel* (Ithaca, N.Y: Firebrand Books, 1993); Jack Halberstam, *In a Queer Time and Place: Transgender Bodies, Subcultural Lives* (London and New York: New York

University Press, 2005); José Esteban Muñoz, *Cruising Utopia: The Then and There of Queer Futurity* (London and New York: New York University Press, 2009); Julia Serano, *Whipping Girl: A Transsexual Woman on Sexism and the Scapegoating of Femininity* (Emeryville, CA: Seal Press, 2007); Sandy Stone, 'The EMPIRE Strikes Back: A Posttranssexual Manifesto' Available at https://sandystone.com.empire-strikes-back.pdf; Susan Stryker, *Transgender History* (Berkeley, CA: Seal Press, 2008).

3. Carolyn Ellis, *The Ethnographic I: A Methodological Novel about Autoethnography* (Walnut Creek, CA: AltaMira Press, 2004); Stacy Holman Jones, 'Autoethnography: Making the Personal Political', in *Handbook of Qualitative Research*, ed. by Norman K. Denzin and Yvonna S. Lincoln (Thousand Oaks, CA: Sage, 2005), pp.763–791; Carolyn Ellis, Tony E. Adams & Arthur P. Bochner, 'Autoethnography: An overview', *Forum: Qualitative Social Research* 12.1 (2011). Available at: http://www.qualitative-research.net/index.php/fqs/issue/view/36.

4. Tony E. Adams and Derek M. Bolen, 'Tragic Queer at the Urinal Stall, Who, Now, Is the Queerest One of All? Queer Theory I Autoethnography I Doing Queer Autoethnography', *QED: A Journal in GLBTQ Worldmaking* 4.1 (2017), 100–113 (p.104).

5. Clair Doloriert and Sally Sambrook, 'Ethical Confessions of the "I" of Autoethnography: The Student's Dilemma', *Asia Pacific Journal of Marketing and Logistics* 4.1 (2009), 27–45.

6. Norman K. Denzin, *Performance Ethnography: Critical Pedagogy and the Politics of Culture* (Thousand Oaks, CA: SAGE, 2003), p.236.

7. Tony E. Adams, 'Mothers, Faggots, and Witnessing (Un)con-testable Experience', *Cultural Studies ↔ Critical Methodologies* 1 (2009), 619–626; Jonathan Wyatt 'What Kind of Mourning? Autoethnographic Fragments', *International Review of Qualitative Research* 2 (2010), 499–512.

8. Tony E. Adams and Stacy Holman Jones, 'Telling Stories: Reflexivity, Queer Theory, and Autoethnography', *Cultural Studies ↔ Critical Methodologies* 11.2 (2011), 108–116 (p.110).

9. *Boys Don't Cry*, dir. by Kimberly Peirce (20th Century Fox, 1999).

10. Jack Halberstam, *In a Queer Time and Place: Transgender Bodies, Subcultural Lives* (London; New York: New York University Press, 2005), p.23. Further references in parentheses in the text.

11. Lucas Crawford, 'A good ol' Country Time: Does Queer Rural Temporality Exist?', *Sexualities* 20.8 (2016), 904–920.

12. Thomas P. McBee, *Man Alive* (Edinburgh: Canongate Books, 2017), p.156.

13. McBee, *Man Alive*, p.157.

14. Carolyn Dinshaw, Lee Edelman, Richard A. Ferguson, Carlo Freccero, Elizabeth Freeman, Jack Halberstam, Annamarie Jagose, Christopher Nealon and Tan Hoang Nguyen, 'Theorizing Queer Temporalities', *GLQ: A Journal of Lesbian and Gay Studies* 13.2–3 (2007), 177–195 (p.182).

15. Elizabeth Freeman, *Time Binds: Queer Temporalities, Queer Histories* (Durham, NC: Duke University Press, 2010).

16. Lee Edelman, *No Future: Queer Theory and the Death Drive* (Durham, NC: Duke University Press, 2005).

17. Freeman, *Time Binds*, p.3.

18. Edelman, *No Future*, p.2.

19. Lisa Duggan, *The Twilight of Equality?: Neoliberalism, Cultural Politics, and the Attack on Democracy* (Boston: Beacon, 2003); see also Halberstam, *In A Queer Time and Place*, and Heather Love, *Feeling Backward: Loss and the Politics of Queer History* (Cambridge, MA: Harvard University Press, 2009).

20. Sara Ahmed, *Queer Phenomenology: Orientations, Objects, Others* (Durham, NC: Duke University Press, 2006), p.554.
21. Muñoz, *Cruising Utopia*.
22. Jay Prosser, *Second Skins: The Body Narratives of Transsexuality* (New York: Columbia University Press, 1998), p.182.
23. Jack Halberstam, *Trans: A Quick and Quirky Account of Gender Variability* (Oakland, CA: University of California Press, 2018), p.136.
24. Mark Doty, 'The Embrace', *Sweet Machine* (New York: HarperCollins, 1998).
25. Mark Hoolboom and Chase Joynt, *You Only Live Twice: Sex, Death, and Transition* (Canada: Coach House Books, 2016), p.123.

Deirdre Flynn

On Being Precarious

'Eight years, if you can stick it out for eight years, you'll make it.'

On one of my first teaching contracts post PhD, a colleague brought me for coffee. He knew I was on an hourly short-term contract, and as a result I would wait two months to get paid, I wouldn't have an office and my name wouldn't appear on the email to welcome new staff, but he said I was now on the ladder. I just had to hold on for eight years. My reward would be a permanent job. In the meantime, I was to say yes to everything, keep the complaining to a minimum, and make sure I used all my spare time to write – remember 'it'll be good for your cv'.

It's been four years since we had that chat. I've taken every contract that came my way, hourly, zero hour, part-time, full-time, fixed-term, specific purpose. I have only survived this long because I have an understanding partner who has a permanent job, sympathetic social welfare employees, and a very generous relationship with the credit union. At the end of every month either my partner or the credit union supplements my income because my wage won't cover my expenses.

When my rent increased by 70% in 2017, the landlord said to me 'sure you're a university lecturer'. I didn't have the heart to tell her that the new rent was now the same as my monthly income, and 50% of that income went towards travelling to and from work. We moved out of the city and now live in rural Ireland. Our main concern in sourcing new rental accommodation was that the rent could be paid on one income, as mine was never dependable, or enough. In fact, things were so tight that year that we cut back on home heating and other basic expenses so we could afford to send me to work. How long more can I ask my partner to put his life on hold to support me in this industry? How do you plan when you live from semester to semester? How do you save, get a mortgage, have children, get married, book holidays, feel secure?

I see myself as lucky – I cannot imagine how I would do this as a single person, a parent, a carer, or with any other barriers seen

Irish University Review 50.1 (2020): 51–54
DOI: 10.3366/iur.2020.0433
© Edinburgh University Press
www.euppublishing.com/iur

or unseen. The odds can be stacked against you if you have caring responsibilities, you're not white, you're a woman, you're not economically secure, you have any health issues. Last year, I had three different contracts in three institutions, meaning I was only out of work for six weeks of the year. The social welfare payment, which is also subject to tax, brought my total income to just above €20,000. That's well below the living wage. Part of that income included 110+ two-thousand-word essays that I corrected for the princely sum of €0.46 a script. In order to make the minimum wage I would have had to correct, assess, give feedback, and upload the grades of twenty-one essays an hour. Still, in 2018 I managed to attend three conferences, two of which were outside of Ireland, and pay my rent (mostly). This year, I'm covering for two full-time staff in two different institutions on opposite sides of the country, and the combined income doesn't equal one full-time salary. I'm thinking of writing a book on how to live on nothing – every publication counts, right?

I recently had the opportunity to calculate all of the work I had done post PhD. Over the course of five years my contracts added up to approximately 115 months. That's nine and a half years of employment over five years. That includes periods of unemployment, but doesn't include any work such as conference organisation, network administration, peer reviewing, applying for funding, conference attendance, conference papers, journal editing, and training. Not included in that calculation is my final year as a box office manager in a theatre, a full-time job that ended in the first year of my academic career. Most of those contracts didn't cover me for the over fifteen publications I published during that period either. Seeing the numbers laid out like that shocks even me. Because despite all this work, I have spent most of the last five years berating myself for not doing enough, not achieving more, disappointed and worried when I had to say no to publications, conferences, opportunities, and events. I felt I was underachieving and should have been working harder. If I didn't work seven days a week, I was lazy, unprofessional, and obviously not motivated and ambitious enough.

But my story isn't unusual. Every week I have the same conversations with disillusioned PhDs and early career researchers in different institutions wondering how they will keep going, or I read another social media post from someone who is leaving academia behind. I'm one of thousands of PhDs, postdocs, early career and not so early career academics. You know us, because we teach most of your undergraduate courses. In one institution I know, fifty percent of all undergraduate teaching is provided by people on precarious contracts. The work is there, but secure contracts are not. New graduates are pumped out on an assembly line to take the place of burned out early career academics that can no longer take it. Their research, their experience, all gone with them.

We get paid to teach, and we research, mentor, administrate (the list goes on) for free. We work on trains, in coffee shops, at evenings, weekends. We choose writing over spending time with family and friends. And when we're not writing, and researching, we're preparing lectures for another new module in another new institution. Or we're in the credit union asking for a loan so we can go to that 'must be seen and network at' conference.

The bar for entry level posts keeps rising. They want an ECR who has supervised PhDs, secured multiple funding streams, published in the right journals, contributed to college committees. These are many of the systems that we are locked out of because we're not long enough in one institution to know where the books we need are in the library. We can't take on PhD students, because we don't know where, or even if we'll be employed next semester, never mind three or four years down the road. And when you do get full-time salaried work, you're put on the lowest point of the scale, because your hourly contracts are judged as much less, and some are deemed 'not relevant' for scale calculation. Years of hourly contracts may equate to less than a year because of thirty-year-old salary and grade calculators that relate to practices long out of date and no longer relevant to the current systems, which depend on low paid exploitative labour. You get demoted because as an hourly-paid employee you are not equal, you are less than the colleagues you work alongside. Those hours you spent preparing lectures, responding to students, completing academic administration and mentoring are worthless, irrelevant. How can you argue the principle of the matter when your academic experience is worthless to them because it is hourly paid?

For those of us who are first generation academics there is a vocabulary, a secret language, a code we weren't aware of that can lock people out of opportunities. There are many more opportunities we have to say no to for financial, caring, parenting, and health reasons. Conferences we can't attend because they don't offer discounts for precarious employees, and asking for discounts can feel demeaning. We don't always speak up because we don't want to be singled out as difficult and troublesome. With huge numbers applying for every job you don't want any negative association with your name. We've all been warned – 'tone it down'. Even writing this makes me nervous, what doors have I closed by being honest?

We need the help of our senior colleagues in secure jobs to shout for us. We need them to say that they will no longer accept an unfair hierarchical system that forces their colleagues to be exploited and pushed into poverty. I've been lucky on many occasions because my colleagues have fought with HR over my remuneration, have made sure I have an office, or that I can claim back conference expenses (I dream of a conference budget!). One of my senior colleagues asked me to share some of my research with her so she could use it in her modules – it was such a simple way to support me, but it meant so much. And we know that many of our colleagues are on below-the-bar contracts, paid up to €20,000 less than their departmental equivalents, and that in reality what exists is a *three*-tier system: precarious, below-the-bar, and permanent.

Our voices need to be represented on the committees, in the meetings – but we are often not included, silencing large portions of the academic staff. Precarious and hourly-paid representatives need to be at departmental meetings, union meetings, network meetings, research meetings. We can't be locked out of funding, of contributing to the organisation we play a vital role in supporting. And while departmental meetings might be boring to some, to us the invite feels like inclusion, it feels like acknowledgement, it feels like we are seen.

Our primary and secondary school educators recently voted for strike action if the same system was not eliminated at their workplaces. Primary and secondary school teachers also have special arrangements with the Social Welfare offices so that each time they are out of work their welfare payments are pre-approved, and the process is swift and straightforward. Our UK colleagues are currently on strike as I write and I'm waiting with bated breath to see the outcome of their action.

And then I think of the students. Do they know the university education they are paying dearly for is staffed by people who sometimes are not even paid for their work? How does the high staff turnover and job insecurity impact on the quality of their degree? I'd like to see them graduate, and achieve, and follow their academic progression but the gig economy won't allow us.

Why do we do it? Why would you put yourself through it? I do it because I love the work: I love teaching, I love research, I get to work with some of the most inspiring people. I just wish the job loved me back. Am I not entitled to be fairly remunerated? Is the work that I and so many other PhDs, postdocs, early career, and hourly-paid academics do not equal? In the current climate it doesn't feel like it.

Emma Creedon

Disability, Identity, and Early Twentieth-Century Irish Drama

INTRODUCTION

From the ancient practice of physiognomy in literature, to contemporary debates on plastic surgery and theories of bodily memory, there is an enduring artistic fascination with corporeal semiotics. The physically disabled, impaired or 'deviant' (non-normative) body has been central to this. Bernadette Sweeney suggests that '[t]he body is [...] responding to and existing within a culturally specific set of parameters which are subject to change' and 'economic and political circumstances, education, gender and sexuality – these and other considerations shape our projections of and on the body within Irish culture and beyond'.[1] There is an increased focus on corporeality in contemporary Ireland and it seems all the more pertinent to discuss bodily representation in Irish culture. The Repeal the 8th Movement, which sought to legalize abortion in Ireland, generated debates on bodily legitimacy and ownership whilst the booming health, beauty, and fitness industries seem to be promoting conflicting ideals of corporeal perfection as the physical ideal – unattainable beauty standards still glamorize skeletal physiques whilst fitness industries are championing the fit, intact, and unblemished body as emulative models. Senator Fiach Mac Conghail, then Director of the Abbey Theatre, said the following at the launch of the 2016 'Waking the Nation' programme to commemorate the centenary of the Easter Rising: 'For over 110 years now the Abbey stage has been a platform for the reflection of Irish society through theatre.... In a year of national introspection, these stories have the power to hold a mirror up to our society'.[2] Mac Conghail's words echo the title of Christopher Murray's 1997 book *Twentieth Century Irish Drama: Mirror up to Nation*, and it is this concept of the 'mirror-image' and its implications of authenticity, that this essay will question. The 'Waking the Nation' programme was met with an onslaught of criticism over gender bias in the proposed 2016 male playwright-dominated billing. The response to the launch of 'Waking the Nation' thus demonstrated a demand in Irish

Irish University Review 50.1 (2020): 55–66
DOI: 10.3366/iur.2020.0434
© Edinburgh University Press
www.euppublishing.com/iur

society for an increased visibility of the marginalized on the Irish stage, with calls for inclusiveness and greater representation of female writers, the LGBT community, and people with disabilities, amongst others.

In drama, the use of stock character-types exemplifies a longstanding literary tradition of identifying characters with disabilities solely by their physical impairment, typecasting those whose bodies do not conform to normative societal bodily standards. Theatrical texts have historically employed characters with disabilities as 'narrative prosthesis', a term coined by David Mitchell and Sharon Snyder to describe how literary narratives have relied on disability to 'len[d] a distinctive idiosyncrasy to any character that differentiates the character from the anonymous background of the "norm"'.[3] Mitchell and Snyder argue that the disabled body provides the healthy body with a symbolic significance by operating as its inverse,[4] leading to the assertion that disability is 'the master trope of human disqualification.'[5] Furthermore, disability in drama is often employed as a synecdoche for a thwarted morality. For example, Sophocles' *Oedipus Rex*, gouged out his own eyes in a self-punishing gesture for the metaphorical blindness that led to sexual transgression and patricide; Gloucester's physical blindness is linked to King Lear's symbolic blindness in the Shakespearean text; in Ibsen's *Ghosts* (1881) the sins of the father are passed on to the son in the form of syphilis as a metaphor for societal ills; and Kattrin's muteness and facial disfigurement designate her as the ultimate innocent victim of war in Brecht's *Mother Courage and her Children* (1941). Irish playwrights have been guilty of this exploitation of physical difference; Irish melodrama notoriously employed characters whose moral fallibility was linked to their physical impairments (examples include James Sheridan Knowles' *The Hunchback* (1832) or the character of Danny Mann in Dion Boucicault's *The Colleen Bawn* (1860)). In the twentieth century, characters such as the Blind Man in W.B. Yeats' *On Baile's Strand* (1904), Mary and Martin Doul in J.M. Synge's *The Well of the Saints*, Johnny Boyle in Sean O'Casey's *Juno and the Paycock* (1924), Dinzie Conlee in John B. Keane's *Sharon's Grave* (1960), Stacia Doyle in *Portia Coughlan*, and Catwoman in *By the Bog of Cats* (1998), both by Marina Carr, or 'Cripple Billy' in Martin McDonagh's *The Cripple of Inishmaan* (1997) all attest to an Irish dramatic tradition of identifying disabled characters by their physical impairment.

THE SOCIAL MODEL OF DISABILITY AND ITS CRITICISMS

In theorizing disability in drama, a consideration of the Social Model of Disability is necessitated here. The Social Model challenges the implication that disability is a digression from a physical paradigm and, as a result, is 'deviant' or transgressive, even threatening to society.

This model suggests that the inequitable treatment of people with disabilities is based on inhibiting social barriers and that 'disability' is socially inflicted whereas 'impairment' refers to the personal experience of the individual. As a result, a person becomes disabled when forced to navigate an unaccommodating ableist society. In the UK, the Social Model of Disability emerged in 1975 from a partnership between Disability Alliance and the Union of the Physically Impaired against Segregation (UPIAS). They produced the document *Fundamental Principles of Disability* (1976), which challenged the Medical Model of Disability's view that disability is an individual issue or 'a set of medical and corporeal 'problems' [and which] works to cure, fix, or eliminate these 'problems' and consequently, disabled people from the population'.[6] The Social Model, principally theorized by the academic Michael Oliver, has been a powerful political tool in addressing issues of inequality in society and disability rights; however, recent disability theorists have criticized its perceived static and one-dimensional approach. Since this model focuses solely on hegemonic societal barriers, it has been criticized for neglecting to include the experience of the embodied individual:

> The social model of disability … fails to adequately theorise disabled people's experiences of impairment, resting on the view that the praxis of solidarity will work in the interests of liberation. In solidarity people may gather and challenge oppression, but there is also little room for recognition of the individual body because this undermines the very ethos of solidarity…. In its current form, the UK social model of disability presumes that all disabled people experience oppression and ignores the variety of lived experiences of impairment.[7]

This argument assumes that the seamless integration of people with disabilities into society renders their experience invisible, thus sanctioning an ableist culture albeit with special conditions or concessions in place. As Paul Darke argues '[t]he call should be for the valuation of difference (abnormality) in itself, as only then will the illusion that normality is a reality be laid to rest'.[8] However, the intersection of performance studies, textual analysis, and disability studies provides new paradigms for analysing Irish theatre and dramaturgical practices. In assessing the shortcomings of the Social Model of Disability, I will address the following critiques as outlined by Mitchell and Snyder:

> (1) social realism assumed that disability tended to be concealed rather than pervasive in literary and film traditions;

(2) the practitioners created a largely ahistorical paradigm that overlooked the specificity of disability representation as an ideological effect of particular periods; (3) social realism presumed that no disability perspective informed the 'inaccurate' images that pervaded the social realists' critique; and (4) social realism projected its own contemporary desires onto the images it sought to rehabilitate.[9]

The first criticism of the Social Model outlined above condemns the model's lack of consideration of culture's role in the formation of attitudes towards disability.[10] Mitchell and Snyder refer to the 'pervasive' presence of disability in literary and film traditions. Similarly, Paul Darke agrees with the view proffered by Martin Norden and Lennard J. Davis that images of disability feature extensively in cinematic and literary spheres[11] and Paul Longmore queries why we ingest such abundant representations of disability in film without analysing them?[12] Indeed, in a case of art reflecting life, Carrie Sandahl and Philip Auslander argue in *Bodies in Commotion: Disability and Performance* (2005) that the representation of disability on stage or as a subject of performance is intrinsically connected to the perceptions of disability in everyday life and vice versa. Similarly, according to Tom Shakespeare, 'the lack of weight given to cultural imagery and difference stems from the neglect of impairment':[13]

> If Social Model analysis seeks to ignore, rather than explore, the individual experiences of impairment (be it blindness, short stature or whatever), then it is unsurprising that it should also gloss over cultural representations of impairment, because to do otherwise would be to potentially undermine the argument.[14]

The danger is that recycled discriminating images of disability can fossilize in the popular mind-set as real. Social norms are reified within the cultural arena. Thus, Mitchell and Snyder have recognised that 'transgressive reappropriation' can potentially destabilise disparaging cultural representations of disability. That '[r]ather than rail against the unjust social exclusion of cripples, scholars have begun to attend to the subversive potential of the hyperbolic meanings invested in disabled figures.'[15] Thus the reappropriation of disability can potentially challenge perceptions of bodily normalcy; within both Irish and international theatrical cultures, this can renegotiate non-disabled perceptions of disability. Additionally, Mitchell and Snyder's identification of 'a largely ahistorical paradigm' within the Social Model can be neutralised by widening the lens of analysis to further consider the textual and performative contexts in which certain derogatory images of disability are produced. In an Irish context, cultural images of disability have been employed to serve particular purposes at different times. For example, deprecating caricatures of Irishness were circulated during the nineteenth century in periodicals such as *Punch* Magazine with the aim of sustaining a culture of imperialism by suggesting the physical inferiority of the colonized. Hence, the Irish Literary Revivalists endeavoured to counteract these images with ideals of heroic physicality, as embodied by the figure of Cuchulain, for example in Yeats' *On Baile's Strand*. Yet the semiotics associated with the figure of Cuchulain were also premised on an image of aberrant physicality. The issue at hand is the metaphorical status of the non-normative body and the readiness with which writers exploit images of disability and readers/audiences accept them. This essay will now reconsider early twentieth century Irish drama through the prism of disability studies to demonstrate how cultural images of the unorthodox body are precarious and open to hermeneutical revision.

DISABILITY IN IRISH DRAMA

The use of disability as metaphor in Irish dramatic literature is further complicated in the context of Ireland's contentious relationship with the body. Images of an 'anomalous' physicality can be traced back to the Irish famine where the aesthetics of starvation and bodily degeneration contributed to the colonial politicisation of the Irish body as inferior. Over a century later, the Irish republican hunger strikers in Northern Ireland in the 1980s capitalised on this association between the abject body and recalcitrance, which had been exploited by colonial propaganda to further promote the Irish body as insufficient and subordinate. Ireland thus has a history of utilising the body as a political tool. The 'abnormal' body in Irish theatre has traditionally been a political one, a pseudo and falsified representation of the truth. Bodily representation on Ireland's stage was further compounded by the ubiquitous influence of the Catholic Church on all aspects of Irish life which, together with stringent censorship laws, have helped to maintain a level of cultural conservatism in Ireland, particularly regarding the body, sexuality and desire. In terms of disability and Irish identity, Mark Mossman provocatively argues that Irishness, when considered in relation to Britishness, denotes a state of disability:

> One could argue that the disabled body and the Irish nation parallel each other in their invention and their function in the work within imperial British culture. The negative disablement of Ireland ties directly into the often allegorical narratives of physical difference that emerge through the nineteenth century as British

imperial organization stretches out and develops into a seemingly complete, networked global enterprise. In this context, individual Irish bodies are perceived, read, and understood within the biocultural dynamics of the social stigma, the statistical chart, the evolutionary narrative, the productive plantation, and the landscape of margin and center.[16]

Mossman is writing specifically on nineteenth century literature and his identification of 'allegorical narratives of physical difference' certainly applies to derogatory caricatures of Irishness that were frequently depicted in nineteenth century periodicals. Cartoons, such as those produced in *Punch* magazine depicted the Irish 'Fenian' male as physically stunted and underdeveloped, animalistic and anarchic, while Britain is often personified as a paternalistic middle-class gentleman who physically dominates the seditious Fenian. These disabling images of nationality operate in a similar manner to the colonizing effects of stereotypes of disability in culture. Ableism, as the dominant stance of society, seeks to colonize the impaired body by categorizing it as 'Other', as 'Dis-', by consigning sympathy, by medical 'corrective' interventions and by infantilization. Often the Fenian's nonconformist body marks him as recalcitrant, devious, and subordinate. Within a cultural context, this relates to Mitchell and Snyder's contention that 'disability serves as an interruptive force that confronts cultural truisms' and that 'disability acts as a metaphor and fleshy example of the body's unruly resistance to the cultural desire to "enforce normalcy"'.[17] In a related argument, Aoife McGrath outlines how a disciplined Irish body was born out of a post-colonial environment as a 'neo-colonial project', and how '[i]n the attempts of ... cultural organisations to liberate Ireland from a colonising power, the body was re-colonised by the nationalist campaign'.[18] During the Gaelic Revival, Irish nationalist organisations promoted a disciplined hegemonic masculinity to counter the feminisation that colonisation inferred. The foundation of the Gaelic Athletic Association, premised on the promotion of able-bodied physical continence and aptitude, was central to this campaign. It followed that any potential disruption to the figurative staging of corporeal fitness would be interpreted as challenging to the nationalist agenda.

The Abbey Theatre was born out of a resurgence of cultural nationalism at the turn of the twentieth century as the Irish Literary Revival sought to create a national Irish identity distinct from England. This was 'an aesthetic program to organise for a native population a sustaining image of itself, its uniqueness, and its dignity, all contrary to the subordinate and submissive identity nurtured by outside administration'.[19] Theatre was chosen as the ideal medium to circulate images of Irishness to a population who, according to William Butler Yeats, read very little but had a distinct tradition of storytelling. The early plays of Yeats, Lady Augusta Gregory, John Millington Synge and others aimed to offset the derogatory images of Irishness as depicted in the caricatures in *Punch* magazine but also in popular nineteenth-century melodramas by playwrights such as Dion Boucicault and J.W. Whitbread. In these plays, Irishness is synonymous with alcoholism, artifice and inferiority and the fact that they were to be staged both in Ireland and abroad contributed to the dissemination of disabling national stereotypes. Lady Gregory's 'Ireland, Real and Ideal', published in *The Nineteenth Century* in 1898, argued the following: 'We have worn the mask thrust upon us too long … we are more likely to win at least respect when we appear in our own form'.[20] This sentiment demonstrates that Lady Gregory was aware of how culture can shape and recast national stereotypes, but it also suggests a commitment to reality that the aesthetics of the Revival failed to deliver. Instead, the early plays produced at the Abbey Theatre foregrounded the 'Celtic' aspects of Irish heritage and folklore. The purpose of Ireland's new national theatre was to halt de-nationalization but it also had a didactic function. On one hand, as Anthony Roche notes, 'The plays written for an Irish national theatre … would show an image of the nation to itself'.[21] Yet, the irony of this lies in the fact that the early plays of Ireland's national theatre contained a residual paganism and reflected a mystic imaginative culture that was far removed from the realities of Irish life. Thus, there was an inherent contradiction at the heart of the Irish Literary Revival.

The imagery promoted by the early plays of the Abbey Theatre relied on the glorification of the Irish peasant and a mythic unworldliness. It was an aesthetic that was packaged as authentic, but which was a vast departure from the realities of Irish life. The first productions of the Abbey Theatre utilized imagery of bodily nonconformity, thus contributing to a theatrical trajectory of employing disability in a metaphorical manner. W.B. Yeats' *On Baile's Strand* (1903), which opens with a conversation between Fintain, described solely as 'a blind man' and Barach, 'a fool', was the first play staged at the Abbey Theatre in 1904, on a triple billing with Lady Gregory's *Spreading the News* (1904), and *Cathleen Ni Houlihain* (1902) by both writers. *On Baile's Strand* was a development of Yeats's poem 'Cuchulain's Fight with the Sea', written 12 years previously, demonstrating an abiding interest in the Irish legend.[22] The play features allusions to 'witchery', 'dragons', 'hags', even 'a unicorn', alongside the characters of the Fool and the Blind Man, who feature in a subplot to the main action between Cuchulain and Conchubar, the High King. In the play, Cuchulain's desire for freedom of self-expression is pitted against Conchubar's appeal for social order.

According to the Blind Man, Cuchulain 'ran too wild, and Conchubar is coming ... to put an oath upon him that will stop his rambling and make him as biddable as a house dog and keep him always at his hand'.[23] As a result, Cuchulain is implored to take an oath of allegiance to the High King and is forced to defeat a Young Man, sent by the warrior Aoife, who threatens their kingdom. In the archetypal role of prophet, the Blind Man has the knowledge, inaccessible to the Fool, that the Young Man that Cuchulain eventually kills at the request of the King, is, in fact, his own son.

Both Philip Edwards and Anthony Roche have noted that Yeats wrote *On Baile's Strand* after attending performances of Shakespeare's five history plays at Stratford-upon-Avon in 1901, including *Richard III*, a character whose disability has been historically linked to his dishonesty. Shakespeare's play is infamously based on Sir Thomas More's unfinished *History of King Richard III*, a text that was also politically motivated to renounce the King. Hence, Yeats would have been familiar with the Elizabethan convention of equating disability and moral deficiency. Indeed, Yeats's utilization of Cuchulain as an emblem of hegemonic masculinity, despite his rhetorical recklessness, is an interesting one. His ascent to power was built solely on his meta-human physical strength, a corporal vigour that was, coincidentally premised on his physical deviancy; according to legend, he could swim like a fish at birth and was born with fourteen fingers and fourteen toes. Thus, his bodily extra-ordinariness seems the ideal counterpart to the Blind Man's perceived physical short-comings. Yet *On Baile's Strand* contains an innate anxiety regarding physical inadequacy or deterioration. The Blind Man's disability was 'punishment' for putting a curse on the wind, Cuchulain criticises Conchubar's children who have 'no pith, [n]o marrow in their bones'[24] while women are pejoratively accused of having the power to 'make a prince decay, [w]ith light images of clay' (p.18). If theatre is, as Martin Esslin suggested in *An Anatomy of Drama*, 'the place where a nation thinks in front of itself',[25] and if the imagery produced by Ireland's national drama was intended to represent the people as they 'appear in [their] own form', where does the disabled body fit into this national identity?

On the other hand, the character of Johnny Boyle in Sean O'Casey's *Juno and the Paycock* provides a fitting example of how physical 'abnormality' was deemed a challenge to nationalism. Johnny's body has been irrevocably marked by the savagery of war – he was shot in the hip during the Easter Rising and he lost an arm in an explosion on O'Connell Street during the Civil War. Although the play as a whole could be read as a scathing critique of the brutality of violence, and Johnny's injury a direct result of his republican involvement, his disability also indicates his worthlessness to the nationalist cause. In fact, he is described as on the cusp of death, his physical inchoateness denoting his bankruptcy: 'His face is pale and drawn; there is a tremulous look of indefinite fear in his eyes. The left sleeve of his coat is empty, and he walks with a slight halt'.[26] Indeed, James Moran draws links between Johnny Boyle and the character of the hunchback, Danny Mann, in Boucicault's *The Colleen Bawn*, noting that each role 'involves being connected with murderous treachery, suffering a physical deformity that indicates moral turpitude and ultimately being shot'.[27] In Boucicault's play, Danny Mann describes himself as a 'cripple' and as 'the shadow of an illegant gintleman like Mr Hardress Cregan' whereas Johnny physically embodies 'the terrible state o' chassis' of the world, frequently denounced by the other characters in the play. The original title for *Juno and the Paycock* was *On the Run*,[28] a metaphor for Johnny's predicament but also an ironic comment on his immobilised physicality. Johnny buys in to the masculinist struggle for Irish independence yet he is rewarded with ostracism and ultimately death. His disability thus operates as a metaphor within the play for a crippled nation – his broken body highlights Ireland's fragmentation and inability to self-govern. In this play, Johnny's disability works as an interruption – it underscores his political uselessness and it determines the end of his military service. It also sanctions his self-motivated withdrawal from the political struggle. As such, it adheres to Sandahl and Auslander's identification of 'the commotion that disability stirs up in narrative',[29] both in the sense of the narrative of the play and the narrative of the nationalist agenda. Petra Kuppers describes the post-colonial condition and the embodied experience of disability in similar terms:

> A disabled person's own 'normality' can be in conflict with the norm of discursive formation. 'Disabled' is the phenomenologically normal experience, but one that is coded as 'periphery' rather than 'center', as 'abnormal' rather than 'normal' from the outside by the ascription of the term and the social status of 'disabled'. Thus, a disabled person experiences her form of embodiment both as primary and secondary at the same time, as she is structured into the certainties and languages of the system (a form of double-consciousness-embodiment that is familiar from post-colonial studies).[30]

In Kupper's words, disability occupies a liminal position, similar to its peripheral yet central positioning within literature. Her identification of a 'double-consciousness-embodiment' also reflects Judith Butler's seminal theories in *Bodies That Matter: On the Discursive Limits of 'Sex'*

(1993) which focused on the abjection of bodies and asked what renders their legibility or liveability. Butler asserts

> it will be important to think about how and to what end bodies are constructed as it will be to think about how and to what end bodies are not constructed and, further, to ask after how bodies which fail to materialise provide the necessary 'outside,' if not the necessary support, for the bodies which, in materializing the norm, qualify as bodies that matter.[31]

Butler calls for an examination of the constructionism, and absence of, specific bodies. And, indeed, the abject body in twentieth century Irish drama has traditionally been treated superficially. Such depictions work to counter representations of the 'normal' body and, in their paradoxical presence-absence, reveal the frailty of ideologies of normality and the constructed-ness of the norm.

CONCLUSION: 'CRIPDRAG'

Disability representation in Irish theatre has traditionally relied on limited narrative representational frameworks of bodily interpretation. Characters in twentieth-century Irish drama are often identified by their disability alone: 'The Blind Man', 'The Lame Man', 'The Hunchback', 'Cripple Billy', the 'Cyclops of Coolinarney', the Douls in Yeats' *The Well of the Saints* (the surname originates from the Irish word 'dall' meaning 'blind'). Disability has been exploited for its metaphoric connotations, resulting in the emergence of two-dimensional character 'types', replete with preconceived theatrical signifiers and operating as melodramatic stratagems. These include, but are not limited to, such caricatures as the Villainous Monster, the Comic Relief, the Inspirational Overcomer, the Prophet, and the Sweet Innocent.[32] Despite the prolific use of disability as a literary tool in Irish drama, there are few examples in Ireland, and indeed internationally, of theatres sourcing actors with disabilities to play these roles, or of ability-blind casting practices. Instead, the conventions of 'cripping up', or 'cripdrag', industry terms describing the practice of an able-bodied actor playing a disabled character, are customary. The term refers to blackface minstrel shows and the now unacceptable practice of white actors donning black makeup to play black characters. By 'cripping up,' an actor demonstrates his/her performative virtuosity, rather than committing to accurate representations of reality. The result is the potential degradation of the disabled body, a stylized performance evoking vaudevillian conventions; performance thus engenders belief in stereotype. This has serious implications regarding preconceptions about normalcy and corporeal perfection; the implication is that disability is performative and that physical impairment is not inherent but a 'deviation' from a corporeal ideal. It is also indicative of an intrinsic social bias. As Carrie Sandahl notes, '[r]arely is an actor of color, a woman, or a disabled person cast against type to play a character from a more dominant social position'.[33] Actors with disabilities expose the exploitation of disability and deny its metaphoric use. They also distract the attention away from mere disability simulation, which, as Kirsty Johnston notes, is often of more interest to audiences and reviewers than the political ramifications of the employment of disability as metaphor.[34] Performance complicates notions of authenticity as it is, by its very nature, contrived. Thus performances of disability by non-disabled actors often become more about the performative (i.e. the actor's competency in imitating the physical disability) than about the character. Performances of disability by actors who are not disabled give visual expression to essentialist sentiments that the able-body is the embodied habitual norm to which the actor returns post-performance. Disability Theatre and performances by actors with disabilities have the capacity to challenge this since the presence of the disabled actor on stage defamiliarizes established norms and challenges perceptions of normativity. Disability performance is emerging in tandem with an increased emphasis on the body and on physicality and a movement away from a text-dependent hierarchy within the Irish dramatic tradition. Realism as mimetic representation has traditionally relied on the able-bodied employment of the senses in its transmission of meaning and yet experimental theatre practices and the employment of actors with disabilities can challenge this. Such potential disruptions caused by the disabled body in performance offer new positive ways of reading disability, subversively defamiliarizing the body in performance and could be used as a template for disability performance in Ireland.

NOTES

1. Bernadette Sweeney, *Performing the Body in Irish Theatre* (Basingstoke: Palgrave Macmillan, 2008), p.15.
2. https://www.abbeytheatre.ie/waking-the-nation-2016-at-the-abbey-theatre/
3. David Mitchell and Sharon Snyder, *Narrative Prosthesis: Disability and the Dependencies of Discourse* (Michigan: University of Michigan Press, 2000), p.205.
4. Mitchell and Snyder, p.215.
5. Mitchell and Snyder, p.3.
6. Ann Millett-Gallant, *The Disabled Body in Contemporary Art* (New York: Palgrave Macmillan, 2010), p.7.
7. Janine Owens, 'Exploring the Critiques of the Social Model of Disability: the Transformative Possibility of Arendt's Notion of Power', *Sociology of Health and Illness* 37.3 (2014), 385–403 (p.389).
8. Paul Darke 'Understanding Cinematic Representations of Disability,' in *The Disability Reader: Social Science Perspectives*, ed. by Tom Shakespeare (London and New York: Continuum, 2002), pp.181–201 (p.188).

9. Mitchell and Snyder, pp.24–25.
10. For similar arguments on the Social Model of Disability's failure to adequately include culture in its analysis see Mairian Corker (1999, 2002), Rob Imrie (1997), Carol Thomas (2010), and Tom Shakespeare (1994, 2010).
11. Darke, p.183.
12. Paul Longmore, *Why I Burned my Book and Other Essays on Disability* (Philadelphia, PA: Temple University Press, 2003), p.132.
13. Tom Shakespeare, 'Cultural Representation of Disabled People: Dustbins for Disavowal', *Disability and Society* 9.3 (1994), 283–299 (p.283).
14. Shakespeare, pp.283–284.
15. Mitchell and Snyder, p.35.
16. Mark Mossman, *Disability, Representation and the Body in Irish Writing, 1800–1922* (Basingstoke and New York: Palgrave Macmillan, 2009), p.39.
17. David Mitchell and Sharon Snyder, 'Narrative Prosthesis and the Materiality of Metaphor,' in *The Disability Studies Reader*, ed. by Leonard J. Davis (New York: Routledge, 2006), 205–216 (p.206).
18. Aoife McGrath, *Dance Theatre in Ireland: Revolutionary Moves* (Basingstoke: Palgrave Macmillan, 2012), p.32.
19. John P. Harrington, ed, *Modern and Contemporary Irish Drama* (New York: Norton, 2009), p.x–xi.
20. Augusta Gregory, 'Ireland, Real and Ideal', *The Nineteenth Century* 44 (1898), 769–82.
21. Anthony Roche, *The Irish Dramatic Revival 1899–1939* (London and New York: Bloomsbury, 2015), p.4
22. *On Baile's Strand* was also based on a chapter titled 'The Only Son of Aoife' in Lady Gregory's *Cuchulain of Muirthemne* (1904), for which Yeats had contributed the introduction, 'Interpretation of the Cuchulain Legend'.
23. *On Baile's Strand* in *The King's Threshold and On Baile's Strand: Being Volume Three of Plays for an Irish Theatre by W. B. Yeats* (London: Chiswick Press, 1904) (accessed via Project Gutenberg on 01/07/2017).
24. *On Baile's Strand*, p.17. Further references in parentheses in the text.
25. Martin Esslin, *An Anatomy of Drama* (London: Abacus-Sphere, 1978), p.101.
26. Sean O'Casey, *Three Dublin Plays* (London: Faber and Faber, 2000), p.71.
27. James Moran, *The Theatre of Sean O'Casey* (Bloomsbury: Methuen Drama, 2013), p.50.
28. Christopher Murray, *Mirror up to Nation* (Manchester Uuniversity Press, 1997), pp.102–103.
29. Carrie Sandahl and Philip Auslander, *Bodies in Commotion: Disability and Performance*, (Ann Arbor, MI: University of Michigan Press, 2005), p.4.
30. Petra Kuppers, *Disability and Contemporary Performance: Bodies on the Edge* (New York and London: Routledge, 2003), pp.14–15.
31. Judith Butler, *Bodies that Matter: On the Discursive Limits of 'Sex'* (New York and London: Routledge, 1993), p.16.
32. See also Carrie Sandahl and Philip Auslander's *Bodies in Commotion: Disability and Performance* (2005), Martin Norden's *The Cinema of Isolation: A History of Physical Disability in the Movies* (1994), and David Hevey's *The Creatures Time Forgot: Photography and Disability Imagery*.
33. Kirsty Johnston, *Disability Theatre and Modern Drama: Recasting Modernism* (London and New York: Bloomsbury, 2016), p. 42.
34. Johnston, n.3 p. 206.

Michael Pierse

Ireland's Working-Class Literature: Neglected Themes, Amphibian Academics, and the Challenges Ahead*

Irish working-class history, culture, and literature are attracting increasing academic interest. With the publication of *A History of Irish Working-Class Writing* (2017), Declan Kiberd could write that its focus on 'an astonishing range of writing – from work-songs and political rhymes to poetry and government reports, from novels and plays to biographies by or about working people', would 'set many of the terms of cultural debate in the decade to come'.[1] As he also noted, 'they could hardly be more timely':[2] while Ireland's post-Crash society came to grips with the inequalities inherent in the injustices of the financial system and the policies of austerity, class sentiment seemed most manifest in, for example, the anti-water charges protests that gained popular support during the recession period. Rory Hearne noted a nascent, post-Celtic Tiger politicisation that had 'in particular mobilised lower income and working class areas'.[3] Of course, this is a politicisation that is still resurgent in various, uneven forms across the globe, from Corbynism to Podemos to Alexandria Ocasio-Cortez, if in an age when the forces ranged against the left (many of them from among the working class) are also on the march. In this context, it was fitting that *A History of Irish Working-Class Writing* was published in parallel with books on British and American working-class literature, and that a chapter on the Irish context will feature alongside studies of

* This article is an extended and revised version of a piece, 'Back to class: Ireland's working-class literature', which was published in the *Honest Ulsterman* in June 2018, and is published here with thanks to magazine Editor, Dr Gregory McCartney.

Irish University Review 50.1 (2020): 67–81
DOI: 10.3366/iur.2020.0435
© Edinburgh University Press
www.euppublishing.com/iur

South African, Swedish, American, Asian, and other working-class writers in a forthcoming follow-up volume to Magnus Nilsson and John Lennon's recent *Working-Class Literature(s): Historical and International Perspectives* (2017).[4] Bringing such diverse perspectives on class and literature together was a feature of recent conferences too, of the international Working-Class Studies Association in Kent, and the European Labour History Network in Amsterdam (both September 2019). 'Class is a relationship, and not a thing', as E. P. Thompson famously declared, and investigating these relationships across space and time enriches our understanding of class globally and locally, in all its complex and contradictory manifestations, providing an important resource for those grappling with class-related scholarly concerns.[5] In Ireland, the experiences of the working class mapped out in history and literature have also empowered those struggling for social change. A sense of continuity with historical struggle was a key resource in recent years, as suggested, for example, by the compelling debates that emerged in Ireland's sometimes clumsy or contentious celebrations of the centenary of the Revolutionary Period.[6] Some of those debates would focus on what James Connolly might have thought of the Ireland that subsequently emerged – his condemnations of capitalism jarring with the tax-haven Republic's inevitably thorny celebration of his legacy; as Timothy White and Denis Marnane noted of the opportunities for the left in the Decade of Centenaries,

> at a time when the Left in Ireland appears to be getting some traction, the legacy of Connolly may at last be able to come in from the cold … his leftist rhetoric that suggested a fundamental redress of economic inequalities is increasingly appealing among many who suffered from austerity policies.[7]

Connolly, as the subject of lore and song, has endured as a semi-mythic figure in Irish working-class life. And 'subliterary' forms such as song have indeed been integral to the formation of working-class culture, but how much effort has been made to unearth, preserve, curate, and indeed complicate our working-class heritage in Ireland, not least in terms of song, poetry, drama, fiction, and life writing? Scholars in recent years have presented, in monographs, edited collections, anthologies – and, increasingly, digitised archives – from across British, American, European, and an increasing range of international contexts, a variety of resources for those who wish to consider how to carry the study on Irish working-class writing onto new terrain.[8] They consider class in relation to matters of form, material production, international comparative contexts, and diaspora experiences, among many other categories and themes, which suggest a range of potential directions in

Irish Studies and class. Many of these scholars focus on British working-class literature and cultural studies, which have been to the fore of international scholarship in this area and provide a range of approaches that Irish Studies scholars can adopt or adapt, even as – as David Convery has noted – we must be careful not to simply map British experiences of class onto Irish ones.[9]

Folk song traditions indeed suggest potential affinities in relation to class and cultural histories across these islands. When *The Full English*, a digital archive of twelve manuscript collections of English folk songs, was launched in 2013 by the English Folk and Dance Song Society, playwright and screenwriter Lee Hall described it as 'the most exciting and significant thing to happen to British folk music in at least a generation.... To give everyone the keys to the archive of our common heritage will be an invaluable inspiration to generations of musicians and writers'.[10] It was interesting that the scriptwriter of a classic film of the northern English working class, *Billy Elliot* (2000), had felt such affinities. Here was an archive – as Billy Bragg also recognised, along with fellow folk musicians and playwrights such as Hall and Neil Leyshon – which was rich with the history of the common folk, the peasant, the working class, and which, Bragg stressed, had relevance for contemporary working-class struggles.[11] Such connections are not merely incidental, but often woven into the very fabric of this kind of creativity. Irish, British, and other folk song traditions share common traits; as John Moulden notes, for example, it is 'widely accepted that, in terms of the repertory of vernacular song, songs in English in Ireland, Scotland and England, and to a marked degree, in North America, Australia and New Zealand, are substantially related.'[12] Folk songs emerged over centuries as a form of popular entertainment that could provide, as well as diversion or levity, wellsprings of resilience and rebellion for the poor.[13] They were easily learned and transcribed, handily stored (often hidden from authorities) and frequently modified, if need be, to chime with the particularities of place and time. In *A History of Irish Working-Class Writing*, Moulden draws our attention to the ways in which, 'from the poorest in society, the Irish working class created, contributed to, transformed and consumed the verbal art that impinged upon them in oral or cheap printed or, occasionally, more substantial form', creating, performing and distributing a folk culture that would transform through space and time.[14] These songs were truly of a 'folk' experience – lamenting injustices or recounting common concerns, such as in 'The Cottager's Complaint', or eulogising exceptional individuals, as in 'Hannah Healy the Pride of Howth', or 'Biddy Mulligan the Pride of the Coombe'.[15] Notwithstanding commendable work such as Moulden's, and that of the Irish Traditional Music Archive, for example, we could do more to trace and disseminate the ways in which this music and song, over centuries, has been part of a tradition that has often mutated and migrated but continually expressed values that can be theorised in terms of class, as well as postcolonial, politics. In a broader sense, we could also do more to consider the scope and substance of the cultural and intellectual life of the Irish working class at home and abroad. Studies such as Christopher Hilliard's *To Exercise Our Talents: The Democratisation of Writing in Britain* (2006) and Jonathan Rose's *The Intellectual Life of the British Working Classes* (2010) suggest possibilities for similar work in Ireland.[16]

The Irish Labour History Society Museum in Dublin and the recently opened James Connolly Centre in Belfast have made strides in this regard, but in the academy, despite the development, over many decades, of a sophisticated and diverse range of critical approaches in Irish Studies, there is still a relative lack of discussion around how class has shaped and shapes the contours of Irish social, political, and cultural life. Class is indisputably at the heart of Irish society, north and south, in its operations, apparatuses, privileges, and anxieties, as scholars such as Liam Cullinane, Colin Coulter, Graham McFarlane, Marilyn Silverman, David Convery, and Christopher J.V. Loughlin have illustrated; it is central to its academies and its intellectual cultures, as others, like Fergal Finnegan, Barbara Merill, and Ciarán Burke have recently shown.[17] And class politics is abundant in literature and the arts. In terms of cultural production, *A History* pointed to the extent of Irish working-class literature, which will provide fruitful material for scholars grappling with matters of culture and class in the time to come. Nils Beese's recent *Writing Slums: Dublin, Dirt and Literature* (2018) suggests potential in the study of literature and working-class space by 'shed[ding] light on the development of slum literature and what one might class Modernist slum aesthetics'.[18] Susan Cannon Harris's recent monograph, *Irish Drama and the Other Revolutions: Playwrights, Sexual Politics and the International Left, 1892–1964* (2017), also conveys, for example, the potential in relation to class and intersectional politics in twentieth-century drama, paving a path, as she puts it, 'to restore to visibility a tradition of left theatre which originated at the intersection between socialist politics and sexual politics'.[19] Cannon Harris looks at New Women and queer socialism in the 1890s, syndicalism and masculinity in the Abbey of the 1910s, and O'Casey's less-explored relationship with post-realism and the Soviet Union, for example. Her book supports the 'pursuit of a truly internationalist understanding' of Irish literature, and that internationalist focus is further enriched by recent scholarship on the Irish emigrant in literature, in which Liam Harte, Tony Murray, Peter Kuch, Margaret Hallissy, John Lutz have been leading the charge, and in which working-class experience is such a strong feature.[20]

Another topic for further investigation is class in the Irish arts infrastructure: we have little research in Ireland on the quantifiably material dynamics behind our cultural and arts institutions and their qualitative impact, though Cultural Policy Observatory Ireland, established in 2015, has been keen to expand the research base in this regard.[21] Britain has, in recent decades, produced significant studies (for example The Warwick Commission Report, which notionally covers the 'UK', but lamentably does not include the northern Irish context) that have pointed to the extent and historical development of class (and race and gender) inequalities and challenges in the arts.[22] In Ireland of late, welcome attention was drawn to gender inequalities in theatre: the #WakingtheFeminists movement revealed, when it emerged in 2015, a staggering bias toward male artists in the Abbey Theatre's 'Waking the Nation' programme. The protests this movement inspired have prompted significant attitudinal and substantive programming changes.[23] But where were working-class women in all of this? As Maggie Armstrong observed, at least one feminist protester felt ill-at-ease during the campaign:

> It was pretty historic. Feminism, so often a stuffy, if not totally threatening, term, was suddenly the New Order. But it was another f-word that had people shifting in their seats, when a silver-haired woman spoke from the crowd. 'A big fair f***s to everyone,' said Cathleen O'Neill, working-class activist. She said she felt proud today, but needed to raise another matter – class. Theatre for the working-class is 'relegated to community arts,' she said. 'Don't forget us, sisters,' she implored the well-heeled theatre-makers on the stage.... Cathleen described how she left the Abbey 'on fire, empowered by it'. But also, 'seething'.... She had gone along to support the women's struggle. But she did not feel as supported by them. She felt that in speaking out about their oppression as women, they had divorced their cause from another, more life-threatening form of oppression – poverty.... 'Theatre is seen as too expensive, exclusive, not for us,' said Cathleen.[24]

There is little data, qualitative or quantitative, produced in this regard. Sandy Fitzgerald's 2004 reader on community arts in Ireland, *An Outburst of Frankness*, grappled, for example, with some of the issues relating to class in the Irish arts scene, such as funding, access and participation, from historical, practitioner and policy perspectives, though it was 'not an academic book' and was written in an environment where data on class and the arts was relatively scarce in comparison with the British context.[25] It did, nonetheless, point up some important issues emerging in late twentieth-century Ireland in regard to class and culture: the 1994 study *The Public and the Arts*, cited in Paula Clancy's chapter, showed that, over the previous thirteen years,

> in relation to certain types of events [in the Republic], and particularly those that form the focus of the publicly funded arts, there was found to be a widening of the class differential, particularly in relation to the semi-skilled/unskilled working class. These events included plays, performances of classical music and exhibitions of paintings and sculptures – art forms that traditionally attracted a middle-class audience.[26]

There were widening gaps too in terms of the purchase of cultural products (including novels, poetry, and music records/tapes), but Clancy points in her chapter to the need for further data on class and region, and this is still very much the case in 2019, leaving many pressing questions unanswered. What are the class dynamics at the Abbey, or in organisations such as the Arts Council, Culture Ireland, Aosdána, or the Dublin Fringe Festival? Who gets funded and supported? Who gets what jobs, and where (in terms of class, ethnicity, gender, and region) do they come from? Who is entertained? The sparseness of thoroughgoing studies on these matters would suggest we have a long way to go in acknowledging the role of class in cultural (and social) production in Ireland.

'CLASS IS ALWAYS IN SOME SENSE PRESENT'

Working-class people don't often get to see themselves in Irish theatres and not enough in television drama or fiction, and when they do, the depiction is often negative. Recently, fiction writers E. R. Murray, Dave Lordan, and Sheena Wilkinson discussed the lack of 'champions for children from poorer backgrounds' in young-adult fiction, for example.[27] According to Murray: 'When we speak about diversity within publishing, we're frequently referring to gender, sexuality, race, language and disabilities. All of these badly need to be represented … but I wonder, where are the champions for the lower socio-economic backgrounds?'[28] Wilkinson's inclusion of working-class characters in her young-adult novels relates to alienating personal experiences: 'I grew up with the only available Belfast narratives focusing on religion and cultural identity, when what I saw around me suggested that the divisions were at least as much to do with social class'.[29] Lordan, from Cork, furthermore points to the difficulty of becoming a working-class writer: 'Class is a huge factor. Many of the successful authors I know around my age and younger receive huge backing from well-off parents over the decade or so it takes to get established'.[30]

Jeremy Hawthorne notes that, 'for some people, "working-class novel" is a contradiction in terms'.[31] He identifies the material barriers to writing for the less well-off: 'such things as literacy, leisure time for reading, publishers sympathetic to their values (not to mention teachers and lecturers), have all been much more easily obtained by upper- and middle-class people than by members of the working class'.[32] Despite the Arts Council and Combat Poverty's joint report, 'Access and Participation in the Arts' (1997), pointing some decades ago to these inequalities in Ireland, little has been done since in terms of research that might support policy change.[33] As a more recent report (2014) highlighted (quoting here Peter Lunn and Elish Kelly):

> While there remains a lack of data about the resources dedicated to cultural inclusion, there is evidence to indicate that people from disadvantaged socio-economic backgrounds with lower levels of educational attainment display equal levels of interest in the arts but are 'many times less likely' to participate in cultural events than their better-off counterparts.... Despite an Oireachtas (Parliamentary) Committee hearing in 2012 to consider how best to support and ensure the participation of disadvantaged groups in cultural life, no recommendations or actions have been issued.[34]

John Kirk begins his study of the British working class in film, literature, and television by observing how 'class is always in some sense present: whether in our refusal to accept it, our inclination to acknowledge it or insist on it or, as in some cases, our being privileged enough not to have noticed it.'[35] It is often when class is least spoken about, or when it is most comfortably acknowledged to be old-fashioned or irrelevant, that it is most pressing in our social machinery and everyday lives, not least in cultural terms. In Ireland, there is nothing of the detailed abundance of work by Mike Savage, in Britain, or Pierre Bourdieu, in France, in the sociological study of class – a lamentable absence that leaves cognate research impoverished.[36]

The general theorisation of social class in Ireland, north and south, is relatively poor, which in turn has hampered connectivity between disciplines in relation to how class manifests itself in things like publishing or arts participation.[37] Some work, by scholars like Marilyn Silverman, Chris Eipper, and, more recently, Fergal Finnegan, for example, has shown how the shame, anger, deprivation and defiant pride that underpin class relations elsewhere are manifest in Irish life.[38] The work of Helena Sheehan on Irish television drama pointed to the extent of the national broadcaster's role in reproducing class inequalities.[39] But Sheehan's trailblazing work has yet to be followed by such significant interrogations of class in RTÉ's more recent decades: what are the unthinking class biases in *Love/Hate* or *Fair City*, for example? As Tom Maguire has recently noted of RTÉ comedy,

> the station has repeatedly presented material the humour of which relies on caricatures of the poor. As an example, Andrew Quirke created two characters, Damo and Ivor initially within a sketch show, *The Republic of Telly* in 2011. In 2013 a stand-alone television show debuted on RTÉ Two. As David Toms comments, the show 'derives its apparent humour from the contrasting of two rather lazy stereotypes of Dublin, one of a northside "skanger" called Damo, and the other of an equally lazy Ross O'Carroll-Kelly imitation called Ivor.' The use of "skanger" or "knacker" in Ireland parallels the use of "chav" within British culture (Jones) to vilify the poor. Quirke's characterisation of Damo exploits the working-class stereotype: stupid, lazy, drunken, foul-mouthed and aggressive. It is notable that Quirke as creator and performer is the son and heir of a millionaire businessman.... The generation of these stereotypes in the media has also found an echo in the wider culture.[40]

Intersectionality is also at issue. While in *An Irish Working Class* (2001) Marilyn Silverman addressed the everyday injuries of class in much more intimate and interpersonal contexts in small-town Ireland, it remains to be asked how have those experiences changed and intersected with issues of race, for example, in recent decades, as newcomers join the Irish working class in unprecedented numbers? And what of those other intersectional experiences documented by scholars like Beverley Skeggs in Britain – the specific manifestations of class for women, or LGBTQ people and BME groups in Ireland? At the intersection of feminism and class-analysis, Nicola Wilson, in her study of British working-class domestic space in fiction, recently noted the continuing merit in Ken Worpole's observation of more than three decades ago that 'the two major traumas that dominate the working class life are, not the strike, not the factory accident, but early and unwanted pregnancy and hasty marriage, or the back-street abortion';[41] such experiences in Ireland are captured in poetry, stories, and plays, by Paula Meehan, Christina Reid, and Roddy Doyle, among others. Recent work by Heather Laird and Tom Maguire is important in opening this matter to further scholarly inquiry. As Maguire suggests, in his exploration of aspects of violence and working-class women on the Irish stage, 'naturalistic dramatic representation of the home as a domestic sphere for poor women may confound nationalist discourses of the country as home, yet may fail to resist the systemic violence of the state against its most precarious citizens'.[42] His focus on popular cultural demonisations of the poor and theatrical responses to them is welcome and chimes with Laird's commentary on representations of motherhood in Irish fiction, both essays, as Laird puts it of her own, laying 'the foundations for much-needed further scholarly work on the representation of working-class Irish women'.[43] Playwrights and novelists such as Doyle, Donal O'Kelly, Ken Harmon, Brian Campbell, Dermot Bolger, Vincent Higgins, Jim O'Hanlon, Bisi Adigun, Charlie O'Neill, Mirjana Rendulic, and Ursula Rani Sarma have been answering questions about immigrant experiences of class in recent years, in often contradictory ways, but few scholars have pointed to this intersectionality.[44] Traveller experiences of class, such as that depicted in Rosaleen McDonagh's *Rings* (2012), are also less considered. Developing interdisciplinary perspectives is difficult when the disciplines are only beginning to communicate on such matters. This was precisely the challenge impelling the foundation of the Irish Centre for the Histories of Labour and Class in 2013, at the Moore Institute in NUI Galway – a commendable forward step in encouraging conversations between historians, sociologists, cultural and literary studies scholars and others in developing broader perspectives on class.

CLASS, CULTURE, AND EDUCATION

Ruth Sherry observed some thirty years ago that 'the concept of Irish working-class writing is not a well-established one.'[45] The same could be said today in general terms, though at the least, through recent and ongoing PhD studies and the publication of scholarly work in the field, it is evident that the language of class politics in Irish literary studies scholarship is here to stay. That Sherry could identify some of the major prose writers of the Irish working class prior to the publication of her article, 'The Irish Working Class in Fiction', in 1985, suggests, however, that the relative neglect of working-class writing since has been inexcusable. Despite book-length studies on Brendan Behan, Seán O'Casey, Sam Thompson, Christy Brown, Stewart Parker, Roddy Doyle and others, research that links such writers together as 'working class' was until recently quite rare and is still in its infancy.[46] Some of this has of course to do with the very structure of our education system; scholarly attention to marginalised and disadvantaged communities is often initiated by people who emerge from those communities into the academy, but what if few outsiders get through? Does the academy buttress the inequality in how cultural (and social, and other forms of) capital are distributed in Irish society, north and south, through the education system?

In a recent comparative study of the experiences of working-class English and Irish university students, Finnegan and Barbara Merrill found promising strides forward through 'widening participation' measures in higher education, but also observed, more depressingly, the endurance of feelings of alienation amongst working-class higher-education students. A high proportion had, at university, experienced 'a feeling of dislocation, or at least a sense of social distance, from the dominant culture in universities', one of the Irish students describing university as 'a foreign country'.[47] Those attending elite institutions were particularly alienated:

> in some cases interviewees discussed going through the difficult and painstaking process of cultural adaptation ... [and] [t]hese accounts of fitting or not fitting in at university were often discussed as something which was felt as embodied and as deeply emotional by the students.[48]

Secondary school can be similarly alienating; Roddy Doyle's Paula Spencer learns in school 'that I wasn't good at all', and that her teachers 'all the same, cunts. Cunts. I hated them.'[49] Such sentiments are frequent in Irish working-class writing.[50]

While questions of access have come to the fore in universities on these islands, how many have asked how the class of people working and studying in universities influences the class of subjects researched and taught, and how they are taught? bell hooks once argued, in a US context, that 'nowhere is there a more intense silence about the reality of class differences than in educational settings'.[51] There has been some quantitative and mixed-method research on the underrepresentation of the working class in Irish higher education in recent decades, but only 'a small number of qualitative studies have explored the potential barriers to HE' in the Republic.[52] Research on teachers has confirmed 'the significant under-representation of, *inter alia*, certain lower socio-economic groups' in the Irish teaching profession, and while I am not aware of similar research on academics, it is not unreasonable to suspect that this more prestigious tier of the education system is just as, if not more, elitist.[53] How does this skewing distort the study and teaching of Irish life? How does it impact curricula and matters of epistemology? If, as Keane, Heinz, and Lynch note, for example, 'research has found that working-class teachers positively impact working-class pupils', what is the impact of a system that produces and embeds classism?[54] This is to say, as Skeggs has, that 'the ability to claim and promote an identity is often based on access to sites of representation such as higher education and the media; the working class (women and men, black and white) have always had restricted access to where these claims are most frequently made'.[55] In Ireland, this is also demonstrably the case, but not a lot of scholars seem to be making that case.

Thus, to adapt a turn of phrase of Terry Eagleton's, there is no need to bring class into literature; it has been there right from the start. In Irish literature, we are beginning to see welcome attention, from a range of thinkers, to the ways in which the canonical has been shaped by class, and the ways in which class has emerged in cultural production – whether in the form of political poems in the pages of the *Irish Worker*, the ground-breaking and controversial novels and TV series of Roddy Doyle, or the mesmeric rap-poetry of Emmet Kirwan. The recent publication of *The Children of the Nation: An Anthology of Working People's Poetry from Contemporary Ireland* (November 2019), edited by Jenny Farrell, and author Paul McVeigh's announcement of his forthcoming collection, *The 32: An Anthology of Irish Working-Class Voices* (scheduled for publication in 2020) are very promising developments too. McVeigh, commenting on the impetus behind his book, which seeks to follow on the success of Kit de Waal's British collection, *Common People: An Anthology of Working-Class Writers (2019)*, explains 'too often, working class writers find that the hurdles they have to leap are higher and harder to cross than for writers from more affluent backgrounds.... *The 32* will see writers who have made that leap reach back to give a helping hand to those coming up behind'.[56] Fittingly, some profits from the publication will be set aside for development workshops with fledgling working-class authors. There is undoubted evidence here of a recent impetus in the exploration and encouragement of working-class cultural production in Ireland. In the academy, this work will hopefully lead to new ways of conceptualising Irish cultural history and indeed of coming to grips with the dynamics of Irish society now and into the future. Often it is being conducted by working-class 'amphibians' – as Michelle Tokarczyk terms them, in her commentary on the study of American working-class writers – those critics from working-class backgrounds who, she argues, 'act as a bridge between working-class and academic sensibilities'.[57] Certainly, in a context of continued austerity, and with growing student expenses at HE in Ireland north and south, these 'bridges' are needed to challenge the ways in which the working class is written, or written about.

NOTES

1. Declan Kiberd, Foreword to *A History of Irish Working-Class Writing*, ed. by Michael Pierse (Cambridge: Cambridge University Press, 2017), pp.xiii–xviii (p.xviii).
2. Kiberd, p.xviii.
3. Rory Hearne, 'The Irish water war, austerity and the "Risen people": An analysis of participant opinions, social and political impacts and transformative potential of the Irish anti water-charges movement', Maynooth University. Published online: https://www.maynoothuniversity.ie/sites/default/files/assets/document/TheIrishWaterwar_0.pdf. Accessed 1 September 2019.

4. Michael Pierse, 'A brief overview of Irish working-class writing', in *Literature(s): Historical and International Perspectives: Volume II*, ed. by John Lennon and Magnus Nillsson (Stockholm: Stockholm University Press, forthcoming 2020).

5. E.P. Thompson, *The Making of the English Working Class* (London: Penguin, 1980), p.10.

6. See Johanne Devlin Trew and Michael Pierse (ed.) *Rethinking the Irish Diaspora – After the Gathering* (Basingstoke: Palgrave, 2018), pp. 251–252. See also, for an example of the controversies that emerged, Anne Dolan, 'Commemorating 1916: How much does the integrity of the past count? "In its own peculiar way, Ireland Inspires quite eloquently expresses the gap between history and commemoration"', *Irish Times*, 2 January 2018.

7. Timothy J. White & Denis Marnane, 'The Politics of Remembrance: Commemorating 1916', *Irish Political Studies* 31.1 (2016), 29–43 (p.33).

8. See for example Janet Zandy, *Calling Home: An Anthology of Working-Class Women's Writing* (New Jersey: Rutgers University Press, 1990); *What we Hold in Common: An Introduction to Working-Class Studies*, ed. by Janet Zandy (New York: The Feminist Press at the University of New York, 2001); *American Working-Class Literature: An Anthology*, ed. by Zandy and Nicholas Coles (New York: Oxford University Press, 2007); *New Working-Class Studies*, ed. by John Russo and Sherry Lee Linkon (Ithaca: Cornell University Press, 2005); *Critical Approaches to American Working-Class Literature*, ed. by Michelle M. Tokarczyk (New York and London: Routledge, 2011); Paul Lauter, 'Working-Class Women's Literature: An Introduction to Study', *Radical Teacher* 15 (1980), 16–26; *Working-Class Literatures: Historical and International Perspectives*, ed. by Magnus Nilsson and John Lennon (Stockholm: Stockholm University Press, 2017).

9. David Convery, 'Writing and Theorising the Irish Working Class', in *A History of Irish Working-Class Writing*, pp.37–56.

10. Katie Bond, 'Folk music archive gains Swindon link', *Swindon Advertiser*, 4 July 2013, https://www.swindonadvertiser.co.uk/news/10524613.folk-music-archive-gains-swindon-link/ Accessed 16 May 2019.

11. Taken from commentary by Bragg on the radio documentary 'Digital Folk: John Kirkpatrick discovers how the digitised archive of England's folk songs is used by Billy Bragg and Lee Hall', broadcast on BBC Radio 4 in 2013. See description online: https://www.bbc.co.uk/programmes/b0383vxr. Accessed 5 June 2019.

12. John Moulden, 'Sub-literatures?: Folk Song, Memory and Ireland's Working Poor', in *A History of Irish Working-Class Writing*, pp.102–121 (p.111).

13. See Georges Denis Zimmermann, *Songs of Irish Rebellion – Irish Political Street Ballads and Rebel Songs* (Dublin: Four Courts Press, 2002), p.2.

14. Moulden, 'Sub-literatures?: Folk Song, Memory and Ireland's Working Poor', p.102.

15. See *A History of Irish Working-Class Writing*, pp.109–110.

16. Christopher Hilliard, *To Exercise Our Talents: The Democratization of Writing in Britain* (London: Harvard University Press, 2006); Jonathan Rose, *The Intellectual Life of the British Working Classes* (London: Yale University Press, 2001).

17. For a summary of the extant research see David Convery, 'Writing and Theorising the Irish Working Class', in Pierse (2017), pp.37–56. See also Liam Cullinane, '"As If You Were Something Under Their Shoe": Class, Gender and Status among Cork Textile Workers, 1930–70', in *Locked Out: A Century of Irish Working-Class Life*, ed. by David Convery (Dublin: Irish Academic Press, 2013), pp.175–191; Colin Coulter, 'The Absence of Class Politics in Northern Ireland', *Capital & Class* 22 (1999), 77–100; Graham McFarlane, 'Dimensions of Protestantism: The Working of Protestant Identity in a Northern Irish Village', in *Ireland from Below: Social Change and Local Communities*, ed. by Chris Curtin and Thomas M. Wilson (Galway: Officina Typographica/Galway University Press, n.d. [1990?]), pp.23–45; Marilyn Silverman, *An Irish Working Class: Explorations in Political Economy and Hegemony, 1800–1950* (Toronto: Toronto University

Press, 2001); Christopher J. V. Loughlin, 'Representing Labour: Notes towards a Political and Cultural Economy of Irish Working-Class Experience', in Pierse (2017), pp.57–71. With regard to educational matters, see Fergal Finnegan and Barbara Merrill's recent essay '"We're as good as anybody else": a comparative study of working-class university student experiences in England and Ireland', *British Journal of Sociology in Education* (5 October 2015). http://www.tandfonline.com/doi/abs/ 10.1080/01425692.2015.1081054. Accessed 12 May 2016. Ciaran Burke, *Culture, Capital and Graduate Futures: Degrees of Class* (London: Routledge, 2015).

18. Nils Beese, *Writing Slums: Dublin, Dirt and Literature* (Oxford: Peter Lang, 2018), p.261.

19. Susan Cannon Harris, *Irish Drama and the Other Revolutions: Playwrights, Sexual Politics and the International Left, 1892–1964* (Edinburgh: Edinburgh University Press, 2017), p.238.

20. Cannon Harris, p.240.; Liam Harte, *The Literature of the Irish in Britain: Autobiography and Memoir, 1725–2001* (Basingstoke, Palgrave Macmillan, 2009); Tony Murray, *London Irish Fictions: Narrative, Diaspora and Identity* (Liverpool: Liverpool University Press, 2012); Peter Kuch, 'Irish Working-Class Writing in Australasia, 1860–1960: Contrasts and Comparisons', in Pierse (2017), pp.226–242; Margaret Hallissy and John Lutz, 'The View from Below: Solidarity and Struggle in Irish-American Working-Class Literature', in Pierse (2017), pp.209–225.

21. See the organisation's website here: https://culturalpolicyireland.org. Accessed 10 September 2019.

22. Jonothan Neelands, Eleonora Belfiore, Catriona Firth, Natalie Hart, Liese Perrin, Susan Brock, Dominic Holdaway, Jane Woddis, *Enriching Britain: Culture, Creativity and Growth: The 2015 Report by the Warwick Commission on the Future of Cultural Value* (Coventry: University of Warwick, 2015). See also Dave O'Brien, Orian Brook, and Mark Taylor, *Panic! Social Class, Taste and Inequalities in the Creative Industries* (Report: 2018); Robert Hewison, *Cultural Capital: The Rise and Fall of Creative Britain* (London: Verso, 2014).

23. See Mary Moynihan, 'Analysis: in three years, the Waking the Feminists grassroots movement has had a seismic impact on Irish theatre and culture', 22 November 2018, RTÉ Brainstorm https://www.rte.ie/brainstorm/2018/1122/1012586-how-waking-the-feminists-set-an-equality-agenda-for-irish-theatre/. Accessed 22 August 2019.

24. Maggie Armstrong, 'Stage: Is Irish theatre now too elitist and middle class', *Irish Independent*, 22 November 2015, https://www.independent.ie/entertainment/ theatre-arts/stage-is-irish-theatre-now-too-elitist-and-middle-class-34217551.html. Accessed 5 August 2019.

25. Sandy Fitzgerald, *An Outburst of Frankness: Community Arts in Ireland – A Reader* (Dublin: TASC at New Island, 2004). Referenced quote is from the back-cover blurb.

26. Paula Clancy, 'Rhetoric and reality: a review of the position of community arts in state cultural policy in the Irish republic', in Fitzgerald, *An Outburst of Frankness: Community Arts in Ireland – A Reader*, pp. 83–114 (p.103).

27. E.R. Murray, 'YA fiction – is it a class act?', *Irish Times*, 27 July 2016, http://www. irishtimes.com/culture/books/ya-fiction-is-it-a-class-act-1.2736395 Accessed 10 June 2019.

28. Murray, 'YA fiction'.

29. Murray, 'YA fiction'.

30. Murray, 'YA fiction'.

31. Jeremy Hawthorn, preface to *The British Working-Class Novel in the Twentieth Century* (London: Edward Arnold, 1984), p.vii.

32. Hawthorn, p.viii.

33. Jeanne Moore, *Poverty: Access and Participation in the Arts* (Dublin: Combat Poverty Agency and The Arts Council, 1997). See also, however, examples

such as: Donal O'Donoghue 'Higher education in art and design: Access participation and opportunity', *Irish Educational Studies* 21.3 (2002), 111–129; Jeanne Moore 'Poverty and access to the arts: Inequalities in arts attendance', *Cultural Trends* 8.31 (1998), 53–73; Fitzgerald, *An Outburst of Frankness: Community Arts in Ireland – A Reader*; Pete Lunn and Elish Kelly, *In the Frame or Out of the Picture? A statistical analysis of public involvement in the arts* (Dublin: National Economic and Social Forum, 2009); ESRI, *Accounting for taste: an examination of socio economic gradients in attendance at arts events*, ESRI Working paper 283 (Dublin: Economic and Social Research Institute, 2009); Nuala Hunt, Gary Granville, Chris Maguire, and Fiona Whelan, 'Academy and community: the experience of a college programme in socially-engaged practice', *International Journal of Education through Art* 8.3 (2012), 271–285. An Arts Council strategic review in 2014 also suggested an awareness of its own failures in this regard, noting arts practice in Ireland's disconnect with 'significant cohorts of the population' and 'almost exclusive emphasis on the production/consumption model of the arts', with 'little emphasis on engagement and participation as a fundamental and valued aspect of the arts in Irish society'. See Arts Council, *Inspiring Prospects: Arts Council Strategic Review 2014 – Report of the Steering Group* (Dublin: Arts Council, 2014), pp.4–5.

34. FLAC, 'Our Voice, Our Rights: a parallel report in response to Ireland's Third Report under the International Covenant on Economic, Social and Cultural Rights' (Dublin: FLAC, 2014), pp.98–99.

35. John Kirk, *The British Working Class in the Twentieth Century: Film, Literature and Television* (Cardiff: University of Wales Press, 2009), p.1.

36. See Mike Savage, *Social Class in the 21ˢᵗ Century* (London: Pelican, 2015); Pierre Bourdieu, *Distinction – A Social Critique of the Judgement of Taste*, trans. by Richard Nice (London: Routledge, 1998).

37. See David Convery, 'Writing and Theorising the Irish Working Class', in Pierse (2017), pp.37–56, esp. pp.50–56.

38. See Silverman reference above; Chris Eipper *The Ruling Trinity: A Community Study of Church, State and Business in Ireland* (Aldershot: Gower Publishing, 1986) and *Hostage to Fortune: Bantry Bay and the Encounter with Gulf Oil* (St. John's, Newfoundland: Institute of Social and Economic Research, Memorial University of Newfoundland, 1989). Fergal Finnegan, Barbara Merrill, and Camilla Thunborg (ed.), *Student Voices on Inequalities in European Higher Education: Challenges for theory, policy and practice in a time of change* (London: Routledge, 2014).

39. Helena Sheehan, *Irish Television Drama: A Society and its Stories* (Dublin: RTÉ, 1987; re-published in a revised edition on CD-ROM, 2004) and *The Continuing Story of Irish Television Drama: Tracking the Tiger* (Dublin: Four Courts Press, 2004).

40. Tom Maguire, 'The State We're in: Violence and Working-Class Women on and off the Contemporary Irish Stage', *Journal of Contemporary Drama in English* 6.1 (2018), 160–175 (p.165).

41. Nicola Wilson, *Home in British Working-Class Fiction* (London: Ashgate, 2015), p.89; Ken Worpole, *Dockers and Detectives: Popular Reading, Popular Writing* (London: Verso, 1983). It is of course significant that the assertion is reiterated more than three decades later.

42. Maguire, 'The State We're in', p.169.

43. Heather Laird, 'Writing Working-Class Irish Women', in Pierse (2017), pp.122–139 (p.139).

44. See Eamon Jordan, 'Multiple Class Consciousnesses in Writings for Theatre during the Celtic Tiger Era', Pierse (2017), pp.378–396. Also, see Michael Pierse, 'The People: Race and Class on the Contemporary Irish Stage', in Paige Reynolds (ed.), *The New Irish Studies: Twenty-First Century Critical Revisions* (Cambridge: Cambridge University Press, 2020).

45. Ruth Sherry, 'The Irish Working Class in Fiction', in *The British Working-Class Novel in the Twentieth Century*, ed. by Jeremy Hawthorn (London: Edward Arnold, 1984), pp.111–123 (p.111).

46. Though see for example Mary M. McGlynn, *Narratives of Class in New Irish and Scottish Literature* (New York: Palgrave Macmillan, 2008); Michael Pierse, *Writing Ireland's Working Class: Dublin after O'Casey* (London: Palgrave, 2009) and Aaron Kelly (ed.), *The Irish Review* (Special Issue: Culture and Class) 47 (December 2013).

47. Fergal Finnegan and Barbara Merrill, '"We're as good as anybody else": a comparative study of working-class university students' experiences in England and Ireland', *British Journal of Sociology of Education* 38.3 (2017), 307–324.

48. Finnegan and Merrill, p.318.

49. Roddy Doyle, *The Woman Who Walked into Doors* (London: Penguin, 1997), pp.25–26.

50. See Pierse, *Writing Ireland's Working Class*, pp.26–30.

51. bell hooks, 'Confronting Class in the Classroom', in *The Critical Pedagogy Reader*, ed. by Antonia Darder, Marta Baltodano, and Rodolfo D. Torres (New York: Routledge Falmer, 2003), pp.142–150 (p.142).

52. Margaret Scanlon, Fred Powell, Pat Leahy, Hilary Jenkinson, and Olive Byrne, '"No one in our family ever went to college": Parents' orientations towards their children's post-secondary education and future occupations', *International Journal of Educational Research* 93 (2019), 13–22 (p.14).

53. Elaine Keane, Manuela Heinz, and Andrea Lynch '"Working-class" student teachers: Not being encouraged at school and impact on motivation to become a teacher', *Education Research and Perspectives* 45 (2018), 71–97 (p.72).

54. Keane et al., p.75.

55. Beverley Skeggs, 'Classifying Practices: Representations, Capitals and Recognitions' in *Class Matters: 'Working-Class' Women's Perspectives on Social Class*, ed. by Pat Mahony and Christine Zmroczek (London: Taylor & Francis, 1997), pp.127–142 (p.127).

56. Lucy O'Toole, 'Paul McVeigh launches *The 32: An Anthology of Working Class Voices* on crowdfunding publisher', *Hot Press*, 4 November 2019. Accessed online: https://www.hotpress.com/culture/paul-mcveigh-launches-32-anthology-irish-working-class-voices-crowdfunding-publisher-22793381 [23 November 2019].

57. Michelle M. Tokarczyk, introduction to *Critical Approaches to American Working-Class Literature* (New York: Routledge, 2014), p.5.

Lisa Fitzpatrick

Contemporary Feminist Protest in Ireland: #MeToo in Irish Theatre

INTRODUCTION

From October 2017 when the accusations against Harvey Weinstein for rape, sexual assault and sexual harassment first went public, through the repealing of the anti-abortion amendment in the Republic of Ireland in May 2018, and on to the recent legalization of abortion in Northern Ireland in November 2019, the women's movement in Ireland and elsewhere has become newly visible and energized. Young women's activism in particular can be seen to shape the priorities of this new feminist moment, using digital technologies to create viral platforms where women can communicate and share personal experiences. One example is #MeToo, which exposed women's experiences of sexual harassment and, by doing so, challenged the stigma and shame often felt by, and attributed to, the victims of this kind of abuse. #MeToo, and #TimesUp,[1] as well as other online activism specific to Ireland[2] created a kind of hunger for change that was noticeable to me in my teaching practice. My female students seemed to become more outspoken and assertive in class; they expressed beliefs in the right to choose abortion, and anger at the conduct of rape trials, and they engaged actively in public protesting and campaigning. This energy was particularly evident in their creative work, which ranged across genres from immersive performance to soundscapes, movement pieces, slam poetry and monodramas, and which explored their experiences of sexual violence from their early teens onwards. The work expressed their acute awareness of, and resistance to, the objectification and sexualisation of women, and the associated misogyny, within their culture. It left me reflecting that I had expected women's lives to be better by now, and that without ever putting the thought into language I had assumed that women of my generation had tolerated nasty behaviour and pushed through difficulties so that succeeding generations would not have to. Seeing that their experiences were not very different, I felt more than sadness: I felt grief. Watching the work,

Irish University Review 50.1 (2020): 82–93
DOI: 10.3366/iur.2020.0436
© Edinburgh University Press
www.euppublishing.com/iur

and discussing it with the students also led me to reflect upon my own responses to sexual harassment, and my failures to challenge unacceptable behaviour. On reading the responses to #MeToo and #TimesUp from Germaine Greer and Catherine Millet's letter in *Le Monde*,[3] I found myself haunted by the question of complicity and by a sense of intergenerational alienation.

#MeToo and #TimesUp gathered popular international support from women (and men) of all ages, with millions of social media users tweeting or posting on various platforms under those signs. Inevitably, there was also a reaction against the movement by a number of feminists including Germaine Greer, whose commentary was provocative but also often thought provoking. The other intervention that attracted media attention was a letter in *Le Monde* in January 2018 signed by one hundred French feminists, characterizing #MeToo as puritanical, anti-sex, and anti-freedom. In fact, it foregrounded problematic but commonplace assumptions about sexual harassment and violence, reinscribing conventional gender roles and power structures that pre-dominantly serve and protect economically privileged men and women while marginalizing others. Yet together with Greer, they raise the insistent question of freedom, with which this essay is also concerned. Greer's commentary interrogated anti-rape activism and proposed Foucauldian-inspired legislative reform that, controversially, appears to minimize rape as 'bad sex' and as a domestic peccadillo. However, in doing so she returns to a foundational idea of the feminist movement: that the personal is the political. This idea is shared by radical feminisms including contemporary feminism that eschews neoliberalism, and is an essential underpinning of the #MeToo movement.

In Ireland, the #MeToo movement became headline news in October 2017 when playwright Grace Dyas blogged about an experience with the Artistic Director of the Gate Theatre, Michael Colgan, and then tweeted 'I've been thinking about Michael Colgan lately...'.[4] In doing so, she broke a silence that had persisted for decades, allowing other women and men to speak about their experiences and the behaviour they had witnessed. In response, the Gate Theatre commissioned a report that generated a set of recommendations. Its findings, and the reporting of the story, highlighted the issue of complicity with abuse and also resonated in quite startling ways with the argument put forward by Germaine Greer, discussed below.

REPORTING SEXUAL HARASSMENT: THE PROBLEM OF CREDIBILITY

Liz Kelly and Jill Radford[5] argue that asymmetric notions of credibility and the limits of representation result in resistance to believing women's experiences of sexual harassment, especially those that stop short of physical violence. They use the phrase 'nothing really happened' (19) to illustrate the minimization of women's experience, pointing out that the victims repeatedly use this phrase themselves: 'On one level all these women were clear that something had happened – they told their stories for that reason, including what the impacts of these encounters were. They were saying "nothing" happened because they know that their perceptions of "something" are unlikely to be validated' (20). More recent scholarship on rape and the law[6] reflects ongoing public tendencies to doubt the credibility of accusers, alongside the persistence of popular myths about rape. The insistence that verbal harassment, unwanted touching, and street harassment are 'nothing' invalidates the victim's perception and experience in favour of that of the perpetrator. Threats thus become harmless flirtation, and stalking is refigured as a compliment to the beauty of the victim. Victims of explicit and enacted violence are also thereby silenced, by the sense of personal and public shame that often attaches to the victim of sexual assault rather than the perpetrator. While there are many reasons why this is so, one significant factor is surely the victim's brutal encounter with her (or his) own vulnerability and the potential of others to use that vulnerability to deny her agency and physical integrity. Vulnerability is often constructed as shameful, as synonymous with weakness, and is strongly associated with femininity even though – as Butler argues – it is an ontological human quality.[7]

Therefore one of the most powerful and disruptive aspects of #MeToo is its unequivocal response to sexual violence across a spectrum of behaviour from unwelcome comments and touching, to rape. It asserts that something did happen, and that none of this behaviour is acceptable. By declaring this publicly and with large numbers of women lending their own stories to the movement, it also asserts that the victims should not be ashamed or silent, because the problem is systemic rather than personal.[8] Or to rephrase: the personal is the political, and the individual experience multiplied by thousands and millions of incidents, is evidence of systemic attitudes and behaviours. By exchanging their experiences, victims also overcome any possible reluctance to appear vulnerable, since the scale of the issue situates vulnerability as a quality shared by many others of different genders.

GREER'S CRITIQUE OF THE MOVEMENT

Germaine Greer was working on two books in 2017: *On Rape* and *On Rage* were both published in September 2018. Earlier that year she debated #MeToo and #TimesUp with Mehdi Hasan on Al Jazeera television, recorded in the Oxford Union, where she is introduced as a 'writer, thinker, and legendary feminist'. She had already argued that #MeToo would make no difference. Ever the contrarian, she criticized the trials of Bill Cosby and Weinstein and the legislation being passed in various countries as futile, saying that the prosecution of Cosby, 'in his 80s, after 60 years of doing what he's been doing' is not a 'victory'. Her recommendation that women should 'slap down' men who harass them ignored the very real material constraints of financial dependence, job insecurity, physical size, and so on that limit the way an individual can respond to abuse. Her interviews in advance of her book *On Rape* make the following assertions: that not all rape is violent; a lot of rape is just 'bad sex'; the burden of proof and the penalties for rape should be lowered, to improve the conviction rate; most rape is domestic, and women are made unreasonably fearful of it. She says, 'of all the crimes in which injuries are sustained, rape is the least impressive. People get hurt all the time, it's mad to pretend to a woman that a penis walking down the street is more dangerous than a knife'.[9]

It is easier to dismiss the letter to *Le Monde* than to dismiss Greer, because in her frequently enraging and outrageous statements there is some truth, and some of what she has to say is important to interrogate and take forward. Her lecture at the Hay Festival on the subject of rape offers a detailed and passionate denunciation of the 'Belfast Rape Trial' for its treatment of the victim, and also offers a strong critique of rape myths.[10] Her analysis of rape law and prosecutorial practices sits easily within feminist discourses, apart from her suggestion that lenient penalties in exchange for lightening the burden of proof would address the very real difficulty of proving or disproving consent. This issue of consent becomes almost impossible to prove in cases of marital and intimate partner rape. One powerful and convincing element in her argument is that most rape is domestic in setting, occurring between intimate partners or spouses. Although Greer is provocative in saying that most rape is only 'bad sex', she explains this as the selfish, unloving forcing of intercourse upon the 'exhausted wife' who does not resist but endures: and to endure or comply is not to consent. And she points out that in many horrifyingly violent rapes the courts have accepted compliance in the face of physical violence and death threats as consent.

THE CASE OF THE GATE THEATRE

The relevance of Greer's comments to the shocking yet widely known information about bullying and harassment at the Gate Theatre, emerges in newspaper articles and interviews with the perpetrator Michael Colgan, and some of his victims. Colgan ran the Gate Theatre for more than thirty years, creating a financially and artistically successful institution with an international reputation. However, he was also allowed to sit on the Board of the theatre, meaning that there was no credible complaints procedure, and his success meant that he had influence and power to help or damage the careers of new and established artists. The accusations against him were of bullying and harassment within the team of Gate employees, and of the misuse of his power in his dealings with independent theatre artists. By the time the allegations became public, Colgan had retired. In a newspaper article for the *Irish Independent* he reflected that he had made mistakes, but insisted he had not committed any 'sex crimes', and he apologised for causing distress to others by his 'politically incorrect' comments.[11]

The women who worked with Colgan describe overt sexual harassment: comments on their hair, bodies, and clothes; comments about his sexual prowess; questions about their own intimate lives; verbal humiliation; unwanted touching, including in one instance a slap on the buttocks in front of other (male) professionals, done to humiliate; tirades of public verbal abuse that could last an hour, amongst other behaviours. Despite this, the women's comments on social media and in the mainstream press reflect their instinct to minimize the abuse. After describing clear instances of workplace harassment including assault, Ciara Smyth writes, '[t]he worst thing for me now is still feeling like I am overreacting. I was slow to write anything down because of that feeling. I imagine other girls and women had far worse experiences'.[12] Another woman says the list of behaviours 'may read as pretty inconsequential' but for an individual it was 'highly destructive, completely demeaning and frankly devastating'.[13] In fact, the behaviour she describes is truly shocking.

Without excusing Colgan's behaviour, or the Gate Theatre for its lack of oversight, the wider context for the abuse as reported by Gaye Cunningham is an arts industry where bullying is common. In a survey of 283 theatre workers in 2016, Irish Equity found that 57% of respondents reported being bullied at work, but 74% did not report it, with 62% of them saying they did not report for fear that it would jeopardise future work opportunities.[14] Within the Gate Theatre itself, the *Gender Counts* report from Waking the Feminists identified that theatre as having low levels of female participation compared to other organizations sampled. 'In the key categories of Director and Author, the Gate Theatre records female representation of 8% and 6% in these roles respectively. ... Looking at the role of Author, the Gate has the lowest level of female participation in the entire sample (6%)'.[15]

The women employed at the Gate Theatre describe classic patterns associated with domestic violence, where Colgan would alternate between kindness and nastiness. Ciara Smyth describes how he would share rare material that he knew interested her as a playwright: 'It was very confusing. Michael had an incredible ability to make you feel so important in one moment and then like dirt in the next'.[16] One woman says that she thought she liked him, but now she realizes that she didn't. A number of those raising complaints say that when they protested to Colgan about his behaviour he would accuse them of lacking a sense of humour, or of being overly politically correct. While the women's reaction to their experiences at the Gate largely supports the findings of Kelly and Radford, Colgan's own statements and reported statements resonate with Greer's analysis of rape as a domestic crime. In both his article in the *Irish Independent* and his interview with Gaye Cunningham for the Gate's review, he repeats the idea that '... it was a small workplace with no hierarchies or structure and he considered that he and the six women there were a team. He believed they were like a family and sometimes if they had a row they had a row and solved it like a family ... and yes, he blurred the lines'.[17]

Colgan's invocation of family relationships and structures in his justification of sexual harassment and bullying resonates with Greer's argument about sexual violence as a domestic issue. Her intervention with that point is crucial to the #MeToo movement and contemporary feminist activism, which reflect the complex power relationships that underpin sexual harassment and discredit the argument that it is merely politically incorrect flirtation. By invoking the domestic space both Colgan and Greer differently foreground the way the sexual violence and the threat of sexual violence act to limit women's agency in the public space, and consign them to the (far more hazardous) private space of the home and family. Underpinning the question of agency is the matter of freedom, and the question of what freedom means, particularly in the face of sexual threat and the fear it provokes.

FREEDOM

#MeToo, #TimesUp, Greer, and Millet *et al*, all open the question of freedom. The *Le Monde* letter declares the freedom to move and act in the world, a freedom which carries with it risks and responsibilities. The freedom proposed by #MeToo shares this vision: to be able to move and act in the world, which it sees as posited on freedom from sexual threat and intimidation. Critics of #MeToo seem to discount this threat, and argue for a freedom *to* act rather than a freedom *from* harassment. They argue that too many accusations are being made about unimportant actions, which should not be experienced as threat. Like Greer, who proposes that women should clout men who bother them, they seem to position themselves as speaking for strong and resilient women who do not have to appeal to men or the law for protection. And, of course, the law does not provide protection, at least not for all women equally, and not in a way that is cognizant of women's freedom as active agents.[18] These competing definitions of freedom underpin differing conceptions of the female subject. While the argument that there is 'freedom from' and 'freedom to' holds some attractions, sexual threat (and the *threat of* sexual threat, which is not the same thing), significantly circumscribes the freedom of girls and women, in all kinds of ways. Women are trained from childhood in all aspects of their embodied behaviours to avoid anything that might draw unwelcome attention from men: the way they sit, move, speak, play, laugh, and so on. This is rarely discussed in terms of freedom. So lived freedom is always embodied, however it is conceived as a philosophical concept, culturally and historically shaped.

The *Le Monde* letter concludes with a defiant statement that women are not reducible to their bodies. But Elizabeth Grosz's work on materialism and Butler's on the calling into being of the human subject quickly contradict this. Grosz proposes that freedom 'is the condition of, or capacity for, action in life'.[19] This is separate from the liberationist understanding of freedom as emancipation from an oppressive system or from unjust constraints or limitations. Instead of freedom from (certain kinds of oppression), the individual has freedom to (take action, exercise agency). Grosz asks, 'Is feminist theory best served through its traditional focus on women's attainment of freedom from patriarchal, racist, colonialist, and heteronormative constraints? Or by exploring what the female – or feminist – subject is and is capable of making and doing?' (141). In her essay, Grosz takes Bergson's concept of freedom because she thinks Bergson might be 'more consonant with a feminism of difference' (142). As she traces this conception of freedom and relates it to the formation of the subject, she is not dismissive of 'freedom from'. In fact, freedom from certain kinds of oppression is the baseline above which the potentialities of 'freedom to' can emerge. But fear and vulnerability inhibit this.

FEAR, VULNERABILITY, AND FREEDOM

Sara Ahmed draws the emotion of fear into her discussion of freedom. Of fear, she writes that it is an embodied experience that 'creates fear on the surface of bodies'.[20] While all bodies feel fear, it is 'felt differently by different bodies' and those bodies are shaped in relation to space and mobility (68). Citing Elizabeth Stanko, Ahmed argues that narratives of fear indicate to women that their safest space in the home, and that public space is dangerous, or at least it is dangerous if the woman is alone. This in turn creates narratives of feminine vulnerability, with vulnerability understood as weakness and susceptibility to harm from others. While this is in opposition to recent work on vulnerability by Butler, Erinn C. Gilson, and Athena Athanasiou who posit it as an ontological human quality, it is an insistent message in the interpellation of the female subject in Western culture. Fear, Ahmed argues, is a response to the awareness of vulnerability rather than actual vulnerability; and it 'restricts the body's mobility; it contains some bodies so that they shrink and take up less space' (69). The shrunken fearful body signals its vulnerability affectively to other bodies, and to itself. Within this discourse of fear and vulnerability, with its objective of placing limitations on women's mobility and access to the world outside the domestic space, it is important to interrogate the security of that domestic space. Statistically, the domestic space is not a safe space for women. On the contrary, it is the space in which they are most likely to experience emotional abuse and physical attack. Furthermore, victims are least likely to report attacks that take place in that forum and are most likely to be disbelieved when they do report.

Ahmed quotes from Jalna Hanmer and Sheila Saunders who wrote in 1984: 'Women's sense of security in public places [including the work-place] is profoundly shaped by our inability to secure an undisputed right to occupy that space. The curtailing of movement is a not infrequent response to violent and threatening encounters in public'.[21] The persistence of women's anxiety about public space is shaped by the dominance of discourses that set freedom (access to the public world, freedom to act) against security (freedom from harassment). These discourses express patriarchal imperatives of heteronormative gender binaries, and use humiliation and violence to punish women who transgress those divisions. Limiting confident access to public space has clear implications for the freedom of the individual subject: physical freedom; economic freedom; freedom to socialize, form relationships, and engage with others in a multitude of ways. This suggests that 'freedom to' is not readily disentangled from 'freedom from'. The argument that the body can be touched, threatened, or harmed without effect on the mind is similarly interrogated by Ahmed's work on affect and emotion. Studies of affect, like Butler's work on vulnerability or on the performativity of gender, suggest deep and abiding effects of emotional and intellectual forces on the materialization of the body. As Laura Kipnis puts it, what happens to the body happens to the person; the self cannot be extracted from the body.[22]

CONCLUSIONS: ACTIVISM AND RESISTANCE

Fear, of further harassment or ostracism, of feeling foolish for over-reacting, or feeling shame for 'inviting' harassment, and knowing that your experience may be disbelieved, all contribute to women's passive endurance of harassment and misogynistic behaviour. But in 2015 with #WakingtheFeminists, and 2017 with #MeToo, women organized visible and active resistance in Ireland and beyond. This also fed other online liberationist movements like those for marriage equality, abortion legislation, and reform of rape trials. These are optimistic, grassroots campaigns, arising from the public sphere, and demonstrating continuity with earlier decades of the women's movement. They indicate freedom to innovate and invent, and the capacity to take action. They return to a core tenet of feminism: that *the personal is the political*.

Writing on young women's engagement with Web 2.0 technologies, scholars like Anita Harris and Jessalyn Marie Keller[23] presciently describe the conditions for the emergence of feminist online activism. Harris notices a shift away from state-oriented feminism towards the transitory, heterogeneous and personal (475). Keller notes girls' engagement with the online world 'in part because of the unregulated nature of online space that nonetheless remains a public way to connect with peer communities and express personal interests outside of adult intervention' (434). Harris notes that 'individual and grassroots practices have come to the fore' in a neoliberal context that emphasizes individual choice and action (478). While the online space may facilitate the spreading of ideas, experiences, and resistant movement, activism seems capable of translating itself from the virtual into the actual world. Online activism seems to be contiguous with the creative learning environment: my students' work speaks to their confidence that personal experience is publicly and politically valuable.

I consider my own position in this debate, and my own lifelong tendency to deal with unwelcome sexual attention by refusing to acknowledge it. I do not describe my experiences as traumatizing; rather, they made me angry; and my friends and I dealt with this behaviour by warning each other and laughing together, bonding as an all-female group against the harasser and thus engaging in mutual support. This is still a tactic that girls and women use, and #MeToo is arguably a more public and therefore more activist digital version of it. At the time, sexual comments, verbal aggression or unwelcome touching seemed to me the price of the freedom to live and work and pursue opportunities for which earlier generations of women had struggled. The harassment expressed disapproval and rage at young women's freedom, clothes, and noise and lack of deference, so I understood my independence as defiant, and oppositional. I suspect that valuing one particular kind of freedom over another underpins the criticisms of some older feminists towards contemporary feminist activism, fed by a sense that young women do not fully comprehend how much the women's movement has fought for and won.

I didn't post under #MeToo, although I admire the movement. I wanted to say 'nothing really happened', even if that sanctioned the negation of my own experience. Harassment is almost always clearly intended to humiliate and bully rather than to seduce; and I believed that distress just rewards the harasser, so it is important to hide your fear. #MeToo, and the memories it provoked, and the work of my students, leads me to reconsider. Not exhibiting any emotion rewards the abuser by allowing him (or her) to continue unrebuked, and naming unacceptable behaviour is in fact essential to feminist and social progress; if it does nothing else, it protects those who come next. Watching students recognize and identify unethical and unacceptable abuses of power, and speak their truth, is a reminder that the 'classroom remains the most radical space of possibility in the academy'.[24]

NOTES

1. It is important to acknowledge that 'Me Too' was an initiative of African-American activist Tarana Burke, who first coined the term in 2006 while working with sexual abuse survivors in Alabama. Burke is a community activist whose roles have included that of senior director of Girls for Gender Equality in New York. The term went viral in 2017 when Alyssa Milano used it to encourage women to tweet about their experiences of sexual harassment. In November 2017 a letter on behalf of the 'approximately 700,000 women who work in the agricultural fields and packing sheds across the United States' was published and a march to 'Take Back the Workplace' followed a few days later in Los Angeles. The farm workers described their own experiences, and affirmed solidarity with the women in Hollywood. *Alianza Nacional de Campesinas*, as the name suggests, represents poor women, the majority of them Hispanic, often migrant workers: women whose livelihoods are particularly precarious. Under the hashtag #TimesUp, this movement was committed to fighting back against sexual harassment in the workplace across a range of industries. Activists like the farmworkers are often denied individual identities and recognition within a women's movement that is disproportionately European / Euro-American and often predominantly middle-class and professional.

2. These very successful examples of online activist networking include: #WakingtheFeminists, which responded to the almost entirely-male Abbey Theatre programme for 2016, celebrating the centenary of the Easter Rising; #InHerShoes and #Repealthe8[th] both supported the repeal of Ireland's near-total ban on abortion; #IBelieveHer expressed public rage at the conduct of a high-profile rape trial in Belfast.

3. The open letter to *Le Monde* signed by Catherine Millet and four others (Chiche, Robbe-Grillet, Sastre and Shalmani) was immediately criticised by the activists behind the French version of #MeToo, named *#Balancetonporc*, and it was subsequently partially retracted by Catherine Deneuve and other celebrity signatories. The full text of the letter is available here: https://www.lemonde.fr. https://www.lemonde.fr/idees/article/2018/01/09/nous-defendons-une-liberte-d-importuner-indispensable-a-la-liberte-sexuelle_5239134_3232.html and here in English: https://www.worldcrunch.com/opinion-analysis/full-translation-of-french-anti-metoo-manifesto-signed-by-catherine-deneuve.

4. Conor Gallagher (2018) 'Michael Colgan ran Gate Theatre as personal fiefdom for decades' *Irish Times* 9 February 2018. Available online at https://www.irishtimes.com/culture/stage/michael-colgan-ran-gate-theatre-as-personal-fiefdom-for-decades-1.3387073. Accessed 11 January 2020.

5. Liz Kelly and Jill Radford '"Nothing Really Happened": The Invalidation of Women's Experiences of Sexual Violence', in *Women, Violence and Male Power*, ed. By Marianne Hester, Liz Kelly, and Jill Radford. (Buckingham: Open University Press, 1996), pp. 19–33. All subsequent references are given in parentheses in the text.

6. Relevant studies include Susan Ehrlich *Representing Rape: Language and Sexual Consent* (London and New York: Routledge, 2001); Conor Hanly, Deirdre Healey, and Stacey Scriver *Rape and Justice in Ireland* (Dublin: Liffey Press, 2009); Amanda Konradi *Taking the Stand* (Westport CT and London: Praeger Press, 2007); Rachel Snyder *No Visible Bruises* (New York: Bloomsbury, 2019).

7. Judith Butler *Precarious Life* (London: Verso, 2004); Butler and Athena Athanasiou, *Dispossession: The Performative in the Political* (London: Polity, 2010).

8. While some of the reports and testimonies have come from male victims of abuse – such as allegations against Kevin Spacey by actor Anthony Rapp – my focus here is on violence against and harassment of women. Although all such cases are based on the abuse of power and the desire to limit the agency and bodily integrity of the victim, social and cultural imbalances of power between men and women further complicate the question.

9. Germaine Greer, in interview with Mehdi Hasan, on Al Jazeera. The transcript is available at https://www.aljazeera.com/programmes/headtohead/2019/01/transcript-germaine-greer-metoo-movement-190107074617210.html.

10. Germaine Greer, interview with Rosie Boycott at the Hay Festival, 30 May 2018. Available online at https://www.hayfestival.com/p-13944-germaine-greer.aspx?skinid=16.

11. Michael Colgan 'Michael Colgan in his own words', *Irish Independent*, 12 November 2017. Available online at https://www.independent.ie/irish-news/news/michael-colgan-in-his-own-words-i-have-been-responsible-for-causing-distress-and-i-am-truly-sorry-36312669.html.

12. 'Barbarian at the Gate' posted by Admin on www.Broadsheet.ie, on 31 October 2017. Available at https://www.broadsheet.ie/2017/10/31/barbarian-at-the-gate/.

13. Deirdre Falvey 'Gate Theatre report: 'I want Michael Colgan to say sorry'', *Irish Times*, 10 March 2018. Available online at https://www.irishtimes.com/culture/stage/gate-theatre-report-i-want-michael-colgan-to-say-sorry-1.3421039.

14. Irish Equity 'Irish Equity Will Support Members in Confronting Sexual Assault and Harassment'. Available online at https://irishequity.ie. The Union policy on sexual harassment is also available at that website.

15. Brenda Donohue, Ciara O'Dowd, Tanya Dean, Ciara Murphy, Kathleen Cawley and Kate Harris *Gender Counts*. (Dublin: The Arts Council / An Chomhairle Ealaíon, 2017), p.46. Full report available online at www.wakingthefeminists.org.

16. 'Barbarian at the Gate' posted by Admin on www.Broadsheet.ie, on 31 October 2017.

17. Gaye Cunningham, *Independent Review: Gate Theatre* (2019), p.11, available from the Gate Theatre. This is a paraphrase of Colgan's response to a question from Cunningham. The report is also available through the *Irish Times* at www.irishtimes.com.

18. I refer here to images published by the *Guardian* on 24 August 2016, accompanying a report by Ben Quinn: 'French Police Make Woman Remove Burkini on Nice Beach'. Available online at https://www.theguardian.com/world/2016/aug/24/french-police-make-woman-remove-burkini-on-nice-beach. The images show a woman in headscarf, leggings and a long-sleeved tunic being required by armed guards to remove the headscarf and tunic. According to the report she received a ticket for wearing clothes that were not "respecting good morals and secularism".

19. Elizabeth Grosz, 'Feminism, Materialism, and Freedom', in *New Materialisms* ed. by Diana Coole and Samantha Frost (Durham and London: Duke University Press, 2010), p.140. All subsequent references are given in parentheses in the text.

20. Sara Ahmed *The Cultural Politics of Emotion* (Edinburgh: Edinburgh University Press, 2004), p.68. All subsequent references given in parentheses in the text.

21. Jalna Hanmer & Sheila Saunders *Well-founded Fear: A Community Study of Violence to Women* (New York: HarperCollins, 1984), quoted in Ahmed (2004), p.39.
22. Laura Kipnis 'Has #Me Too gone too far, or not far enough?', *Guardian*, 13 January 2018. Available online at https://www.theguardian.com/commentisfree/2018/jan/13/has-me-too-catherine-deneuve-laura-kipnis.
23. See, for example, Anita Harris, 'Mind The Gap', *Australian Feminist Studies* 25.66, (2010), 475–484, and Jessalyn Marie Keller, 'Virtual Feminisms', *Information, Communication & Society* 15:3, (2012), 429–447. Further references are given in parentheses in the text.
24. bell hooks, *Teaching to Transgress* (London and New York: Routledge, 1994), p.12.

Anne Mulhall

The Ends of Irish Studies?
On Whiteness, Academia,
and Activism

I
'Solidarity is not a market exchange.' Robin D.G. Kelley[1]

What is the place of the political in contemporary literature and criticism and, more specifically, in the contemporary field of Irish Studies? At the IASIL 2019 conference 'The Critical Ground' in TCD marking the fiftieth anniversary of IASIL, the political seemed at times to be an artefact of a glorious but receding past. The sense of originary energies since dissipated tinged several roundtables and plenary sessions. This feeling was captured in a comment from the floor following the opening plenary roundtable, noting the dwindling of political intensities since the high tide of the 1980s and 90s, and lamenting the decline of Irish Studies as a field where muscular contention and vituperative public exchanges indicated its political significance.[2] Along with this intermittent nostalgia for a lost political purpose, the conference also witnessed the occasional refusal – sometimes angry, sometimes louche – of the imposition of the political. John Banville in conversation with Fintan O'Toole, for instance, repudiated the idea of political literature, naming Brecht as the template of 'pure politics masquerading as art.'[3]

This investment in art as a space of freedom from the corruptions of the political is of course nothing new but has perhaps a new (political) traction and a more desperate emotional and psychological appeal in times of accelerating global crisis. At the 2016 IASIL conference at UCC, a roundtable on the work of Frank O'Connor addressed, among other things, the political obligations of the writer and of literature. Of the five writers who took part – Sara Baume, Rob Doyle, Madeleine D'Arcy, Thomas Morris, and William Wall – only Wall insisted on the political agency of both. Participants, some more vociferously than others,

Irish University Review 50.1 (2020): 94–111
DOI: 10.3366/iur.2020.0437
© Edinburgh University Press
www.euppublishing.com/iur

rejected the idea that the writer might have a political voice that should be used, seeing it as a form of censorship, an unbearable imposition of obligations hostile to the creative imagination, a tethering of the wild energies of the literary instinct, a craven bowing to 'identity politics'.[4] Again in 2016, in a special issue of *Poetry Ireland Review* marking the centenary of the 1916 Rising, editor Vona Groarke asked the featured poets to respond to a questionnaire: '30 questions for the Rising Generation'. One question, 'If someone described you as a political poet, what would your reaction be?', garnered interesting and varied responses. Several poets welcomed the description. Others gave thoughtful reflections on the relationship between politics and poetry. Julie Morrissy observed that 'it is difficult to speak at all without being "political"'.[5] Stephen Sexton made a distinction 'between political poetry, and a political poet'.[6] Emma Must, reflecting on her former full-time involvement as an activist, noted that while poetry can 'deal with political issues' or 'be used in the service of political ends', this is different to the work of activism. As she puts it, 'if you want to generate specific political change, you'd be better off devising a strategy, writing a press release, organising an action, and... and... and... You won't have time to sit and write poetry.'[7] Many poets expressed an aversion toward political poetry, even some poets whose work would be considered political. For Christodoulos Makris, for instance, 'the political poet brand carries echoes of polemic. A kind of writing steeped in certainty, its purpose to force the reader into assent.' Similarly, Paula Cunningham is 'leery of the didactic in the political. I dislike being told what to think, especially in a poem'; Mary Noonan dislikes poetry that is 'too obviously in the service of a cause or an agenda', Roisin Tierney objects to poetry that feels 'as if you are being lectured to', with Brecht again cited as an example; while Declan Ryan rejects 'sloganeering', 'bombast or loudspeakers. I don't like the school assembly voice.'[8] In that vein, Groarke herself expressed dislike of 'political poetry' in an interview with Ciaran Carty in the *Irish Times* the following year: 'I come out in a rash at the idea of being a political poet. If you want to change things, stand for election.' Groarke's emphasis on electoral politics is itself politically interesting given the contempt she expresses for street protest and mass mobilisation in the same interview: '"Everyone was chanting 'Heigh ho, heigh ho, Donald Trump has got to go'.... The automatic full rhyme hurt my ears, and the sense of it offended me even more ... why use language that you know is empty of meaning?"'[9]

The attribution of 'political' can be a way of dismissing certain kinds of work, certain 'categories' of artist, ideological commitments, and forms of critique. At its most anodyne, this repudiation may express itself in terms of declarations of a borderless literary citizenship that renders critique of the asymmetries of power and access in the literary and cultural world impolite and divisive. Within the Republic of Letters, all difference is transcended and allegiance is pledged to the universality of art, the antithesis of so-called 'identity politics'.[10] While the last couple of years has seen an amplified focus on 'diversity and inclusion' in literary, cultural, and academic institutions in Ireland, this focus has not necessarily curbed suspicion of the 'political'.[11] Addressing the systemic issues of class, race, sexual orientation, and gender within these institutions requires more than an 'add-on' approach, where marginalised writers and artists are added into a programme line-up or table of contents. It requires a redistribution of power and access that would change the structures of these institutions – and redistribution of the means of production, including cultural and literary production, is always political. The US-based artist Juliana Huxtable speaks of the add-on approach as 'sabotage' – a hijacking of the 'minoritized' artist to fulfil diversity requirements, to give an event or an institution the right 'look'. She argues that 'the sabotage is to invite two trans artists to an event, to post the image on Instagram, to share the Facebook article, and to not actually deal with the structural aspects.' Gossett responds: 'It makes me think of visibility as a deadlock, you know? It's representation, sort of, but not really. It's a scattering of people without any redistribution of power.'[12]

The function of literary criticism as (political) critique has been an issue of ongoing contention for the last century, and the last decade or more has seen strong arguments for 'weak theory' that moves away from critique and toward what Rita Felski calls 'post-criticism'.[13] In an essay on 'Critique and Anti-Critique', Ronan McDonald notes the turn toward the post-critical, a critical attitude that spans from re-valorizations of the literary and its affective power, to practices of 'surface reading' – reading with rather than against the text – to the development of forms of enquiry that lend a scientific objectivity to literary research (for instance, in projects in narrative medicine, or distant reading, or other varieties of digital humanities or arts-science collaboration).[14] In her 2012 book *Object Lessons* Robyn Wiegman (a key figure in the polemical vanguard of anti-critique) queries the 'political belief' in 'critical practice as an agency of social change' in the fields of what she calls 'identity knowledges' – for instance, critical race studies, gender studies, queer studies, 'nation' studies – to explore how such fields 'become disciplinary instead of interventionist, and mimic radicality instead of teaching how to become politically undone'.[15] In another key publication of the 'anti/post-critique' turn, Sharon Marcus and Stephen Best question the effectiveness of literary criticism as radical political action. 'Where it had become common for literary scholars to equate their work with political activism', they note, 'the disasters and triumphs of the last decade have shown that literary criticism alone is not sufficient to effect change.[16]

'What does "the political" mean in those academic domains that take critical practice as the means and measure for pursuing justice?' Wiegman asks, and although I suspect our motivations for asking such a question come from different ideological positions, I nonetheless agree that it is a question worth dwelling on.[17] The belief that literary criticism is a form of political activism requires much hubris to sustain itself. Perhaps the problem lies in part with the terms 'activism' and 'activist'. These words have become meaningless with overuse, and their overuse diminishes the (often invisible and unacknowledged) work toward emancipatory justice that many are engaged in, whether people who live at the sharp end of multiple forms of systemic violence and injustice or those who work in solidarity, who may or may not call what they do or how they live 'activism'. The forms of academic or academic-adjacent work I admire as having made real contributions to transformative change have involved academics working in close collaboration with social movements (as distinct from taking social movements or 'subaltern' people as the subjects of their research). In the abortion rights and reproductive rights movement; the migrant justice and asylum activist movement; in campaigns to address racial stratification in hiring practices in the university and across labour markets; in campaigns for justice and reparations for women and children incarcerated in Ireland's institutional gulags; in the housing movement; in organising against casualisation and precarious work; in work that develops truly emancipatory pedagogies and seeks to make education accessible for all in real, material ways: in all of these movements and campaigns, some few academics have made truly significant contributions. This work is informed by, and actively part of, collective social movements and it is alien to the managerialist institutional belief that (to quote from a public address by a diversity manager in my own institution), 'change has to be top down; small committees of decision-makers can effect change more effectively.' Priorities matter because they define the purpose, process, and consequences of what we do: engagement with social justice as a theme or object of enquiry, as a commodity or brand, as a research funding opportunity or smart promotional move, prioritises the career of the academic and the status of the institution rather than demonstrating any real commitment to actual transformative change.

'The political' is perhaps difficult to escape if your existence is itself politicized. There is an expectation that the BAME writer or writer of migrant background will or should write on particular themes and experiences, or that the writer is happy to be categorised as a representative of a particular community. As a 'political' critic and as an activist I have made such assumptions about shared political agendas or positions and have read people's work within particular frames – the 'migrant' frame, the 'race' frame, the 'multicultural' frame – whether or not writers would welcome their work being placed within these frames (and many do not). As poet and academic Sandeep Parmar has written, 'BAME poets themselves must set the boundaries and the agenda, individually and collectively, for discussions about race and British poetry, and how this relation is impacted by individual experience and racial, religious, and regional identities', and needless to say this must also be the case in literature and literary criticism in Ireland where settled white writers, publishers, editors, and critics remain in position as gatekeepers.[18] Irish Studies has been slow to address the overwhelming whiteness of the field though this is coming under increasing pressure to change. At 'Are We Doing Diversity Justice? Challenging Whiteness in Irish Literary Spaces', an event held during IASIL 2019, some of these issues were addressed. It is important to note that this event was not part of IASIL's own programming but was an intervention co-organised by Chiamaka Enyi-Amadi and Emma Penney in response to the whiteness of the programme, and made possible by Enyi-Amadi's inspired curation, the collaboration of Skein Press, and the brilliant work and analyses of the writers and performers who took part. Speaking to the burden of being continually addressed in terms of race and ethnicity, Philomena Mullen, researcher, activist, and writer observed, to vocal recognition from all panellists, that 'I don't want to be busy being Black'; Enyi-Amadi, Nidhi Zak/Aria Eipe, Oein DeBhairduin, Christie Kandiwa, and Chinedum Muotto spoke about (among many other things) writing as a space for joy and a state of being that can afford freedom from the burdens of living as a black or minority ethnic person in a racist white nation.[19]

This insistence on writing as a space of freedom is not the same as (usually white) claims about the Republic of Letters as a solvent of the corrupting pressures of the political. It does not exonerate those in positions of power and privilege within a racial capitalist patriarchal system from responsibility to anti-racist action and critique or to the redistribution of the means of cultural production. In this vein, Chinedum Muotto challenged the majority audience assembled in the Royal Irish Academy – that fine white institution, as Muotto described it – to consider: What does it mean to be an ally? What does solidarity mean to you? One response articulated during the writers' discussion is that solidarity at the very least entails challenging an order of things of which most of us working in Irish academic institutions and in Irish Studies more widely are beneficiaries and that in doing so we may free up some space for people to do the creative and intellectual world-making that only they can do.

II

Two types of borders divide the global world. The first and most obvious type is the national border, which separates different nation-states. The second and less obvious type is a racialized class border, which separates two different experiences of mobility in the world of national borders.... On the one hand, we have a world where a 'third-world-looking' transnational working-class and underclass citizens live, and are made to feel that national borders are exceptionally important and difficult to cross.... On the other hand, we have a world experienced as open, in which people move smoothly across national borders, experiencing the world as almost borderless. This is the experience enjoyed by the largely White upper classes, who are made to feel truly at home in the world.

Ghassan Hage, *Is Racism An Environmental Threat?*[20]

One area we might expect to find 'identity knowledge' and critique at work in Irish Studies is in work on culture, literature, and contemporary migration. While much excellent work has been done in this field, engagement with critical race scholarship (as distinct from migration studies scholarship) has been lacking in the analysis of the writing and representation of 'multicultural' Ireland. In a 2016 special issue of *Irish Studies Review* edited by Pilar Villar-Argaiz and Jason King on 'multiculturalism in crisis' in Irish Studies, Ronit Lentin critiques the dominance of the vocabulary of interculturalism, multiculturalism, integration, and other policy buzzwords in the Irish Studies field. For Lentin, these words echo the rhetoric of the State and 'the cultural turn and the rhetoric of intercultural encounters that predominates in the discourses about immigration.'[21] This rhetoric disavows the necropolitics that buttress the migration regime in Fortress Europe (including, or course, the Irish state). Likewise, Alana Lentin has argued that in what she calls the 'MEM field' (Minority/Ethnic/Migration research), 'the voices of (racialised) migrants are in the main absent, the epistemic orientation of the scholarship reproduces hegemonic white frames by not engaging with critical race scholarship, and the work is set in an institutional context that emphasises normalising goals such as integration or even migration control.'[22] While both critiques speak from the field of sociology, their (political) observations are important for Irish literary and cultural studies. Consciously or unconsciously, the dominance of these terms and frameworks can have the effect of downplaying or sliding past what Nicholas de Genova pinpoints as 'the precisely racial specificity of what is so commonly and casually euphemized across Europe as "migrant" or "of migrant background".'[23]

Those terms – 'migrant', 'of migrant background' – are deeply politicized terms with specific referents and consequences in what Ghassan Hage describes as the global apartheid system of the racialised border regime. The category 'migrant writer' threatens a confinement that the writer may find difficult to escape, a segregated silo adjacent to the literary mainstream. Kasia Lech emphasises the importance of representation, agency, and not being confined within 'that migrant frame':

> It's about representing. It's about agency, first of all, of how migrants are represented: so both migrants having agency over their representation…. But it's also about allowing spaces for migrants to be represented beyond their migrant identity … without that migrant frame. It's about working towards that.[24]

The 'stickiness' of that migrant frame is racialised, and this racialisation carries over into the field of literary and artistic production. As Fatima El-Tayeb notes, regardless of how many generations particular communities have lived in Europe, 'communities of color continue to be perceived as "foreign matter," stand-ins for the masses beyond the continent's borders'.[25] In addition, as Carla de Tona and Elena Moreo point out, the deeply racialised nature of contemporary migration regimes 'as well as media, political and everyday discourses, tend to construct some migrants as *more migrants* than others (who may alternatively be called ex-pats, international professionals or not considered migrants at all) based on legal status, ethnicity, language, religion, occupational status and class'.[26]

Multiculturalism and interculturalism may be perceived as forms of integration from below but these frameworks are inseparable at this point from policy objectives and the governmental and carceral purposes of migration and diversity management. In her study of migration and contemporary Irish performance, Charlotte McIvor pointedly associates interculturalism as it has been adopted in many EU and Irish institutions with the nexus of migration, integration, and arts policy strategies. Interculturalism in the Irish context has primarily been a policy response to migration, putatively valorizing seemingly depoliticized gestures towards 'dialogue', 'understanding', 'exchange', 'participation', and so forth, between minority and majority communities. As McIvor outlines, the role of the arts has been central, at least rhetorically, to 'interculturalism as integration' strategy and diversity management.[27] The adoption of 'interculturalism' can do the ideological work of disavowing state racism by foregrounding culturalist approaches that celebrate 'diversity' and valorise an individualist charitable ethos that masks structural violence and works to delegitimise collective political action. For instance, the Department of Justice, which presides over an increasingly punitive migration and asylum regime in Ireland, and that keeps people segregated in the apartheid ghettoes of Direct Provision, is the same government department that controls the EU-funded Communities Integration Fund. This provides small pots of funding to 'organisations such as local community groups, sports clubs, faith-based groups, arts groups, schools, theatrical and cultural organisations wishing to carry out activities to promote the integration of migrant and host communities, foster mutual cultural respect and encourage migrant participation in civil and cultural life'.[28] This is perhaps the key instance of how 'interculturalism as integration' 'opens up cultural spaces of inclusion *as a substitute* to effective inclusion in mainstream political processes' as Ghassan Hage says of what he calls White Multiculturalism, with its dual faces of 'multicultural tolerance' and 'multicultural extermination'.[29] The limits of interculturalist approaches that lack a grounding in political realities come into sharp focus at critical moments. To take one example, happening as I write, in 2019 the Arts Council held a two-day conference, 'Places Matter: Building Inclusion in the Arts' at which it launched its new Equality, Human Rights, and Diversity Policy. The conference was part of the Council's aspiration 'that arts and culture should be accessible to everyone, irrespective of origin, place of residence, religious beliefs, economic or social background.'[30] One of the contributors to the conference was spoken word and hip-hop artist Theophilus Ndluvo who has been in Direct Provision in Galway since 2016. In the last week, Ndluvo has been issued with a deportation order by the Department of Justice. What obligations do arts, academic, and cultural organisations have for the people they recruit as legitimating participants in their diversity and inclusion projects? What is the point of events celebrating and deliberating over diversity and inclusion if there is no reciprocal solidarity with those we want to 'include'? As Mary Ann DeVlieg notes in 2019 in conversation with Evgeny Shtorn, one problem with institutional diversity talk is that it has little cognizance of the legal, economic, and socio-cultural obstacles that stand in the way of artists at risk. These obstacles are political, not accidental, and cannot be magically resolved through nicely worded policy documents. DeVlieg observes:

> for the last couple of years I have been seeing what I would call hypocrisy: a certain rhetoric in arts policies, especially around cultural diversity, which speaks about openness, about new voices, about support for everybody, but when we look at relocated artists, those who I am calling 'artists impacted by

displacement', there are multiple obstacles and legal restrictions such as the prohibition to work and earn money, for people seeking asylum.[31]

This hypocrisy extends to institutions seeking to 'include' and commodify artists seeking asylum while failing to learn about and confront the brutal political realities of the asylum and deportation machine that are ever-present contexts of such artists' lives.

All this said, there are creative projects that, even though led by majority culture artists, nonetheless work collaboratively with 'communities of interest' and explicitly centre these lived political realities. For instance, choreographer and dancer Catherine Young has worked intensively with people seeking asylum in Ireland in her productions over the last five years. These include *The Welcoming Project*, a collaboration between 'migrants, refugees, asylum seekers and local Irish', including professional dancers, people with no dance background, and well-known musicians, which has produced *Welcoming the Stranger*, *It Takes A Village*, and *Le Chéile*.[32] In 2018 CYD (Catherine Young Dance) premiered *State of Exception*, which is going on tour again in 2020. This production is inspired by Young's work with people who have sought asylum in Ireland and the resulting understanding of the necropolitics at work in the asylum and deportation system, captured in the work's title, taken from Giorgio Agamben's analysis of the biopolitics of the modern state: 'The camp is the space that is opened when the state of exception begins to become the rule'.[33] The grounding of creative production in lived, political realities and 'knowledge from below' arises from the collective's commitment to collaborative grassroots work – and to each other. This was manifest during CYD's contribution to an anti-deportation assembly organised by Donal O'Kelly in the Abbey during the 2018 production of *Jimmy's Hall*, a play based on the deportation from the state of Jimmy Gralton in 1933. One of the dancers who performed in an excerpt from *It Takes A Village* was Vicky Khokar, a man from Pakistan who had been served a deportation order and was due to leave Ireland that evening to return to the country he had fled in search of protection. As O'Kelly wrote, Khokar was persuaded to join the post-performance discussion:

He spoke with a calm resigned benevolence about Ireland, expressed the hope that he would see us again, and his last words were: 'I want you to promise me you will help these others so what is happening to me doesn't happen to them'. He looked around at the other dancers, many in tears. Indeed, most of the gathering was in tears, a mixture of sadness, futility, anger and commitment to resist.[34]

The disparity between representation of and on behalf of the presumed multicultural 'other' and the self-representation of the oppressed is a key aspect of the dynamics of White Multiculturalism and one point at which cultural and political representation intersect. The need to control or mediate the self-representation of the oppressed is at the core of the conflict between NGOs and radical self-organised movements. The account of the asylum-seeker led organisation ARASI by Ronit Lentin and Elena Moreo in *Integration From Below* is illustrative of this conflict of interests and of the long-standing charitable-colonial ethos in the migrant advocacy NGO sector, strongly associated at its beginnings in Ireland with religious and missionary orders. ARASI, established in the late 1990s by people in the asylum system, was subjected to what founder Kensika Moshengwo describes in interview with Lentin as a 'colonial takeover'. With support from the UNHCR who considered ARASI to be 'too aggressive' and 'too African', the organisation SPIRASI was established and UNHCR funding for ARASI was henceforth brokered via the Spiritans Fathers, leading eventually to a full displacement of ARASI by SPIRASI.[35] The colonial dynamic has persisted in the relationship between NGOs involved in asylum advocacy and the communities they represent. MASI organiser Bulelani Mfaco describes how MASI was born from a collective refusal on the part of people incarcerated in the Direct Provision system to stay in a space of dependency and powerlessness implanted by both the asylum regime and (largely white) NGO gatekeepers. Describing the residents' ten-day protest in autumn of 2014 in Kinsale Road Accommodation Centre in Cork, Mfaco notes that 'the mood changed from that of an obedient asylum seeker ... to a strong, courageous and defiant asylum seeker.' He continues:

> The women, men and children who made placards and blocked the entrance ... reclaimed a political space that had long been occupied by NGOs advocating for asylum seekers. It sent a message to them that asylum seekers can actually speak.... When they speak, it comes with a lot of pain and takes courage.[36]

The politics of representation and self-representation is intrinsic to what Didier Fassin calls humanitarian governance. At the heart of this governance is ambivalence: the 'tension between inequality and solidarity, between a relation of domination and a relation of assistance, is constitutive of all humanitarian government.'[37] The social relations between giver and receiver, between rescuer and victim, are underwritten by material, historical, and ontological conditions that constitute the fundamental inequality of those relations. These conditions, Fassin argues, 'make compassion a moral sentiment with no possible reciprocity.'[38] When compassion is exercised in the public space, it is therefore always directed from above to below, from the more powerful to the weaker, the more fragile, the more vulnerable. Any kind of reciprocity involved in humanitarian reason is not reciprocity at all but a further articulation of the profound inequalities that structure the exchange: reciprocity 'in the form of an obligation linking the receiver to the benefactor – for example, the obligation on the receivers sometimes to tell their story, frequently to mend their ways, and always to show their gratitude'.[39] There is a further political problem here. In terms of the politics of the asylum regime, foregrounding the traumatic story or the speaking wounds that validate the claims of the asylum seeker to compassion works through 'humanising' the person to those with more power. However, as Fassin notes, 'the very gesture that appears to grant them recognition reduces them to what they are not – and often refuse to be – by reifying their condition of victimhood while ignoring their history and muting their words'.[40] The full existence and complexity of the living person is buried, subject to erasure and non-recognition.

Resistance against this erasure and non-recognition is central to the political voice that organisations such as MASI have fought to create for some of the most oppressed people living in the Irish state. The creative spaces of art, literature, dance (as we have seen), and performance can also be spaces of political articulation, resistance, and forms of emancipation. For instance, the dynamic that Fassin articulates in theory is articulated with deeply effective poetic clarity by Insaf Yalçınkaya in her poem 'A Worthless Life', where the poet captures the dehumanizing logic of the asylum process, and the life-and-death- interview with the International Protection Office that determines whether her claim will be accepted or rejected:

> Around a table
> We strike a bargain for my life
> They think
> I'm just a number
> my life is worthless
>
> I put my knowledge up for sale
> my art, my poems, my music
> They are not interested in them
> They are worthless
>
> I put my happiness up for sale
> They don't want happy people
> Happiness is worthless

I put my hopes up for sale
My future, my dreams
Their border is priceless
My hopes are worthless

I put my sorrows up for sale
my tears, my deep griefs
They want to buy them
to pretend they are merciful
They should take pity on me
Their mercy is priceless
But my humanity is worthless[41]

Caoimhe Butterly, a migrant justice and peace activist based in Dublin, has turned to documentary as a means to co-create spaces of self-agency, self-narration, and self-authorship with people subject to the brutalities of border regimes. Butterly questions the ethics of the representation of the suffering of others, particularly given the extremities of vulnerability, violation, humiliation, erosion of personhood, and social and actual death that are inflicted on people on the move and seeking refuge in Europe. Butterly's reflections on accountability in the representation of people seeking a place to live in safety extends to other forms of representation whether in campaigning or in literature, commentary, performance, and art:

> Nuanced exceptions to documentation that isolates, and often over-exposes, vulnerability have also been present over the past years – work that is complex, empathetic, and that often provides platforms for advocacy and action. However, there is work, even when motivated by deep solidarity, that can still lack deeper insight into the struggle of those seeking refuge to make meaning of their experiences, experiences which can be overwhelming by their sheer injustice and lived humiliations. It is this existential process, of meaning-making, of the 'speculative space' of identity within borderlands, of 'belonging, (self) representation and (dis) identification' which can perhaps only truly be accountably represented by those who have lived to self-narrate the journey and whose self-authorship, and by extension self-agency, are so very powerful.[42]

Among examples of such work, Butterly cites work by two artists living on the island of Ireland – Vukašin Nedeljković's *Asylum Archive*, an online and multimedia documentation of and resistance against the

Direct Provision and deportation system, and Nandi Jola's poem 'Ink' – as demonstrating the 'gravitas' of self-authored representation in articulating the experiences of living in the state of exception.[43] Asylum Archive's refusal to use individuals' stories or images is a refusal of the neo-colonial dynamics that inform the asymmetrical relations that allow advocates, artists, journalists, academics, and others to reduce the person seeking asylum to passive object of charity and commodified image. In Jola's poem 'Ink', the gap between what is said and unsaid marks the corrosive indefinite waiting of asylum limbo and the constant threat of forced removal. The closing line, 'I am here', nonetheless finally attests to survival and endurance:

> The letter came too today.
> Ten years late, but it arrived
> Telling me that I now am a Citizen.
> I will breathe the same air
> Walk the same streets of Belfast without fear
> Roam Ireland like a bird.
>
> I am no longer a case number, a statistic
> My anger will disappear,
> Fear will be the thing of the past.
> I must be grateful
> The letter came today, ten years late,
> I'm not on the next charter plane, from
> detention to deportation.
> I am here.[44]

In 'The Unknown', Owdunni Ola Mustapha articulates the same corrosive effects of waiting without knowing when or how the waiting will end, as six months becomes five years.

> I set my reminder to six months
> With the hope that I'll be living
> in a 3-bedroom house.
> ...
> Six months roll by quickly.
> It's the 60th month and I
> await the unknown,
> The unknown decision from the IPAT.
> I'm unsure if this will be
> the end to the wait, but
> I'm anxiously awaiting the unknown.[45]

Finding or re-finding a literary or artistic agency is perhaps inherently political when asserted against the weight of such unbearable oppression, erasure, and fear. Self-representation is crucial in art and literature as it is in political action for people who are routinely denied that agency in multiple ways.

III

It is undeniably human, this want: to seek shelter, to take refuge, to belong. There are so many storms, after all, and all I can give you are words. But words allow me to stand in the doorway, hold out a hand, invite you into a rush of intimacy. *Listen*, they let me say, *trust me*: language is body, language is mother, language is love. We can lay down in secret with it, sound its soft syllables out in our mouths. We can make ourselves known through it, announce ourselves present. We can come in from the rain, sing clear into the night. *Listen; call it home* – and we can find our way back, together, through this dark.

Nidhi Zak/Aria Eipe, 'l'amour/la mort: a stunted symphony'[46]

The field of Irish Studies was constituted in the late 1970s at the intersections of the conflict in the North, the felt need to reclaim the high modernist triumvirate of Yeats-Joyce-Beckett for Irish literature, and the desire to foment a specifically Irish postcolonial critique. Thinking again about that remark from the floor at IASIL last summer, lamenting the lack of political energies and conflicts in Irish Studies *now* compared to *then*, perhaps the real issue is – why is the mainstream of Irish Studies so disconnected from, or oblivious to, where these political energies, conflicts, arguments, and communities of solidarity are now gathering, now being fought, now coalescing? Several decades after its inauguration, does Irish Studies itself now need to be decolonized? Unfortunately as it is currently constituted, in its whiteness, its conservatism, and its elitist and hierarchical attachments, it is quite possible that the field of Irish Studies does not appear particularly hospitable or relevant to present and future BAME critics, thinkers, researchers, and writers, most particularly people living and working in Ireland.

Irish Studies, Irish literature, and Irish academia are implicated in the same the systemic, institutional whiteness. In relation to the mainstream literary culture in Ireland, the statistics are stark. Research on race and ethnicity in UK and Irish poetry publishing has found that between 2012 and 2018, none of the Irish magazines included in the study 'came close to meeting the country's 4.9% figure for BAME people: *The Stinging Fly* (1.6%), *Poetry Ireland Review* (2.3%), and *Southword* (2.6%)', thus falling far short of 'even the most basic measures of inclusivity'.[47] The situation in poetry criticism in Ireland is outlined in the recent MEAS report 'Poetry reviews in the *Irish Times* 2013–2018', where Kenneth Keating and Ailbhe McDaid found that only four of 187 books reviewed were by BAME poets and all reviews, including those by twenty-two guest reviewers, were by white critics. In terms of non-Irish authors reviewed, this amounted to just three out of thirty-five poets over six years – six years that saw work by Claudia Rankine, Danez Smith, Ocean Vuong, Vahni Capildeo, Sarah Howe, Roger Robinson, Warsan Shire, among many others receiving major poetry awards and international acclaim.[48] Sandeep Parmar who, with Susan Howe, established the Ledbury Emerging Poetry Critics initiative in the UK in 2017, notes that 'critical whiteness' diminishes the work of BAME poets even where it does receive critical attention. She observes:

> The lens of what can only be described as critical whiteness fixes on the poet of color as an anomaly and seizes on their writing as a direct expression of their racial otherness.... [I]n the long-term, a real and meaningful shift in cultural value must come with critics whose first loyalty is to the work at hand, to reading it knowledgeably and with an awareness of the structural power within which works of literature are produced and received. It is my strong sense that critics of color bring with them a complex awareness of this structural power that is so desperately needed.[49]

The extent of the deep structural and institutional transformations required in relation to knowledge production and cultural production in and about Ireland are substantial. The work of initiatives like the student-led UCD Decolonizing the Curriculum Platform, the work in many different spaces of writers and thinkers including the artists involved in the 'Are We Doing Diversity Justice?' intervention, the work of writers and editors involved in Skein Press and other publishing initiatives (including Chiamaka Enyi-Amadi's co-editing of the recently published Dedalus Press anthology *Writing Home*) indicate where some transformations are happening in Ireland, but whether Irish Studies is the place where such work can be most productively realised is a moot question.[50]

When I was invited to write this piece, Emilie Pine suggested I address some connections between activism, academia, migration, and writing. On a personal and political level, the connection for me is quite clear. I have been transformed by the people I have met and worked alongside in the migrant justice movement in Ireland. In particular, working with MASI, an autonomous grassroots movement organised by people with lived experience of the asylum, direct provision, and deportation regime, unfunded by political choice, has radically transformed my priorities and understanding of the structures and institutions I inhabit, how I construe knowledge and knowledge production, and how I conceive of the obligations and purpose of what my priorities should be as an educator and person with immense privilege. One thing I have learned is that if we are truly committed to real emancipatory transformation, we must take our lead from the people who we would too often speak for, especially as academics used to having the floor. As academics, we are not inclined to sideline our status as experts, to listen rather than speak, to hold space for others without prioritizing our own benefit. Sara Ahmed's observations on resistance and the necessity of listening to challenges we may not want to hear and examining attachments that many no longer serve are worth reflecting on:

> Sometimes we have an idea of place because of our own histories: a place seems inclusive, radical, open, because that place was open to us, because that's how it seemed to us. But that is not how everyone experiences that place... [T]he resistance we might have to hearing the stories, our resistance, mine too, might be because of how they challenge our most profound attachments. To hold onto an idea of a place as good might even require not listening to those who have a different idea. But I think: to make our attachments – to education, to a college, to a project, to equality, to feminism – meaningful we have to listen to those who seem to get in the way. It is the only way.[51]

NOTES

1. Robin D.G. Kelley, 'Solidarity is not a market exchange: An interview with Robin D.G. Kelley', *Black Ink*, 16 January 2020. Available at: https://black-ink.info/2020/01/16/solidarity-is-not-a-market-exchange-an-interview-with-robin-d-g-kelley/?fbclid=IwAR1u4Ov8_y76sO2ffMgUeheC62oeyVbkDY2_Jgg1ASYzPhVfHxcz9rwFPoc

2. Plenary Panel – '50 Years of The Critical Ground', IASIL 2019, 'The Critical Ground', Trinity College Dublin, July 2019.

3. John Banville and Fintan O'Toole in conversation, 'The Danger and the Glory: Irish Writers on the Art of Writing', IASIL 2019, 'The Critical Ground', Trinity College Dublin, July 2019.

4. Frank O'Connor Reading and Roundtable, IASIL 2016, 'Change', UCC, 25 July 2016.

5. Julie Morrissy, 'Questionnaire', *Poetry Ireland Review*, Special Issue 'The Rising Generation', ed. by Vona Groarke 118 (2016), p.111.

6. Stephen Sexton, 'Questionnaire', *Poetry Ireland Review* 118 (2016), p.156.

7. Emma Must, 'Questionnaire', *Poetry Ireland Review* 118 (2016), pp.116–117.

8. 'Questionnaire', *Poetry Ireland Review* 118 (2016), pp.101, 41, 165, 126 and 151.

9. Ciaran Carty, 'Vona Groarke: "If you want to change things, stand for election. Poems aren't part of that."' *The Irish Times*. 28 March 2017. Available at: https://www.irishtimes.com/culture/books/vona-groarke-if-you-want-to-change-things-stand-for-election-poems-aren-t-part-of-that-1.3017368

10. For an incisive recent analysis of whiteness and literary institutions, see Claudia Rankine and Beth Loffreda, 'Introduction: On Whiteness and the Racial Imaginary', in

The Racial Imaginary, ed. by Claudia Rankine and Beth Loffreda (New York: Fence Books, 2015), pp.13–22.

11. See, for instance, the Arts Council's Equality, Human Rights and Diversity Policy (2019) and Poetry Ireland's 'Inclusion and Diversity Strategy (2018). Available at: http://www.artscouncil.ie/Publications/All/Equality,-Human-Rights-and-Diversity-Policy-2019/ and www.poetryireland.ie/content/files/PoetryIreland_InclusionDiversity2018-20.pdf. Create's Summer School on Cultural Diversity and Collaborative Practice which has run for two years now is noteworthy. For more details, see: https://www.create-ireland.ie/activity/aic-scheme-summer-school-on-cultural-diversity-and-collaborative-practice/

12. Juliana Huxtable and Che Gossett, 'Existing in the world: blackness at the edge of trans visibility', in Trap Door: Trans Cultural Production and the Politics of Visibility, ed. by Reina Gossett, Eric A. Stanley, and Johanna Burton (Boston and London: The MIT Press, 2017), 39–55 (p.45).

13. Rita Felski, The Limits of Critique (Chicago: University of Chicago Press, 2015).

14. Rónán McDonald, 'Critique and anti-critique', Textual Practice 32.3 (2019), 365–74.

15. Robyn Wiegman, Object Lessons (Durham: Duke University Press, 2012), p.10, p.12.

16. Sharon Marcus and Stephen Best, 'Surface Reading: An Introduction', Representations Special Issue: 'The Way We Read Now', 108.1 (Fall 2009), 1–21 (p.2).

17. Wiegman, Object Lessons, p.5.

18. Sandeep Parmar, 'Not A British Subject: Race and Poetry in the UK', Los Angeles Review of Books, 5 December 2015. Available at: https://lareviewofbooks.org/article/not-a-british-subject-race-and-poetry-in-the-uk/

19. 'Are We Doing Diversity Justice? Challenging Whiteness in Irish Literary Spaces', IASIL 2019, 'The Critical Ground', Trinity College Dublin, July 2019. Co-hosted by UCD Centre for Gender, Feminism & Sexuality (CGFS).

20. Ghassan Hage, Is Racism An Environmental Threat? (Cambridge: Polity Press, 2017), Kindle edn, loc. 605.

21. Ronit Lentin, 'Asylum seekers, Ireland, and the return of the repressed', Irish Studies Review Special Issue: 'Multiculturalism In Crisis' 24.1 (2016), 21–34 (p.29).

22. Alana Lentin, 'Postracial Silences: The Othering of Race in Europe', in Racism and Sociology, ed. by Wulf D. Hund and Alana Lentin (Berlin et al.: Lit Verlag, 2014), 69–106 (p.80).

23. Nicholas de Genova, 'The Migrant Crisis as Racial Crisis: Do Black Lives Matter in Europe?', Ethnic and Racial Studies Special Issue: 'Race and Crisis', 41.10 (2018), 1765–1782 (p.1768).

24. Kasia Lech, quoted in Language and Migration in Ireland (Dublin: Immigrant Council of Ireland, 2017), p.51.

25. Fatima El-Tayeb, '"The Birth of a European Public": Migration, Postnationality, and Race in the Uniting of Europe.' American Quarterly 60.3 (September 2008), 649–670 (p.652).

26. Carla de Tona and Elena Moreo, 'Theorizing Migrant Led Activism', in Migrant Activism and Integration From Below in Ireland, ed. by Ronit Lentin and Elena Moreo (Basingstoke: Palgrave Macmillan, 2012), pp.21–41 (p.30).

27. See Charlotte McIvor, Migration and Performance in Contemporary Ireland: Towards a New Interculturalism (Basingstoke: Palgrave Macmillan, 2016), pp.1–19.

28. 'Communities Integration Fund 2019', Office for the Promotion of Migrant Integration, Department of Justice and Equality http://www.integration.ie/en/ISEC/Pages/WP19000006,

29. Ghassan Hage, White Nation, p.112.

30. Arts Council, 'Places Matter: Building Inclusion in the Arts' (Dublin: The Arts Council, 2019). Available at: 'Places Matter Conference 2019', http://www.artscouncil.ie/Arts-in-Ireland/Local-Arts/Places-Matter-Conference-2019/

31. Mary Ann DeVlieg, 'Helping Artists At Risk: Mary Ann DeVlieg in conversation with Evgeny Shtorn'. *Cassandra's Voices*. 5 December 2019. Available at: https://cassandravoices.com/articles/helping-artists-at-risk-evgeny-shtorn-in-conversation-with-mary-ann-devlieg/?fbclid=IwAR3zWVJOS4Fh7WS9qvvf6sYFonmDcZhcg3LUGJ_xIlLkIOaiHL73PFsz9zk

32. See: http://www.catherineyoungdance.com/index.php/the-work/thewelcoming-project

33. Giorgio Agamben, *Homo Sacer: Sovereign Power and Bare Life*, trans. by D. Heller-Roazen. (Stanford: Stanford University Press, 1998), p.168.

34. Donal O'Kelly, 'Jimmy's Hall Today: A Theatrical Response to Direct Provision'. *RTÉ.ie* 3 September 2018. https://www.rte.ie/culture/2018/0904/991317-jimmys-hall-today-a-theatrical-response-to-direct-provision/

35. Ronit Lentin, 'There Is No Movement: A brief history of migrant-led activism in Ireland', in *Migrant Activism and Integration From Below*, pp.41–70 (p.55).

36. Bulelani Mfaco, 'Introduction', *Correspondences: an anthology to call for the end of direct provision*, ed. by Jessica Traynor and Stephen Rea (Dublin: Sprint, 2019), p.xi.

37. Didier Fassin, *Humanitarian Reason: A Moral History of the Present* (Berkeley: University of California Press, 2012), p.3.

38. Fassin, *Humanitarian Reason*, p.3.

39. Fassin, *Humanitarian Reason*, p.3.

40. Fassin, *Humanitarian Reason*, p.254.

41. Insaf Yalçınkaya, 'A Worthless Life?', *MASI Journal 1*, ed. by Irma Bochorishvili, Lucky Khambule, and Anne Mulhall (Dublin: MASI, 2019), 102 (p.102). See also *Correspondences*, p.53.

42. Caoimhe Butterly, 'Journeys', *Studies in Arts and Humanities* 4.2 (2018), 179–183 (p.180).

43. See Vukašin Nedeljković's Asylum Archive online: http://www.asylumarchive.com/. See also the print version of the Asylum Archive: Vukašin Nedeljković, *Asylum Archive* (Dublin: Create/Arts Council of Ireland, 2018).

44. Nandi Jola, 'Ink', *Baobab Vol 4: Solidarity*, (Dublin: Anti-Racism Network, 2018), 26 (p.26).

45. Owodunni Ola Mustapha, 'The Unknown', *MASI Journal*, 114 (p.114).

46. Nidhi Zak/Aria Eipe, 'l'amour/la mort: a stunted symphony', *MASI Journal*, 122–123 (p.123).

47. [Dave Coates], 'The State of Poetry and Poetry Criticism in the UK and Ireland Jan 2012–Mar 2018'. Available at: https://www.liverpool.ac.uk/new-and-international-writing/emerging-critics/poetry-report/

48. Ken Keating and Ailbhe McDaid, *Poetry Reviews in the Irish Times 2013–2018* (MEAS 2020), pp.8, 9–10, 10. Available at: https://measorg.com/interim-reports/irish-times-poetry-reviews/gender-race-and-publishers-in-irish-times-poetry-reviews-2013-2018-3/

49. Sandeep Parmar, 'A Q&A with Sandeep Parmar: Supporting Emerging Poets of Color'. *Poets.org* January 24 2019. Available at: https://poets.org/text/qa-sandeep-parmar-supporting-emerging-critics-color

50. For more details, see the Skein Press website at: https://skeinpress.com/about/ and see *Writing Home: The 'New Irish' Poets*, ed. by Chiamaka Enyi-Amadi and Pat Boran (Dublin: Dedalus Press, 2019).

51. Sara Ahmed, 'Equality Credentials', *Feminist Killjoys* 10 June 2016. Available at: http://feministkilljoys.com/2016/06/10/equality-credentials/

Chiamaka Enyi-Amadi and Emma Penney

Are We Doing Diversity Justice?
A Critical Exchange

This critical exchange is based on a conversation between the authors which took place during the *Irish University Review* Roundtable Discussion: Displacing the Canon (2019 IASIL Conference, Trinity College Dublin). As authors we give first-hand accounts of our experience writing, editing, and teaching in Ireland, attempting to draw out concerns we have for the future of Irish literature and Irish Studies that specifically relate to race. In our practice we both aim to explore the theoretical and political implications of white heteropatriarchy, racial capitalism, and coloniality in Ireland. We appreciate the opportunity to trace some of the implications of this politics on literary value systems and on how black and minority ethnic writers and editors are treated by the literary establishment in Ireland. We hope that the inclusion of our conversation in the 50th anniversary issue of the *Irish University Review* will disrupt social relations of domination in Ireland which play out along colour lines. The conversation here suggests that race directly impacts what we consider valuable in our literary culture. We both require decentring universalism as a governing literary critical concept and insist on the urgent application of critical race analysis to the construction of literary value systems in Ireland.

EP: Have you experienced alienation in the literary canon?

CEA: Yes, I experienced it during secondary school in Ireland. I encountered poets from a western canon who inspired me to write but I had to go beyond the curriculum to find writers from the African canon. I found a body of literature, namely through the African Writers Series, which held sentiments similar to mine, experiences similar to mine, and I was excited but also unsure of why this literature wasn't being discussed or valued for the insights it brings.

Irish University Review 50.1 (2020): 112–119
DOI: 10.3366/iur.2020.0438
© Edinburgh University Press
www.euppublishing.com/iur

EP: How did that neglect make you feel?

CEA: Not only was I going through the transition of settling into a new country but also the transition of becoming a young adult. You are already so emotionally charged. You already encounter so much resistance in daily life between what society wants you to be and the way you want to be. And to go in to literature, a place I thought of as a solace, and discover the way blackness is written, or often is absent completely. ...It exacerbated the alienation I was feeling – made me believe my story didn't matter.

Thankfully, early on in my childhood my dad introduced me to two books that helped me understand what it meant to be a black person in western society: *Invisible Man* by Ralph Ellison and *Black Boy* by Richard Wright. So, I can talk about it now, though it still isn't easy to write my own experience down.

EP: Why is talking about this easier than writing it?

CEA: I think talking is fundamental to the work that goes into decolonising society. The decolonial practice is easier for me when I am in a relational situation with another person rather than alienated in front of the page. Written word is more colonial than spoken word in this way. It's not just a blank page, it's the entire historical narrative of 'fuck you you're a savage, you are irrational, you can't create knowledge'. I have very little to turn to when going to the archives of people like me who have done similar work and I feel that dearth when I go to write, particularly when it is a personal story I am telling – the processes themselves can speak words of alienation.

For instance, I recently co-edited *Writing Home: The 'New Irish' Poets*.[1] I was given two weeks to write an introduction. So there is no editor's introduction from me, no words on the page.

EP: Do you feel discomfort in front of the blank page?

CEA: There is a general discomfort for writers around the blank page but it becomes more chronic when one is confronted with an entire literary culture in Ireland that invalidates the written experience of black and ethnic minorities. As if to say, ethnic minorities and black narratives are only valid or interesting when they take the form of folklore. I suppose because it is entertaining when it's wrapped around the idea of spectacle. Where nothing has to change. The event of speaking is enough to appeal to the individual in a moment, but it stops there at that moment of representation – it doesn't go further into restructuring the wider socio-economic and cultural infrastructure.

There is a difference in Ireland between how the spoken and written words of black and ethnic writers are received. There is this question of: 'is the writing good or is it just black? They'll invite me to come speak at events, about my experience as a black woman and a migrant in Ireland, but nothing is said about my writing. If you look at all the media coverage around *Writing Home*, I am asked about what it's like being black and a migrant in Ireland, but not about my writing or my editorial process.

So yes, you are giving black and ethnic minorities a space, but are you really? Is my knowledge truly valued? Coverage of the anthology highlights white European writers – reviewers are not picking out work by writers of colour. It is still a very western lens so I am left feeling like, what was the point of this book? Is it just about western migration?

EP: Is there a 'right' kind of migrant?

CEA: Massively so. I mean from a literary context some written accounts are less threatening. My co-editor shaped the narrative of the book to circulate around the themes of emigration and immigration. If you look at white immigration it is much more similar to Irish emigration. So this is what has been picked up in coverage of the book. I think people are more comfortable exploring sameness rather than difference.

EP: Where does that discomfort come from?

CEA: It is coming from a little bit of shame and defensiveness. When you send in poems that challenge the social status quo as an immigrant of colour, you're not stroking the national ego, you're not being 'grateful'. You might actually bring a discussion of whiteness into an understanding of Irish identity, power, and cultural representation.

EP: How does black and ethnic minority writing challenge the status quo?

CEA: The writing can challenge what Ireland claims to be which is welcoming and that there is no racial discrimination. I wanted the anthology to be a space where I could address everything that I was struggling with when it comes to facing the blank page, which is facing the power of whiteness in Ireland, as well as the denial of that power. I want to emphasise this… because what we have in the anthology is different from what motivated me to do it in the first place.

EP: You have talked about the idea of wanting to create a safe space, did the anthology achieve that?

CEA: Yes, but I faced a lot of challenges in attaining that. I spoke to Anne Mulhall, an activist with MASI and a UCD lecturer. I wanted someone to tell me if my vision for the book was worthwhile, not crazy or controversial – I was struggling with the idea of positive discrimination. She told me not only was it a valuable approach but it was fucking necessary. As a body of work, it is a safe space. I really believe that.

EP: Do you think there was pressure for poems to be about the popular experience of migration?

CEA: There was conflict around the subtlety and complexity of the migrant experience that I had to negotiate with my co-editor. Poems were supported where there were explicit representations of being a migrant, an outsider, the experience of culture shock, and they were good poems – articulated clearly. Where difficulty arose was when there were more subtle waves of discomfort, alienation, or isolation – under the surface of a poem.

EP: Were those subtle poems less likely to be chosen?

CEA: They caused the most disagreement. I heard the words 'that's not relevant' a few times. If a poem didn't have the word migrant or the words 'céad míle fáilte' it wasn't deemed relevant enough. Whereas I believe that the experience of being other and being othered can be felt in any kind of a poem. If that poem is successful, if the language is utilised well, it conveys the tension and resistance between one human being and another.

I can talk to you about my own poems; in particular, 'How'.[2] I had to defend its relevance. The poem illustrates a moment of intimacy between the speaker and a lover, but weaving beneath the intense vulnerability, warmth, and familiarity that is shared between the two figures is a profound sensation of isolation and alienation, because that is something that is carried everywhere you go, like trauma. You carry it around with you and it creates tension in the psycho-social relations you have with the outside world. The body remembers that it's alone, that it carries pain as well as pleasure and that pain needs to be spoken, it needs a stage, a spotlight, a safe place to stay: 'I give in, allow my body take centre stage / announce my pain out loud, / and you reach for me again, the harmony / of skin on skin ... my body in distress.'[3]

EP: So, in this poem there is a more subtle expression of connection or disconnection?

CEA: The poem's speaker is engaged with a loved one who is making significant efforts to make her feel wanted and loved. The speaker has an experience of a menstrual period which appears suddenly and unexpectedly. This is how alienation is experienced. It is insidious, sudden, confronting, undeniably marking you. It is not a direct commentary on migration but a meditation on how alienation can intrude on intimacy. But also ... maybe ... how connection can be a mode of healing.

EP: Do you think there was a willingness to make the migrant experience a theme but not the everyday racism that black and ethnic minority people experience in Ireland?

CEA: There was this distinction in the editing process between the event of migration and everyday racism. Focusing on the event of migration itself meant that the core focus of the book was on tracing and even celebrating cultural connections between white Irish migration and all other migration. However, this left very little space to explore the experience of institutional racism in the Irish state and everyday interactions with Irish people where racial stereotypes persist. Everyday feelings and sensations of being a minority are political and, in order to actually give space to this experience, it is necessary not to erase difference in pursuit of connection.

EP: Do you think focusing on the 'event' of migration and racism was politically safe?

CEA: It is definitely socially safe. A deliberate attempt to make it 'relevant' and easy to digest. You can explain it on the RTÉ Poetry Programme, on RTÉ Arena, and in the *Irish Times*. You can't have every black person talking about racism in such an abstract way – racism has to be digestible for white Irish people. White Irish people are more comfortable hearing about overt acts of racism because it is easier to deny responsibility for racial violence and discrimination when the event has an obvious perpetrator and victim. But more subtle forms of racism are part of how whiteness sustains itself as a dominant cultural logic within the literary canon in Ireland.

EP: In Pat Boran's introduction to the anthology he talks about possibly having ancestral ties to the Boran people of Kenya. This 'African Connection', as he calls, it provides him with a sense of connectedness to others and gives us the reassuring notion that we are all from somewhere. How useful is this kind of universalism?

CEA: When you're trying to do an anthology of new Irish poets this is not useful. When you start to try and make connections between experiences that have yet to be given the space to demonstrate their distinctiveness it can cause cultural collapse, erosion, and silence. Some attempts to connect are alienating and culturally destructive. We can lose a linguistically rich and diverse experience, and in doing so we sacrifice knowledge for power.

We know that 'New Irish' refers to ethnically diverse communities. Having it in inverted commas was prescriptive to me as an editor to help guide me in delineating the kinds of poems I was looking for – which had to encompass the conflicting energy and tensions that an amalgamation of identities brings onto the page. But now that the anthology has launched, I don't think the inverted commas around 'New Irish' fit. I never intended those inverted commas to appear in the title, they were an editorial tool. Dropping the inverted commas gives the work more authority: rather than *The 'New Irish' Poets* it would have been *The New Irish Poets*.

EP: What is preventing critics from seeing black and ethnic minority writers as representative and part of Irish literary culture?

CEA: There is an Igbo proverb – which I believe aptly illustrates that issue of creative authority – that tells of how 'Only an old woman is offended when dry bones are mentioned'. The adage highlights that it is those who are aware of their receding creative vitality that are worried about obsoleteness, fearing they will be replaced soon and keen to avoid being reminded of the fact - the people who are enforcing the status quo and deriving power. This brings our discussion from my editorial practice to your teaching practice, especially where you have tried to teach about the specificity of Irish racism.

CEA: You teach Irish Cultural Studies at UCD, do you think there is a resistance to the idea of a racist Irish state within the literary, historical, and cultural canon?

EP: Yes, in my first year as a tutor in UCD I taught the canonical film Robert Flaherty's *Man of Aran*. I knew, vaguely, that it was about a pure and untouched Irish identity and that it was associated with Fianna Fáil (Eamon de Valera's cabinet attended the Dublin premiere in 1934). The enthusiastic reception accorded the film in Ireland was summed up by nationalist historian and close supporter of de Valera, Dorothy Macardle, who saw in its portrayal of the heroic struggle of the Aran Islanders 'nothing less than the rehabilitation of the Irish people in the eyes of the world'.[4] The film spent a year showing in Irish cinemas and, on the Irish Film Institute website, it is still listed amongst the most important cinematic depictions of western Ireland.[5] More recently, Fintan O'Toole argued that Flaherty's ethnographic documentary could be read 'as a party political broadcast on behalf of de Valera's Fianna Fail'.[6]

To prepare for the class, I did a bit of research and discovered that *Man of Aran* had won top prize at the Mussolini Cup in 1934 (a major Fascist film award in Europe). I was eager to explore the relationship between the film's ideological significance in the Free State and its success in fascist Europe. In exploring the film further I came across Brian Winston's recent reflection on how the film's "vision of a pure and noble civilisation surely impressed [in fascist Europe]".[7] Based on this, he describes its success in Ireland as "worrying".[8] I was inclined to agree, and I decided to bring this concern to the class.

CEA: What was your immediate reaction upon discovering this relationship between an Irish cultural text and European fascism?

EP: I wondered why we were still watching and teaching this film – but then I reflected on how the alignment of Irishness with whiteness needs to be taught so that students can use their critical tools to look at past and present racism. The heroic masculinity portrayed in *Man of Aran* acted as a rehabilitation of the image of a weakened colonised Irishman. The film won the Mussolini Cup because those characteristics which it promoted as 'distinctly Irish' were also racialised as white and accruing power globally as fascism was on the rise. I asked students to look at the film in relation to Susan Sontag's understanding of fascist aesthetics and to identify in it 'the cult of beauty'; 'the fetishism of courage', 'the dissolution of alienation in ecstatic feelings of community', 'repudiation of the intellect', 'the family of man' (under the parenthood of leaders).[9] The point in looking at aesthetics and the power of aesthetics is that we need to identify whiteness even when it isn't explicitly stated – by looking at the values, concepts, and images through which whiteness has accrued power (which is always a power over others).

CEA: Has this experience had any further influence on your teaching practice?

EP: Our conversations in class moved toward an examination of the 'west' in the Irish cultural and political imagination. Fintan O'Toole describes the myth of the west as conferring 'Ireland's mythic unity before the chaos of conquest ... where Ireland can be encountered in its purest, most primeval state'.[10] Read this way, the 'west' is revealed as a racializing force through the twentieth century. In class we explored how this representation was not disconnected from contemporary forms of governmentality that used force to keep people of colour out of sight in Ireland (like Direct Provision or the 27th Amendment for example). We have been making a prize of whiteness in our political and cultural imaginary for well over a century. The fact that Ireland has the second-lowest rate of granting asylum in Europe is a reflection of a violently asserted white culture in Ireland.

Eventually the class found that for much of the twentieth century there was an attempt to draw some kind of baseline of pure authentic Irishness – what Ebun Joseph has referred to as 'cashing in' on the 'currency of Irish whiteness', which, I believe, was central to the aesthetic power of the 'Gael'.[11]

CEA: Do you think there is a reluctance to bring critical race theory to bear on Irish Studies?

EP: I think it is typical of an Irish exceptionalism that some people find it hard to understand the racial power of Irish culture and politics. It's harder because we have not always been able to derive power from the phenotypic whiteness of most Irish people – because of how we were historically racialized by the British. Racialisation was a powerful cultural programme executed by the British but, following independence, Ireland was able to cash in on the currency of whiteness so effectively because we knew how to orchestrate a powerfully racialising aesthetic – we had witnessed it and had been the subjects of it.[12] I realised that in teaching students to think about whiteness, I was asking them to consider how the idealisation of the west and racism still overlap today. As a result, they started to become more reflexive in regards to their curriculum and how it was taught. I think this is key for the future of Irish Studies.

NOTES

1. *Writing Home: The 'New Irish' Poets*, ed. by Chiamaka Enyi-Amadi and Pat Boran (Dublin: Dedalus Press, 2019).
2. Chiamaka Enyi-Amadi, 'How', in *Writing Home*, p.29.

3. Enyi-Amadi, p.29.
4. Martin McLoone, 'Man of Aran' in *The Cinema of Britain and Ireland*, ed. by Brian McFarlane (New York: Wallflower Press, 2005), p.45.
5. Kevin Coyne, 'Man of Aran', entry on the *Irish Film Institute* website. Available at:. *https://ifi.ie/film/man-of-aran-4/*, accessed 4 December 2019.
6. Fintan O'Toole, 'An Island Lightly Moored', *The Irish Times*, 29 March 1997, p.18.
7. O'Toole, 'An Island Lightly Moored'.
8. Martin McLoone, *Irish Film: The Emergence of a Contemporary Cinema* (London: British Film Institute Press, 2000), p.43.
9. Susan Sontag, 'Fascinating Fascism', in *Under the Sign of Saturn* (New York: Picador, 1980), pp.73–105.
10. O'Toole, 'An Island Lightly Moored'.
11. Joseph, Ebun. 'Whiteness and Racism: Exploring the Racial Order in Ireland', *Irish Journal of Sociology* 26.1 (2017), 46–70.
12. The idea that we learned our particular racism from the British is something that Ronit Lentin and Robbie McVeigh point out in *Racism and Anti-Racism in Ireland* (Belfast: Beyond the Pale Publications, 2002).

Cóilín Parsons

Oceans Apart: Amitav Ghosh, John Millington Synge, and Weak Comparison

There is a book that should sound very familiar to readers of this journal. It is the account of a student of anthropology who finds himself an object of curiosity to an isolated community into which he arrives to study its language and its culture. As an ethnographer, the narrator of the story finds himself awkwardly placed – torn between observation and participation; between revulsion and desire; between condescension and admiration; between his deeply informed scholarly and archival research and his inability to reconcile what he has found there with what he sees on his travels. This complex, ambivalent position comes to a head at a celebration, where the narrator finds himself awkwardly on the edge, beguiled by the music, sexually attracted to the women dancing, and yet unable to enter the scene. The account, in a book that is a genre-bending mix of historical research, ethnographic observation, and creative non-fiction, is structured as a series of vignettes, moving back and forth across time, with little sense of when they begin and end, resulting in a timeless narrative landscape. It is suffused, and problematically so, with romanticized ideas of a unified past torn apart by the forced integration of this part of the world into a developmental paradigm that privileges national economic progress and imperial power over pre- or sub- or supra- or counter-national systems of allegiance. It transpires over the course of the book, however, that the community being described is nowhere near so isolated as the traveller at first imagines. Indeed, the life of the village where the narrator stays is sustained by remittances from the village's children, who travel overseas to earn money in a far wealthier place. And what appear to be idiosyncratic local religious beliefs are, in fact, transoceanic, syncretic forms that are the result of an occluded cosmopolitanism.

No, the book I am describing is not John Millington Synge's *The Aran Islands* (1907), though every detail of the description above could fit Synge's formative account of island and oceanic life. Or at least, not only

Irish University Review 50.1 (2020): 120–130
DOI: 10.3366/iur.2020.0439
© Edinburgh University Press
www.euppublishing.com/iur

The Aran Islands. This description belongs also to Amitav Ghosh's *In an Antique Land* (1992), an account of the travels of an Indian scholar (mostly indistinguishable from Ghosh himself) in Egypt, where he is undertaking fieldwork that will form the basis of his doctoral thesis in anthropology. This scholar encounters what appear at first blush to be two quite separate stories – the life of the villagers of Nashâwy and Lataîfa, and the story of a Jewish trader and his unnamed slave who is mentioned in a manuscript from the mid-twelfth century found in the Cairo Geniza. The latter story, of manuscripts in Arabic written in Hebrew script, of an Indian slave given free reign to conduct the business of a Jewish trader from North Africa in the Indian Ocean port of Aden and on the Malabar Coast of India, functions as a nostalgic tale of a deeply cosmopolitan Indian Ocean world of fluid and multiple allegiances, connected by the unfettered trade in goods. This free trade fantasy is seen in some of Ghosh's other work too, and is not uncommon as a strand of Indian Ocean scholarship – a fantasy that was fatally interrupted by the arrival in the 'Arab lake', as the Indian Ocean was known at one point, of European navies, establishing what Janet Abu-Lughod diagnoses as 'European hegemony'.[1] Ghosh both laments the death of this cosmopolitanism, and finds unexpected traces of it in the lives of the Egyptian villagers, as the cosmopolitanism of twelfth-century travel and trade recurs in the oil-driven gulf economy of the 1980s that gathers into its sphere workers from southeast Asia all the way to north and east Africa, creating new affective communities problematically supported by the extraction of fossil fuels.

Why begin with a discussion of Ghosh's Egyptian travelogue in an Irish studies context where Synge is a more familiar reference point? What does it mean, and what could it yield, to read together these two non-fictional, semi-anthropological accounts of oceanic lives at the opposite ends of the twentieth century and from distinct continents and oceans? And what conclusions, or comparisons, can we draw when there are so many differences between the texts? Part of the answer to these questions lies in the narrative form itself: Ghosh's yoking together of twelfth and twentieth century, Mediterranean and Indian Ocean, and cosmopolitan and nation-centric worlds, challenges us to make exactly these kinds of transhistorical comparisons. Indeed, Ghosh's lamentation for the passing of a time when people and objects far apart in space thought of themselves as intimately connected, and not divided, by oceans drives us to be more imaginative critics. It is a conception of the world echoed by one of Synge's ubiquitous informants, known simply as 'old woman'. This woman's son had emigrated to America, and was moving from New York City to Albany, which she found incomprehensible – as long as he was in New York City she felt that he was only on 'the other edge of the Atlantic'.[2] In short, location (or what we might think of as context) are far from defining characteristics of these two texts, or even of the peoples and cultures described in them. When read together, Ghosh and Synge foreground, from very different positions, the instability and historical contingency of nation as a meaningful identifier of peoples and as a meaningful category of literary analysis.

* * *

These are also not just travelogues, as the subtitle of Ghosh's book announces: 'History in the Guise of a Traveller's Tale'. Time looms large, as both authors seek to capture a culture before it disappears, indeed to capture a culture that has become invisible, and, in doing so, to write from the peripheries of both the modern and the modernist. If it is in the Aran Islands that Synge can see the presence of the past in everyday life, it is in the villages of Nashâwy and Lataîfa that Ghosh can see traces of what he thought was a long lost, and barely lamented, cosmopolitan past. As a result, in both we see more fully defined the scope of peripheral modernisms that engage energetically with a modernity marked by the radical presence of the past. That sense of the irruptions of the past in the present is what makes these two texts so unsettling, for both Synge and Ghosh struggle to contain it.

Equally, *In an Antique Land* and *The Aran Islands* both emerge out of a deep immersion in, and a discomfort with, the discipline of anthropology, of which both Synge and Ghosh were students.[3] One, at its outset and before its Boasian heights, the other in the waning of its days of innocence, as the discipline came in for criticism from Talal Asad and other postcolonial critics.[4] For both Synge and Ghosh, anthropology is a discipline in dispute, and one in which neither of them feels at home. And in this shared discomfort and engagement with the emerging and changing discipline of anthropology, a new conjunction of modernism and postcolonialism emerges. Seeking and failing to establish the ground of locality, or to identify and objectify a pure culture, both Synge and Ghosh are forced to rethink the territorial and cultural assumptions of their work, turning to oceanic frames to understand the forces at work in the villages they make their object of study. Synge, for example, finds in the Aran Islands an ostensibly simple, pure culture subtended by complex networks of trade (their fish being sold in markets in France, their lobsters travelling all over Europe); travel (Synge got there from Paris in just a few days); migration (the islanders have a complex sense of the geography of the US, since so many of them had lived there); and scholarship (many of the best known ethnographers, antiquarians, and folklorists from across the Atlantic world had visited the islands). The islands are untouched and pure, and fully integrated into systems of exchange, travel, and knowledge. Ghosh both expects and finds much the same, and we find an uncanny similarity between the two texts at the level of content. These parables illustrate the positioning of the writer in relation to the object that he describes and desperately desires, for that object represents for Synge and Ghosh a sort of indigeneity that they see slipping from grasp, and that they are both also clear-headed enough to recognise as never having been anything other than syncretic and fluid.

Here, first, is Ghosh, describing a party in Nashâwy:

> The crowd pressed closer with the quickening of the beat, and as the voices and clapping grew louder, the girl, in response, raised an arm and flexed it above her head in a graceful arc. Her body was turning now, rotating slowly in the same place, her hips moving faster while the crowd around her clapped and stamped, roaring their approval at the tops of their voices. Gradually, the beat grew quicker, blurring into a tattoo of drumbeats, and in response her torso froze into stillness, while her hips and her waist moved ever faster, in exact counterpoint, in a pattern of movement that became a perfect abstraction of eroticism, a figurative geometry of love-making pounding back and forth at a dizzying speed until at last the final beat rang out and she escaped into the crowd, laughing.
>
> 'Where have you been all this while?' a voice cried out behind me. 'We have been looking everywhere for you – there's so much still to ask'.
>
> Turning around I came face to face with the man who had demanded to see my identity card.[5]

And here is JM Synge, describing a dream he has had while on the islands:

> Last night, after walking in a dream among buildings with strangely intense light on them, I heard a faint rhythm of music beginning far away on some stringed instrument.
>
> It came closer to me, gradually increasing in quickness and volume with an irresistible definite progression. When it was quite near the sound began to move in my nerves and blood, and to urge me to dance with them.
>
> ...
>
> Then the luring excitement became more powerful than my will, and my limbs moved in spite of me.
>
> In a moment I was swept away in a whirlwind of notes. My breath and my thoughts and every impulse of my body, became a form of the dance, till I could not distinguish between the instruments and the rhythm and my own person or consciousness.

For a while it seemed an excitement that was filled with joy, then it grew into an ecstasy where all existence was lost in a vortex of movement. I could not think there had ever been a life beyond the whirling of the dance.

Then with a shock the ecstasy turned to an agony and rage. I struggled to free myself, but seemed only to increase the passion of the steps I moved to. When I shrieked I could only echo the notes of the rhythm. (pp.54–55)

Here, in these two passages, is on full display the erotic affinities of two travellers in strange lands and times, each caught up in an economy of sexual and cultural desires, each longing to travel in times long lost to them in their everyday worlds, and each ultimately frustrated by interruption, desiring and clinging to and losing an affiliation with cultures not theirs that hold out the promise and possibility of travelling in other worlds.

* * *

Contrapuntal literary criticism of this kind enables us to think about interoceanic comparison, but in this case we find not the interoceanic movement of people or goods that frequently defines oceanic studies. Instead we see here the punctuated emergence of a genre, or perhaps even a form, of oceanic or of hydrocolonial writing in two locations across the decades of the twentieth century.[6] These tales of syncretism and synthesis, of deep and unbroken time, are themselves fractured, fragmented, temporally promiscuous, and logically paratactical – they stretch the imagined historical moment and locations of modernist writing.

One model for thinking about this emergence might be to turn to world systems theory, which has a storied history in the study of the Indian Ocean through the pioneering work of K.N. Chaudhuri.[7] A method of accounting for notable similarities across the works of Synge and Ghosh might see Ireland at the turn of the last century, even its most recalcitrant edges, having reached a position in the world economic system enjoyed by India and Egypt only in the latter half of the century. The resulting semi-ethnographic and auto-ethnographic narrative of oceanic living and crossing would then be facilitated by this structural position. I will not be the first to point out the possible inflexibility of this systemic thinking, since it implies (even as its best work persuasively disavows) a stagist or developmental model of history.[8] Indeed, Ghosh is alive to this problem, his semi-autobiographical character Amitav getting into some scrapes when he tries to negotiate and define the relative developmental stages of India and Egypt, enacting in the name of cross-cultural friendship a new kind of developmental paternalism (p.200). And we can already discern in Synge's relentless insistence on the continued existence of the past in the present an unease with linear models of time and history. The tenuous and yet inescapable echoes between *The Aran Islands* and *In an Antique Land* call for a looser, less certain form of comparative thinking that emphasises incompatibility and yet contiguity over structural positioning.[9]

The radically different locations of the composition of *In an Antique Land* and *The Aran Islands* enables comparison rather than foreclosing it, and the books 'hail each other across the lines of a century' (to borrow a phrase from a recent essay by Melanie Micir and Aarthi Vadde), allowing a form of comparative analysis that is weak yet attends to fragile similarities traced across expansive spaces and times.[10] This weak comparison stretches and expands the definition of context that literary critics have long taken for granted, in ways that Wai Chee Dimock took issue with over a decade ago.[11] Dimock, writing more recently of 'the strength of weak ties' continues to search for a method of comparison that can acknowledge similarity but allow differences to remain fluid, generative, contradictory, messy.[12] A weak approach to comparison offers a (suitably) tentative model for holding Ghosh and Synge at a distance but yet in balance, or for resisting the need to account for their connectedness and yet recognising their formal similarities across time.[13]

Where Ghosh might show us the way towards a speculative practice of weak comparison across distant places is in those very frustrating places where he gives up all conceit of objective history that he had taken on in his essay in Subaltern Studies: 'For all we know', he writes, repeatedly, foregrounding his own Quixotic historical practice (p.162 and *passim*). Later, as Ghosh tries his hand at a history of emotions, reconstructing the relationship between Ben Yiju and his wife, the pages are littered with phrases signalling dubiousness: 'there can be no doubt', 'This could mean', 'the date must have preceded', and more (pp.226-227). As frustrating as these passages are, they leave us constantly questioning the simple assertions that pepper the latter half of the book, as Ghosh's imagination runs wild. Ghosh foregrounds and thematises the impossibility and yet the necessity of an imagination called to oceanic thinking – a loose structure, if that is not a paradox, of modernity in the wake of empire that demands a new kind of fluid and contingent comparison. It is a hesitancy that is not yet fully formed in Synge's work, which still clings to vanishing certainties – reading Ghosh alongside Synge brings this latent uncertainty to the surface.

* * *

But what is the value of an Indian Ocean-inflected approach to the study of Ireland's modernity? It is, as with any oceanic approach, a question of scale bending and scale jumping – geographic, temporal, species scales. In rethinking the scale of 'Irish' literature, we decentre Ireland, and in decentering Ireland from the study of its own modernity we can find opportunities to compare sometimes non-contiguous and discontinuous objects. While scholars of Irish literature might now be familiar with the Green and Black Atlantic, and with Caribbean-Irish connections (and this work has been groundbreaking for the study of Irish modernity), what would it mean to make more distant comparisons that are not authorized by a shared colonial archive or by migrations that establish long-distance relations?[14] A shift from thinking of Ireland in the Atlantic or archipelagic frame brings us to other oceanic formations that offer new questions – the Indian Ocean world, for example, is built around deeper and longer cultural intermingling that offers a long-standing corrective to the nation-dreaming of the Global North. The new oceanic studies can, if carefully construed, bring perspectives 'from and on the Global South' to what is sometimes called the blue humanities, as Hofmeyr and Bystrom point out in a recent issue of *Comparative Literature*, and these perspectives can also enliven the work of Irish Studies.[15]

For our purposes, an oceanic perspective transposed from the Indian Ocean asks us to take into account the deep time of Synge's imagined world, in which Fir Bolgs cavort among the islanders in a way that has been read as a primitivist impulse, but might also be read as an engagement with occluded scales of time that historicize and diminish the dead hand of the modern empires. At the same time, these oceanic reading practices forged in the Global South emphasize routes over roots, or affiliation over filiation, to use Edward Said's resonant terms. *The Aran Islands* in this reading can be a text of mobility and fluidity rather than a desperate attempt at fixing and holding. Its oceanic impulses are what impel it into the 'big world', almost against Synge's own desires.[16]

There is a danger in some oceanic thinking – and Ghosh himself is guilty here – that this could become a Deleuzian deterritorialization, as we celebrate the rhizome over the root with little sense of the power relations at play in what appears to be a fluid world. Oceans have become overdetermined as sites of restless movement, cosmopolitanism, deep history – of connection and circulation. Rather than simply celebrating the movement of goods, capital, and people under the power of states and empires we must be alive to the need to push back against the idea that oceans must be necessarily fluid, or pre-globalised. Nathan Hensley and Tommy Davis address this concern with regard to the ever-expanding machine of 'global modernism' of which Synge and Ghosh may form parts by asking 'if expansion, flexibility, and unmooring are also the salient traits of ... global capitalism, what intellectual tools might craft alternative logics to those that have underwritten and emerged from ... capitalism's drive toward this liquid modernity?'[17] The challenge for the critic working in this field is to be fully alive to the capacities of oceanic thinking without succumbing to the logics of fluidity and freedom offered to us by global capital.

A weak comparative rather than a connective framework holds this difficulty in mind. It may be wary of the siren calls of connection and fluidity, but it does not set either the national or the local over the global. Indeed, in the field of Irish literature, the pull is the opposite – there is a continuing, if not deepening, investment in a localism that was the bedrock of nationalism in the early twentieth century but that is returning today as a form of counter-globalism, especially in the environmental humanities. So, two fields here – Indian Ocean studies struggling against regionalism, if not globalism, and Irish studies fighting the demons of localism – represented by two books. One (*Antique Land*) flouts its fluidity and its regional and global scales, and the other (*Aran Islands*) has been read as providing a bedrock of national authenticity. Coming at opposite ends of the twentieth century, these desires can hardly be surprising. The racial violence at the heart of the century had not yet been unleashed when Synge went in search of the Irish race, while Ghosh's tale is all too aware of just what that hardening of ethnic differences can lead to, given its central set-piece describing the violence unleashed at the partition of India and Pakistan in 1947 (pp.204–210).

* * *

Synge is not the only Irish writer of the early twentieth century who has been recently transplanted to the shores of the Indian Ocean, nor the only one whose newly established contexts are inextricably linked with the nostalgic imagination of the Indian Ocean as a zone of peace and cooperation. If there could be said to have been one foundational political moment for the academic study of the Indian Ocean as an integrated system, it was the 1955 Afro-Asian conference that took place in Bandung, Indonesia, and that kick-started the Non-Aligned Movement. The rhetoric of Sukarno, Nehru, and the other leaders of the Global South who met in 1955 was focused on solidarity and horizontality – on shared feelings and non-hierarchical relations that could be seen to be reflected in a long history of Indian Ocean migrations, circulations, and exchanges. But the fine sentiments and the days of the Non-Aligned Movement appear to be waning in our world. The political power of the NAM has been ebbing since the

127

beginning of the 1970s, when UN General Assembly Resolution 2832 declaring the Indian Ocean a 'zone of peace' became obsolete almost as soon as it was passed, and India and Pakistan made it clear that they had nuclear ambitions and were willing to take *de facto* sides in the Cold War.[18]

In 2003, the members of the NAM met in Kuala Lumpur, on the eve of the US- and UK-led invasion of Iraq. While the president of the 2003 summit of the NAM, Mahathir Muhamad of Malaysia, lamented the fact that 'the world is in a terrible mess', Thabo Mbeki of South Africa offered a more poetic diagnosis.[19] At the opening ceremony, delegates were treated to a long speech by Mbeki carefully structured around W.B. Yeats's 'The Second Coming'.[20] The recognition that things are falling apart was not, of course, new in the context of African literature, but its being carried over into the Indian Ocean world by an African head of state, and retooled for the twenty first century, extends the geographical and historical reach of Yeats's poem. The contextual landscape of 'The Second Coming' – hysteria over the rise of Communism in Russia and a fearful look at the politics of Ireland in the late 1910s – is stretched to accommodate the dissolution of the power of the NAM and the invasion of Iraq in 2003. The poem's footprint and the meanings it makes have migrated and expanded.[21]

But not all of the monuments of Irish modernism have been so lucky. In March of 2019, I had the chance to have dinner with Amitav Ghosh. It was a stuffy affair, though Ghosh himself is far from stuffy. He had just given a keynote lecture at the American Comparative Literature Association annual meeting at Georgetown University, and he was relaxing into the evening with a glass of wine. I leaned over and asked him whether he had ever read *The Aran Islands*. He shook his head – no, he had not even heard of it. I recommended it to him, and I was secretly relieved that he hadn't read it. The delicacy of the web of Ghosh/Synge connections across oceans and centuries remained undisturbed by influence or interest. Irish literature had not, in this case, travelled transnationally or transoceanically, but neither are its concerns and its forms either necessarily Irish or indisputably singular. The result of transnational and comparative work is not an unthought universalism, but should be the careful disaggregation of Irish literature and its Irishness, of writing and nationhood.[22]

NOTES

1. Janet Abu-Lughod, *Before European Hegemony: The World System A.D. 1250–1350* (Oxford: Oxford University Press, 1991). For a critique of Ghosh's free-trade nostalgia see Gaurav Desai, 'Old World Order, Amitav Ghosh and the Writing of Nostalgia', *Representations* 85.1 (2004), 125–148.
2. John Millington Synge, *The Aran Islands* (London: Penguin, 1992), p.62; further references in parentheses in the text. On these questions of the bending and shifting

scales of life in the Aran Islands, see Cóilín Parsons, *The Ordnance Survey and Modern Irish Literature* (Oxford: Oxford University Press, 2016), pp.119–152.

3. On the anthropological stakes of Synge's writing see Gregory Castle, *Modernism and the Celtic Revival* (Cambridge: Cambridge University Press, 2001), pp.98–133; and Sinéad Garrigan Mattar, *Primitivism, Science, and the Irish Revival* (Oxford: Oxford University Press, 2004), pp.130–184.

4. The story that Ghosh tells of Indian Ocean crossings is published almost simultaneously in *In an Antique Land* and in the journal *Subaltern Studies*, signalling his disciplinary discomfort. Amitav Ghosh, 'The Slave of MS. H.6.' in *Subaltern Studies No. 7: Writings on South Asian History and Society*, ed. by Partha Chatterjee and Gyanendra Pandey (Oxford: Oxford University Press, 1993), pp.159–220.

5. Amitav Ghosh, *In an Antique Land: History in the Guise of a Traveller's Tale* (New York: Vintage, 1992), p.202. Further references in parentheses in the text.

6. Isabel Hofmeyr defines a new field of inquiry called 'hydrocolonialism', signalling 'an affinity with postcolonialism while declaring an intention to shift the intellectual center of gravity away from a purely land-focused one'. Isabel Hofmeyr, 'Provisional Notes on Hydrocolonialism', *English Language Notes* 57.1 (2019), 11–20 (p.13).

7. K.N. Chaudhuri, *Trade and Civilisation in the Indian Ocean: An Economic History from the Rise of Islam to 1750* (Cambridge: Cambridge University Press, 1985).

8. For the most considered of this work see Warwick Research Collective, *Combined and Uneven Development: Towards a New Theory of World-Literature* (Liverpool: Liverpool University Press, 2015).

9. For a more in-depth discussion of the comparison of incompatibles see Natalie Melas, *All the Difference in the World: Postcoloniality and the Ends of Comparison* (Palo Alto, CA: Stanford University Press, 2006).

10. On difference enabling comparison see Melanie Micir and Aarthi Vadde, 'Obliterature, Toward an Amateur Criticism', *Modernism/modernity* 25.3 (2018), 517–49 (p.519).

11. Wai Chee Dimock, *Through Other Continents: American Literature Across Deep Time* (Princeton, NJ: Princeton University Press, 2006).

12. Dimock's phrase is borrowed from sociologist Mark Granovetter. Wai Chee Dimock, 'Weak Network, Faulkner's Transpacific Reparations', *Modernism/modernity* 25.3 (2018), 587–602 (p.590).

13. The conversation appears in a recent issue of *Modernism*/modernity edited and introduced by Paul Saint-Amour. See Paul K. Saint-Amour, 'Weak Theory, Weak Modernism', *Modernism/modernity* 25.3 (2018) 437–459. In an early iteration of this idea, Wai Chee Dimock turns specifically to Irish literature to help her weave a theory of weak connections. Wai Chee Dimock, 'Weak Theory: Henry James, Colm Tóibín, and W.B. Yeats', *Critical Inquiry* 39.4 (2013), 732–753.

14. See, for example, *The Green and Black Atlantic, Cross-Currents of the African and Irish Diasporas* ed. by David Lloyd and Peter D. O'Neill (Basingstoke: Palgrave Macmillan, 2009); Maria McGarrity, *Washed by the Gulf Stream: The Historic and Geographic relation of Irish and Caribbean Literature* (Dover, DE: University of Delaware Press, 2008); Michael Malouf, *Transatlantic Solidarities, Irish Nationalism and Caribbean Poetics* (Charlottesville, VA: University of Virginia Press, 2009).

15. Isabel Hofmeyr and Kerry Bystrom, 'Oceanic Routes: (Post-it) Notes on Hydro-Colonialism', *Comparative Literature* 69.1 (2017), pp.1–6. Oceanic approaches to Irish literature are themselves gathering pace, with a renewed focus not just on ocean crossing, but on oceanic inhabitation and littoral lives. See Nicholas Allen, *Ireland, Literature, and the Coast: Seatangled* (Oxford: Oxford University Press, 2020); *Coastal Work: Cultures of the Atlantic Edge*, ed. by Nicholas Allen, Nick Groom, and Jos Smith (Oxford: Oxford University Press, 2017); Claire Connolly, 'Turbulent Water: A Cultural History of the Irish Sea', *The Irish Times*, 4 May 2019; Nels Pearson, *Irish*

Cosmopolitanism: Location and Dislocation in James Joyce, Elizabeth Bowen, and Samuel Beckett (Gainesville, FL: University Press of Florida, 2015). See also the body of work by Maebh Long, which traverses Irish literature and the Pacific Ocean, though mostly separately.

16. This is the term that Maurya, in *Riders to the Sea*, uses to describe the world beyond her island. John Millington Synge, *The Collected Works, Volume III: Plays I*, ed. by Ann Saddlemyer (London: Oxford University Press, 1968), p.13.

17. Nathan K. Hensley and Thomas S. Davis, 'Scale and Form: Or, What was Global Modernism?', *Modernism/modernity Print Plus* 2.4 (2018), available at: https://modernismmodernity.org/forums/scale-and-form. Accessed 11 October 2019.

18. See Christopher Lee, 'The Indian Ocean during the Cold War: Thinking through a Critical Geography', *History Compass* 1.17 (2013), 524–530.

19. Don Hill, 'World: Non-Aligned Movement Summit Opens in Malaysia', *Radio Free Europe Radio Liberty*, 24 February 2003. Available at: https//www.rferl.org/a/1102321.html. Accessed 11 October 2019.

20. I am grateful to Daniel Mulhall, ambassador of Ireland to the United States for bringing to my attention this speech, which Mulhall heard when he was ambassador to Malaysia. See Daniel Mulhall, 'The Non-Aligned Port: "The Second Coming" of W.B. Yeats', *New Straits Times*, 5 March 2003. Infoweb Newsbank. Accessed 11 October 2019.

21. In making this argument about the occluded and expansive geographies of 'The Second Coming', I am thinking of the generative work of Jahan Ramazani, especially in 'The Local Poem in a Global Age', *Critical Inquiry* 43.3 (2017), 670–696.

22. My thanks are due to many who have heard drafts of and given their responses to longer versions of this paper, including Rogaia Abusharaf, Nicholas Allen, Anne Bang, Uday Chandra, Pamila Gupta, Isabel Hofmeyr, Jeanne-Marie Jackson, Ronan McDonald, Nels Pearson, Sangeeta Ray, Meg Samuelson, Aparna Vaidik. Thank you also to Emilie Pine for sharp-eyed and generous editing.

Patricia Kennon

Reflecting Realities in Twenty-First-Century Irish Children's and Young Adult Literature

The past four decades in Ireland have seen profound cultural, political, economic, social, sexual, and religious transformations that have propelled the country's process of reinventing itself from an inward-looking, conservative, predominantly rural, Catholic country to becoming a multicultural, metropolitan, and secular nation. The story of Irish childhood has powerfully intersected with this series of transformative events in modern Irish history. Indeed, children and the conceptualisation and treatment of childhood have been central to these transitions as well as the associated scandals which catalyzed challenges to the authority of the old order and the Catholic Church's traditional dominance. These controversies included the clerical child-abuse scandals, the Ireland-US adoption scandal, the death of Ann Lovett in 1985, the X case and subsequent landmark Irish Supreme Court ruling regarding Irish women's right to an abortion, and generations of injustices against pregnant women and girls sent to Magdalene Laundries and mother-and-baby homes. Global images of Ireland moved from 'De Valera's dream of a nation of romping, sturdy children, athletic youths and comely maidens, to one in which innocent boys and girls were incarcerated in industrial and reformatory schools where they were demeaned, abused, and brutalized';[1] locally and nationally, Irish institutions and individual citizens grappled and continue to grapple with inconvenient truths about historic and contemporary dissonances between the idealized regime of untroubled childhood innocence and the demanding social and political realities in which Irish young people live.

Childhood is constructed and mediated within a myriad of power relationships, contexts, identities, nostalgia, historical legacies, and socio-cultural forces: 'If we want to understand the way in which a culture envisions itself, we might look no further than the stories adults tell and retell to their children'.[2] Cultural representations of

Irish University Review 50.1 (2020): 131–142
DOI: 10.3366/iur.2020.0440
© Edinburgh University Press
www.euppublishing.com/iur

young people and texts for young audiences are intertwined with ambivalent desires, hopes, and anxieties around the status of young people, children's agency, and the adult management of youth's radical potential. Observing the emancipatory and regulatory histories and impulses of children's literature, Kimberley Reynolds argues that these texts provide 'a curious and paradoxical cultural space... [that] is simultaneously highly regulated and overlooked, orthodox and radical, didactic and subversive'.[3] There has been a rich Irish tradition of writing and storytelling for children for more than three centuries with authors such as Maria Edgeworth, Jonathan Swift, Lady Mount Cashel, L.T. Meade, Padraic Colum, Sinéad de Valera, Patricia Lynch, Cathal O'Sandair, and Eilís Dillon imagining and exploring the evolution of Irish childhood. However, the turn of the twenty-first century witnessed a 'vast and vivid achievement in writing for children'[4] which accompanied the contemporaneous oscillating financial, social, and cultural expansion and contraction of Ireland and its increasing presence and confidence in international arenas during the last two decades. As Jane Elizabeth Dougherty states, 'this common trope, of an Ireland being reborn or coming of age, was matched by an outpouring of Irish maturation narratives ... [and] as the nation came of age, so too did the Irish child'[5].

Links between the past and the present have been dominant concerns 'in much contemporary Irish writing and in Irish culture in general' yet 'the focus on the Irish past has also been accompanied by an obsession with Irish childhood'.[6] In 1997 Robert Dunbar remarked that 'the world of Irish children's literature is a strange, complex, and fascinating place',[7] and a distinctive aspect of Irish youth literature's strangeness and complexity then and now involves the negotiation and mediation of history alongside the potential of young people for embodying, envisioning, and enacting change. Reflecting upon developments in Irish publishing and how children's literature was increasingly engaging with change, continuity, and the realities of modern Irish society during the first decade of this century, Valerie Coghlan suggested that Irish children's literature was 'achieving a new degree of maturity– that it can be "of Ireland" while not necessarily preoccupied with a traditional Ireland'.[8]

WOMEN'S WRITING, WOMEN'S VOICES AND ENVISIONING GIRLHOOD

A key development in this recent literature 'of Ireland' has been the increasing visibility of women's writing and the interrogation of traditional representations and regimes around women's and girls' histories, voices, and lived experiences in Irish history, media, and culture. Over the last decade, the elision of Irish girls, women, and women's writing has been challenged and defied by increased visibility, publication, public discourse, and grassroots activism around women's reproductive rights, such as the Repeal the Eighth campaign, the representation of women in Irish theatre (Waking the Feminists), marriage equality, and systematic gender biases in literary, cultural, and political institutions. Although there has been a long tradition of Irish women children's authors as well as a robust wave of novels during the 1980s and 1990s which explored the travails and preoccupations of girlhood (by writers such as Joan O'Neill, Marita Conlon-McKenna, Siobhán Parkinson, Elizabeth O'Hara, and Maeve Friel), 'in Irish literary tradition ... childhood has become a male genre' and 'by contrast, few readers, whether casual or scholarly, can readily name an example of the Irish literary girlhood'[9].

In 2004 Patricia Coughlan pronounced that 'much unfinished business remains to be done in Irish psyches'[10] particularly when it comes to women's narratives or those of other silenced and elided voices. During the last fifteen years, Irish youth literature has been increasingly engaged with proclaiming the importance, and advocating for due recognition, of Irish girlhoods.

There have been many works by Irish male authors of youth literature which involve girl protagonists (e.g. Aubrey Flegg's 2003 historical novel, *Wings Over Delft*, Roddy Doyle's exploration of four generations of girls and women in the 2011 novel, *A Greyhound of a Girl*, and the headstrong Valkyrie of Derek Landy's *Skulduggery Pleasant* series comprising twelve books to date). However, few of these are explicitly feminist or even pass the Bechdel test (a measure of representation of girls and women in cultural works, examining whether the work features at least two named women who talk to each other about something other than a man). A recent exception involves Peadar Ó Guilín's horror duology *The Call* (2017) and *The Invasion* (2018) which recognises the empowering importance of female relationships and presents multiple young female characters with complexity, vulnerability, and agency.

Recent years have seen a momentum of explicitly feminist and social-change-oriented publications for children and authored by Irish women. Drawing upon the centenary anniversary of Irish women's suffrage in 1918 as a platform for education and awareness-raising of all-too-often neglected or erased women's creative and cultural histories and voices, publications such as Sarah Webb and Lauren O'Neill's *Blazing A Trail: Irish Women Who Changed the World* (2018) and Siobhán Parkinson's *Rocking the System: Fearless and Amazing Irish Women Who Made History* (2018) aim to provide inspiring role models for girls, and to explicitly recognise and respect the vibrancy, diversity, and importance of girl characters and their creators. In the same year Children's

Books Ireland presented its 'Bold Girls' national project, which celebrated twenty contemporary Irish women writers and illustrators for young people, provided anti-sexist recommended reading lists promoting gender equality, and nationally advocated for girls' agency, voices, and empowerment.

Susan Cahill has argued that recent post-Celtic Tiger writing by Irish women such as Eimear McBride's *A Girl Is A Half-Formed Thing* (2013) alert 'us to the ways in which Irish literature refuses to see or hear the teenage girl'.[11] Contemporary Irish women creators of young-adult (YA) literature have been especially committed to exploring and disrupting what Cahill terms the 'critical invisibility'[12] of teenage girls in Irish culture and literature. Since its emergence in the US publishing sector in the late 1960s, YA literature usually involves at least one teenage protagonist, is preoccupied with adolescent desires, anxieties, and scenarios, and is widely marketed and packaged for 12–18-year-olds rather than younger children. While YA has evolved, and issues around its classification and audience are debated (e.g. due to adults now comprising a significant proportion of readers of YA texts), narratives of 'coming of age' constitute the generally agreed markers for YA literature. Indeed, what Alison Waller has called the 'very in-betweenness or liminality'[13] of YA literature echoes the liminality and transitional status of adolescence itself. Conceptualized as unstable, transitional, dynamic, and ostensibly naturally rebellious, adolescence is regarded as 'an othered subjectivity' with adolescents 'watched at all times for signs of "impurity", and ... scapegoated as unclean things, ejected from the social body if they are seen to make the wrong moves of identification within the webs of ideological signifiers laid before them'.[14] Adolescent female bodies are subjected to even further surveillance, regulation, and adult ambivalence due to their unsettling liminal position between the borders of childhood and womanhood, purity and fertility, and innocence and experience, as well as their 'striking biopolitical potential ... [to] physically and metaphorically embody the future because their bodies will birth the next generation'.[15]

Although Irish YA fiction can be traced back to the 1990s, early Irish YA novels such as Margrit Cruikshank's *Circling the Triangle* (1991) were reluctant to recognise or engage with adolescent sexuality or desire: there was 'no mention of the protagonist's awareness of his body or physicality, his desires or gratifications' in that novel.[16] While works such as Jane Mitchell's *When Stars Stop Spinning* (1993) did address some 'taboo' aspects of youth experience such as homelessness, violence, and drug abuse, Irish youth literature in the 1990s and 2000s was slow to recognise or address subjects such as teenage pregnancy, the realities of female embodiment, reproductive freedoms, and institutional child abuse in past and contemporary Irish society.

Marita Conlon-McKenna's 2003 historical novel set in the 1960s, *A Girl Called Blue* (the only Irish book for children to date set in a religious institution), does describe harsh aspects of this experience, 'but in deference to the age of her readers, mainly in the 10 to 13 age group, her use of the binary cruel nun/kind nun ameliorates the vicious punishments inflicted on the girls'.[17]

This sanitising approach and the adult desire to protect young people's 'innocence' from dark and disturbing topics and truths tends to dominate much of late twentieth-century Irish youth literature into the first millennium. Siobhan Dowd's works during this first decade of the twenty-first-century provide powerful exceptions to what Pádraic Whyte in 2011 called the 'continued refusal at a cultural level' in Irish YA fiction up to that time 'to engage with some of the more controversial subjects common to YA fiction'.[18] Set in a claustrophobic Irish village in 1984, Dowd's first novel, *A Swift Pure Cry* (2006) was loosely based on a true story of teenage pregnancy, potential incest, and dead babies that rocked the country's complacency and religious hypocrisy. Dowd's posthumous novel, *Bog Child* (2008), which won the Carnegie Medal, was also set in the 1980s amidst the backdrop of the Troubles. Unsentimentally confronting the Ireland of prehistory, violations of female bodies, and the multigenerational ripple effects of trauma and violence, *Bog Child* explores borders, ideas of nation, conflict, self-sacrifice, human frailty, love, death, and the potential of redemption.

Dowd's work is no longer a rare or isolated example of confronting difficult topics in YA literature. The last decade has witnessed the emergence and success of a cohort of Irish women YA authors such as Sarah Crossan, Louise O'Neill, Deirdre Sullivan, Möira Fowley-Doyle, and Sarah Maria Griffin who continue this exploration of the nexus of power, sexuality, and adolescent female embodiment. Their works pose uncomfortable, important questions around power, abuse, trauma, misogyny, and historic as well as contemporary discriminations and violence against teenage girls and women in Ireland. For example, Louise O'Neill's best-selling novel, *Asking For It* (2015) – inspired by real-life Irish and international rape trials, sexual assaults, and misogynistic uses of social media – helped catalyse national conversations and debates in its unflinching confrontation with rape culture, slut-shaming, revenge porn, and consent. Throughout the novel, O'Neil emphasises the hypocrisies and double-standards around adolescent sexual activity and the lack of sex education available for Irish young people – a controversial issue, which the recently-designed Relationships and Sexuality Education (RSE) programme in Irish primary and secondary schools is designed to address. Her 2014 dystopian novel, *Only Every Yours*, and her 2018 novel, *The Surface Breaks* (a feminist retelling of 'The Little Mermaid'), also address toxic masculinity, patriarchal power, and adolescent female agency.

TWENTY-FIRST-CENTURY IRISH YOUTH LITERATURE AND THE GOTHIC

Much of this Irish women's YA writing engages with the Gothic, understandably so, considering Catherine Spooner's assertion that 'the body at the centre of many contemporary Gothic narratives is definitively an adolescent one'.[19] There has been a long Gothic tradition in Irish literature with contemporary Irish children's authors such as Darren Shan, Derek Landy, and Peadar Ó Guilín drawing upon Gothic tropes in their explorations of childhood innocence, resilience, vulnerability, and curiosity. The Gothic's fascination with the body, unequal power relationships, family secrets, and trauma holds particular affinity with Irish youth literature when contextualised within 'the wake of successive revelations of physical, psychological and sexual abuse of children at home and in state-funded institutions' and the 'Gothic nightmare ... of fear, terror, and enforced silence' that characterised 'childhood in Ireland during the twentieth century'.[20] 'Teen Gothic'[21], as Glennis Byron and Sharon Deans have termed a recent phenomenon in YA Gothic texts, possesses an intriguing potential for empowering its adolescent protagonists and for envisioning and enacting transformative change regarding inherited hegemonic norms and power relationships. Refuting Roberta Seelinger Trites's argument in her influential book, *Disturbing the Universe: Power and Repression in Adolescent Literature*, that although 'the surface intention of most YA novels is ostensibly to legitimize adolescence', mainstream YA fiction teaches 'adolescent readers to accept a certain amount of repression as a cultural imperative',[22] teen Gothic, instead, depicts how adolescent agency and power can challenge, subvert, and successfully defy existing hegemonic power structures.

The last few years have seen a flourish of Irish YA writing that may be classified as teen Gothic along with its empowering vision of adolescent might. Three novels by Irish YA women authors (all published during 2019) particularly embody teen Gothic's capacity and commitment to bestow to the teenage reader 'an alternative viewpoint which allows them to see the world in a different way and crucially allows them to escape the didactic and instructive nature of "realist" texts'.[23] Sarah Maria Griffin's *Other Words For Smoke*, Moïra Fowley-Doyle's *All The Bad Apples*, and Deirdre Sullivan's *Perfectly Preventable Deaths*. All three novels are explicitly set in and engage with Irish history and culture, and this intensifies the disturbing resonance of the violent histories and traumas that their female characters must survive. In a 2007 essay, Celia Keenan reflects on how 'all culturally specific references' in the majority of turn of the millennium Irish youth literature had either been eliminated or rendered parodic, and she ruefully concludes that 'the local has ceded to the global'[24] and that this globalizing trajectory would likely continue and even intensify. These works of Irish YA 'witcherature' (literature of the fantastic with witch characters) defy that homogenizing impulse in their devoted, explicit sense of Irishness, their many Irish historical and cultural references, their details of Irish landscape and setting, and their use of Hiberno-English. Literary witches hold a 'perennial literary fascination ... [and] in a #MeToo world, where Donald Trump – a fan of the term "witch-hunt" – is US president, it is really no surprise that female writers are examining the role of the witch in new ways'.[25] The symbolic resonance of the witch is further intensified when merged with female adolescence, ambivalences around the potential power of teenage girls, and the backdrop of Irish histories of injustice against women and girls.

In the 'Acknowledgments' for *Other Words for Smoke*, Sarah Maria Griffin muses that 'if a whole country could be a haunted house, [she] can think of no more accurate site'[26] than Ireland. Like Fowley-Doyle and Sullivan's novels, *Other Words for Smoke*s excavates the haunting of Ireland's past and present by institutional misogyny, the denial of female bodily autonomy and reproductive rights, the Irish state's complicity with the Catholic Church, and the macabre history and legacy of mother-and-baby homes. Griffin skilfully deploys time shifts, narrative frames, and perspectives to create a lyrical anatomy of the costs of power, control, obsession, rivalry, and desire in a small Irish town which is 'pleasant, but for the disquieting presence of the old Magdalene laundry by the river ... leering history'.[27] A generation before the novel begins, 'some nameless girl' died 'in childbirth beneath the statue of the Virgin Mary' and the monstrous 'wrong of it tore a cut in things'[28] through which two monstrous supernatural predators arrive: one feeds on fear and the other on love. Griffin sensitively presents the ordeals and journeys of her queer witch characters while starkly delineating the realities of homophobia and the purity-policing of female bodies and sexualities in both 1970s and modern-day Ireland.

Similarly, sixteen-year-old Maddie, the lesbian protagonist in Deirdre Sullivan's lyrical *Perfectly Preventable Deaths*, discovers her witchcraft while grappling with internalised shame, family traumas, and living in a town where teenage girls have mysteriously gone missing for generations in the surrounding mountains: 'so many missing girls, lines and lines of them, like beads on strings.... A girl can turn into an ellipsis so easily'.[29] A particularly stark confrontation with Irish historical abuses and ongoing, contemporary violations of female bodies involves Maddie, her mother, and her sister encountering the list of names of all the girls whom a supernatural predator has abducted, murdered, and mutilated across generations. The devastating list spans three and a half pages, comprising the names of women who infamously died due to Irish medical and legal institutions and whom Ireland failed, including the name of Savita Halappanavar, an Indian woman living in Ireland whose death led to the passing of the 2013 Protection of Life During Pregnancy Act. Sullivan's novel, while unwavering, is also concerned with the importance of hope and ultimately presents the potential for young people to effect change on both an individual and collective level.

Moïra Fowley-Doyle's *All the Bad Apples* is likewise committed to re-inscribing queer women, confronting multigenerational traumas, and repudiating Ireland's long tradition of stigmatizing and erasing non-conforming female 'bad apples'. In exploring the curse on her family tree, protagonist Deena unearths the stories of her female ancestors and traces a centuries-long familial and national trajectory of marginalization and violation of women and girls. A pivotal moment occurs when Deena and her friends spend the night in an abandoned former mother-and-baby home which uncannily combines openness and enclosure, the past and the present, destruction and the possibility for transformative change: 'the front door was open: a great black mouth.... It looked like there were building works going on during the daytime. As if they planned to tear the place down or build it up, start anew'.[30] After conversing with the ghosts of the young women committed there, Deena is compelled to give voice to their silenced stories, realising that 'there are no bad apples.... The curse isn't on our family.... It's on every woman in this country. Kept in shame and silence for generations. Kicked out, locked up and taken away. Their children sold in illegal adoptions; their babies buried in unmarked graves'.[31] The teenagers agree that the only way to break this toxic cycle is to 'tell your story and the story of your family. You speak your truth. You shatter the stigma'.[32] In the Author's Note, Fowley-Doyle states that this novel 'was, in part, fuelled by rage'.[33] While the novel is indeed fiery and nears being polemical at times, her protagonists successfully harness outrage and advocacy 'in order to bring necessary secrets to light, to heal wounded families, and to affect the world around them'.[34] The novel ends with Deena enacting feminist activism within her family and her school, coming out as a lesbian on her own terms, wearing a Pride pin, and organizing a student petition to secularize Irish education and separate church and state.

THE POTENTIAL FOR QUEER NARRATIVES AND CHALLENGING RACIAL HEGEMONIES

Although Whyte noted that representations of homosexuality 'in YA fiction in Ireland are limited'[35] apart from rare exceptions like

Tom Lennon's 1993 *When Love Comes To Town* (considered the first Irish YA novel to involve a gay protagonist), Irish youth literature has been demonstrating a slow but gradually increasing recognition and representation of queer identities and sexualities since the legalisation of same-sex marriage by popular vote in 2015. In addition to the queer characters in *Other Words For Smoke*, *All The Bad Apples*, and *Perfectly Preventable Deaths*, Claire Hennessy's *Like Other Girls* (2018) features a young bisexual woman facing an unplanned pregnancy, and Meg Grehan's *The Space Between* (2017) involves a teenage lesbian narrator. In Shirley-Anne McMillan's 2019 YA novel, *Every Sparrow Falling*, her queer teenage characters grapple with Northern Ireland's social and religious conservatism and homophobia, as well as the threat of reparative therapy. The youngest queer character to date in Irish youth fiction is Stevie, the eleven-year-old protagonist of Grehan's 2019 verse novel, *The Deepest Breath*, and this sensitive exploration of a child's coming-out experience offers an exciting potential for challenging heteronormativity in Irish children's literature.

As welcome as these texts and their disruptions to sexism and heteronormativity are, the population of Irish youth literature has been and continues to be overwhelmingly white and written by majority-culture authors. While there are some examples of people of colour and intersectionality in recent Irish YA fiction (for example, the biracial and bisexual Finn in Sullivan's *Perfectly Preventable Deaths* and Nell, the bisexual girl of colour protagonist of Griffin's 2016 debut novel, *Spare and Found Parts*), whiteness is all too often presumed and practised as 'a master signifier … the screen against which any "other" culture is projected; it embodies the universal, making any other ethnicity the particular, the curious, the deviant'.[36] In her 2016 study of the pervasiveness of whiteness and the racialization of Irish identity in Celtic Tiger Irish children's fiction, Clíona Ó Gallchoir states that the 'relative silence in the field of Irish children's literature on the subject of race since 2004' is 'arguably suggestive of a lack of faith in a truly inclusive Ireland'.[37] This 'relative silence' of Irish youth literature is particularly significant in light of recent debates on social media and advocacy movements in UK and US youth literature publishing. Since 2014, awareness-raising campaigns and non-profit organisations such as #reflectingrealities, #weneeddiversebooks, and #ownvoices have sought to challenge white privilege, ethnocentricity, and embedded norms around gender and sexualities, and class and able-bodiedness, while seeking to promote anti-racist, intersectional, and authentic writing and illustration which respects and recognises the diverse experiences and identities of all young people. According to the 2018 *Reflecting Realities: Survey of Ethnic Representation within UK Children's Literature* report published in September 2019, only seven percent of books feature a Black, Asian, or Minority Ethnic (BAME) character and only four percent of books involve BAME characters as protagonists.[38]

The representation of the 'new Irish', characters of colour and marginalized ethnic minorities such as Irish Travellers, in Irish youth literature is similarly troublingly deficient. While Lucy Caldwell acknowledges in her 2019 collection, *Being Various: New Irish Short Stories*, that 'it has never been more apparent' that 'Ireland is going through a golden age of writing', she describes how she would like 'to look, too, at where the new ways of Irish writing might take us' and 'to read, in future iterations of [that] anthology, stories by Polish-Irish, Syrian-Irish, Traveller voices'.[39] Twenty-first-century Irish youth literature, while admirably dynamic in its engagement with girlhood and increasingly evolving in its recognition of diverse sexualities, still suffers from what Ebony Elizabeth Thomas terms 'an imagination gap'[40] around race, ethnicity, and intersectionality. Acknowledging and addressing this gap would involve a committed and systematic review, re-conceptualization, and re-design of the ideologies, infrastructures, and power systems of youth publishing and youth storytelling, including the active commissioning of new stories, mentoring diverse talent, and the decolonizing of systems of reviewing, literacy education, editing, book retailing, marketing, and librarianship. As Thomas states, this radical, emancipatory process ultimately 'requires decolonizing our fantasies and our dreams'.[41] Irish children's and young-adult literature to date has demonstrated an exciting and deepening potential for posing important questions around power, relationships, identities, and experiences, yet there are still more tales to tell, new storytellers to speak, and a wider range of realities to reflect.

NOTES

1. Tom Inglis, 'The Global and the Local: Mapping Changes in Irish Childhood', *Éire-Ireland* 46.3–4 (2011), 63–83 (p.63).

2. J. Zornado, *Inventing the Child: Culture, Ideology, and the Study of Childhood* (New York: Routledge, 2006), p.3.

3. Kimberley Reynolds, *Radical Children's Literature: Future Visions and Aesthetic Transformations in Juvenile Fiction* (Houndmills: Palgrave Macmillan, 2007), p.3.

4. Declan Kiberd, 'Literature, Childhood and Ireland', in *Expectations and Experiences: Children, Childhood and Children's Literature*, ed. by Clare Bradford and Valerie Coghlan (Lichfield: Pied Piper Publishing, 2007), pp.13–26 (p.23).

5. Jane Elizabeth Dougherty, 'Coming of Age in the 1990s: Mary Robinson and the Irish Literary Childhood', in *Children, Childhood and Irish Society, 1500 to the Present*, ed. by Maria Luddy and James M. Smith (Dublin: Four Courts Press, 2014), pp.339–356 (p.339).

6. Pádraic Whyte, *Irish Childhoods: Children's Fiction and Irish History* (Newcastle Upon Tyne: Cambridge Scholars Publishing, 2011), p.xii.

7. Robert Dunbar, 'Rarely Pure and Never Simple: The World of Irish Children's Literature', *The Lion and the Unicorn* 21.3 (1997), 309–320 (p.309).

8. Valerie Coghlan, 'Questions of Identity and Otherness in Irish Writing for Young People', *Neohelicon* 36.1 (2009), 91–102 (p.101).

9. Jane Elizabeth Dougherty, 'Nuala O'Faolain and the Unwritten Irish Girlhood', *New Hibernia Review* 11.2 (2007), 50–65 (p.50).

10. Patricia Coughlan, 'Irish Literature and Femininity in Postmodernity', *Hungarian Journal of English and American Studies* 10.1–2 (2004), 175–202 (p.180).

11. Susan Cahill, 'A Girl Is A Half-Formed Thing?: Girlhood, Trauma, and Resistance in Post-Tiger Irish Literature', *Lit: Literature Interpretation Theory* 28.2 (2017), 153–171 (p.161).

12. Cahill, p.156.

13. Alison Waller, *Constructing Adolescence in Fantastic Realism* (New York: Routledge, 2009), p.14.

14. Joseph Campbell, '"The Treatment for Stirrings": Dystopian Literature for Adolescents', in *Blast, Corrupt, Dismantle, Erase: Contemporary North American Dystopian Literature*, ed. by Brett Josel Grubisic, Gisèle M. Baxter, and Tara Lee (Waterloo: Wilfred Laurier University Press, 2014), pp.165–180 (p.172).

15. Alison Garden, 'Girlhood, Desire, Memory, and Northern Ireland in Lucy Caldwell's Short Fiction', *Contemporary Women's Writing* 12.3 (2018), 306–321 (p.308).

16. Emer O'Sullivan 'The Development of Modern Children's Literature in Late Twentieth-Century Ireland', *Signal* 81 (1996), 189–211 (p.206).

17. Valerie Coghlan, '"What Foot Does He Dig With? Inscriptions of Religious and Cultural Identity', in *Irish Children's Literature and Culture: New Perspectives on Contemporary Writing*, ed. by Valerie Coghlan and Keith O'Sullivan (London: Routledge, 2011), pp.55–69 (p.63).

18. Pádraic Whyte, 'Young Adult Fiction and Youth Culture', in *Irish Children's Literature and Culture: New Perspectives on Contemporary Writing*, ed. by Valerie Coghlan and Keith O'Sullivan (London: Routledge, 2011), pp.71–83 (p.71).

19. Catherine Spooner, *Contemporary Gothic* (London: Reaktion Books, 2006), p.87.

20. Anne Markey, 'Walking Into the Night: Growing Up with the Gothic', in *Irish Children's Literature and Culture: New Perspectives on Contemporary Writing*, ed. by Valerie Coghlan and Keith O'Sullivan (London: Routledge, 2011), pp.129–144 (p.141).

21. Glennis Byron and Sharon Deans, 'Teen Gothic', in *The Cambridge Companion to the Modern Gothic*, ed. by Jerrold E. Hogle (Cambridge: Cambridge University Press, 2014), pp.87–104.

22. Roberta Seelinger Trites, *Disturbing the Universe: Power and Repression in Adolescent Literature* (Iowa City: University of Iowa Press, 2000), p.83.

23. Byron and Deans, p.101.

24. Celia Keenan, 'Divisions in the World of Irish Publishing for Children: Re-Colonization or Globalization?', in *Divided Worlds: Studies in Children's Literature*, ed. by Mary Shine Thompson and Valerie Coghlan (Dublin: Four Courts Press, 2007), pp.196–208 (p.202).

25. Rhiannon Lucy Cosslett, 'From Baba Yaga to Hermione Granger: Why We're Spellbound by "Witcherature"', *The Guardian* 12 August 2019, <https://amp.theguardian.com/books/2019/aug/12/dark-charms-why-writers-are-spellbound-by-witches?utm_term=Autofeed&CMP=twt_gu&utm_medium=&utm_source=Twitter&__twitter_impression=true>, accessed 25 September 2019.

26. Sarah Maria Griffin, *Other Words For Smoke* (London: Titan Books, 2019), p.vii.

27. Griffin, p.10.

28. Griffin, pp.164, 161.

29. Deirdre Sullivan, *Perfectly Preventable Deaths* (London: Hot Key Books, 2019), p.98.

30. Moïra Fowley-Doyle, *All The Bad Apples* (London: Penguin, 2019), p.180.

31. Fowley-Doyle, p.328.

32. Fowley-Doyle, p.328.

33. Fowley-Doyle, p.339.
34. Susan Cahill, 'Bold Girls: A Literary History of Wild Irish Girls', *The Irish Times* 9 March 2018, <https://www.irishtimes.com/culture/books/bold-girls-a-literary-history-of-wild-irish-girls-1.3421134>, accessed 9 March 2018.
35. Whyte, 'Young Adult Fiction and Youth Culture', p.73.
36. Karen Coats, *Looking Glasses and Neverlands: Lacan, Desire, and Subjectivity in Children's Literature* (Iowa City: University of Iowa Press, 2004), p.125.
37. Clíona Ó Gallchoir, 'Whiteness and the Racialization of Irish Identity in Celtic Tiger Children's Fiction', *Breac: A Digital Journal of Irish Studies*, August 2016, <http://breac.nd.edu/articles/preface-to-childrens-literature-changing-paradigms-and-critical-perspectives-in-ireland-and-beyond/>, accessed 10 September 2016.
38. The Centre for Literacy in Primary Education, *Reflecting Realities: Survey of Ethnic Representation within UK Children's Literature 2018* (London: The Centre for Literacy in Primary Education, 2019).
39. Lucy Caldwell, 'Introduction', in *Being Various: New Irish Short Stories*, ed. by Lucy Caldwell (London: Faber and Faber, 2019), pp.1–6 (p.4).
40. Ebony Elizabeth Thomas, *The Dark Fantastic: Race and Imagination from Harry Potter to the Hunger Games* (New York: New York University Press, 2019).
41. Thomas, p.169.

Margaret Kelleher

Irish Culture(s): Hyphenated, Bilingual, or Plurilingual?

'ANGLO-IRISH', 1966

In 1966, Roger McHugh was appointed the first Professor of Anglo-Irish Literature and Drama at University College Dublin, the first such academic chair in 'Anglo-Irish' literature to be established worldwide. His papers, as held in UCD Archives, illuminate the long campaign conducted for the post's establishment. In 1949, soon after his appointment as statutory lecturer, McHugh submitted a memorandum to the President of UCD wherein he sharply criticised the paucity of attention to 'Anglo-Irish Studies' in the university, 'despite the potential wealth of this field and despite the fact that it is one of the chief cultural bonds we have with our people all over the world.'[1] The international benefit of fostering such studies was a key tenet of his argument, in particular the potential to advance cultural relations between Ireland and North America. 'A greater appreciation by English speakers throughout the world of Ireland's distinctive contribution to literature in English cannot but enhance her prestige', he wrote with some considerable prescience.[2]

McHugh's vision for the teaching of 'Anglo-Irish literature' was markedly inclusive in pedagogical terms: featuring the 'Gaelic tradition', 'Irish speech in English', as well as the 'comparative treatment of Anglo-Irish literature with English and American literature' – the latter he viewed as having a 'similar need to break away from the over-mastering prestige of English literature.' It is clear from the 1949 memorandum that he was especially exercised by the absence of opportunities for students to encounter Irish writing in English in their undergraduate course (then the subject of only a 'handful of lectures' in their third year). The short-term result of his lobbying, as a handwritten note on the memorandum bluntly records, was 'some reform in courses, otherwise continued myopia.' But in the longer term, and bolstered by events marking the 100th anniversary of W.B. Yeats's birth in 1965, McHugh's campaign was successful and the inauguration

Irish University Review 50.1 (2020): 143–152
DOI: 10.3366/iur.2020.0441
© Edinburgh University Press
www.euppublishing.com/iur

of the Chair in 1966 was quickly followed by the introduction of an MA in Anglo-Irish Literature, whose first students graduated in 1967.

The phrase 'Anglo-Irish literature' can now seem a fusty term, and partial in cultural scope; in 1998 the International Association for the Study of Anglo-Irish Literature shortened its adjective and pluralized its noun (now IASIL, the 'study of Irish literatures'), and in 2018 we at UCD changed the title of our masters programme to the MA in Irish Literature and Culture. But it is worth recalling the radicalism of McHugh's assertion: that Irish literature in English is a 'distinctive' tradition, different to American, Canadian, Australian, and indeed Scottish, English, or Welsh writing. And a further advantage of the term is the signal of cultural hybridity it delivers – albeit with some considerable historical baggage.

The epithet 'Anglo-Irish' as the description of a political class has a long history but its cultural application a much shorter one: some of the earliest instances of its use to classify language or literature date from the *Nation* writers of the 1840s. In the preface to his 1845 collection *The Ballad Poetry of Ireland*, Charles Gavan Duffy argued that 'There is an Anglo-Irish language as easily discriminated from London English as the dialect of Saxon spoken in the Lowlands of Scotland.... It is a dialect fired with the restless imagination, and coloured with the strong passions of our nation.'[3] Reviewing Duffy's collection that same year, Davis identified 'Anglo-Irish ballads' by Samuel Ferguson and others as a distinct and new poetic category.[4] A generation later, in his early anthologizing work, Yeats strategically deployed this duality of tradition and innovation to present Irish literature in English as the 'newcomer' to the cultural scene.[5]

By the late 1970s, an explicit critique of the term 'Anglo-Irish' was apparent; in the preface to his groundbreaking work *Synge and the Irish Language* (1979), Declan Kiberd noted that, while the epithet had been used for decades 'to describe the particular brand of English spoken in rural Ireland, under the historic influence of the Irish language', the more correct linguistic term was rather 'Hiberno-English' – English 'conditioned by the Irish *substratum*.'[6] Hiberno-English had proved to be the most successful linguistic legacy of the Irish Revival, and a means through which an Irish literary tradition, in English, could continue to be animated by the energy and flexibility of linguistic difference. However, in the decades after the Revival, this success also brought the increasing occlusion of Irish as a literary language, within celebratory accounts of national culture. And for readers and audiences, both at home and abroad, the pleasures of encountering Hiberno-English have rarely extended to an interest in engaging more substantially with its lesser-known linguistic progenitor.

This is very often the fate of a hyphenated culture: where parity of esteem is illusory or transient. But, in the light of both contemporary creative practice and historical antecedents, it is worth musing now on the possibilities extended by reconceptualising Irish literature and culture as bilingual (even plurilingual): not only as a 'backward look' but also as a means of securing more hospitable and open fora for cultural creativity in our present.

BILINGUAL IRELAND: A HISTORICAL VIEW

The historical reality of prevalent and persistent bilingualism in many regions of Ireland into the late nineteenth century has yet to find the attention it deserves within Irish literary and cultural scholarship. The 1891 census recorded the existence of 38,121 Irish-speaking monoglots in the country, a figure regularly invoked as proof of the near-death of the Irish language. Yet that same census also registered a figure of over 642,000 bilingual speakers, representing 13.6% of the population, and significantly before the Irish language revival could have made any significant imprint. And, even more significantly, the composition of bilingual speakers, English monoglots and Irish monoglots varied greatly from region to region. According to the census of 1881, the barony of Ross, home of Myles Joyce (who a year later would become the victim of a miscarriage of justice linked to the infamous Maamtrasna murders), had a population of 8,260 people, 7,350 of whom were recorded as Irish speakers and just under half of these were bilingual.[7]

Bilingualism was often a transitional social condition for individuals and families, and domestic scenes of quite dramatic language shift, where grandparents spoke limited English and grandchildren little Irish, feature in many nineteenth-century social commentaries. As historian Joe Lee has remarked, arguments regarding language change in Ireland tend to account for the acquisition of English rather than loss of Irish, and the possibility of enduring bilingualism can be seen as one of the great might-have-beens of Irish cultural history.[8] Rich evidence of bilingual practice, among individual speakers, and of 'languages crossing', in social and political occasions, exists throughout eighteenth-century and nineteenth-century Irish fiction, for example.[9]

Moving to the present, laudable efforts have been made in recent decades to broaden the census questions regarding language use, but on occasion their results have been invoked to support some disturbing forms of cultural sectarianism. Since 1996, the question on the Irish language in the Republic of Ireland census has comprised two parts: the first asks 'can you speak Irish?' and the second asks respondents to declare their frequency of speaking the language (within the education system or without: daily, weekly, less often, or never). In 2011 1,774,437 people, or 41.4% of respondents, indicated they could speak Irish; in

2016 the figure was 1,761,420, representing 39.8% of the population, a decrease of 13,017 on the 2011 figure.[10]

In 2011, the Republic's census schedule introduced a new question on 'foreign languages,' and, for those who answered 'yes' to speaking a foreign language at home, a query as to level of ability in speaking English. Polish emerged as the most common foreign language spoken at home, with a total of 119,526 self-declared speakers (followed by French 56,430 and Lithuanian 31,635). Five years later, in the 2016 census, Polish was again in first place, and of its 135,895 'home speakers', 27,197 were born in Ireland. Chinese and Arabic were in ninth and tenth place respectively, with recorded numbers of 17,584 and 16,072 speakers at home. Both in 2012 and 2017, the publication of these census results received considerable media coverage and comparisons with the Irish-language figures were frequently drawn. While a lone few commentators sought to convey the complexities of the census structure – wherein the speaking of Polish and the speaking of Irish were differently measured – the simplistic slogan that 'Irish is now the third most spoken language in Ireland' has gained much political currency.

The census for Northern Ireland in 2011 is especially revelatory regarding the still contested subjects of language and identity. In that year new questions were introduced concerning national identity, main language, ability to speak English (for those who entered a language other than English as 'main') and ability in Ulster-Scots.[11] From a population of 1.7 million aged 3 and over, 10.65% of respondents declared they had some ability in Irish; and 8.08% in Ulster-Scots. The categories employed within the tabulated report are at first reading quite unwieldy and on second reading quite startling: 'understand, but cannot read, write, or speak Irish/Ulster-Scots', 'speak but do not read or write Irish/Ulster-Scots', 'speak and read but do not write Irish/Ulster-Scots', 'speak, read, write and understand Irish/Ulster-Scots', and 'other combination of skills.' Most strikingly, a footnote accompanies both tables, warning that 'An ability to speak, read or write Irish/Ulster-Scots does not imply an ability to understand Irish/Ulster-Scots unless stated. Persons in these categories may or may not have the ability to understand Irish/Ulster-Scots.' This convoluted formulation, quite bizarre in its socio-linguistic implications, is itself an eloquent testimony to the ever more politicized arena of language affiliation on this island.[12]

THE *IUR*'S BILINGUAL INVESTIGATIONS

Reviewing the publication history of the *Irish University Review* over the last fifty years, two articles stand out as agenda-setting interventions with respect to further work in the area of Irish bilingualism. The first,

Michael Cronin's article, 'Babel's Suburbs: Irish Verse Translation in the 1980s', was published in 1991, as part of a special issue on the Contexts of Irish Writing. Here Cronin provided an incisive overview of what he termed 'the Irish translation risorgimento' in two forms: firstly the extensive translation of Irish-language poetry into English, and secondly the publication of translations by Irish poets from other languages into English (by Raven Arts Press and Dedalus Press). Notwithstanding the high number of such publications, he persuasively highlighted the paucity of 'public theoretical reflection on the art and more particularly the science of translation'. This absence contrasts, quite surprisingly, to the prevalence of such commentary in the nineteenth century which was distinguished, as Cronin notes, by a 'constant sensitivity to the complexity and specificity of translation.' In the years since this article was published, and despite Cronin's own leading contributions to the field, that specificity of textual and theoretical attention is still rare, and bilingual editions are greeted more as social contributions – the recognition of two or more cultures – than as linguistic and aesthetic advances worthy of detailed engagement.

The second article, by Carolina P. Amador-Moreno, published in the Spring/Summer issue of 2009, is entitled 'Remembering Language: Bilingualism, Hiberno-English, and the Gaeltacht Peasant Memoir' and is distinguished by close textual readings of a bilingual body of work. The range of memoir extends from works by Mící Mac Gabhann and Séamus Ó Grianna, first written in Irish, to novels by Patrick MacGill written in English. As a group of texts, these works vividly illustrate how language borrowings and cultural transfers took place in the early twentieth century, and in both directions: not only borrowings from Irish into English-language usage but also vice versa. As she notes, these novels and memoirs have deep social and socio-linguistic value, as 'our best available source for Gaeltacht speech practices, discourse and conversation analysis, the ethnography of speaking, and ethnostylistics around the turn of the twentieth century', and capture in vivid detail how language change occurs in spoken practice.[13]

Amador-Moreno's work also provides an excellent remedy to the bifurcation of language traditions and literary careers that bedevils many surveys of Irish writing. The case of Brendan Behan is a notable instance; for many years, critical attention to his writings in English was isolated from his Irish-authored work. The comparative reading given of An Giall and The Hostage by Michael Pierse in his 2014 IUR article is an important exception and points to the value of more such translingual studies, of the work of Éilís Ní Dhuibhne, Michael Hartnett, Celia de Fréine, Pearse Hutchinson, and Doireann Ní Ghríofa to name just some bilingual writers. Similarly, the IUR section dedicated to the work of de Fréine in 2018, including an interview with Lia Mills and article by

Luz Mar González-Arias, is a model worth emulating in future issues.[14] Useful theoretical models may be gleaned more generally from recent comparative analyses of the French and English work of bilingual Beckett (which also provide suggestive insights on his use of Hiberno-English and references to Ireland). As Sam Slote has remarked regarding Beckett's trilogy of *Molloy, Malone meurt*, and *L'Innommable*, 'the three novels and their translations are a kind of linguistic atopia, neither French, nor English, nor Irish.'[15] Relatedly, Chiara Montini has provided an illuminating account of Beckett's pre-war writings, viewed as 'polyglot monolingualism' ('la monolinguisme polyglotte').[16]

BILINGUAL AND PLURILINGUAL CREATIVE PRACTICE TODAY

Many contemporary Irish writers are bilingual speakers, and some plurilingual; consequently their works, even if apparently monolingual with respect to the language of publication, are richly polyglot in their range of reference, and contain a diversity of idiom which critical studies can struggle to comprehend fully. The author Eiléan Ní Chuilleanáin is a compelling example: the intricate register of her poetry draws from her translation work in Irish, Italian, and Romanian as well as her career-long commitment to the greater dissemination of bilingual work and writings in translation. In her poem 'Gloss/Clós/Glas', the meditation on language use offers the following suggestive epithet: 'The rags of language are streaming like weathervanes, / Like weeds in water they turn with the tide'.[17] In a recent interview with UCD doctoral student Jennifer Preston, Éilís Ní Dhuibhne commented: 'I think I would like to be able to write a text that was totally bilingual, that is in both languages, but that's an unacceptable thing to do from the point of view of readers it seems.'[18]

Current discourse regarding Irish creative practice and the language of creation fails in particular to acknowledge the plurilingualism of many Irish-language writers, as Máirín Nic Eoin has observed. Her 2019 IASIL plenary on 'Directions in Twentieth-Century Irish-language Literary Criticism' includes the following valuable insights: 'Many of the best-known contemporary writers, and a majority of our literary scholars, are plurilingual. Many of them spent formative or extensive periods of their lives outside of Ireland, and not solely in Anglophone countries. In fact, in certain cases motivation to write in Irish can be traced to those periods of immersion in other languages and cultures. I would argue that a full understanding of what is happening in Irish-language writing, especially over the last fifty years, calls for a broad comparative literary approach, one that transcends or at least complicates the Irish/English binary.'[19]

The traditional structures and monolingual modes of literary publication in Ireland have also posed significant obstacles to writers choosing to write bilingually and such challenges have now become especially pressing as contemporary literary production moves beyond an Irish/English binary. The creative work produced by the newest generation of Irish writers brings both a plurality of language (Hindi, Igbo, Polish, etc) and a diversity of genre (performance poetry, digital poetry, memoir), factors which require ever more versatility on the part of contemporary publishing platforms. In 2018 the Arts Council published a short but incisive 'Literature Policy and Strategy' document, the first for this specific area in many years, in which it states the Council's interest in bringing to the fore voices that are 'new, risky or experimental'. The document contains a laudable commitment to sustain 'diverse platforms – journals, pamphlets, new media' given what it rightly terms commercial publishing's 'increasingly risk-averse nature.'[20] In addition, it recognizes the particular vulnerability of Irish-language literature and its publishers (evident in the closure of a number of fora, including publisher Cois Life, in recent years): 'This vulnerable sector faces a significant number of challenges, including audience development, readership, translation, partnerships, promotion and critical writing.'[21]

However this strategy is more sparse in detail regarding concrete measures, and recognition of the richly bilingual and multilingual practice among many young writers is conspicuously absent. Looking to the future, more proactive plans and considered thinking will be needed to bridge the large gap that continues to exist between the publishing establishment – its modes of production, funding models, and editorial authorities – and artists from families and communities more recently-established in Ireland. To date much of this writing has been supported and mentored by online publishing platforms and by smaller publishers such as Banshee Press (also publisher of the dynamic literary journal *Banshee*), Skein Press (publisher of Melatu Uche Okorie's *This Hostel Life*), and Dedalus Press (publisher of *Writing Home: The 'New Irish' Poets* edited by Pat Boran and Chiamaka Enyi-Amadi). Especially urgent is the provision of sustained funding that can allow these excellent initiatives to achieve more than a passing impact, to become visible to wider audiences, and to become embedded in our educational curricula.

The hyphenation of Irish culture is now more interestingly 'Irish-Nigerian' or 'Lithuanian-Irish', though such terms have as yet a limited currency. In the introduction to *Writing Home*, an anthology featuring fifty poets with countries of origin ranging from Angola and India to Nigeria and Pakistan, Boran acknowledges his editorial discomfort with 'New Irish' as a label: 'The most distinguished practitioners push beyond the limitation of labels to make something new. For instance we might reasonably ask: When do the "New Irish" become the "Old Irish" or just the "Irish", without any need for qualification? That said, a little unease is not unusual (or entirely useless) at the start of a journey. If nothing else, it quickens the heartbeat and ensures that we pay attention.'[22]

I close with one selection from this anthology, written by Chiamaka Enyi-Amadi, a recent BA graduate from UCD's School of English, Drama and Film. Her poem not only ensures that readers 'pay attention' but is also a welcome reminder to us as teachers of the vital forces of creative change that our students continue to provide:

> Once upon a time a little girl turns eleven and is transformed into a new EU citizen. But then she spends her first Irish winter desperate, weeping, her mother shrouding her in a floral duvet, her stalk-thin, pre-teen body pressed against the radiator in the hallway of their new house all one frosty night ….

> And ever after? – a delicate time,
> Spent in the trauma of self-
> renewal, preparing
> to be whole again. (from 'Women and Other Flowers')[23]

NOTES

1. The President of UCD at this time was Michael Tierney; Jeremiah J. Hogan was Professor of English and also Dean of the Faculty of Arts (Hogan would later serve as Registrar from 1953 to 1964 and President 1964 to 1972). Roger McHugh became Professor of English in 1965 and first Professor of Anglo-Irish Literature and Drama in 1966; he retired in 1978 and died in 1987. Source: Roger McHugh Papers, University College Dublin Archives, LA51/1. My thanks to Fiona McHugh and the McHugh family for permission to reproduce this quotation.

2. Other correspondence points to McHugh's larger objective to establish a 'centre of Anglo-Irish studies in Dublin'. In May 1948, Celtic scholar D.A. Binchy wrote from Corpus Christi College, Oxford, supporting his suggestion in the following glowing terms: 'I can think of nothing that is as badly wanted. It is a disgrace to Ireland that such a centre was not established years ago. Even still it could do invaluable work while a number of survivors of the heroic age are at hand to give information which will otherwise certainly perish and can never be recovered.' Source: private papers of Roger McHugh held by his family; my thanks to Fiona McHugh for this reference.

3. Charles Gavan Duffy, *The Ballad Poetry of Ireland* (1845; Dublin: Duffy, 1857), p.xxii.

4. See Matthew Campbell, 'Poetry in English, 1830–1880', in *Cambridge History of Irish Literature*, 2 vols, ed. by Margaret Kelleher and Philip O'Leary (Cambridge: Cambridge University Press, 2006), vol. 1, pp.500–543 (p.518).

5. In 'Modern Irish Poetry', a prefatory essay to his anthology *A Book of Irish Verse*, Yeats dates the emergence of a poetic voice for 'English-speaking Ireland' to the early nineteenth century; *A Book of Irish Verse* (London: Methuen, 1900), pp.xviii–ix.

6. Declan Kiberd, *Synge and the Irish Language* (London: Methuen, 1979), p.x. Kiberd went on to suggest that Anglo-Irish 'as a technical term' would more appropriately be

applied 'to that brand of Irish, known as "Béarlachas", which has been greatly contaminated by English usage.'

7. For more information on the history of bilingualism in nineteenth-century Ireland, see chapter two of Margaret Kelleher, *Maamtrasna Murders: Language, Life and Death in Nineteenth-Century Ireland* (Dublin: University College Dublin Press, 2018), pp.28–59.

8. J.J. Lee, *Ireland 1912–1985: Politics and Society* (Cambridge: Cambridge University Press, 1989), pp.662–3.

9. See Tom Dunne, '"On the boundaries of two languages": Representing Irish in novels in English, 1800–1950', in *Culture and Society in Ireland since 1752: Essays in Honour of Gearóid Ó Tuathaigh*, ed. by John Cunningham and Niall Ó Ciosáin, (Dublin: Lilliput Press, 2015), pp.44–63.

10. See http://www.cso.ie/en/census/census2011reports/census2011thisisirelandpart1 (accessed 28 January 2017). Irish is compulsory in primary and secondary schools in the Republic of Ireland; therefore, the figure for respondents who said they used Irish outside of the education system is a more accurate reflection of usage: 77,185 daily (from a population of 4.57 million), 110,642 weekly, and 613,236 less often. Of the 77,185 daily Irish speakers not in the education system, 54,010 lived outside the Gaeltacht areas (government recognized Irish-speaking districts).

11. See http://www.nisra.gov.uk/Census/key_report_2011.pdf (accessed 28 January 2017). In 1991, a question on ability to read, write, or speak in the Irish language was added to the Northern Ireland census, ending an eighty-year gap in the asking of this question for that region (since the last all-island census of 1911).

12. A census is taken every five years in the Republic of Ireland and every ten years in Northern Ireland. The 2011 results showed that the second 'main language' of Northern Ireland was Polish, with 17,731 respondents or 1.02% of the population; 'Irish (Gaelic)' came fourth, after Lithuanian, at 0.24 (4,130 residents), and Ulster-Scots was in forty-fifth place with sixty-five residents citing it as their main language. Some of the more detailed demographic breakdowns reveal interesting patterns of language use and gender: of the 184,898 people who declared some ability in Irish, 88,352 were male and 96,546 were female; conversely for Ulster-Scots the 140,204 speakers included a majority of male speakers (74,406) and a minority of female speakers (65,798).

13. Amador-Moreno has extended this work in her 2019 monograph *Orality in Written Texts: Using Historical Corpora to Investigate Irish English 1700–1900*, published in the Routledge Applied Corpus Linguistics series (London and New York: Routledge, 2019).

14. See *Irish University Review*, 48.2 (2018), pp.169–201, comprising 'In Full Voice: Celia de Fréine in Conversation with Lia Mills', two poems by de Fréine, and 'Impossible Returns: The Trope of the Soldier in Celia de Fréine's Poetry' by Luz Mar González-Arias.

15. Sam Slote, 'Bilingual Beckett', in *The New Cambridge Companion to Samuel Beckett*, ed. by Dirk Van Hulle (Cambridge: Cambridge University Press, 2015), pp.114–125, p.122.

16. Chiara Montini, *La bataille du soliloque: Genèse de la poétique bilingue de Samuel Beckett* (Amsterdam: Rodopi, 2007), p.24.

17. Eiléan Ní Chuilleanáin, 'Gloss/Clós/Glas', from *The Girl who Married the Reindeer* (Oldcastle: Gallery Press, 2001), p.46.

18. Interview with Éilís Ní Dhuibhne conducted by Jennifer Preston as part of her doctoral dissertation, *Idir Eatarthu: Between or Both? A Study of Contemporary Irish Creative Literary Bilingualism*; my thanks to Jennifer Preston for this reference.

19. Máirín Nic Eoin, 'Margins or Thresholds? Directions in Twentieth-century Irish-language Literary Criticism', Plenary Paper, IASIL Conference, Trinity College Dublin, 23 July 2019. I am very grateful to Professor Nic Eoin for sharing the text of her address with me.

20. 'Literature Policy and Strategy' can be accessed at http://www.artscouncil.ie/Publications/All/Literature-Policy-and-Strategy-2018 (accessed 13 October 2019).

21. 'Literature Policy and Strategy', p.4.

22. *Writing Home: The 'New Irish' Poets*, ed. by Pat Boran and Chiamaka Enyi-Amadi (Dublin: Dedalus Press, 2019), introduction, p.xiv.

23. *Writing Home*, pp.30–31. My thanks to Chiamaka Enyi-Amadi and Dedalus Press for permission to quote this extract.

Éilís Ní Dhuibhne Almqvist

Reflections on Memoir
as a New Genre

1. 'OUR LIKE WILL NOT BE SEEN AGAIN.'

'*Scríobhas go mionnchruinn ar a lán dár gcúrsaí d'fhonn go mbeadh cuimhne i bpoll éigin orthu... mar ná beidh ár leithéidí arís ann,*' ('I have written very accurately about many of our activities so that they would be rememberered in some corner or other ... because our like will not be seen again') is one of the closing lines of Tomás ó Criomhthain's book, *An t-Oileánach,*[1] one of the first of a rich series of regional memoirs written in Irish in the mid-twentieth century. Yet though, arguably, the great classics of twentieth-century Irish language prose are memoirs, the genre is considerably less significant in the canon of Irish literature in English, during the same period. The outstanding works of twentieth-century Anglo-Irish prose have been novels and short stories. Some of these classics take the form of Bildungsromans, such as James Joyce's *Portrait of the Artist as a Young Man* (1917), Edna O'Brien's *The Country Girls* (1960), John McGahern's *The Barracks* (1963) and so on – they are auto-fiction. But auto-fiction is not memoir, it is fiction which uses some autobiographical material. It does not purport to be factually 'true', but the opposite. Given this inheritance, what is the relationship now between Irish writers writing in English and the memoir?

2. A MEMOIR BOOM?

My impression is that, in Ireland, the English language memoir has emerged as a key genre of literary prose recently in the twenty-first century, and as part of an international trend. And it is a fashion which I have followed. Recently, after a lifetime of writing fiction, auto-fiction and other kinds of fiction, I wrote a memoir, which will be discussed later in this essay. Already in 2001 Claire Armitstead, literary editor of *The Guardian*, identified 'the rise and rise of the memoir':

> Why are memoirs so popular? What exactly is a memoir? These are questions that prompt some head-scratching.[2]

Irish University Review 50.1 (2020): 153–163
DOI: 10.3366/iur.2020.0442
© Edinburgh University Press
www.euppublishing.com/iur

And Jack Smith, writing in *The Writer* in 2018, has this to say:

> Once upon a time, fiction ruled the market. Today, however, nonfiction is just as heavily competitive – and memoir is a key corner of that genre.[3]

Meanwhile, Neil Gelzlinger expressed a curmudgeonly view of the genre's trendiness:

> A moment of silence, please, for the lost art of shutting up.
>
> There was a time when you had to earn the right to draft a memoir, by accomplishing something noteworthy or having an extremely unusual experience or being such a brilliant writer that you could turn relatively ordinary occurrences into a snapshot of a broader historical moment....
>
> These days, if you're planning to browse the "memoir" listings on Amazon, make sure you're in a comfortable chair, because that search term produces about 40,000 hits, or 60,000, or 160,000, depending on how you execute it.[4]

But is the general impression of the memoir boom borne out by the facts?

A quick search of the catalogue of the National Library of Ireland reveals that in the period 2000–2019, 431 memoirs were catalogued. (These are books which include the word memoir somewhere in the title or subject description.) 331 memoirs were catalogued in the 20 years 1980–2000, and 350 in the period 1960–80.Since the National Library of Ireland has had a policy of acquiring only books 'of Irish interest' – i.e. books by Irish authors, or about Ireland – since about 1960, it isgenerally safe to assume that all memoirs catalogued since then are by Irish writers or dealing with life in Ireland. We can also assume that all books published in 2019 have not yet been catalogued so the figure for 2000–2019 will be somewhat greater than 431. It must be borne in mind also that as well as getting current publications, the Libray acquires old books, to fill gaps in the collections, so the figures are not a precise record of publications in any specific period. Nevertheless they provide a rough guide thereto. The number of Irish memoirs from the 21st century so far would thus appear to be about 25% higher than the figure for the previous forty years. This does not really support the view that there has been a recent huge explosion in memoir writing, that the 'market is saturated.' So why do we believe the genre has 'taken off'?

It may be that critics and readers are paying more attention to it, and that memoirs are receiving more publicity than hitherto. Or is it rather that a new kind of memoir is emerging, a kind of memoir which was not common in the past, and which is developing aesthetically and artistically, in a manner which allows it to compete with the novel?

3. CATEGORIES: FROM THE REGIONAL ADULT
TO THE ORDINARY CHILD

There are many categories of memoir, just as there are many kinds of novel, or of play, or of folktale – or any genre of 'literature'. In the context of Irish literary history, the regional memoir forms a distinct sub-genre. Alice Taylor's extremely successful *To School Through the Fields* (1988) can possibly be shelved in the same category as the Irish language regional literature. The memoir of rebels is another early 20th century Irish sub-genre: Dan Breen's *My Fight for Irish Freedom* (1924) might be the prototype. The most common kind of memoir, though, was until recently the celebrity memoir, a sub-type which continues to thrive.

What has been growing in popularity recently, however, is what Neil Gelzlinger disparages as the'non-celebrity memoir', what we could more neutrally term life writing which describes and analyses the everyday experiences of people who are not famous – in other words, its subject matter is similar to that of the novel. Some memoirs of this kind have always been with us, particularly those written through the lens of 'childhood'. Mary Carberry's *The Farm by Lough Gur* (1937) is an early Irish example, as is, arguably, David Thomson's *Woodbrook* (1974). But in Ireland since the 1990s the memoir of childhood has flourished, and is perhaps the harbinger of the later sub-genres of personal memoir.

Childhood is an experience we have all had – and writers in particular may never quite grow up. Nevertheless, children do not as a rule write books about themselves (some children have been published writers, but they are few and far between, and usually have not written memoir or autobiograpy, but stories about vegetables or animals or fairies). Childhood is therefore an area of life which we experience and know, but which is dependent on adults for documentation. Writers of fiction frequently draw on the well of childhood experience: any random catalogue of novelists or short story writers provides rich examples of prose inspired directly or indirectly by childhood memories (and this may be particularly true of Irish writers, from James Joyce to Claire Keegan to Sally Rooney). It is the well that keeps giving, the territory which is both intensely familiar and a foreign island that demands exploration. Ross Skelton, a writer and psycholanalyst, writes, in his magnificent memoir, *Eden Halt:*

> My relationship with my parents … had never been good, but now that they were dead I could not turn to them for help. Yet I kept writing what would eventually become this memoir of childhood. I now realize that every day I spent in their ghostly company was invisible mending; that finally I was beginning to understand, to love them and at last to see myself in them.[5]

The most well-known of all recent memoirs of Irish childhood is Frank McCourt's *Angela's Ashes* (1996). A work which straddles the border between fiction and autobiography, this account of the childhood of an unknown schoolteacher was published in 1996, won the Pulitzer Prize, and became an international best-seller. Nuala O' Faolain's *Are You Somebody* (1998), dealing very much with her childhood and young adulthood, appeared two years later – though not such a huge international success as Frank McCourt's memoir, it enjoyed considerable success in Ireland. Alice Taylor's *To School Through the Fields* (1994), while it has something in common with the 'regional memoirs' in Irish, is also a childhood memoir – romanticizing the rural idyll, in sharp contrast to the painful memories of McCourt and O'Faolain. Carlo Gebler – one of Ireland's most prolific memoirists – published *Father and I* in 2000. This is a childhood memoir, but one with a foot in the celebrity category, since Carlo is the son of Ernest Gebler and Edna O'Brien, one of Ireland's most famous novelists.

Memoirs of childhood continue to be popular. Recent examples which come to mind – because they are on my bookshelves – are Mary Rose Callaghan's *The Deep End: a Memoir of Growing Up* (2016), Colbert Kearney's *Down by the Liffey Side* (2019), and Thomas Kilroy's *Over the Backyard Wall* (2019).

The very newest kind of memoir deals not with childhood, happy or miserable, however, but with specific adult life events of a traumatic nature. Topics which recur are illness, mental health, drug abuse, death, and bereavement. Lia Mills' *In Your Face* (2007) deals with her own experience of cancer; Ruth Fitzmaurice's *I Found My Tribe* (2017) describes her husband's illness and death and her reactions to the challenges posed by both; Sinéad Gleeson's collection of memoir-essays, *Constellations* (2019), focuses in particular on her own lifelong illnesses. Emilie Pine's *Notes to Self* (2018) is a collection of essays about the difficulty of coping with a parent's serious illness, growing up as the child of divorced parents, the tragedy of childlessness, and other challenging aspects of female life in Ireland. Like the best of the memoirs, the experiences recounted and analysed are simultaneously intensely personal and universal.

In the hands of a skilled writer, the memoirs of illness, or of grief and loss, use the techniques of the novelist. McCourt's *Angela's Ashes* is a good example – his memoir has a clear narrative structure, characters are vividly drawn, there is a great deal of dialogue. Some of Pine's essays in *Notes to Self* are similarly novelistic. The opening essay, 'Notes on Intemperance', has a clear narrative arc, strongly drawn characters, and plenty of tension. All the essays employ arresting dramatic opening lines:

'I pee on sticks and into sample cups'[6]

'My parents separated when I was five and my sister was a baby.'[7]

'I'm not here. That is what I'm thinking as his hands are on me, his hands and mouth and the rest of him...'[8]

'Famously, the trick of good writing is bleeding onto the page.'[9]

These first lines all have an element of surprise, or shock, but also a concrete physical image, indeed a concrete anatomical image, appropriately for a book which is much concerned with the body – pee, baby, hands, blood. Although Pine has said in interviews that she never considered using the raw material of her essays for fiction – novel or short stories – the techniques of the fiction writer are evident in the essays. This is characteristic of the 'new' memoir genre. We have always had well-composed literary memoirs which share the novel's techniques – for example, Thomson's *Woodbrook* – and novels and short stories which are close to memoir or life writing. But perhaps in the twenty-first century there are more of both. Memoirists acknowledge that memory is selective and their books are constructs. The relationship with fact in each case exists, but is complex.

4. LIKE A NOVEL

Some readers have commented that my memoir, *Twelve Thousand Days*,[10] reads like a novel – a comment which I found flattering. Although I don't want to write a critique of my own book, it occurs to me that it is more like a collection of connected short stories than a novel – and that that resemblance would have come about spontaneously since I am primarily a short story writer.

Twelve Thousand Days was written in response to the sudden death of my husband in 2013. In my decision to write and publish it, I was influenced by several previous works: Mills' *In My Face*, for example, was a 'hospital memoir' which provided a model for writing about illness and hospitals; but books about death and grief were to the forefront: Joyce Carol Oates' *The Widow's Story* (2011), Joan Didion's *The Year of Magical Thinking* (2005), C.S. Lewis's *A Grief Observed* (1961), and Julian Barnes's *Levels of Life* (2013).

In the aftermath of my husband's death, I had no wish to write fiction. Instead I wrote a journal. I had begun this already when he was in hospital, during the five days before he died. I was not writing this diary for therapeutic reasons – I don't think so – but in order to have a record of what happened, and of my reactions to what was happening. I knew I would forget the details of the events and the details of the emotions surrounding the events, if I did not document them as they occurred. Obviously, the practice of writing autobiographically at this difficult time also fulfilled my everyday need, born of habit, just to write something. At the time, documenting reality was easier than inventing fiction.

Why?

Making things up is a kind of child's play. But it's not easy for an adult, because it is harder to move from the real world into the world of make believe when you are older. Except when you *are* asleep, the transition requires an act of will – such as, the act of will you need to make before diving into a deep pool from a cliff top, or jumping out of a plane with a parachute attached to your back. Instinctively you resist taking the plunge; you want to stay safe on land. And then, when you jump, if you are writing fiction you must stay in the otherworld for a reasonable time. It's not a ten second dip. You have to give yourself up to the game, totally. You need to explore the depths for hours at a time.

It's never easy to perform this switch from the 'real world' to the world of imagination and, for at least a year or so after the death of my husband, I couldn't do it. Real life at this time of traumatic transition was more powerful and extraordinary than anything I could imagine. I was stuck. My feet were in a grave, his grave, and I didn't have the will, or the wish, to get out of there.

And so, I stayed and engaged in 'life writing'.

After a few months, as well as jotting down notes on my experiences and emotions as a bereaved person, I began to write about my life with my husband – our first days together. The diary notes written in the months after his death dealt with his absence. By remembering and writing times past I was able to relive the days when he was alive and so to keep him with me. I was aware of this as a motive – a cowardly motive – while I was engaging in the writing. So it was a form of escapism, after all. It was magical thinking, magical writing, it was a false sort of conjuring trick which I played on myself. But I didn't have to invent the story, because it was my own story. All I had to do was remember.

The idea of remembering specific days, and constructing the memoir in days, came from Philip Larkin's poem, 'Days', which I quote as a promethium to the memoir.[11] It's a poem which frequently plays in my memory and so I am used to thinking of life as a sequence of days. Since I like to locate short stories in very limited periods – a few hours, or a day or a night – it is natural for me to create narratives confined by the frame of a day, rather than more protracted periods, such as thirty five years (the length of my relationship with my husband). And, indeed, memoir in general deals with selected moments in a life, rather than with the whole life – the challenge, and the frequent downfall, of biography and autobiography. It is not possible to narrate everything, and the stricter the chronology in a biography the harder it is to create a readable work.

While I began to use the pattern of days, selected from the beginning and end of our life together, quite early on in my drafting of my book, at first I wrote exactly what came into my head. For the latter days, I had my notes written as events had occurred. For the early days – in the 1970s – I was relying on my memory. So the book is a combination of facts recorded on the spot, and 'fact' remembered from several decades earlier. 'What is remembered' is the title of a short story by Alice Munro.[12] What does anyone remember? Definitely not everything. In fact, as I was writing the book I became more and more aware that most of my life is completely forgotten. What is remembered is a limited selection of days, moments, people, episodes. And how is that selection made?

Randomly?

Sometimes, yes. Some of my memories seem pointless (my daughter-in-law, a Lacanian psychoanalyst, would probably tell me that they are the ones to pay attention to). But on the whole what is remembered are the moments, or days, which are of obvious emotional significance. I did not actually remember the day I first met my husband, because it was not very important, although I remember vividly the day I first heard about him, as it happens (a random memory, it seems to me, involving not him but characters who were vivid, but who played a minor role in my life. Unless…) I remember the first time I felt attracted to him. I remember the first date, the first night together … many firsts. But most of the days of our life are forgotten, all those ordinary good and bad days when we went to work, ate dinner, washed the dishes.

Only a writer like Karl Ove Knausgaard can write about the small details of ordinary life, because he documents it as it happens, just as I documented exactly what was happening between 2 November 2013 and sometime in mid-2014. For the most part, the long-term conscious memory holds on to the more dramatic moments. Insofar as it does this, memory is akin to a storyteller, or a playwright. Falling in love, having children (or not having them), being ill, dying, are commonplace experiences. But they are significant commonplace experiences. They constitute the drama of the 'ordinary' life. And these moments are what make their way into most memoirs, including mine. That is why a memoir may read like a novel.

Memory itself is a kind of novelist. I don't think that is a fanciful claim. Like a novelist, or a storyteller, or a writer of soap opera, memory extracts from the vast expanse of a life the main plot points, the moments of high comedy or tragedy, and inscribes them on the mind. In addition, memory is quite clever at providing settings. It pinpoints locations of significance. It even selects characters. The main protagonist in memoir is usually the author of the story, so the hero is conveniently close at hand. Other characters with their traits and quirks people the narrative memory has written – principal characters, anti-heroes, and indeed minor characters who are remembered because they are quirky and colourfully eccentric: the Mr Micawbers and Mrs Flytes and Sam Wellers of our lives. Remembered not because they are important, but because they are, well, just memorable.

That is what is remembered.

What is not remembered, at least not by me, is that key component of fiction or drama, namely dialogue. Rarely can I recall exactly what anyone said thirty or forty years ago. There are exceptions – fixed forms of expression, such as proverbs, or jokes, that certain people used – my husband as it happened had many such formulae. Or unusual memorable lines uttered at key moments, or occasionally lines remembered because they were hilariously funny, or absurdly ridiculous, or hurtful. When I was writing my memoir, I had to invent the dialogue, based on what seemed likely for the character and the occasion. It is in the creation of dialogue that memoir most blatantly overlaps with fiction. This occurs in oral anecdote narration as well as in written life writing. Good narrators of personal anecdotes usually enliven their accounts with dialogue. But the only recorder which documents dialogue accurately is a tape recorder. Most of the dialogue in memoir is made up.

Did I find the writing of my memoir therapeutic? This is the question I am most frequently asked. And the answer has to be, yes. It was therapeutic in the early days in the way that any activity or work on which I concentrated, could concentrate, was therapeutic. It passed the time. It helped me get through the days as I moved through time towards the light at the end of the tunnel. So did walking, swimming, watching movies, reading memoirs, reading novels which deal with bereavement (like the Brontë's novels), being with friends, going on holidays. Teaching creative writing. I don't think it was more therapeutic than any of those activities, but I could be wrong.

When the time came to shape the raw material into a book, into 'the memoir', I was much recovered from the shock of bereavement. Craft, artistic decisions, editing, were definitely helpful in assisting me on my journey back to normality, back to 'being myself.' Art in that way is always therapeutic, no matter what any writer tells you. That its primary function is something else – to make a good book – does not alter the therapeutic value of the process for the creator.

Publishing the memoir was a different story. I am always nervous about publication, but publishing something which tells the factual truth is much more terrifying than publishing fiction. There is no fig-leaf to protect the writer or those she is writing about. A memoir may be artistically shaped, well written, it may 'read like a novel'. But it is presented as the truth. I knew from the experience of other memoirists that even the most benign memoir has the potential to offend and annoy some people, for a variety of reasons. Either their memories do not coincide with those of the writer, or they would prefer not to have family linen washed in public – or they simply don't want a memoir relating to their family to exist at all. Writers of fiction contend with some of this sort of reaction, but writers of memoir are much more exposed. Reaction to my memoir was very enthusiastic, among critics and friends. Admirers included several close friends of my husband. But inevitably and predictably there were a few malcontents. As a writer, and particularly a writer of memoir, one must be prepared to suffer the critics. It's one of the risks you take.

5. NOT QUITE STORIES

The final four works in this book are not quite stories. They form a separate unit, one that is autobiographical in feeling, though not, sometimes, entirely so in fact. I believe they are the first and last – and the closest – things I have to say about my own life.[13]

Thus Alice Munro, in what is – alas – probably her final collection of short stories, *Dear Life*.

Alice Munro has written fourteen collections of short stories, about 200 stories in all. Many are clearly entirely fictional. Others appear to draw on settings, feelings, and to some extent characters inspired by 'real life'. Some of the content of the final four 'not quite stories', for instance, can be matched, partially, with fictional short stories. (For example, the girl called Diane in 'Dear Life' corresponds in some ways to a girl called Frances in a short story 'Fathers'.)[14] The piece 'The Eye' includes a setting faintly reminiscent of a house in 'Thanks for the Ride' in *Dance of the Happy Shades*.[15] Many of the settings of the short stories correspond to places in Southern Ontario, where the author was born and lives. I had been longing for a long time for some sort of memoir from Alice Munro, a memoir like John McGahern's, which explained to an extent the connection between his life story and his fiction. But, interestingly, she has declared that what she will offer in the way of autobiography is this minute suite of four 'not quite stories'.

Perhaps, though, it is in this interesting borderland that the newly emerging genres of memoir and novel are located. The straight memoir and many kinds of traditional novel thrive. But in the newest kind of work the boundary between fiction and life-writing seems to be breaking down. Knausgaard's *Min Kamp* can be read as a novel or as a memoir. Rachel Cusk's trilogy of novels – *Outline* (2014), *Transit* (2016), and *Kudos* (2018) – cross the border between fiction and non-fiction. Well-crafted memoirs 'read like novels' and utilize the techniques of fiction. Readers, far from demanding that the stories they read are entirely invented and 'novel', seem to be looking for the opposite. True life stories. And 'true life stories' are no longer summarily dismissed as some sort of third-rate literature, but as works of literary merit.

One can speculate about the reasons for this new appetite for writing and reading memoir, for life writing. One answer is that the phenomenon of 'sharing' – on blogs, social media, and other means of self-publication – has encouraged the production, publication, and reading, of personal memoir. People are becoming more open, transparent, and unafraid to reveal themselves, or the truth about illness, grief, death. (It is telling that one of the greatest grief memoirs, and one which has attained the status of classic, Lewis's powerful *A Grief Observed*, was first published under a pseudonym because the writer did not want to be identified – even though he was clearly compelled to write and publish the book.) It is also worth considering that as fake news, falseness, embroidering of facts, and lying, become more commonplace among public figures, in newspapers, and on social media, that readers, thinking people, are becoming more desirous of truth in the books they read. If so, the emergence of the personal memoir as a literary genre would be a positive by-product of the era of public mendacity. It is likely that there are several reasons for the popularity of memoir. What seems clear is that a new way of writing prose and of composing stories and not quite stories is in the process of evolution. That is rather exciting for the story of literature.

NOTES

1. Tomás Ó Criomthain, *An t-Oileánach* (Dublin, Talbot Press, 1973), p.256. (First edition, 1929).
2. Claire Armitstead, 'The rise and rise of the memoir', *Guardian*, 27 January 2001. Available https://www.theguardian.com/books/2001/jan/27/biography
3. Jack Smith, 'Is the memoir market oversaturated?', *The Writer*, 6 August 2018. Available at https://www.writermag.com/get-published/the-publishing-industry/memoir-market/.
4. Neil Gelzlinger, 'The Problem with Memoir', *New York Times*, 28 January 2011.
5. Ross Skelton, *Eden Halt: An Antrim Memoir* (Dublin: Lilliput Press, 2013), p.14.
6. Emilie Pine, *Notes to Self* (Dublin: Tramp Press, 2018), p.37.
7. Pine, p.79.
8. Pine, p.119.
9. Pine, p.97.
10. Eilis Ni Dhuibhne, *Twelve Thousand Days* (Belfast: Blackstaff, 2018).
11. Philip Larkin, 'Days', in *Whitsun Weddings* (London: Faber, 1964).
12. Alice Munro, 'What is Remembered', in *Hateship, Friendship, Courtship, Loveship, Marriage* (London: Chatto and Windus, 2001).
13. Alice Munro, *Dear Life* (London: Chatto and Windus, 2012), p.256.
14. Alice Munro, 'Fathers', in *The View from Castle Rock* (London: Chatto and Windus, 2006).
15. Alice Munro, *Dance of the Happy Shades* (Toronto: Ryerson Press, 1968).

Eric Falci

Rethinking Form (Yet Again) in Contemporary Irish Poetry

Debates about form in contemporary Irish poetry seem at once overdone and undercooked. Overdone because it often feels like the same story has been told for a while: that there is a vibrant though hegemonic mainstream that adheres to relatively conservative formal practices and to the notion of the 'well-made poem' as both *sine qua non* and ultimate aspiration, and a very small group of Irish experimental poets who have been systemically ignored by the mainstream and yet who continue to produce important work in inhospitable conditions. Yeats remains if not an actively overbearing influence then a foundation stone for mainstream writers, while the more 'innovatively-minded' figures look to earlier formations of 'alternative' Irish poets as well as to the traditions of American and European modernism and certain experimental practices emerging from Britain. In this story, the mainstream's centre of gravity remains in Northern Ireland, or at least features most heavily Northern Irish poets. Over several generations, poets from the North have tended to draw the most attention within the institutions of mainstream literary culture both in and beyond the island of Ireland, although of course a large number of poets from the Republic have built important careers and bodies of work during the same stretch, including nearly all of the key figures among the marginalized experimentalists. Such are some of the major lineaments of the narrative, one that perhaps has had more staying power because of the relatively small size of the field. It sometimes feels as though the structure of the argument about form in Irish remains hitched to a binary – raw vs. cooked, open form vs. closed – that has long since dissipated in, say, North American poetry, if only because the sheer size of that field of literary production makes it impossible to sustain any single overarching narrative that doesn't end up misrepresenting or missing a great deal of significant work.

At the same time, the argument about form in contemporary Irish poetry remains, on the whole, undercooked. Not because there aren't individual scholars doing important work – there are.[1] And not because

Irish University Review 50.1 (2020): 164–174
DOI: 10.3366/iur.2020.0443
© Edinburgh University Press
www.euppublishing.com/iur

there aren't individual poets making work whose formal interest exceeds or eschews the terms of the binary suggested above – there are. But because, on the whole and in part because of the relatively small body of work upon which these arguments have been conducted, working concepts of form itself have not been sufficiently elaborated. In a scholarly moment when form is once again a central concern across a number of literary fields, and in which its dimensions and implications are being newly theorized and contextualized, it is an auspicious moment for critics to fashion revitalized and more capacious understandings of the particular formal dynamics of Irish poetry.[2]

In part, the problem is one of nomenclature. If *mainstream* and *traditional* almost always enfold a pejoration that isn't necessarily earned, then the terms on the other side of the debate – *experimental*, *innovative*, or *alternative* – are often just as misleading, especially the first two. It is no longer clear just what kind of purchase the terms *experimental* or *innovative* provide, for poets or readers, especially when the rhetoric of poetic experimentation and newness is more than a century old (and Pound took his influential phrase, 'Make It New,' mediated via several sources, from Confucius), and when broader concepts of innovation have been so thoroughly captured by the ideologies of capitalism.[3] Often, those terms function as a proxy for another: *difficulty*. If it is sometimes difficult to determine just what kinds of experiments or innovations are being conducted in poems tagged as *experimental* or *innovative*, then it is usually safe to say that such poems are 'difficult,' although the way that they might be difficult might not be innovative or experimental. There are, for example, numerous examples of contemporary difficult poems whose difficulty is at least partly a function of their adherence to or expansion of a style of open field poetics 'discovered' by modernists such as Pound and William Carlos Williams and theorized most famously by Charles Olson in an essay first published in 1950.[4] If we describe such contemporary reflexes of open field poetry as *experimental* or *innovative*, then both terms seem sapped of conceptual and historical force. Under such a usage, nearly any poem can be said to be an experiment, in the sense that every act of literary composition is an experiment – a test, a trial, a process, a tentative procedure. Embedded in this discourse is also a set of ideological assumptions and implications: just as it is sometimes reductively suggested that mainstream, traditional, or conventional poetry is politically conservative or ideologically mystifying, so is it reductively thought that experimental, innovative, or difficult poetry necessarily emerges from the political left or is automatically disruptive or critical of ideological conditions. It has been said many times in many ways, but it is worth saying again: a particular poetics doesn't necessarily entail a particular politics.

A few examples from the contemporary Irish context may help to concretize these larger matters. Paul Muldoon and Medbh McGuckian, each central within a body of Northern Irish poetry that takes up a lot of space in the mainstream, are occasionally recruited into conversations about experimental or innovative tendencies within late twentieth- and early twenty-first-century Irish poetry. In both cases, this recruitment is premised upon the difficulty of each writer's poems. Muldoon's hyper-formalist, data-rich, constitutively associative work and McGuckian's hermetic, metaphorically-recessive, fluctuational poetry model different species of postmodern lyric. Muldoon's difficulty is most often a problem of unknown or obscure reference, as he trawls dictionaries and incorporates words, phrases, and references from a number of lexical and discursive galaxies. And because his work is so deeply associative – with rhyme-pattern, morphology, phonology, etymology, and whim often governing the unfolding of stanzas – the referential challenge is compounded. The difficulty of McGuckian's poetry is also due to its obscurity, but this usually isn't a problem of reference or knowledge: her word-hoard tends to be less outlandish and willfully bizarre, but her method of radical juxtaposition (one often reliant on large-scale borrowings from other texts) estranges lines from those around them and from themselves. Unless one posits a central speaker and attributes the wavering, often impenetrable imagery to the fluxes of consciousness, memory, impulse, or dream, then it is difficult to find a way to make texts cohere with themselves. Similarly, reading the intensely paratactic textures that emerge from Muldoon's high-wire verbal inventions most frequently necessitates the positing of an author-maker holding it all together, one who experiments by leveraging a seemingly inexhaustible word-hoard in the service of the elaboration of baroque or novel rhyme schemes.

Two points are worth making about this – admittedly ragtag and cursory – sketch of Muldoon's and McGuckian's work. The first is that precisely those aspects of their work most likely to be tagged as experimental or innovative are those that lead back to a relatively familiar or conservative mode of lyric reading: the supposition of a centripetal speaker. This doesn't mean that the work becomes more interesting or less, or more conventional or less, but only that the tendency to read literary innovation and experimentation as entailing textual difficulty thoroughly muddles our ability to reckon with these texts on their own terms. The second is this: the fact that I am able – however ineffectually or unsatisfactorily – to offer a summary of Muldoon's or McGuckian's practices suggests that what might have been experiments at one point have become signature styles – or that what have been understood as the innovative or experimental aspects of their work have simply become their preferred or default compositional approaches. Again, this is not to suggest that the work is more or less interesting or important than it otherwise is. The development of a recognizable, distinctive style has long been understood as a measure of aesthetic success. The gravitational pull of one's style is seen as an indication of its influence or force. But while the development of a style is certainly a process of authorial experimentation or innovation at a granular level, those terms – *experimentation, innovation* – don't quite scale up without a significant loss – or even inversion – of connotative freight. What seems to be an intriguing or particularly poignant innovation or experiment within the context of a single author's or artist's career is unlikely to be read as *Experimental* or *Innovative* in the context of the much larger field of artistic and cultural production. There is an aporia within our broad use of those terms within literary-critical and literary-historical contexts. (To take a perhaps too convenient example: if our data set were only the poems of Seamus Heaney, we would discover hundreds of innovations and experiments at multiple scales – within a single poem, over the course of a volume, over the arc of his career. But no one, or, nearly no one, would argue that Heaney was an experimental writer in the larger context.)

Muldoon and McGuckian are particularly clear examples of these matters. From the publication of *New Weather* (1971), Muldoon's poetry has been characterized by thematic and tonal obliquity and formal ingenuity, and one way to plot the course of his work is to understand it as a ceaseless ratcheting of that obliquity and ingenuity through his works of the 1990s – *Madoc-A Mystery* (1990), *The Annals of Chile* (1994), and *Hay* (1998) – at which point the major formal features and processes are fully established and elaborated. What to do, then, with the work of the past two decades? The most ungenerous reading is that he has been repeating himself. Such a reading is available because Muldoon's experiments and innovations have been developed over several decades of practice and by now their lineaments are recognizable. Any reader of Irish poetry, or (considering Muldoon's prominence) contemporary poetry in general, knows, by now, what a Muldoon poem looks like and how it moves. A twenty-first-century Muldoon poem remains difficult, formally intriguing, and (at least locally and within the context of the whole of his work) often inventive, but it can't be said to be experimental or innovative, either in general or in the overall context of his whole body of work. At this point, the innovative or experimental Muldoon poem is the one that doesn't have a rhyme scheme, such as 'The Landing' (in *Horse Latitudes*), or one that would proceed by some compositional method other than the stunningly dexterous completion of a formal procedure based on the patterning of line-end words.[5]

A similar set of considerations applies to McGuckian's work. Her first book, *The Flower Master* (1982), is metaphorically and imagistically dense and at times cryptic, but it was legible enough at the time to win significant praise.[6] As in Muldoon's case, the experiments undertaken in her first book were intensified and extended in her subsequent books, but they weren't fundamentally altered. Even as she became less tethered to normative patterns of grammar, syntax, and sense, and even as she began to draw more heavily from texts she encountered as word and phrase banks, her formal shapes remained consistent: reliably stanzaic, but not in regular or uniform stanzas; composed in non-metered lines, with occasional rhyme; and comprising a seemingly placid lyric surface that held radical juxtapositions. Like Muldoon, McGuckian seems to have fully established her central form in the 1990s, and her work since then has – in large part – remained committed to that form. At this point, and based on the history of her work, the most 'innovative' McGuckian poem is the lucid, narrative text – such as 'The Rainbow Division' (from *Blaris Moor*) – that commits to a particular thematic or narrative path rather than activating the diegetic, figural, and rhetorical torsions to which her readers have become accustomed. So, Muldoon and McGuckian have been – in broad terms – considered within the realm of experimental or innovative practices in Irish poetry, but the innovations of each can be posited as conventional: both within the terms of broader lyric practice and of each of their careers. Analogous readings might be fashioned for several other poets, on either side of the spectrum. Depending on the scale at which we are looking – the poem, the volume, the career, the whole field – our understanding of ideas about experimentation and innovation have to be reformulated and must remain pliable if they are not to simply lapse into reified and increasingly empty critical gestures that one set uses to berate another. Additionally, the use of terms like *experimental* or *innovative* as proxies for *difficult* or *not-clearly-accessible* also tends to obscure the actual experiments that poets undertake, as well as what the stakes of those experiments might be.

Along with McGuckian and Muldoon, Ciaran Carson is often positioned as a kind of toggle-switch within accounts of contemporary Irish poetry. His work can be placed in relation to and as a departure from the work of earlier Northern Irish poets (Heaney, Longley, Mahon) and he existed within many of the same literary-critical and institutional formations as those earlier poets (Gallery Press, Queen's University Belfast), and so he might be considered as a central figure within the putative mainstream. At the same time, his work has been described by many as experimental, innovative, or postmodern, especially after the publication of *The Irish For No* (1987) and *Belfast Confetti* (1989), whose long, winningly digressive lines were something new in

Irish poetry: they modeled all at once the wandering style of the *seanchaí*, the reels and accretive cadences of Irish traditional music, and the tense and shifting paths that constituted everyday life in Troubles-era Belfast. Unlike, say, Muldoon, who has not fundamentally remade his style, Carson's work after those two signal volumes seems catalyzed by the desire to experiment on – and so largely refashion – the precise formal feature upon which the distinction of those volumes was premised: the long line. He keeps the long line in his books of the 1990s – *First Language* (1994) and *Opera Et Cetera* (1996) – but often submits those long lines to the demands of rhyme and so alters the texture of the poems quite significantly: from the lyric realism of the 1980s volumes to one that is much more noticeably absorbed in its own linguistic confections. The rhymes, as though to work against any lessening of effect because of the long lines, are often comically mannered. *Breaking News* (2003) unmakes and remakes the long line once again: by arraying it down the page as a series of very short lines, most of which are models of clarity and documentary precision. This volume experiments by radically adjusting the relation of the line to the sentence that had structured the four previous volumes. The next volume, *For All We Know* (2008), reinstitutes the long line as the dominant form, but the gains of the previous volume are redeployed within the terms of a pseudo-epistolary lyric romance. The digressions and hijinks that typified his earlier long-line poetry have been abandoned for a double sequence in lucid couplets in which a tragic love story is unfolded. Once again overturning his previous mode, the next two volumes – *On the Night Watch* (2009) and *Until Before After* (2010) – splay sentences over extremely short lines of just a word or several. The narrative, novelistic momentum that Carson allowed to build in *For All We Know* (itself a transposition of the narrative strategies of his earlier volumes) is anatomized, as each word and phrase is made to take its own weight. The redistribution of the weight and energy of sentences according to shifting logics of lineation is, from this angle, the crux of Carson's practice of formal experimentation over several decades. Even as his central topoi and themes have remained relatively stable, they have been remade again and again within the crucible of a stylistic restiveness that is based on an urge to continually rethink – to conduct new experiments on – the formal bind at the heart of poetry: the relation between lines and sentences.

Looking at Carson's work from this angle opens up a few different ways of understanding how Irish poets have experimented or innovated within their compositional practice, and so might provide a different sort of purchase on our working concepts of poetic form. More straightforwardly, it is perhaps a spur to thicken concepts of experimentation or innovation by examining them at the scales of the individual book (as a compositional process rather than an aesthetic artifact) and of the career. More implicitly, it offers new frames and perspectives through which we might pitch our interpretive endeavors. What if, for instance and building from the Carson discussion above, we understand poetic experimentation in contemporary Irish poetry within the rubric of sentence-making and grammar? How might our use of the term *form* within discussions of that poetry change if we centralized the sentence? What new aspects of individual poems might we notice and how might our critical map of the field be reconstellated?

This is, of course, not a revolutionary suggestion – it's barely a novel one. And its function, at least within the terms of a brief essay, must needs remain speculative or heuristic. But I do think it would both thicken and concretize the notion of *form* at work in discussions of Irish poetry. For instance, the seemingly centrifugal energies of Muldoon's work – where an ever more abstruse or tenuous connection is always about to be made – look different when we attend to the repeating syntactic figures and phrases to which those connections are often tethered. His poems – think of 'Incantata' – become at once simpler and stranger. Thus, one might approach the broader field by considering how poets reckon with or avoid grammatical subordination. Sinéad Morrissey's formal restlessness, for instance, might be newly seen as not only an attempt to eschew a recognizable style, or as a large-scale dialectical study of the relation between lyric poetry and expression, but also as an extensive compositional survey of the ways in which lines interact with sentences. Focusing only on her most recent volume, *On Balance* (2017), one finds experiments with run-on sentences ('The Millihelen'), extended sub-ordination ('Receiving the Dead'), unpunctuated sentences ('Platinum Anniversary,' 'Perfume' part 2, and 'My Life According to You'), and single-sentence poems ('Perfume' part 1 and 'Very Dyspraxic Child'), to name only the most notable instances. More broadly, we might consider a differently-inflected series of formal questions: about the implications of how line- and stanza-endings converge and diverge with sentence-endings, about the movement between long and short sentences, about the importance of non-sentence sentences (i.e., those without verbs) for several poets (Muldoon and Heaney in particular), or about species of hypotaxis and parataxis.

Perhaps more importantly, reframing the critical conversation about mainstream and experimental poetry by centralizing a mundane formal feature like the sentence provides a means to concretize the achievements of those poets who constitute the experimental formation within the field of Irish poetry, as well as to understand their work in relation to the so-called mainstream, rather than as merely a refusal or avoidance of it. One way to approach the work of such poets as

Catherine Walsh, Trevor Joyce, and Maurice Scully – at least as compared to figures representative of mainstream Irish poetry – might be to emphasize their collective refusal of or ongoing resistance to the normative, hierarchical sentence. Throughout their work, although not apparent in all of it, we see examples of what Roland Barthes described as 'what is eternally, splendidly, *outside the sentence*'.[7] If, for Barthes, 'the Sentence is hierarchical' because 'it implies subjections, subordinations, internal reactions', then the sentence-based experiments of poets like Walsh, Joyce, and Scully seek to find a working space *'outside the sentence'*.[8] This feature roots what is presumed to be their difficulty, which then – of course and illogically – both precedes and explains their place outside of the Irish mainstream. However, we have tended to both monumentalize and under-examine this aspect of their work, such that it becomes both pretext and explanation. If we understood particular volumes and texts by Walsh, Scully, or Joyce as undertaking extended experiments on the shapes, substances, and ideologies of sentences, and began a critical investigation from that point, we have both diffused the mystifying connotations that swirl around terms like *experiment* and *innovation*, and set a path by which we might actually read the work on its terms. This wouldn't neutralize the quite real difficulty that their poetry presents to readers, but it would provide an interpretive perspective from which it is possible to reckon concretely with it. We might even come to understand such work as more accessible – or, at least, more amenable to readerly participation – than Muldoon's poetry, or a good deal of McGuckian's and Carson's work (and even some of Heaney's). Poetry by Walsh, Scully, or Joyce typically does not feature the wide range of reference that is fundamental to Muldoon's practice, but it does tend to demand a kind of open-ended attention to the words on the page and a willingness to think alongside them. Their poems do not promise formal closure or aesthetic satisfaction, but rather open processes of provisional and always fluctuating thought. And the concrete manifestation of what we too easily think of as their rebarbative nature is their constitutive upsetting of the normative patterns of sentences.

What might also emerge from such a turn in attention is a comparative or relational view of work that is usually kept on either side of the critical divide. The relative formal consistency of Scully's poetry – both that comprising his multi-volume, multi-decade project *Things that Happen* (1981–2006) and what he has published since then – might be productively juxtaposed with Muldoon's penchant for a reliable cache of lyric shapes (the sonnet, the quatrain). Scully's work is, in so many ways, utterly different from Muldoon's, but Scully too has depended on a relatively small set of shapes: short-lined stanzas that tend to move between tercets and quatrains, and longer-lined verse blocks or paragraphs. Scully's career-long play with generic categories – titling poems 'Sonnet' that bear no formal relation to a conventional sonnet – might be seen as a persistent critique of the staid generic conventions of poets like Heaney or Muldoon (for each of whom a sonnet will always act like a sonnet), but also as the production of something like generic anti-matter. Analogously, Walsh's poetry, so dependent on the anatomization of sentence parts and their amalgamation into unpunctuated runs of text that remain 'outside the sentence', might be taken as a more radical form of Carson's regular refashioning of the long line. Her volumes of the 1980s and 1990s, culminating in *City West* (2005), tended to literalize her disruption of normative syntax and grammar by placing words and phrases in various configurations all over the page, such that a single path of reading is often debarred by text running along multiple and unconventional paths on the printed page. A shift occurs in *Optic Verve: A Commentary* (2008), in which discrete phrases and unpunctuated sentences are, not always but more often than previously, fused into quasi-stanzaic text blocks. *Astonished Birds Cara, Jane, Bob and James* (2012) generally moves between pages of short-lined poems and those made of denser blocks of text, and at times Walsh reintroduces the accoutrements of normative sentences (capitalization, punctuation) while inhibiting typical modes of sense-making to coalesce. This volume also expands the range of Walsh's experiments 'outside the sentence' by including an extended fiction, although one that eschews most typical features of narrative and novelistic discourse as it continually touches down on one of its four featured characters, 'Cara, Jane, Bob and James'. Most recently, Walsh has again restructured her approach: *The Beautiful Untogether* (2017) consists of sixty isolated seven-line stanzas (two per page) that once more eschew sentences, followed by a long single-stanza text entitled 'In Form'. Even as she continues to refuse the sentence as a governing structure and even as the particular form of difficulty that her poems produce has remained relatively consistent, the shape of that refusal has shifted massively over nine volumes. Finally, we might understand the formal restlessness of a handful of mid-career Irish poets – Morrissey centrally, but also David Wheatley, Justin Quinn, and Catríona O'Reilly – quite differently if placed next to Trevor Joyce's propensity to devise regularly new formal and procedural shapes. Unlike Walsh, for whom the space outside the sentence is the constitutive zone of poetic composition, Joyce moves among poems that adhere to normative sentence structures (such as 'Hopeful Monsters' or 'The Peacock's Tale'), those that eschew or at least severely problematize sentences within a phrase-based structure (such as 'Syzygy' or 'Saws'), and those that maintain grammar and syntax while abandoning punctuation (such as the thirty-six word poems, a form initially devised as part of a collaborative online project called *offsets*, that feature prominently in *What's In Store* (2007) and exclusively in *The Immediate Future* (2017)). Joyce's penchant for devising complex procedures to generate poems adds a further dimension to what seems to be a more widespread commitment among contemporary Irish writers to attend to poetry's basic tangle between the unit of the line and that of the sentence.

I have moved swiftly and haphazardly through a number of poets in order to sketch one way in which a renovated approach to the question of form in contemporary Irish poetry might help to disrupt some of the usual critical paths. In addition to offering new perspectives on individual Irish poets and on particular formations within Irish poetry, such a turn can help us to clarify connections between contemporary Irish poetry and other national literatures, and – more crucially – the ways in which Irish poetry relates to (and doesn't) larger tendencies within Anglophone literature and poetry across the globe. Focusing on a particular concrete feature across the field of Irish poetry, such as the sentence, allows us to see that prominent modes of experimentation among Irish poets – both those of the mainstream and those outside it – don't necessarily draw from dominant trends in North American poetry: there is little evidence, for instance, of the kind of 'new sentence' that was at the compositional and theoretical heart of Language poetry. On the other hand, the kind of pressure that Walsh or, at times, Joyce place upon the sentence might be thought about next to the pulverizations that typify J.H. Prynne's late work. And far from removing questions of politics and history from view, such investigations into crucial but often unnoticed aspects of poems – how do they use or avoid sentences? – lead onto a much broader consideration of the ideological implications of particular modes of linguistic construction and discursive representation. I suggested earlier that specific forms or styles don't inherently embed particular politics, but the corollary to that claim is that no aesthetic forms are free of ideologies and histories. Moving away from worn-out abstractions like *experimental* or *innovative, mainstream* or *traditional* and working along different trajectories will help us to reckon with the kinds of compositional practices that Irish poets across the spectrum have been undertaking, thus revitalizing yet again what is simultaneously the most fusty and the most vital term in the literary-critical lexicon: form.

NOTES
1. The *Irish University Review* has been a crucial outlet for much of this scholarship. See in particular special issues on Brian Coffey (5.1 (Spring 1975)); the Long Poem (13.1 (Spring 1983)); Thomas Kinsella (31.1 (Spring-Summer 2001)); Eiléan Ní Chuilleanáin (37.1 (Spring-Summer 2007)); Poems that Matter, 1950–2000 (39.2 (Autumn-Winter

2009)); Poetry Cultures, 1930–1970 (42.1 (Spring-Summer 2012)); and Irish Experimental Poetry (46.1 (May 2016)).

2. For a variety of accounts, see Caroline Levine, *Forms: Whole, Rhythm, Hierarchy, Network* (Princeton, NJ: Princeton University Press, 2015); Denise Gigante, *Life: Organic Form and Romanticism* (New Haven, CT and London: Yale University Press, 2007); Angela Leighton, *On Form: Poetry, Aestheticism, and the Legacy of a Word* (Oxford: Oxford University Press, 2007); and Susan Wolfson, *Formal Charges: The Shaping of Poetry in British Romanticism* (Stanford, CA: Stanford University Press, 1997). Also see Marjorie Levinson, 'What Is New Formalism?', *PMLA* 122.2 (2007), pp.558–569; and Jonathan Kramnick and Anahid Nersessian, 'Form and Explanation', *Critical Inquiry* 43 (Spring 2017), pp.650–669. Many of the essays included in the March 2000 special issue of *Modern Language Quarterly* (61.1), edited by Susan Wolfson, remain influential (an expanded version of the issue, edited by Wolfson and Marshall Brown, was published by the University of Washington Press in 2006).

3. For a rich account of Pound's encounter with and redeployment of the phrase, see Michael North, *Novelty: A History of the New* (Chicago and London: University of Chicago Press, 2013), pp.162–171.

4. See Charles Olson, 'Projective Verse,' in *The New American Poetry*, ed. Donald Allen (New York: Grove Press, 1960), pp.386–397.

5. 'The Landing', a wonderful poem that might be described as an unrhymed sonnet, contains several rhymes, part-rhymes, buried rhymes, and pararhymes (and reversed pararhymes), but it doesn't contain a systemic rhyme pattern (as far as I can tell) or else the pattern is so thoroughly 'fuzzy' that it is nearly inapprehensible. On Muldoon's 'fuzzy rhymes', see Andrew Osborn, 'Skirmishes on the Border: The Evolution and Function of Paul Muldoon's Fuzzy Rhyme', *Contemporary Literature* 41.2 (Summer 2000), pp.323–358.

6. The volume won the Alice Hunt Bartlett Prize from the Poetry Society and the Rooney Prize for Irish Literature. 'The Flitting,' one of the volume's anchor poems, won the 1979 National Poetry Competition (McGuckian submitted it using a male pseudonym).

7. Roland Barthes, *The Pleasure of the Text*, trans. by Richard Howard (NY: Farrar, Straus and Giroux, 1975), p.49.

8. Barthes, *The Pleasure of the Text*, p.50.

Marie-Louise Coolahan

New Technologies of Research and Digital Interpretation for Early Modern Irish Studies

It is now unthinkable for an early modernist working on Irish or British culture at any remove from a major research library not to reach first for *Early English Books Online* (*EEBO*), the online repository of digital facsimiles of printed books published between 1473 and 1700. So ingrained has *EEBO* become that it seems strange to recall that it was launched as recently as 1998, arriving to Irish universities a few years later (so naturalised, indeed, that researchers rarely feel the need to draw attention to its use when citing early printed books). *EEBO* was a vital cog in the wheel of primary-source digitisation, the first major impact of new technologies on early modern research. The provision of digital versions of primary sources vastly expanded access and revolutionised the breadth, depth, and speed with which research is conducted (notwithstanding that its distribution behind a paywall compromises the democratisation of access). The teleological trajectory of the digital humanities has run from the 'making visible' entailed in online access, to enhancement and creation of newer resources to fill further gaps, and an aggregating thrust that aims to scale up by making resources interoperable (able to speak to each other), as well as enabling users to extract and manipulate data themselves. It has changed the kinds of research we can conduct, manifesting patterns we did not know were there and allowing us to see problems at a different scale.

This article outlines the vastly expanded ecosystem of digital projects and resources of use to researchers of early modern Ireland. The tumult of the sixteenth and seventeenth centuries – reiterated cycles of warfare, colonial encroachment and resistance, religious reformation, plural ethnicities – mean that such research has to be interdisciplinary, drawing in not only historicist and literary approaches but also language specialists, palaeographers, archaeologists, and geographers. Digital modes of representation have opened up this interdisciplinarity, which remains to be fully exploited by researchers. The discussion

Irish University Review 50.1 (2020): 175–186
DOI: 10.3366/iur.2020.0444
© Edinburgh University Press
www.euppublishing.com/iur

encompasses early digitisation projects, many of which are enhanced on an ongoing basis with features that add value and enable researchers to envisage new kinds of research on early modern Ireland. Not all are self-evidently Irish-focused resources; early modern Ireland was a multilingual, contested place. But all offer new possibilities for enterprising researchers and new perspectives on the field in terms of generation as well as use; the creation of resources for the study of early modern Ireland should itself be considered an act of research-in-practice.

EEBO – avowedly focused on English books – is one of a number of online reference resources that enjoy first-port-of-call status. Initially designed as an online repository of digital surrogates for printed books, it has since evolved substantial full-text searchability via the Text Creation Partnership, an initiative that ran from 1999 to 2015 and has, to date, converted 41% (over 60,000 texts) of *EEBO*'s digital surrogates into searchable, TEI-compliant SGML/XML texts.[1] A further evolution of the resource has arisen from its migration to the new *Early Modern Books* platform run by *ProQuest*. The original resource – in itself invaluable – has evolved from an online site where researchers could search and read digital facsimiles and download individual pages to a resource that enables scholars to search for individual words or phrases across the entire collection of 146,000 texts, easily download entire books, and cross-search against other in-house databases like *Early European Books*. The capacity of the resource has moved on from substituting digital for physical access (and virtual for textual materiality) to facilitating text mining and the exportation of results, among other features. In other words, access and scale have enabled the kinds of quantitative research that have been nigh impossible for humanities researchers.[2]

The major online reference resources are increasingly turning to this kind of enhanced functionality. The British State Papers, which contain all kinds of documents relating to the operations of the English state in Ireland as well as letters and petitions addressed to or intercepted by the English government have been digitized by Gale-Cengage as *State Papers Online, 1509–1714* (SPO).[3] This tool enables users to view manuscript images and calendar pages, and search via collection, date, letter writer/recipient, and keyword, although without transcriptions or downloadable options.

The promise of online access is not so easily delivered when the primary materials are early modern manuscripts. The *1641 Depositions Project* (2007–2010) is a prime example of how to surmount this barrier.[4] Previously accessible only to specialists familiar with (hastily written) seventeenth-century secretary and italic scripts, able either to travel to Trinity College Dublin or purchase microfilms, these manuscripts are a unique research resource. Comprising approximately 8,000 witness testimonies supplied by protestants fleeing the violence that broke out in October 1641, the collection is now fully digitised, with high-quality digital images and, crucially, diplomatic transcriptions of all the texts. In this case, the born-digital led to the print edition, now underway with the *Irish Manuscripts Commission*. The online repository is hosted on a fully searchable database. The original data taken down by the commissioners included occupation and location as well as name; these are among the search fields available, as well as free-text search of the deposition transcriptions. Barbara Fennell's linguistic analyses of the texts advertise one route for innovative large-scale research facilitated by the resource.[5]

Another means of representing manuscripts digitally is evident in the 'Perdita Project' (1994–2007) on early modern women's manuscripts. Perdita arose from feminist recovery research, which saw in technological developments a dream opportunity to retrieve and promote women's writing. The earliest such project, *Women Writers Online (WWO)*, was founded in the mid-1980s to establish a textbase – electronic versions of texts by women in print from 1526.[6] Like *EEBO*, this resource contains items of Irish interest but these are not separated from other materials. Of 416 texts in *WWO*, items of Irish interest include Elizabeth Cary's *Tragedy of Mariam* and *History of Edward II*, twenty three works by the pamphleteering prophet Eleanor Davies, and *Poems* by Katherine Philips.[7] The list privileges print and anglophone culture: one would not know of these women's Irish connections without prior knowledge. Cary lived in Dublin as Lord Deputy Falkland's wife from 1622 to 1625 (infamously converting to catholicism on her return to London); Davies from 1609 to 1619 as wife to attorney-general John Davies (whose death she accurately prophesied when they fell out over her publications); Philips from 1662 to 1663 in pursuit of a land claim (which failed but was outweighed by having her play *Pompey* performed publicly to great acclaim).

'Perdita' drew from the work of scholars such as Margaret Ezell, who demonstrated that print represented only a fraction of the evidence for early modern women's writing, manuscript remaining the medium of choice for women writers into the eighteenth century.[8] Focusing on women compilers, 'Perdita' brought to light approximately 500 manuscripts, ultimately producing two digital resources: an open-access XML-tagged database in 2005 and a second, enhanced version published by Adam Matthew in 2008.[9] Both resources foreground the material, formal, and historical contexts for each manuscript, supplying a biography for each compiler, a bibliographical description of each manuscript, and a detailed contents list. (It should be noted that not all full entries were complete by the time of the project's conclusion.)

The Adam Matthew version supplies all this, linked to digital images of 230 of the 500 manuscripts. Thus, the text is visually inserted, enhancing the user's sense of the manuscript's materiality, but without textual editorial intervention. As with *WWO*, there are a number of women of Irish interest, including Anne Southwell (Munster planter and poet), the intellectual mover and shaker, Katherine Jones, and diarist and autobiographer, Mary Rich (the latter two born in Ireland as daughters of Richard Boyle, first earl of Cork).

Cutting-edge digital editions are emerging in ever-growing sophistication from such material. Just as Perdita was getting off the ground, a new discovery was made in the Brotherton Library of a hitherto-unknown manuscript containing 120 poems and a prose romance by Hester Pulter. This is an important body of accomplished work, which has made a big impact in the fields of women's writing and digital editing and, happily, there is an Irish connection to justify its inclusion here: Pulter was born in Dublin because her father James Ley was chief justice of the king's bench in Ireland from 1604 to 1608.[10] Launched in 2018, 'The Pulter Project: Poet in the Making', led by Leah Knight and Wendy Wall, is an innovative collaborative project that invites users to all stages of the editorial process.[11] At the time of writing, sixty five of Pulter's poems are edited in multiple ways: an 'elemental' edition presents a modernised text with minimal notes; an 'amplified' edition presents the same text edited by a different scholar and with scope for more wide-ranging contextual interpretation. These editions are supplemented by high-resolution digital facsimiles and contextual 'curations' and 'explorations'. The 'compare editions' function enables users to juxtapose the editions and contemplate their consequences for the poem's representation. The commitment to transparency and multiplicity is reflected in the open call for proposals from users, as the full corpus of poems is edited. Thus, the user encounters born-digital resource creation.

English, of course, was not the main language spoken in early modern Ireland; a number of text-based resources address the very same access issues by digitising sources in Irish. *The Corpus of Electronic Texts (CELT)*, founded in 2003, has assembled an online, searchable corpus of multi-lingual texts that range from Old Irish to the nineteenth century.[12] The Bardic Poetry Database is a catalogue of bardic poems, searchable by first line, poet's name, metre, and motif (among other categories) with access to the texts, and further updates underway. *Irish Script on Screen (ISOS)*, founded in 1999 by Pádraig Ó Macháin, makes available digital surrogates of Irish manuscripts held in collections scattered across Ireland, the UK, and in private ownership.[13]

The language barrier itself is being tackled by the *Léamh* project at the University of Connecticut. The brainchild of Brendan Kane, this is an online resource that supports non-specialists in acquiring reading competence in early modern Irish. The site offers 'guided translations of a wide range of texts and genres, a grammar with basic paradigms and descriptive summaries, and a searchable reference glossary'; a guide to early modern Irish paleography is also envisaged.[14] Designed as a tool of self-instruction, the project challenges monolingual researchers to redress the Anglocentric thrust of much scholarship on early modern Ireland and it aims to provide the tools for ameliorating that bias: 'The overarching goal of this method is that users work closely with a variety of texts, and in doing so, they accumulate a body of experience and skills – that is, a working knowledge – that they can then apply to reading other Early Modern Irish texts, a process assisted by returning to the Léamh site so as to consult the grammar and glossary features'.[15] The project promotes practical competence, thereby encouraging scholars of disciplines other than Irish to engage with the full range of sources relating to early modern Ireland, many of which remain untranslated.[16]

Biographical databases, whether born-digital or revised for digital consumption, have proven both authoritative reference resources and, increasingly, the foundation for newer resources and analysis. *The Oxford Dictionary of National Biography*, thoroughly revised and relaunched in print and online in 2004, has enhanced its preeminent status as the reference resource for biographies of those operating in Ireland and Britain during the early modern period.[17] Recognising the gender and class bias of the original nineteenth-century print publication, 16,300 newly commissioned biographies of women and men were added to the 2004 version. Such work is ongoing, as exemplified by the inclusion of twenty two new biographies of early modern nuns led by Victoria Van Hyning in May 2014, and twenty five new biographies of early modern women led by Anders Ingram in May 2019, both of which initiatives included Irish women.[18] The *Dictionary of Irish Biography*, launched by the Royal Irish Academy in 2009, focuses solely on Ireland.[19] Like the *ODNB*, it was published online and in print, is regularly updated, comprising 11,000 lives at the time of writing.

Similarly, the 'Who Were the Nuns?' project (2008–2013) may be probed for Irish women.[20] Covering the period from the foundation of the first post-Dissolution convent for English women on the Continent through to their return in the aftermath of the French Revolution, this is a prosopography, searchable by secular name, religious name, convent, profession date, or place. Numbers of Irish women joined the exiled English convents, as researchers working with this database have shown.[21] Many Irish women, of course, entered religious life in indigenous convents in Iberia, France, and the Low Countries but that evidence is scattered and not yet exploitative of digital technologies.

Perhaps the most important development in the field of digital resource creation has been data exchange between projects, as new resources are imagined and created. Rather than reinventing the wheel, major resources such as the *ODNB* are sharing their metadata with others. This is mutually beneficial: it saves time by avoiding duplication but also directs users back to the donating resource. For example, the social network project, Six Degrees of Francis Bacon, built its biographical dataset from the *ODNB*. This became the foundation for a network visualisation platform, which displays connections between people operating in early modern Britain and Ireland.[22] However, as Christopher Warren (co-founder of 'Six Degrees') has observed, the generation of one resource from another should be alive to the peculiarities of its foundations: 'Considering digital resources in their entirety and as historically contingent artifacts demystifies the means of collection and more clearly delimits the knowledge-making that a particular data infrastructure allows and constrains'.[23] Similarly, the work of Ruth Ahnert and Sebastian Ahnert on Tudor networks of power is grounded in metadata sourced from the *State Papers Online*. The application of network-analysis algorithms enabled the authors to identify broad patterns in the transmission of information, to the extent of developing a model that could predict which correspondents were engaged in espionage, and analyse government surveillance practices.[24] Most recently, Ahnert and Ahnert have been leading the Networking Archives project, which is merging the metadata relating to correspondence contained in *Early Modern Letters Online* – an international union catalogue for early modern correspondence – and the *State Papers Online* to create an aggregated metadata archive for early modern letters.[25]

Also drawing on existing resources, *MACMORRIS* (*Mapping Actors and Contexts: Modelling Research in Renaissance Ireland in the Sixteenth and Seventeenth Centuries*) is an exciting new project led by Patricia Palmer, David Baker, and Willy Maley and funded by the Irish Research Council. This project aims to rebalance the Anglocentric perspective of literary-historical scholarship on early modern Ireland by creating a resource 'that maps significant cultural figures (of whatever ethnicity) writing in, or engaging with, Gaelic, English, Latin, Scots, Spanish, Italian, Portuguese, and Dutch, in late 16th and early 17th century Ireland'.[26] Reminding us that this historical moment precedes the political and linguistic dominance of English, its goal is to reinstitute that landscape; to capture 'the full-screen, surround-sound of a rich and complex culture on the brink of transformation' and recover 'the cultural and linguistic plurality of a period before all that is swept away'. Their proposed method is the creation of a database with biographical and bibliographical information for 'every political figure and cultural producer active in Ireland between 1541 ... and 1691'.[27] In its preliminary phase, the project drew on metadata from the *ODNB* and *Bardic Poetry Database* to build a relational database of '338 people associated with Ireland in the early modern period'.[28] As its instigators argue, the risk of re-use lies in the replication of biases inherent in the original dataset: if the source dataset is flawed, so is the new resource built on it. In order to mitigate this effect, *MACMORRIS* aims to diversify, drawing additionally from the *Dictionary of Irish Biography* and 'Six Degrees'. Transparency about such complicating methodological factors is crucial to the scholarly rigour of digital resources and, consequently, to quantitative analysis based on these tools. However, it must be said that no digital resource will be all-inclusive or fully comprehensive. To be aware of our parameters both shapes the questions we can ask and pinpoints further gaps for future research.

New resources are also interacting with each other to produce better understandings of the field. With an eye to adding value to such resources, and the shift from simple digitisation toward an enhanced functionality that permits researchers to extract and manipulate the data they contain, the ongoing development of the 'Down Survey of Ireland Project' (2011–2013) aims to showcase the interdisciplinary and scalable research potential of linking databases and datasets.[29] Reconstructing the land survey conducted in the 1650s (which was tasked with identifying lands for redistribution from catholics to English adventurers and soldiers), the project assembled and digitized all the surviving maps, geocoded them, and cross-referenced them with lists of all landowners. In itself this is a valuable resource, bringing together all known surviving maps in the face of archival losses in fires in 1711 and 1922. (Thomas Herron's 'Centering Spenser' project, with a 3-D recreation of Kilcolman Castle, home of the poet and administrator Edmund Spenser, offers another innovative re-imagining of the spaces of early modern Ireland, including interactive diagrams and animated fly-throughs.[30]) As an experiment in linking with other databases, the team then geo-referenced all murders mentioned in the Ulster Deposition volumes, overlaying this with the seventeenth-century roads depicted in William Petty's atlas, *Hibernia delineatio* (1685). The result 'graphically illustrates how many of the recorded murders followed along the major transportation routes, a fact not recorded in the witness statements'. On this basis, Ó Siochrú and Brown advocate for the transformation of image repositories into 'active research platform[s], exploiting recent technological advances to enable the user to begin asking the types of questions that hitherto would have been impossible to address, let alone answer'.[31]

As the recovery of women's writing has gained pace and space in the academy, attention has shifted from production to reception. *Women Writers Online* has supplemented its textbase with resources such as 'Women Writers in Review', a collection of eighteenth- and nineteenth-century reviews of women's writing. Julia Flanders and Sarah Connell have recently mined this data to experiment with topic modelling (training algorithms to identify clusters of words) in order to ascertain patterns in the language of reviewing in periodical culture. Their findings suggest that the vocabulary of literary evaluation was charged with anxiety about mass literacy that mapped onto gender and class biases.[32]

The 'Reception and Circulation of Early Modern Women's Writing' (RECIRC) project (2014–2020), of which I am principal investigator, is essentially a study of intellectual impact, producing a large-scale, quantitative analysis of reactions to, and transmission of, women's writing between 1550 and 1700.[33] Having first designed a database so that team researchers could store information about reception in a single online location, and structured according to taxonomies that would enable us to compare findings, we ultimately designed a new user interface in order to share our findings with a wider public. The project's remit is to consider reception in the English-speaking world; it therefore includes women with Irish connections, writing in any language, as long as they were received or circulated. The open-access version enables users to search almost 5,000 instances of reception evidence, filtered by categories that include date, place, and source, as well as reception type, circulation type, and three categories of person: the female author, the receiver, and the owner/compiler/scribe of the volume in which the instance of reception occurs. Crucially, and in common with the added functionality entailed in the projects described above, we aim to empower users to generate their own results and visualisations in order to provoke new research that reaches beyond our own approaches to reception history and women's writing. Thus, users' search results will be displayed via visual formats (network graphs, tables); individual results will encompass digital image, transcription, and relevant metadata; and exportable formats (e.g. .csv) will enable users to manipulate a richer complexity of information. For example, users may wish to run their own network analysis by exporting a dataset to run on a software programme such as Gephi, as team researchers Evan Bourke and Bronagh McShane have done.[34]

Discoverability – the need to ensure resources can be found amidst their proliferation – is increasingly an issue. Furthermore, as we move from the provision of electronic versions of primary sources to encouraging users to do things with them, how do we ensure that these changes to the research outlook are taken on board? Ellen Rooney has warned against the 'additive approach' to feminist scholarship, cautioning us to be wary of simply adding formerly excluded authors and texts without thinking through their integration and adoption into our narratives of literary history.[35] Contemplating this in relation to the now-extensive number of electronic versions of female-authored texts, Jacqueline Wernimont observes that digital availability alone is insufficient; it requires the curation of entry routes and contexts: 'In a moment where so many texts are available, sometimes through multiple sources, we need digital archives to help users discover and make sense of women's writing'.[36] Elsewhere, she and Julia Flanders ask: 'how does the simple, apparent "visibility" of the entire *WWO* collection translate into an actual perceptual shift in a reader's understanding of the landscape of gender and authorship?'[37] These are, in themselves, questions about intellectual impact – and surely empowering users with the capacity to build and refine their own datasets begins to close the circle between producing a digital resource and thinking about what to do with it. Interoperable platforms and infrastructures offer one answer, as does the increasing impetus to facilitate users in working themselves with the metadata and electronic texts that are made accessible. There is an already advanced shift underway from digitising sources, so they can be read anywhere – which replicates the kinds of reading scholars have always done, changing their physical location (and this is transformative in itself) – to thinking in new ways about what constitutes a dataset and what can be done with it. Distant reading, network analysis, topic modelling are just some of the possibilities that are taking root. The interoperability advocated by Ó Siochrú and Brown directs us towards the future possibilities of linked open data (the structuring of data according to open-source ontologies that can be read by machines, enabling automated data exchange) to expand both speed and range. On the other side of the spectrum, materiality eludes digitisation; as these resources become digital artefacts in themselves, they cannot replicate the material experience and insight of working with early modern manuscripts and books.

We inherit an emancipatory vision of digital humanities as transcending obstacles of restricted access – rarity, the ownership of private hands, the distance of far-flung repositories. What factors determine the openness or closedness of our digital resources? What can we live with, in the service of widening access and recovery research? The politics of 'open access' stretch into funding, as 'open science' becomes mandatory and impact agendas come to the fore. Of the resources discussed here, *DIB, ODNB, 'Perdita', WWO, EEBO*, and *State Papers Online* offer access that is restricted to subscribers. On the one hand, the paywall publishing model provides commercial backing and a vested interest in maintaining software legibility (at least as long as the publisher survives).

On the other, the adoption of open-source software in building digital resources is seen to ensure that future designers and users can integrate with, and build from, existing resources. Sustainability involves different outcomes for finite resources such as 'Perdita', 'RECIRC', and the 1641 Depositions Project, which have completed their work, and resources that benefit from ongoing development, such as the *ODNB* and *EEBO*. Complete digital resources require investment to ensure their continuing legibility; not to do so is to squander the original commitment. Currency and relevance are key to durability, as an ecosystem of valuable resources grows and cross-fertilises. This interconnectedness in itself contributes to preservation. 'Beyond 2022', for example, a digital reconstruction of the building and collections of the Public Record Office, burned down in 1922, will offer further capacity for the field.[38] *The Digital Repository of Ireland* is a Trusted Digital Repository, certified as trustworthy in terms of sustainability and sustained access, at which member institutions can deposit digital resources for long-term preservation and sustained access.[39]

Finally, and pragmatically, autodidactism is a major feature of the digital humanities, for often logistical reasons; it is hard to recruit computer science specialists in today's job market, where the financial rewards are far greater in industry than the humanities. The time cost can be substantial, and production challenges such as data cleaning and disambiguation labour-intensive. However, the scholarly rewards should be evident from the widespread adoption and endemic use of digital surrogates as primary sources, of online biographical reference authorities, and of the selection of useful tools discussed above. The reality that has crept up on us is that we are all digitally engaged scholars now.[40]

NOTES

1. https://support.proquest.com/articledetail?id=kA11W000000bn1pSAA. *Early English Books Online*: https://search.proquest.com/eebo/index (subscriber-only).
2. See, for example, Heather Froelich, 'Thus to Make Poor Females Mad: Finding the "mad woman" in Early Modern Drama', The Pragmatics and Stylistics of Identity Construction and Characterisation. Studies in Variation, Contacts and Change in English, vol 17, ed. by Minna Nevala, Ursula Lutzky, Gabriella Mazzon & Carla Suhr (University of Helsinki: VARIENG e- publication series, 2016), http://www.helsinki. fi/varieng/series/volumes/17/froehlich/; Hugh Craig and Brett Greatley-Hirsch, *Style, Computers and Early Modern Drama: Beyond Authorship* (Cambridge: Cambridge University Press, 2017).
3. *State Papers Online*, 1509–1714: https://www.gale.com/intl/primary-sources/state-papers-online (subscriber-only).
4. 1641 Depositions: http://1641.tcd.ie/index.php (open access).
5. Mark Sweetnam and Barbara Fennell, 'Natural Language Processing and Early-modern Dirty Data: Applying IBM to the 1641 Depositions', *Literary and Linguistic Computing* 27 (2012), 39–54; Nicci McLeod and Barbara Fennell,

'Lexico-Grammatical Portraits of Vulnerable Women in War: The 1641 Depositions', *Journal of Historical Pragmatics* 13 (2012), 259–90.

6. *Women Writers Online*: https://www.wwp.northeastern.edu/wwo/ (subscriber-only).

7. Eighteenth-century works such as Mary Barber's *Poems on Several Occasions* (1734) and Sarah Butler's fiction, *Irish Tales* (1716) are also available.

8. Margaret J. M. Ezell, *Writing Women's Literary History* (Baltimore: Johns Hopkins University Press, 1993), and *Social Authorship and the Advent of Print* (Baltimore: Johns Hopkins University Press, 1999).

9. 'Perdita' (frames-based version): https://web.warwick.ac.uk/english/perdita/html/ (open access); 'Perdita Manuscripts, 1500–1700': https://www.amdigital.co.uk/primary-sources/perdita-manuscripts-1500-1700 (subscriber-only).

10. For a discussion of this date, which differs from Mark Robson's biography in the *ODNB*, see Alice Eardley, 'Introduction', in Hester Pulter, *Poems, Emblems, and The Unfortunate Florinda*, ed. by Alice Eardley (Toronto: Iter, 2014), pp.1–21.

11. Leah Knight and Wendy Wall, gen. eds., 'The Pulter Project: Poet in the Making' (2018): http://pulterproject.northwestern.edu (open access).

12. By 5 June 2019, this amounted to 1,629 texts: https://celt.ucc.ie/faq.html.

13. *Bardic Poetry Database*: https://bardic.celt.dias.ie/; Irish Script on Screen: https://www.isos.dias.ie/ (both open access). See also Sarah E. McKibben, 'Bardic Close Reading', in *Early Modern Ireland: New Sources, Methods, and Perspectives*, ed. by Sarah Covington, Vincent P. Carey, Valerie McGowan-Doyle (London and New York: Routledge, 2019), pp.96–112 (pp.97–100).

14. *leaṁ: Learn Early Modern Irish*: léamh.org/ (open access).

15. Brendan Kane, 'Making Early Modern Studies Irish? Teaching, Learning, and Researching Early Modern Irish in a Digital Age', in *Early Modern Ireland*, pp.79–95 (p.89).

16. Countering the argument that the same problems pertain to the marginalisation of writing in Latin (which is receiving a print boost through the editions that have emanated from UCC's Centre for Neo-Latin Studies), Kane suggests this is a 'category error' that equalises the insular vernacular language of Irish with Latin, 'the register of international and classical forms and genres'; Kane, 'Making Early Modern Studies Irish?', p.84.

17. *Oxford Dictionary of National Biography*: https://www.oxforddnb.com/ (subscriber-only).

18. For an introduction to the 2019 update, see https://www.oxforddnb.com/fileasset/AMT/ODNB%20Introduction%202019%20May2.pdf.

19. *Dictionary of Irish Biography*: https://dib.cambridge.org/ (subscriber-only).

20. 'Who Were the Nuns? A Prosopographical Study of the English Convents in Exile 1600–1800' https://wwtn.history.qmul.ac.uk/ (open access).

21. See Marie-Louise Coolahan, 'Archipelagic Identities in Europe: Irish Nuns in English Convents', in *The English Convents in Exile, 1600–1800: Communities, Culture and Identity*, ed. by Caroline Bowden and James Kelly (Burlington, VT.: Ashgate, 2013), pp.211–28; Bronagh McShane, *Irish Women in Religious Orders, c.1530–1756* (forthcoming with Boydell & Brewer).

22. 'Six Degrees of Francis Bacon': http://www.sixdegreesoffrancisbacon.com/?ids=10000473&min_confidence=60&type=network, 9/16/2019 (open access).

23. Christopher N. Warren, 'Historiography's Two Voices: Data Infrastructure and History at Scale in the *Oxford Dictionary of National Biography (ODNB)*', *Journal of Cultural Analytics* (2018), DOI: 10.22148/16.028, paragraph 21.

24. Ruth Ahnert and Sebastian E. Ahnert, 'Metadata, Surveillance and the Tudor State', *History Workshop Journal* 87 (2019), 27–51.

25. *Early Modern Letters Online*: http://emlo.bodleian.ox.ac.uk/ (open access); Networking Archives: https://networkingarchives.org/.
26. David Baker, Willy Maley, Patricia Palmer, 'What ish my network? Introducing MACMORRIS: Digitising Cultural Activity and Collaborative Networks in Early Modern Ireland', *Literature Compass* 15 (2018): doi.org/10.1111/lic3.12496, 4.
27. Patricia Palmer, David J. Baker, Willy Maley, 'Enter MacMorris', *Dublin Review of Books* 114 (2019): https://www.drb.ie/essays/enter-macmorris.
28. Baker, Maley, Palmer, 'What ish my network?', 6.
29. *Down Survey of Ireland*: http://downsurvey.tcd.ie/index.html.
30. *Centering Spenser*, http://core.ecu.edu/umc/Munster/virtual-tour.html.
31. Micheál Ó Siochrú and David Brown, 'Mapping the Past: Geographical Information Systems and the Exploitation of Linked Historical Data', in *Early Modern Ireland*, pp.301–320 (pp.314, 315, 303 respectively).
32. Julia Flanders and Sarah Connell, 'Writing, Reception, Intertextuality: Networking Women's Writing', *Journal of Medieval and Early Modern Studies*, special issue: 'The Dynamics of Cultural Reception in Early Modern Europe', 50 (2020), pp.161–80.
33. RECIRC: http://recirc.nuigalway.ie/ (open access).
34. Evan Bourke, 'Female Involvement, Membership, and Centrality: A Social Network Analysis of the Hartlib Circle', *Literature Compass* 14 (2017), 1–17, https://doi/10.1111/lic3.12388/ (subscriber-only); Bronagh McShane, 'Visualising the Reception and Circulation of Early Modern Nuns' Letters', *Journal of Historical Network Research* 2 (2018): 1–25, https://doi.org/10.25517/jhnr.v2i1.32 (open access).
35. Ellen Rooney, 'Introduction', *The Cambridge Companion to Feminist Literary Theory* (Cambridge: Cambridge University Press, 2006), pp.1–26 (p.4).
36. Jacqueline Wernimont, Whence Feminism? Assessing Feminist Interventions in Digital Literary Archives', *digital humanities quarterly* 7 (2013): paragraph 5, http://www.digitalhumanities.org/dhq/vol/7/1/000156/000156.html.
37. Jacqueline Wernimont and Julia Flanders, 'Feminism in the Age of Digital Archives: The Women Writers Project', *Tulsa* 29: 2 (2010), 425–435 (pp.425–6).
38. Beyond 1922: Ireland's Virtual Record Treasury: https://beyond2022.ie/.
39. *Digital Repository of Ireland*: https://dri.ie/.
40. Research for this article was funded by the European Research Council under the European Union's Seventh Framework Programme (FP/2007–2013)/ERC Grant Agreement n. 615545.

Lucy Collins

Hidden Collections: The Value of Irish Literary Archives

As definitions of Irish Literature change, the roles that archives play in preserving literary history, in changing perceptions, and in opening new areas for exploration, are more important than ever. Archival Studies in Ireland is founded on loss: with the burning of the Four Courts during the Civil War, documentary evidence of seven centuries of our rich and contested history was destroyed.[1] Yet this is not perhaps as disastrous as it might seem; for archives are always fragmentary, made up of what happens to have survived. They are also dynamic; they preserve existing treasures and renew their collections with manuscript and print acquisitions. In Ireland, the National Archives and the National Library are constantly improving their holdings, supporting the work of literary scholars through the archiving of key documents of the Irish past as well as by collecting the personal and literary papers of Irish writers, editors, and publishers. By facilitating the preservation and arrangement of documents, they support new way of interpreting and communicating historical and artistic processes to a wide audience.

CRITICAL FUTURES

Any discussion of a literary archive needs to take into account the relationship between the recording of the creative past and the shaping of a critical future. Collections, rather than functioning purely as a source of materials, are rewarding subjects of study in their own right, and illuminate the construction of our literary heritage. Irish Studies archives have inevitably prioritised the acquisition of documents relating to our own history and culture, and to the political and artistic expressions of the independence struggle. The value placed on these materials is reflected in the holdings of national institutions, as well as in the continuing prominence of documents and artefacts from the revolutionary period in online sales and auctions.

The existence of these materials continues to offer rich contextual resources for scholars of revivalist culture, but also to highlight the operation of dominant narratives in our intellectual traditions.

Irish University Review 50.1 (2020): 187–197
DOI: 10.3366/iur.2020.0445
© Edinburgh University Press
www.euppublishing.com/iur

Likewise, for many literary critics, canonical figures still hold a privileged place in teaching and research, and these are the writers whose archives attract significant scholarly attention. Institutional and private collectors still invest in the books and manuscripts of W.B. Yeats, James Joyce, and Samuel Beckett, with a significant consolidation of these materials outside Ireland. The State University of New York at Buffalo holds the largest collection of Joyce materials, while the Beckett Collection at the University of Reading represents the most significant holdings of Beckett's papers. The gathering of materials linked to Joyce's time in Paris – including his personal library and the papers of his publishers and associates, B.W. Huebsch and Sylvia Beach – testifies to the importance of bringing together diverse resources in order to best represent the varied interactions of the writer's life.[2] Joyce's awareness of the importance of his manuscript materials helped to ensure their survival, and this in turn has shaped the critical methodologies applied to his work. For both Joyce and Beckett, the genetic approaches that have fostered close scrutiny of creative process are made possible by the preservation of work in draft form. The same is true of W.B. Yeats, whose legacy is more directly linked to the formation of Ireland's modern literary identity.[3] Owing to the importance of the Yeats family as a whole, the lives of W.B. and his siblings can be traced through archival materials in the National Library of Ireland and the National Gallery of Ireland, as well as through the Royal Irish Academy, Trinity College Dublin, and University College Dublin. Such diversity is expressive of the creative versatility of the Yeats family as writers and artists, as well as of the significance of this period in the formation of Ireland's modern aesthetic. The state's failure to secure further items prior to an auction of Yeats family material in 2017 was widely interpreted as evidence of a lack of commitment to Ireland's significant cultural heritage.[4]

Market forces play an important role in the fate of manuscripts, but there are reasons why individual artists, or their descendants, may wish to maintain control over their own archives, or to ensure that their papers are held in an institution with which they have personal ties. While the first step in securing the artistic legacy of an author may be inclusion in a major repository, materials must be catalogued before they can be used by scholars for research or teaching. The cost of this cataloguing can be considerable, so that even if papers have been donated to an institution, they may remain inaccessible for some time. The problem is especially acute for the archives of minor literary figures or for material in less mainstream areas of scholarship, for which demand is not high. Brenda Donohue, a scholar of Irish theatre, considers that this tendency has clear political implications: 'Where women's theatre practice has entered the archive, it has often been kept safe in a repository, whilst remaining buried, hidden, unexposed to interested human eyes and not benefiting from interaction with scholars'.[5] The extent to which the artist, or his or her executors, maintain a relationship with the institution and participate in activities around their material legacy often determines the visibility of the archive. Digital and print exhibitions can also help to raise the profile of writers, both among scholars and in the wider community. The papers of Edna O'Brien, held at UCD Special Collections, became the focal point for several events celebrating the selection of *The Country Girls Trilogy* as 'Dublin: One City, One Book' for 2019. Five contemporary Irish fiction writers were invited to explore and respond to these materials; the result was fruitful creative engagement between writers and the literary archive in a session entitled 'Infamous, Influential, Beloved: Irish Writers Celebrate Edna O'Brien'.[6]

The relationship between archives in Ireland and those overseas is an increasingly significant one, given the limited funding for acquisitions by Irish institutions, and the demand for Irish materials in key universities abroad including the Harry Ransom Center at the University of Texas and Emory University. Opinions differ on the relative merits of preserving the papers of a writer in the place – or at least the country – with which that writer has the closest association, especially when this might render the materials more difficult to preserve or access. However, there are times when the popularity of the writer may play a significant role in the retention of the archive. Patrick Kavanagh's papers were collected and curated by his brother Peter, who expressed a strong preference that the materials be kept in Ireland. To this end, a national fundraising campaign was launched by Professor Gus Martin in 1986, and £100,000 was raised, a quarter of which was paid by the Irish government.[7] While Kavanagh scholars have used these papers,[8] their full potential for researchers interested in mid-century literary production has yet to be realised. In Ireland, as elsewhere, digitisation projects and grants to support travelling researchers are instrumental in ensuring close links between archiving and scholarship and in maintaining the profile – and value – of certain collections.

The Kavanagh archive not only sheds light on the creative career of the poet himself, but also reveals much about the place of the writer in the newly-formed Free State. An overlooked dimension of the literary archive is its potential to inform our understanding of cultural networks; even apparently marginal figures can have a wide range of contacts, making their correspondence a rich resource for cultural historians. Interesting conjunctions between writers also enhance the research value of the single archive: poet and playwright Austin Clarke was a friend of F.R. Higgins, who was also a poet and director of the Abbey

Theatre (1935–41). An examination of their papers, both held in the National Library of Ireland, provides a greater understanding of literary allegiances and enmities during the early Free State years than the record of any individual figure could reveal. Regional affinities can also be clarified in an archive, as is demonstrated by comparing holdings north and south of the border. Collaborative projects and the digitising of resources increasingly allow dialogue between these different repositories. The Northern Ireland Literary Archive, which is part of the Linen Hall Library, is a digitisation project that brings materials from nine key writers associated with Northern Ireland to a wider audience.[9] Spanning generations and genres, these authors were chosen to represent the variety of the library's literary holdings, yet they reveal instead the essentially close-knit character of the artistic community in Northern Ireland. While this archive, like so many others, is structured around the work of key authors, the business of literary production and the operation of networks of friendship and collaboration may be better understood through assembling the broadest range of material possible. Publishers' archives, such as the Dolmen Press archive in Wake Forest University and Trinity College Dublin, the archive of Carcanet Press at Manchester's John Rylands Library, or the Archive of British Publishing and Printing at the University of Reading, tell us much of the mechanisms of selection and publication that shape the careers and the legacies of Irish writers. Recent work by Eve Patten and Conor Linnie, in collaboration with the Library of Trinity College Dublin, has revealed the aesthetic and political considerations involved in the publication of poetry in modern Ireland. The rarity of many of the items in their *Poetics of Print* online exhibition makes the choice of a digital format ideal from both a curatorial and pedagogical perspective.[10]

Papers may be held at particular repositories for reasons of geography or economics, but such decisions may also reflect a larger sense of institutional identity. The relationship between an individual collection and the overall aims of the library is important, and initiatives to facilitate the acquisition of new material by institutions already in possession of noteworthy collections from a named writer helps to make these materials more readily accessible to a scholar travelling to use them. In this respect it is significant that both Trinity College Dublin and University College Dublin are members of the Group for Literary Archives and Manuscripts (GLAM), as is the National Library of Ireland. The National Library has, since the early 1990s, made a particular effort to collect the papers of living Irish writers, and existing archives relating to W.B. Yeats, James Joyce, Brian Friel, and Seamus Heaney have raised the profile of the holdings among international scholars, as well as among writers and their executors. Similarly the concentration of poetry materials, both in print and digital modes, at UCD Special Collections has helped to shape their holdings. These include many print items relating to W.B. Yeats, and the personal libraries of Thomas Kinsella and Dennis O'Driscoll. The presence of a few important archives in a repository can attract others, and this in turn fosters teaching and scholarship both within the institution and further afield. This is an important reminder of the relationship between the scholar and the archivist, and the active roles that library staff play in the formation of the scholars of tomorrow.

THE SHAPE OF THE LITERARY ARCHIVE

Archives often trouble the boundary between public and private worlds in ways that are both challenging and productive. A literary archive is not a defined entity and its capacity to extend our understanding of what the writer is can also challenge canonical norms within a subject area. Most literary archives contain a range of materials including both print and manuscript drafts of work, correspondence with publishers, and writing notebooks, but they may also include personal diaries and private correspondence that shed light on an individual's relationships and development as a writer. In the case of theatre archives, the development of collaborative relationships and of specific roles within the performance space may be traced through the records, as the rich gathering of theatre materials at NUI Galway attests.[11] It is the relationship between these materials, and their capacity to extend – or even contradict – existing versions of the subject that are often most illuminating for a scholar. The archive not only provides contextual detail for the study of literary figures, but also allows us to reflect directly on the relationship between the printed or performed work and the larger context of its production. Literature plays a role in mediating complex political and social worlds, yet is also intrinsic to the formation of identity and to social change. Archives enable our understanding of this relationship, and reveal much of both the aesthetic and practical choices of the author.

One of the key principles of the archive is that the materials should be preserved in the order in which they were used or maintained by their creator. However, as Jennifer Douglas and Heather MacNeil have argued, this understanding needs to be problematised in the case of personal archives, which often lack a systematic arrangement.[12] As well as giving insight into the writer's process,[13] archives also testify to the randomness and disorder of the creative life, as Carolyn Steedman has suggested: 'The Archive is made from selected and consciously chosen documentation from the past and also from the mad fragmentations that no one intended to preserve and that just ended up there'.[14] If the papers were assembled by someone other than their original creator, the decisions that shaped their retention and organisation may not be fully understood. Instead, these documents may express the journey these objects have taken through the hands of family members and executors, as well as informal handling by scholars or enthusiasts. A changed arrangement of this material releases new interpretations that may or may not be justified – this is the 'added value' that the archivist's knowledge and experience brings to the records' original context of creation.[15] Yet this desire to create 'an orderly seamless narrative from what were once scattered and discontinuous fragments',[16] can also be a cause of anxiety among archivists. It is impossible to exclude interpretative process from the archive: by its nature it draws attention to the relationship between the individual artefact and the collection, positing 'the existence of an affinity between abstract wholes and material parts' that is intuitive as well as systematic.[17]

Digitisation has brought new attention to the material text.[18] It reminds us of the unique character of archival materials – what we find in a notebook or manuscript draft is not found elsewhere and, though it may be digitally reproduced, not every aspect of its original meaning can be replicated. Yet in spite of the democratising character of the digital archive, our reliance on it risks limiting, or even destroying, swathes of our print heritage. Shafquat Towheed notes that some digitisation projects have led directly to the destruction of the printed materials, resulting in unique records of ownership and reading being lost.[19] In other ways too, examining the digital image is a distinctly different experience from our encounter with the original archival object. The uniformity of the screen version compromises our understanding of the physical attributes and contexts of production of the original: diverse publications may be given the same level of attention and size of visual presentation, obscuring the key differences in the conditions under which these were originally printed and read.[20] For these reasons digital processes have a complex relationship with the paper archive, and Jerome McGann cautions against using them to 'replicate our procedural, as opposed to our reflexive, powers and faculties'.[21] Yet at their most effective they make entirely new ways of reading possible. In the Irish context, the *Industrial Memories* project, which uses digital tools to analyse the Report of the Commission to Inquire into Child Abuse, more commonly known as the Ryan Report, offers access to a vast body of material and brings hitherto unknown patterns of experience to light.[22] Such initiatives create an innovative form of archive, not just replicating existing printed text, or analysing the data derived from it, but generating new objects, both in digital and paper formats, to enlarge the interpretative potential of the text.[23]

WOMEN WRITERS IN THE ARCHIVE

Writers today have an acute sense of the potential of their documents to accrue both scholarly and monetary worth but previous generations – and especially those unsure of their reputation and legacy – are much less securely positioned as archival subjects. The contention that major repositories have been until recently inhospitable to the papers of women writers is linked to questions of canon formation: arguably then, the neglect of the materiality of the woman writer is indicative of an approach that prioritises the major writer and seeks to enhance those holdings at the expense of more diverse materials. This policy serves present and future scholars of recognised writers of achievement, but fails to acknowledge the importance of minor writers, and – just as significantly – of networks of creativity, in the formation of cultural traditions. This process is often underpinned by deeply practical concerns: Judi Cumming notes that 'archival repositories do not want to acquire private archival fonds that take up valuable shelf space and will require processing and conservation, if those fonds do not serve the research needs of their clientele'.[24] The need for repositories to actively prioritise certain acquisitions can therefore lead to reinforcement of areas in which they already have strengths, rather than the opening of new fields. Archival collections may lag behind research priorities and thus, obliquely, direct them through omission. Conversely readers may have the opportunity to empower archivists to make the case for acquiring and cataloguing diverse materials.

Yet in spite of a deepening interest in the work of Irish women writers, reinvigorated by #WakingTheFeminists (2016) and 'Fired! Irish Women Poets and the Canon' (2017), the archival profile of individual women writers has not been significantly raised. Fired! draws particular attention to the neglect of earlier generations of Irish women poets, and to the fact that their work is both out of print and largely unrepresented in the archive. When I began work on Poetry by Women in Ireland: A Critical Anthology 1870–1970 (2012), only two of the fifteen women I chose had named archives in institutional repositories: Katharine Tynan in Southern Illinois University and Sheila Wingfield in the National Library of Ireland. Materials relating to the other women were very limited: some papers of Dora Sigerson Shorter's were held in Leeds University and in Trinity College Dublin; Eva Gore-Booth could be traced through items in the National Library of Ireland and at University College Dublin. For these women, as for so many others, representation is often in the archives of male poets and editors, where the specifics of their own creativity are obscured.

The material traces left by these women continue to be fragmentary, falling short of the ideal archival representation of the complete life. There are many reasons for this. Often, women poets do not systematically collect their manuscripts, either because they have not been encouraged to think of these as valuable, or because periods of comparative creative inactivity may prevent them from seeing their artistic career in a singular or continuous way. Not every aspect of their creative life may be judged as of equal importance – papers relating a key work may be retained, while others are discarded, a fact that may encourage critics to give continued attention to only that one part of the writer's output. The presence of ephemera that bears only a tangential relationship to the creative work may represent an unwelcome excess of material, while in privileging the documentary or printed archive we may overlook elements that cannot be captured in this way – the meetings, conversations, and performances that may be as important, both in the formation and reception of the writer, as the written text.

This pattern of exclusion has serious repercussions for the role of the archive in accurately documenting the literary contribution of women to modern Irish society. Archival theory has tended to privilege document collections that contribute to our understanding of public history but, in the Irish context in particular, women bear an uneasy relationship to the state, a fact that has limited their engagement with formal archival processes and may specifically inhibit them from seeking to place their work in a national repository. Exploring the fate of the woman writer's archive in Canada, Linda Morra and Jessica Schagerl have observed:

> since archival papers that were considered worth keeping usually related directly to the official process of nation building, with which women could only have had a limited part, the material retained tended to perpetuate women's marginalisation.[25]

This issue is pertinent to the work of Irish women: materials collected are shaped by prevailing assumptions, which are perpetuated by the versions of female experience expressed through existing materials and acknowledged by generations of scholars. Thus, for example, poetry archives are influenced by the standing of women poets in the wider cultural community, and go on to shape how we evaluate and teach women poets. Éilís Ní Dhuibhne, in her reflection on the collecting policy of the National Library of Ireland, remarked:

> The [National] Library tries, correctly and unsurprisingly, to acquire the papers of Ireland's most important writers and poets – its greatest poetic treasure obviously being the Yeats Collection. One might ask that it also try to identify poets of less exalted stature whose work could be of interest to research. As usual, women writers are notable by their absence in the manuscript collections relating to Irish poetry, here as in the US,

even though the National Library's holdings have a better gender balance than those of Emory University or Boston College, which is not saying much, however. And it is clear that male writers, even minor ones, stand a much better chance of making it to a National Library manuscript list than females.[26]

THE LIVING ARCHIVE

The need to tell more diverse stories of Irish social and literary identities has meant greater attention to the concept of the living archive in recent years. The importance of securing documentation and online records relating to landmark events is demonstrated by the reception of archival materials relating to the 2015 Marriage Equality referendum into the National Library of Ireland.[27] This complements the Irish Queer Archive currently held there and marks a welcome effort to rebalance the scholarly treatment of neglected narratives. These archives not only extend our understanding of the experiences and creative acts of the past, but challenge the monumentality of the archive – the ways in which it represents exceptional lives and work. Individual efforts to place marginalised experience on the record, and to address the importance of material traces in contemporary life can also be found in Vukašin Nedeljković's *Asylum Archive*, which documents the experience of Direct Provision in Ireland.[28] These projects have literary analogues too, most notably in Kimberly Campanello's MOTHERBABYHOME – a 796-page production from zimZalla.[29] This work, which engages with a multiplicity of documentary and media representations of the Tuam Babies controversy, both responds to – and rethinks – the preservation and visibility of the lives of all citizens. Printed on semi-transparent acetate sheets, and presented in a wooden box, the project, which is both formally and typographically innovative, draws attention to the extent and duration of institutional abuse as well as to the need for adequate commemoration of the children who died. MOTHERBABYHOME is both in and of the archive, derived from printed sources and drawing on the cumulative nature of these materials. In January 2020 Campanello performed a durational recording of the complete work for the Irish Poetry Reading Archive, thus voicing the names of the dead and the processes of research and writing for viewers all over the world.[30]

CONCLUSION

As we have seen, Irish archives express the freedoms and limitations of our wider society, which in turn influence the methodologies adopted by textual scholars. The ongoing importance of the archive in the field of Irish literary studies lies in its potential to extend the subjects of our research and offer new perspectives, even on established writers and themes. In building a bridge between past and future, archives challenge monolithic versions of Irish literature and pave the way for new interpretations of our cultural past. Barry Houlihan identifies the latent power of the archive in 'its potential to effect change, knowledge and accountability',[31] thus positioning the literary archive as uniquely capable of linking the close scrutiny of text and performance to the politics of literature and its institutional relationships. At a time when the power structures of our cultural foundations are under scrutiny, support for the principle and practice of the archive will at once facilitate change, and record the challenging process of achieving it.

NOTES

1. *Beyond 2022: Ireland's Virtual Record Treasury* is a collaboration between Trinity College Dublin and the National Archives of Ireland, the National Archives (UK), the Public Record Office of Northern Ireland, and the Irish Manuscripts Commission to create a virtual reconstruction of the Public Record Office of Ireland lost in the Four Courts fire during the Civil War, accessed 28 January 2020, https://beyond2022.ie

2. 'Collection Overview', James Joyce Collection, State University of New York at Buffalo, accessed 11 January 2020, https://library.buffalo.edu/jamesjoyce/collection-overview/

3. The Cornell Yeats prints the manuscript materials of all W.B. Yeats's major work. See http://www.sfu.ca/~curtis/CornellYeats/

4. Sarah Bardon, 'State to purchase a number of items from Yeats family collection', *Irish Times*, 27 September 2017, accessed 23 January 2020, https://www.irishtimes.com/news/politics/state-to-purchase-a-number-of-items-from-yeats-family-collection-1.3235018

5. Brenda Donohue, 'Women and the Archive: What Vision of the Present will be Preserved for the Future?', *Navigating Ireland's Theatre Archive: Theory, Practice, Performance*, ed. by Barry Houlihan (Oxford: Peter Lang, 2019), pp.163–81 (p.164).

6. 'Infamous, Influential, Beloved: Irish Writers Celebrate Edna O'Brien' was held at UCD on Monday 17 September 2018, organised by Dan O'Brien and Eve Kearney, accessed 23 January 2020, https://www.ucd.ie/englishdramafilm/newsandevents/irishwriterscelebrateednaobrien/

7. RTÉ reported on the acquisition of the manuscripts: 'Patrick Kavanagh Papers Return', accessed 23 January, https://www.rte.ie/archives/2016/1216/839405-patrick-kavanagh-manuscripts/

8. See, for example, Úna Agnew, *The Mystical Imagination of Patrick Kavanagh: A Buttonhole in Heaven?* (Dublin: Veritas Publications, 1999; rev. ed. 2019) and Antoinette Quinn, *Patrick Kavanagh: A Biography* (Dublin: Gill and Macmillan, 2003).

9. The archive features manuscript materials from John Boyd, Samuel Ferguson, Robert Greacen, Sam Hanna Bell, John Hewitt, Joan Lingard, Louis MacNeice, Stewart Parker, and W.R. Rodgers. See https://www.niliteraryarchive.com.

10. *The Poetics of Print: The Private Press Tradition & Irish Poetry*, accessed 11 January 2020, https://www.tcd.ie/library/exhibitions/poetics/

11. Accessed 23 January 2020, https://www.nuigalway.ie/drama/theatrearchivesandre-searchresources/. See also Barry Houlihan, ed., *Navigating Ireland's Theatre Archive: Theory, Practice, Performance* (Oxford: Peter Lang, 2019).

12. Jennifer Douglas and Heather MacNeil, 'Arranging the Self: Literary and Archival Perspectives on Writers' Archives', *Archivaria* 67 (Spring 2009), 25–39 (p.27).

13. Catherine Hobbs argues that archival materials may be capable of representing an author's 'mental map' and therefore of illuminating his or her processes of thought and creation. Hobbs, 'Re-envisioning the Personal: Reframing Traces of Individual Life', *Currents of Archival Thinking*, ed. by Terry Eastwood and Heather MacNeil (Santa Barbara, CA: Libraries Unlimited, 2010), pp.213–41 (p.231).

14. Carolyn Steedman, *Dust* (Manchester: Manchester University Press, 2001), p.68.

15. Peter Horsman, qtd in Jennifer Douglas, 'Original Order, Added Value? Archival Theory and the Douglas Coupland Fonds', in *The Boundaries of the Literary Archive: Reclamation and Representation*, ed. by Carrie Smith and Lisa Stead (London: Routledge, 2016), pp.45–59 (p.45).

16. Maryanne Dever, 'Reading Other People's Mail', *Archives and Manuscripts* 24 (May 1996), 116–29 (p.121).

17. Douglas and MacNeil, 'Arranging the Self', p.27.

18. Maryanne Dever and Linda Morra, 'Literary Archives, Materiality, and the Digital', *Archives and Manuscripts* 42.3 (2014), 222–6 (p.223).

19. Shafquat Towheed, 'Reading in the Digital Archive', *Journal of Victorian Culture* 15.1 (2010), 139–43 (p.141).

20. Towheed, 'Reading in the Digital Archive', p.142.

21. Jerome McGann, *Radiant Textuality: Literature After the World Wide Web* (New York and Basingstoke: Palgrave Macmillan, 2001), p.214.

22. *Industrial Memories* is an IRC-funded project led by Associate Professor Emilie Pine (UCD School of English, Drama and Film) and Professor Mark Keane (UCD Insight Centre), accessed 11 January 2020, https://industrialmemories.ucd.ie.

23. *Survivors' Stories* is an oral history project that has collected some of the stories of victims of abuse in Irish institutions, and placed these in the National Folklore Archive at UCD. Led by Emilie Pine and Críostóir MacCárthaigh, the project was awarded the UCD Research Impact Award for 2019.

24. Judi Cumming, 'Beyond Intrinsic Value: Towards Development of Acquisition Strategies in the Private Sector', *Archivaria* 38 (Fall, 1994), 232–39 (p.233). The term 'fonds' denotes a group of documents that come from the same source.

25. Linda M. Morra and Jessica Schagerl, 'Introduction: No Archive is Neutral', in *Basements and Attics, Closets and Cyberspace: Explorations in Canadian Women's Archives*, ed. by Linda M. Morra and Jessica Schagerl. Toronto: Wilfrid Laurier Press, 2013, pp.1–19 (p.2).

26. Éilís Ní Dhuibhne, 'Poetry in the Archive: Reflections of a Former Archivist on the Manuscripts of Twentieth-century Irish Poets in the National Library of Ireland', *Irish University Review* 42.1 (2012), 155–68 (p.165).

27. The Marriage Equality Referendum took place on the 22 May 2015. It proposed an amendment to the Constitution of Ireland to permit marriage between two persons without distinction as to their sex. It was approved by 62% of the voters and came into force on 16 November 2015.

28. Accessed 11 January 2020, http://www.asylumarchive.com. See Vukašin Nedeljković, 'Reiterating Asylum Archive: Documenting Direct Provision in Ireland', *Research in Drama Education: The Journal of Applied Theatre and Performance*, 23.1 (2018), 289–93.

29. zimZalla is a publishing project that releases literary objects. It is administered by Tom Jenks. See zimzalla.co.uk.

30. The Irish Poetry Reading Archive is a national digital repository of poetry readings, interviews and lectures, based at UCD.

31. Barry Houlihan, 'Introduction: The Potential of the Archive', *Navigating Ireland's Theatre Archive*, p.11.

Irish Studies Internationally

Dianne Hall and Ronan McDonald

Irish Studies in Australia and New Zealand

Internationally, Irish Studies tends to thrive where the Irish diaspora settled: Boston, New York, Liverpool, London, Montreal. Yet one could not say that Irish Studies in Australia is especially robust, particularly when looked at comparatively.[1] We will attempt to answer why that is so in this brief survey, addressing institutional and cultural factors and also the historic relationship between Ireland and Australia, which has produced a strange mix of familiarity and distance between the two countries.

While Australia received far fewer Irish migrants than the more proximate Britain and USA, the proportionate Irish influence in Australia is unmatched. In 1901 at the time of the Federation of the separate colonies that made up Australia, one quarter of the white population of 3.8 million were of Irish birth or descent. Among the white European population, the Irish were second only to the English, forming a substantial and important minority.[2] Visiting Irish politicians now refer to this by routinely calling Australia the 'most Irish country outside of Ireland'. There is, then, great overlap between the story of the global Irish and that of the development of the Australian nation since European settlement. Australia is far from Ireland geographically, but much closer culturally.

In Australia the majority of the Catholic settlers were Irish, and the majority of Irish were Catholic, arriving into a majority Protestant colony. This was different to Canada, which also attracted a significant proportion of Irish Protestant migrants and had a substantial ethnically French Catholic settler population. New Zealand attracted fewer Irish Catholics proportionally than Australia, with substantial and influential Irish Protestant migration schemes. So there are historical differences

Irish University Review 50.1 (2020): 198–205
DOI: 10.3366/iur.2020.0446
© Edinburgh University Press
www.euppublishing.com/iur

between Irish settlement in Australia and New Zealand as well as the rest of the British world. Catholics in Australia were overwhelmingly of Irish birth or descent until the post-war migrations from Catholic southern European countries. Therefore, until the 1950s, to be Catholic was to be Irish in Protestant Australia, with all the implications for discrimination this sectarian otherness implied. The Irish in Australia were often suspected of disloyalty, especially at times of national or international crisis, such as the Land Wars and the First World War. Upwardly mobile Irish had to negotiate their bonds to Ireland with the suspicion of British Australia: this impacted how Irish Australia affiliated with the cause of Irish political nationalism. Because of their place within the British Empire and later Commonwealth, Irish Catholics in Australia and New Zealand were less likely to take up radical positions on Irish nationalism and republicanism than their compatriots in the United States. Furthermore, as very few refugees from the Famine settled in Australia or New Zealand, because of the distance and cost involved in the journey, the general degree of grievance against the English for their treatment of the Famine Irish was less overt. Certainly, many Irish and their children in Australasia felt strongly about their connections with Ireland, and were prepared to donate money and attend events supporting Irish causes throughout the nineteenth and into the twentieth century. But they were generally content with their position in Australia or New Zealand as part of the British Empire and this muted their response to the Irish political situation. In general, Irish constitutional nationalism and home rule was favoured. The assertion of autonomy was one thing, but it was not in the interests of Irish Australia to declare its absolute difference from the British establishment. This culture of integration, or limited separateness, had long term implications in how Irish-Australia saw itself and for Irish Studies within Australia.

While the sectarianism of the nineteenth century, that had erupted into overt discrimination periodically, simmered away through the first half of the twentieth century, from the late 1980s it was largely suspended alongside the continuing arrival of new and more different migrant groups.[3] So the Irish appeared, by comparison with Italians, Greeks, Vietnamese, and Lebanese, and, later, Africans, all in all *less* different. The distinct story of Irish assimilation, and the tenacious idea of an 'Anglo-Celtic' Australia, stymied the idea of Irishness as a distinct, autotelic object of inquiry. It could be one reason why, in Australia, Irish Studies remained relatively muted in the academic mainstream.

During the time when Australian and New Zealand universities were expanding in the 1960s, there was little appetite for looking towards Ireland for intellectual inspiration, the direction of the outwards gaze was firmly towards the ivory towers of Oxbridge or the Ivy League, where Irish interests were also usually marginal. Today's universities are to some extent at least the products of the aspirations and intellectual backgrounds of those who came of age in the 1960s and 70s, often with degrees from English or American universities.[4]

What of the state of Irish Studies now? While North America, including Canada, boasts vibrant Irish Studies centres offering specialised qualification, there is not a single one in Australia. No university in Australia offers an Irish Studies BA minor or an MA. In the whole of Australasia only the University of Otago offers a designated minor in Irish Studies. Thanks to the gift of an Irish businessman who made his fortune in New Zealand, the Eamonn Cleary Chair of Irish Studies was endowed at Otago, which subsequently saw the establishment of the Centre for Irish and Scottish Studies. In Australia, there is only one permanent, devoted post, also the product of diasporic philanthropy – the Gerry Higgins Chair in Irish Studies at the University of Melbourne. Yet educational philanthropy is still comparatively undeveloped in Australasia and, these two initiatives apart, Irish Studies has no devoted institutional presence in Australia and New Zealand (apart, that is, from Celtic Studies or European Studies). While to some extent this can be explained by the smaller population, with less scope for specialised majors or degrees in many of the topics available in larger countries, Australian and New Zealand universities are moving increasingly to broader degrees with less subject choice as a way of maximising numbers and staffing in an increasingly hostile economic climate. The current climate in the universities, including the funding and legitimacy challenges facing arts and humanities more generally, would not seem to favour Irish Studies.

Even though the university landscape for Irish Studies is problematic, Irish Studies has long benefitted from the dedication, passion, and industry of numerous individual scholars working inside and outside the third level sector. Lone academics with an interest in Irish history or literature, or less commonly, political science, music, and archaeology, form trans-institutional clusters and collaborations, some long standing. The Irish Studies Association of Australia and New Zealand (ISAANZ) is the main academic association in the region and was established in 2006. It took under its umbrella the long-standing Irish-Australian conference series which was begun in Canberra in 1980 by Oliver MacDonagh and W.F. Mandle.[5] The proceedings of these conferences were often published as stand-alone volumes, with Val Noone producing important bibliographic essays on the conference series from 1980 until 2007.[6] Bob Reece at Murdoch University in Western Australia established the *Australian Journal of Irish Studies* in 2000, and in 2006 the journal moved to Melbourne and was renamed the *Australasian Journal of Irish Studies* to reflect the inclusion of New Zealand Irish

Studies scholars into ISAANZ. *AJIS* is a peer reviewed academic journal published annually and distributed to university libraries and individuals around the world.[7] It provides a formal academic platform for Irish Studies in Australia and New Zealand, while also keeping activity in the Antipodes connected to international academic Irish Studies.

Other avenues for sharing Irish Studies scholarship have developed and continue to thrive. As part of a collaboration that includes the Gerry Higgins Chair of Irish Studies, Newman College at the University of Melbourne provides funds for an annual Irish Studies Fellowship based in their library which houses the internationally significant O'Donnell collection centred around the library of Australian-born Gaelic scholar Dr Nicholas O'Donnell (1862–1920). This fellowship, offered annually since 2010, has attracted high calibre Irish Studies scholars from Australia, Ireland, and the United States from a wide range of disciplines including Irish language, music, and history.[8] The O'Donnell Fellows share their research findings by giving a seminar in the long running Melbourne Irish Studies Seminar series, organised by a committee of Irish Studies scholars in Melbourne, and publish their findings in *AJIS*. Joyce's 'Bloomsday' is celebrated on 16 June each year in parts of Australia. In Melbourne, for example, since the 1990s a group of enthusiasts led by Frances Devlin-Glass has been organising readings and discussions of Joyce's work, as well as staging dramatized episodes from *Ulysses*.[9] (Joyce and other major Irish writers are staples of the literary curriculum in Australia, though rarely as part of devoted Irish courses.) Melbourne's Celtic Club also hosts the annual 'Brigidfest' held to coincide with St Brigid's feast day in February. This popular event hosts a speaker on a topic relevant to Irish or Irish Australian women. In Sydney, study days and conferences associated with Celtic studies usually include Irish material and have been organised first by the late Anders Alqvist and then by Jonathan Wooding, holders of the Chair of Celtic Studies at the University of Sydney as well as independent scholars such as Dr Pamela O'Neill. Sydney is also the home of the Aisling Society, a society that for some sixty years has advanced the study of Irish and Irish-Australian history and culture. The numerous Irish and Celtic clubs around the country also, typically, have a heritage remit as part of their mission. There are other extra-academic organs for Irish interest material, such as *Tinteán*, previously a print and, since 2012, an online magazine published by the Australian Irish heritage network. Language classes and cultural activities thrive all around the country, and there are well attended annual events such as Daonscoil in rural Victoria. The Australian Irish Heritage Association, based in Perth, Western Australia and founded in 1993 by the late Joe O'Sullivan, organises annual lectures, writers' awards, commemorations, and publications. These activities are organised and sustained by dedicated volunteers and signal that there is a healthy appetite for Irish language, literature, and history among many Australians and New Zealanders, as well as Irish ex-pats.[10]

So perhaps as a side effect of the relative lack of university support for Irish Studies, Irish Studies in Australia is notable for often productive synergies between academic and non-academic wings, between professional historians based in universities and scholars with other (or no) institutional allegiances. ISAANZ conferences typically feature a high proportion of papers by local historians, genealogists, journalists, or trade writers. Associations, community groups, and Celtic clubs in the major cities have long invested time and resources in cultivating and promoting the study of Irish history, culture, music, and language and it is not unusual for Irish studies initiatives and collaborations to emerge from these sites.

Conversely, as these connections might indicate, Irish Studies in Australia confronts a local version of a transnational tension. While Australasian Irish Studies has forged productive alliances outside the university institution, Irish Studies is nonetheless sometimes required to negotiate conflicting images amongst its stakeholders. For example, Irish Studies specialists scrutinize, with all requisite critical scepticism, nostalgic, or sentimental ideas of Irish identity, to which the wider culture, including the Irish-heritage philanthropists who might fund it, are often quite attracted. In other words, there are tensions as well as possibilities in the extra-academic quality of Irish studies in Australia.

Internationally, Irish Studies must also confront a more troubling dilemma. Its success is inseparable from circuitries of power that emerge from geopolitical asymmetry. The Irish brand around the world trades off a marketable sense of acceptable alterity. Its attraction to students comes from the sense that, while the Irish might be different, they are not *too* different. Ireland was sufficiently of the West not to be threatening, and also sufficiently *not* of it to be exotic and alluring. The Irish in Britain, the United States, and Australasia had certainly suffered persecution and oppression. But as the 1980s ceded to the 90s, Irishness and by extension Irish studies, enjoyed a revamped reputation and glimmered with cultural allure, especially as economic success finally arrived in Ireland. An Anglophone culture, with a huge diasporic presence in the major cultural powers in the world, Ireland enjoyed visibility out of proportion to its population. Ireland and Irishness became known through capitalist image making or, more troublingly, with the whiteness and the assimilability of the Irish compared with dumped and disregarded ethnicities around the globe. In that respect at least, though the story of Ireland often seems ill-fated, the story of Irish studies seems blessed, ideally positioned to thrive in the world's academic and cultural networks.

This feature has, in a sense, been inverted in Australia, where Irish Studies has lost ground to areas where difference to the dominant culture is more marked. Irish studies in Australia enjoyed a fillip in Australia during the 1990s, when the Chairs in Otago and Melbourne were founded. During this period, the peace process meant Ireland was not far from international headlines and the booming Celtic Tiger and its cultural analogues meant Ireland had a sheen of Cool Hibernia. But Irish studies in Australia has lost some of its energies since then for a number of reasons, not least because Australian intellectual and academic culture has increasingly sought to address long neglected issues of race, post-war immigration, and, perhaps above all, its festering and unresolved Aboriginal question (unlike New Zealand, no treaty currently exists with Australian indigenous people). Australia needed to wake up to its geography rather than its history, to recognise its regional location in south east Asia and address its neighbouring national cultures. In this context, the Irish question seemed less urgent and the Irish less different. To be sure, as Elizbeth Malcolm and Dianne Hall's recent new history has forcefully reminded us, Australian history has often been marked by sectarian division and discrimination against Irish Catholics.[11] But this division has long subsided and it is easy to group the Irish with the British under the catch-all phrase 'Anglo-Celt' or 'White Australian', obscuring the history of division in those falsely unifying categories. It has made the Irish less visible to the Australian academy, and Irish history and culture more easily assimilable to British courses, which is where much 'Irish' politics, literature, and history in Australia is studied. This has been exacerbated by the relative neglect of significant relevant Irish Australian scholarship, such as the very important work of the late Patrick O'Farrell, by Australian historians and academics.[12]

One of the challenges ahead for Irish Studies in Australasia is to confront the part that Irish settlers played in the brutal colonial frontiers and the ongoing discrimination of people of colour in Australia and New Zealand. The comfortable popular perception is that because the Irish were oppressed in Ireland and discriminated against in Australia, and New Zealand, then they were kinder, less brutal, to the Indigenous peoples that they encountered when they moved outside to the antipodes.[13] This is certainly the premise behind the Australian movie *The Nightingale* (2019) in which a young Irish woman is subject to violence by English settlers and forms an alliance with a similarly brutalised Aboriginal man. However, as Larissa Behrendt, an Eualeyai/Kamillaroi lawyer, academic, novelist, and film-maker, recently wrote in her review of the film in the *Guardian*, the processes of colonisation involving previously marginalised peoples such as Irish Catholics coming into contact with Indigenous peoples were more complex than this and need much more nuanced analysis and research.[14] It is a pity that *The Nightingale* has received greater mainstream attention than the sensitive low budget documentary directed by Paula Keohe, *An Dubh ina Gheal: Assimilation* (2015) which featured interviews with Indigenous Australians of Irish descent as well as Indigenous activists on Irish-Indigenous relations. It is, however, encouraging that Malcolm and Hall's *A New History of the Irish in Australia*, with an explicit agenda to begin to tackle some at least of these issues, was not only published by a mainstream Australian publisher with subsequent healthy sales, but was also funded by the main government funding body, the Australian Research Council and has been short-listed for an Australian literary prize. It is also encouraging that scholars such as Malcolm Campbell from New Zealand and Barry McCarron from New York are now researching the complex role of the Irish in the colonisation of the Pacific and Asia.

There are many other opportunities for Irish-Australian studies, which have not yet been tapped. The Australian national imaginary, the 'larrikin' figure and rebel perhaps most famously incarnated in the bushranger Ned Kelly, owes much to images of Irishness. This amounts to a common truism, yet it still awaits theoretically sensitive investigation and careful scholarly genealogy, deploying the latest insights of diaspora studies. What does it mean to speak of Irish-Australian identity and how does it relate to transnational circuitries of Irishness? Can we talk of a discrete tradition of Irish-Australian literature, running from from Frank the Poet, via Joseph Furphy to Vincent Buckley, Tom Kenneally, and Thea Astley? Despite its distance and its occasional invisibility in Ireland, Australia has been blessed by the attentions of some of Ireland's greatest modern historians, such as Oliver MacDonagh (1924–2002) and David Fitzpatrick (1948–2018). There is a sizeable and growing scholarship about Irish-Australasia. Yet many rich seams across the Irish Studies disciplines await investigation.

NOTES

1. For other detailed surveys of Irish Studies in Australia and New Zealand see Elizabeth Malcolm, '10,000 Miles Away: Irish Studies Down Under', *Ireland Beyond Boundaries: Mapping Irish Studies in the Twenty-First Century*, ed. by Liam Harte and Yvonne Whelan (London: Pluto Press, 2007), pp.39–47; Philip Bull and Elizabeth Malcolm, 'Irish Studies in Australia and New Zealand, 1980–2013', *Australasian Journal of Irish Studies* 13 (2013), 29–44, and Elizabeth Malcolm, 'Searching for the Irish and Irish Studies in Australia', *Estudios Irlandeses* 14 (2019), 207–217.
2. C.A. Price, 'The Ethnic Character of the Australian Population', *The Australian People: An Encyclopedia of the Nation, its People and their Origins*, ed. by James Jupp, 2nd ed. (Cambridge: Cambridge University Press, 2001), pp.78–85.

3. Jeff Kildea, *Tearing the Fabric: Sectarianism in Australia, 1910–25*, (Sydney: Citadel Books, 2002).
4. Malcolm, 'Searching for the Irish and Irish Studies in Australia', p.209.
5. Bull and Malcolm, p.30.
6. Val Noone, 'Irish-Australian conference publications: content and context', pp.349–366, in *Ireland and Australia 1798–1998: Studies in Culture, Identity and Migration*, ed. by Philip Bull, Frances Devlin Glass and Helen Doyle (Sydney, Crossing Press, 2000); 'Recent Australian Irish research papers, 1998–2007', Paper for 15th Irish-Australian Conference La Trobe University, 23–26 September 2007. Both papers are available at http://isaanz.org/conference/irish-australian-conference-series-1980-2007/.
7. See http://isaanz.org/ajis/.
8. For more on this fellowship, see https://www.snac.unimelb.edu.au/news/.
9. See <bloomsdayinmelbourne.org.au>.
10. Malcolm, 'Searching for Irish and Irish Studies in Australia' has a more comprehensive account of various activities.
11. Elizabeth Malcolm and Dianne Hall, *A New History of the Irish in Australia* (Sydney: NewSouth Publishing, 2018 and Cork: Cork University Press, 2019).
12. Patrick O'Farrell, *The Irish in Australia*, 1st ed. (Sydney: University of New South Wales, 1986). Elizabeth Malcolm has discussed this point in detail in her surveys of Irish Studies in Australia, see Malcolm, 'Searching for the Irish and Irish Studies in Australia', and Bull and Malcolm, 'Irish Studies in Australia and New Zealand'.
13. Malcolm and Hall, pp. 22–47.
14. Larissa Behrendt, '*The Nightingale* review – ambitious, urgent and necessarily brutal. But who is it for?' *The Guardian*, 20 August 2019. Available at: https://www.theguardian.com/film/2019/aug/20/the-nightingale-review-ambitious-urgent-and-necessarily-brutal-but-who-is-it-for.

Andrew Fitzsimons

The English Language Issue:
Irish Studies in Japan

The position of the English language within the Japanese education system is both the enabling and limiting condition for Irish Studies. The study of Ireland would not take place on the scale that it does were it not for the prominence of English-language requirements within third-level education in Japan. At the same time, the study of Ireland is bounded by the strictures of Ministry of Education guidelines for the study of the English language, which are driven by market-led demands for 'internationalization.' In this brief article, I will outline the institutional context and climate within which Irish Studies scholars operate in Japan, present a brief account of the history and achievements of, and specific challenges faced by, IASIL Japan, and finally, look very briefly at the problems posed in Japan by the primacy of an English-language, Anglo-American paradigm in academic discourse.

THE INSTITUTIONAL CONTEXT

In Japan, Ireland, when considered at all, is seen as one of the lesser known of the 'English-speaking countries'. The United States is dominant, and its variety of English is the one featured in the textbooks students encounter in the education system. The USA is followed in awareness by Britain, Australia, and Canada. Entering university, students have studied English for at least six years, but would have very limited knowledge of any of these countries, even the United States, and most would have never been abroad. Within any course on English literature, students engage with material that is challenging at the most basic linguistic level, very distant from their own experience, and that emerges out of a cultural context far different from their own. Most students, even those who have chosen to study English in university, would never have read a book in English, their reading of 'foreign literature' having taken place through Japanese translation. Many, if not most, of the classes they will take on English language and literature at university will be taught through the medium of Japanese, with English texts used as exercises in Japanese translation.

Irish University Review 50.1 (2020): 206–214
DOI: 10.3366/iur.2020.0447
© Edinburgh University Press
www.euppublishing.com/iur

The development of Irish Studies in Japan is constrained in a number of ways: most of those specializing in Irish Studies do not teach in departments with language and literature at their centre. They teach in departments of Law or Economics, for instance, where the remit is to impart the English language to students of those fields rather than to teach 'content' classes in their own field. Most do not have their own 'zemi' (a two-year seminar of third- and fourth-year students dedicated to a topic chosen by the teacher), nor graduate classes related to their research, and so have no students dedicated to further study in the field. Thus, there is little possibility of institutional support for the expansion of what individual courses on Irish topics there are, let alone the establishment of a section solely dedicated to Irish Studies. In April 2015, Waseda University, however, as a result of internal re-organization, established an Institute of Irish Studies, under the directorship of Hiroko Mikami, as part of a new Organization for Regional and Inter-Regional Studies (ORIS).

When teaching about Ireland in a university, each individual teacher *is* Irish Studies, and the material to be covered can be overwhelming. With Ireland a topic so off the main drag, the temptation is to stick to the canonical, in the case of literature, to those Irish authors firmly established within the institutional study of English. With so much background information to be filled in, this can lead to the presentation of literature chronologically, in sharply defined contexts, as a byproduct of society and history, and to the presentation of individual authors almost exclusively in terms of identity and biographical detail. With the distance between the languages so great, the cultures so different, identity, the socio-historical, and biographical, as well as the technical, and, historically, the philological – today the linguistic – have been the dominant modes of Japanese inquiry into the literature of the English language. New Historicism has further enhanced this tradition, and the fall off since the 2000s in the numbers of students applying to literature departments, a collateral effect of the problem of the declining birthrate in Japan, has seen many change name to departments of Cultural Studies.

The Japanese academic year begins in April, the first semester ends in late July (early August in some universities); the second semester begins in September and ends in late January/early February. This schedule, allied to the obvious difficulty of geographical distance, makes attendance at conferences abroad, particularly when most of these take place in North America and Europe, problematic. The numbers of Japanese scholars attending the IASIL International Conference, for instance, tends to fluctuate according to date: if held earlier in July, there will be fewer Japanese capable of attending.

Given the obstacles facing Japanese scholars, it is remarkable what *has* been achieved. Every October since 1984, IASIL Japan has held a conference. The roll call of guests includes Daniel J. Albright, Ciaran Carson, Evelyn Conlon, Gerald Dawe, Bernard O'Donoghue, Dennis O'Driscoll, Paul Durcan, James W. Flannery, Seamus Heaney, Brendan Kennelly, Declan Kiberd, Julie O'Callaghan, Timothy O'Grady, Michael Longley, Deirdre Madden, Medbh McGuckian, Sinéad Morrissey, Paul Muldoon, Glenn Patterson, Matthew Sweeney, among others. A substantial list. Recent conference themes have included 'History and Healing in Irish Writing', 'Offshore Irelands: Irish Influence and Influence', 'Echo Chambers: Reverberations in Irish Writing', 'Here and/nor There: Locating Ireland,' and in 2019, 'Borderlands,' with the invited guests Eoin McNamee and Aileen Douglas. The first conferences did not have set themes. At the third conference, held at Shimonoseki in 1986, for instance, according to the 'Member's Report' by James E. McElwain:

> there were four papers on Yeats, two on Synge, one each on Joyce and Shaw, and one on the mythical presence of Finn in literature. These were well-researched and presented papers that at times drew spirited discussion from the floor. One would hope that they could be better circularized, even in abstract form, to all IASAIL members.[1]

That hope has turned into a reality. The Newsletter became a Bulletin, and is now since 2001, a peer-reviewed journal, the *Journal of Irish Studies*, which is distributed to major libraries in Ireland, Britain, and the USA, and has become the most significant resource for Japan-based scholarship on Irish literature.

Most Japanese scholars are practicing translators, and are as engaged in the translation of contemporary Irish writing and scholarship as in publishing their own research. The range of Irish writing currently available in Japanese is extraordinary. When it comes to research, the problem of geographical distance and access to material has, of course, been lessened by developments within digital humanities. The problem of the institutional isolation of individual scholars has also been lessened by the network of personal contacts and by relations fostered within and by IASIL Japan (and IASIL itself), among other societies, and the publication opportunities afforded by the *Journal of Irish Studies*.

One of the corollary effects of IASIL Japan's existence has been its indirect contribution to a significant number of creative works written by Irish authors as a result of their experiences in Japan, including Paul Muldoon's *Hay* (1998), Michael Longley's *The Weather in Japan* (2000), and Glenn Patterson's *The Third Party* (2007). There has also been a major anthology of Irish poetry with Japanese themes, *Our Shared Japan* (Dedalus Press, 2007), and a monograph exploring the influence of Japan on Irish poetry, *The Japanese Effect in Contemporary Irish Poetry* by Irene De Angelis (Palgrave, 2012). It has not all been one way: the eminent Japanese poets Mutsuo Takahashi and Mikiro Sasaki have written work inspired by their visits to Ireland. In 2019, Dedalus Press published Sasaki's *Sky Navigation Homeward: New and Selected Poems*, translated by Mitsuko Ohno, Beverley Curran, and Nobuaki Tochigi, and a new edition of Takahashi's *On Two Shores: New and Selected Poems*, translated by Mitsuko Ohno and Frank Sewell.

From its beginning in 1984, the Japan branch of IASIL had, and continues to have, a membership drawn from all over the country. 'Irish Studies' signifies a loose affiliation of individual, often institutionally isolated scholars, attached to academic societies such as the Yeats Society, the James Joyce Society (which celebrated its thirtieth anniversary this year), the Ireland-Japan Society, and IASIL Japan itself. Many of these scholars are emblematic of the larger story of change within the study of Irish literature. In their own ways they have moved from seeing Yeats, Joyce, and Swift solely in the contexts provided by their supervisors and the institutions in which they first studied; that is to say, from reading Irish writers solely in the context of English literature, or in literary-historical contexts such as Modernism, eighteenth century satire, etc. In later, independent research, through visits to places associated with their research subject, through conferences, and through personal interaction, these scholars have discovered the complex relations to Ireland and Irishness that marked the achievements of these authors. In more recent years, Japanese scholars have closely followed the changes within Irish society and Irish writing, and significant in contemporary Japanese scholarship and translation is the attention that has been given to the Irish language and to writing by women. Indeed, writing by women, in particular by Nuala Ní Dhomhnaill and Eavan Boland, and the achievements of the women's movement in Ireland, has given impetus and example to female Japanese scholars in their examinations of their own society.

THE ENGLISH CONTEXT: JAPAN AND ENGLISH-LANGUAGE LITERARY SCHOLARSHIP

IASIL Japan is unique in Japan in that it is the only literary organization whose proceedings, conference, meetings, newsletters, and journal are all conducted through the medium of English. The English Literary Society of Japan, the largest literary organization in the country does not use English to conduct its affairs, nor indeed do any of the other

Irish-associated societies mentioned previously. The Ireland-Japan society, for instance, shares many of the same members as IASIL Japan, but conducts its affairs entirely in Japanese.

So why does IASIL Japan use English? The decision had a degree of necessity deriving from IASIL Japan's status as a subsidiary to the main body of IASIL. There were also other factors, however, as Mitsuko Ohno outlines: 'it was also a deliberate choice by the founders, because they believed IASIL Japan meetings should be a fostering ground for younger scholars to be more international and linguistically adept.'[2] From the beginning the decision to use English had a galvanizing effect. Ohno was one of the initial group of IASIL Japan members, and she remembers the effect of the use of English at that first IASIL Japan conference, held at Waseda University in 1984:

> having a conference on broad topics of Irish literature, all in English in Japan, was like attending an international conference abroad. Also, it was the first occasion when Irish literature was claimed as independent from English literature, and Irish identity of formerly English writers was reclaimed.[3]

By 1990 the Japan Branch had so established itself that the International Conference of IASAIL was held at Kyoto, with Seamus Heaney as guest, and with a special address given by Toki Koizumi, the grandson of the greatest link between the two countries, Lafcadio Hearn, better known in Japan by his adopted name, Yakumo Koizumi. Tetsuro Sano, then incumbent President of the Japan Branch, in his opening address spoke of Irish Literature and its changing profile in Japan:

> A few days ago a press reporter asked me what we meant by Irish literature. He knew the name of Yeats, Joyce, Wilde and others, but to him they were all part of English literature. It is natural for him to think so, for things Irish were by no means well-known in Japan, and Yeats and Wilde, who were popular with a sizeable group of readers, were accepted as representing the atmosphere of the fin-de-siècle period.
>
> But things began to change. Thanks to the efforts of people in the fields of arts and literature, business, diplomacy, and sports, the name of Ireland is now familiar to Japanese ears. It is no longer confused with Iceland[.][4]

The effect of this conference was immediate and lasting: Japanese academic interest in Ireland increased and widened; at the International Conference held at Trinity College Dublin the following year, in 1991, thirty Japanese scholars attended, with thirteen presenting papers.

Some of their topics showed Japanese interests moving beyond Yeats and Joyce: Charles Maturin, Lafcadio Hearn, Louis MacNeice, Jennifer Johnston, Nuala Ní Dhomhnaill and John McGahern.

The original publication of the society was given the name *The Harp*, at the suggestion of Ken'ichi Matsumura, the first secretary of the organization, who also later served as President. The first issues were called Newsletters and were rudimentary productions in magazine format, very much linked to the annual conference: they consisted of approximately thirty pages and contained details of the schedule and abstracts from the previous year's conference, occasionally including full papers.

By 1991, *The Harp* had become a Bulletin, still in magazine format and still linked to the conference in its contents but without including programme details and with a higher concentration of full papers and thus an increase in pages; issues now exceeded fifty pages. In 2000, under the editorship of Peter McMillan, the format changed to something close to its current form. In 2001 it was decided that a change of name was due and a change of editorial policy: *The Harp* would become the *Journal of Irish Studies*, and would from then on be a peer-reviewed journal. The move signaled serious intentions and a desire to raise the standards and profile of the organization, and the credibility of its academic achievements. By 2004 the format and look of the *Journal* had reached its current state.

The continual and constant challenge, in the future as in the past, is financial. At present there are approximately 144 members of IASIL Japan, the largest single grouping within IASIL. The society over the years has received enormous help and financial support from the Embassy of Ireland, the Department of Foreign Affairs, the Arts Council of Ireland, and Culture Ireland, and in earlier years support also came from the British Council, in particular when invited guests were from Northern Ireland.

The other challenge involves the need to provide a forum for the work of our membership. There are few venues for literary scholarship in English in Japan. The respected magazine *Eigo Seinen/The Rising Generation*, though aimed at researchers and students of English literature, publishes only very occasional pieces in English, has ceased print publication, and now appears only in an online version. Most of the venues for literary scholarship in English that do exist are in what are called *kiyoo*: journals produced by university faculties and devoted to research by faculty members, not specifically members of English departments and not specifically in English. *Studies in English Literature*, the journal of the English Literary Society of Japan, publishes one issue in English of the two issues they publish annually. As can be seen, then, the *Journal of Irish Studies* is an unusual venture in the context of Japan, and this has brought with it some complex issues. In the 'Notes for Contributors' the *Journal* stipulates:

> Contributors whose first language is not English should have their paper checked by a literate native speaker of English before submission.

There was some agonizing over the decision to state so boldly this English-language requirement. To give some of the background: there are contributors to the *Journal* whose English is of a very high standard indeed and which needs little, if any, grammatical fine-tuning, but it had become clear that certain contributors had come to regard the submission process as an opportunity for a 'native check' of grammar etc, rather than as a review of the intellectual quality of their scholarship. In publishing an academic journal in a language not native to most of the contributors the problem frequently arises – how to judge the quality of scholarship and thought when a paper lacks comprehensibility at the fundamental level of the sentence? Yet what criteria do we, or can we, create for this situation? Are we imposing inappropriate, unfair codes and standards upon contributors when the discourse structures from which they come may not correspond with culturally specific expectations derived out of the Anglo-American academic sphere? What are we missing by a too-strict adherence to approaches and standards 'naturalised' through long-practice but themselves culturally specific?

I do not think, in the case of the *Journal of Irish Studies*, that unique voices have been stifled by a requirement to write an artificial and imposed idea of what constitutes a 'comprehensible level of English'. Our reviewers have shown tolerance for the infelicitously expressed but also for writing which required more of a grammatical helping hand. Criteria of comprehensibility occupy a sliding scale, and often it is clear that though a piece of writing in English may need large-scale revision, it is also academically solid and valuable, and after revision viable as a published paper.

Which bring us to the next issue raised in the editing process: how far to push this revision and re-writing process? Should a reviewer allow the retention of non-native features true to the voice of the contributor? This is a delicate issue, and one familiar from theories of translation influenced by post-colonial studies, which argue that for a translation to have integrity it should retain some of the foreignness of an original text. Not only are all reviewers different in their approach to this question, so too are the contributors: some contributors want a firm hand guiding their English toward native or near-native fluency, others want to retain as much of their own voice and signature as possible while not sacrificing comprehensibility.

Ireland's relationship with English is complex, and this has been one of the main attractions of Irish Studies for contemporary scholars whose first language is not English but for whom English is a professional requirement. Many of our contributors have taken as their subject writers for whom issues of language and power have been paramount. Brian Friel's *Translations* acknowledges the fact of the linguistic moment in nineteenth-century Ireland when English was in the ascendant as the *de facto* language of the country, yet also laments that things have turned out to be so. Many parts of the modern world are living through a similar linguistic moment, if in a different key. For good and for ill, the criteria of 'internationalization' in the global ranking of universities, in reality, means publication in English. As this *Japan Times* editorial writes:

> Asian universities are gaining on their western counterparts, according to the recently released *Times Higher Education* rankings. The annual evaluations of world universities found Asian universities doing better than ever before in the annual global rankings.... The best showings in Asia were in the areas of science, health, engineering and technology. *Asian universities did not fare so well in arts and humanities or social sciences.* Perhaps the results of investment take more time to show up in those areas, but also *the issue of language continues to hold back some Asian countries in these areas. Publishing research papers in English has become the world standard, so efforts to improve the level of learning in English must be more fully supported.*[5]

To lament this emphasis on English is just, and to say that the criteria for these university rankings emerge out of the Anglo-American institutional world and thus the results have an Anglo-American bias is true. However it is also in some senses a flight from the realities we in the non-Anglophone world find ourselves facing.

One final point that is perhaps so obvious it need not be made: most of the academic work done on Ireland in Japan, by historians, economists, and literary scholars, in the past and currently, in journals, magazines, and at conferences and symposia, is in Japanese. For the English-speaking audience within Irish Studies, there is a great deal we have not yet heard, from Japan, and from other countries. Translation works in both directions: isn't it time we engaged with what has been said, and is being said, about us in other places, in other tongues, on other people's ground, on their own terms?

NOTES

1. *The Harp: IASAIL-Japan Newsletter* Vol. II (1987), n.p.
2. Mitsuko Ohno, 'Re: IASIL Japan History.' Message to Andrew Fitzsimons. 1 December 2012. Email.
3. Ohno, as above.
4. *The Harp: IASAIL-Japan Bulletin* Vol. VI (1991), 1, n.p.
5. 'Asian universities catching up', *Japanese Times* 17 October 2012, emphasis added.

Ondřej Pilný

Irish Studies in Continental Europe

The origins of significant interest in Irish culture on the part of continental Europeans date back at least to the late eighteenth century, when James Macpherson's 'Ossian' became one of the most widely read authors in Europe for several decades. Ossianic verse caused an excitement about so-called Celtic poetry, and exercised a seminal influence on European romanticisms. This was followed by the general popularity of Thomas Moore's Irish melodies with revivalists across Europe seeking political emancipation from authoritative forms of government in regions as diverse as the German speaking countries, France, Italy, Bohemia, and Hungary. The interest in 'Celtic literatures' was further boosted by the work of Ernest Renan in France and Matthew Arnold in England in the 1850s and 1860s, who laid the foundations of the first academic framework for the study of writing from Celtic-language areas, including the establishment of the first Chair in Celtic Studies at Oxford in 1874, and at the Collège de France in 1882.

What made Ireland the focus of early research was also the development of comparative, particularly Indo-European linguistics: the Irish language became the object of study of French and German linguists in the early nineteenth century, with individual professors at German universities teaching Celtic philology from the 1840s and seminal publications such as Johann Kaspar Zeuss's *Grammatica Celtica* appearing in the 1850s. As much as the interest of most of these philologists (who later included scholars from Denmark, the Netherlands, and elsewhere) may have been on language only, rather than literary aesthetics or culture, they played a seminal role in the preservation and publication of manuscript material, and made Ireland the destination of visits by researchers, who thus enhanced the ranks of early European tourists.[1]

Indeed, it was travel writing that made another vital contribution to the kindling of interest in Ireland in early to mid-nineteenth-century Europe. Travel narratives frequently adopted a popular tone, such as the *Briefe eines Verstorbenen* (1830–31) by the larger-than-life aristocrat Hermann von Pückler-Muskau, allegedly the most widely read book

Irish University Review 50.1 (2020): 215–220
DOI: 10.3366/iur.2020.0448
© Edinburgh University Press
www.euppublishing.com/iur

in nineteenth-century Germany.[2] Others, however, were politically motivated and revolved around the emancipatory activities of Daniel O'Connell, who became a model for constitutional nationalists and militant radicals alike. O'Connell's work was followed and commented upon by most European travellers to Ireland of the 1830s to the 1850s, with the Irish situation being offered as a parallel to the vast regions of continental Europe living under monarchical or imperial dominance.[3]

Virtually concurrent with the rise of Celtic Studies as a scholarly discipline was the establishment of English Studies: while the earliest lecturers in English language appeared at the universities of Greifswald and Jena as early as the late seventeenth century, it was only in the 1850s to the 1870s that regular Chairs of English language and literature were established at Zurich, Strasbourg, Vienna, Christiania, and Berlin; and English Studies first truly flourished around the turn of the century.[4] The literature curricula often included prominent Anglo-Irish authors such as Jonathan Swift or Oliver Goldsmith, and later the two most popular contemporary English-language playwrights of the era in Europe, Oscar Wilde and George Bernard Shaw. However, their work was discussed almost exclusively in the context of English literature. The Irish Literary Revival became the subject of keen interest of intellectuals in small nations suffering from oppression, particularly in Galicia, the Basque Country, Catalonia, the Czech Lands, and Poland, being perceived as analogous to their own struggle; but the poetry of W.B. Yeats and the plays of J.M. Synge were also admired and translated in dominant cultures such as French or German. Notwithstanding that, once they entered curricula at universities, they were again taught in the context of English, rather than as a product of an autonomous national culture. The absence of focused research in and teaching of Irish literature and culture indeed lasted well into the second half of the twentieth century: as much as Irish writing in English had been widely translated and popular across the European continent, the work of Yeats, James Joyce, and Samuel Beckett was discussed in the broader contexts of world literature (or theatre), European modernism, or English literature, the tradition of the Irish Gothic in the context of English Gothic fiction, Irish playwrights from Farquhar to Behan in the framework of English or British drama, and so on.

The current situation of Irish Studies research and teaching in continental Europe has been largely determined by these historical origins. Independent departments of Irish Studies that would comprise Irish literature, history, politics, economy, and culture in its broader sense do not exist, and even in terms of literary studies alone, neither do departments that would comprehensively cover the literature of the island in both of its official languages. This has been the result of the existing delimitations of disciplines, whereby different aspects of Ireland have been studied in departments of comparative linguistics, Celtic Studies, English, history, archaeology, or music, and, given the relative marginality of Irish culture, conditions have never been favourable to the establishment of comprehensive interdisciplinary departments or programmes of study, including in the contemporary era where interdisciplinarity may be a favourite buzzword.

That being the case, about a dozen continental universities feature Irish Studies centres or units within their English departments at the moment, a few of which offer dedicated Masters programmes focused mostly on Irish writing in English in its broader contexts, including an Irish-language element (Sorbonne Nouvelle – Paris 3, Rennes 2, Lille 3, Charles University Prague). As much as Celtic Studies has regrettably been on the wane since the 1990s, a few European universities still offer degree programmes based in Celtic philology (MA in Lublin, Poznań, Marburg, Utrecht, and Vienna; BA in Bonn, Brest, and Uppsala). Several research centres have emerged between the late 1990s and 2017 in Aarhus, Dalarna, A Coruña, Leuven, and Granada that are interdisciplinary to a varying degree, and two inter-university Irish Studies centres have recently been formed, The Budapest Centre for Irish Studies, joining scholars from five universities based in the city, and BANNA/BOND comprising scholars from the universities of Burgos, Deusto, La Rioja, and Zaragoza. None of these offer specialised degrees to students, however, which is also true of the smaller, semi-independent Irish Studies centres or units at universities in Austria, Poland, Hungary, Portugal, Italy, Finland, Norway, France, Germany, Belgium, the Netherlands, Romania, and Russia. Apart from these research groups, there are several hundred individuals working in history, politics, literature, language, archaeology, music, dance, and other aspects of Ireland at universities and research institutions from the Baltic states and Croatia to the Western edge of the European mainland. While the institutional grounding of Irish Studies may thus be far from ideal, the overview above provides ample evidence of enthusiasm and dedication on the part of individual scholars, who can, moreover, focus on supervising PhDs on Irish topics, raising future generations of academics and educators.

What must also be apparent is that collaboration within international networks is fundamental to the future of Irish Studies. In the current atmosphere of marginalization of the humanities by technocrats and populist politicians alike, which has brought about an often critical lack of funding and precariousness of jobs in academia and non-applied research, focus on allegedly marginal areas such as Ireland is often discouraged; for instance, many English departments treat an Irish specialism – or are made to by university management – as one of those unnecessary frills that should be shed whenever there is a need to cut, since students really need to focus on the English language and the main Anglophone cultures, that is to say English and American, only. Irish Studies experts thus have to justify their existence by bringing in funding and producing 'measurable' outputs in the form of international projects and publications – and professional Irish Studies networks have played a seminal role in this effort.

The first of these to affect Europe was IASAIL/IASIL, set up in 1969 'to encourage research and study in all aspects of Anglo-Irish literature and to act as a link between the many scholars working in the field in all parts of the world'.[5] The conferences of the association became meeting places for literary scholars in Irish literature in English and have generated many joint research projects and long-term collaborations, as well as facilitating contact with members of the American Conference (originally Committee) for Irish Studies (established in 1960), the Canadian Association for Irish Studies (founded in 1973), and scholars working outside the European and North American continents. In France, where Irish Studies has traditionally been strong not only in literature but also in history and social sciences, a national association, SOFEIR, was set up in 1981 to facilitate dialogue across the disciplines and provide a backing to individuals scattered across French universities. In 1998, a group of researchers based mainly in France instigated the creation of EFACIS, a European federation of Irish Studies scholars with similar objectives to SOFEIR; within a few years, EFACIS featured a balanced representation of a range of European countries on its executive, and began to play a vigorous role in spearheading cooperation in Irish Studies and promoting Irish culture across Europe. The Scandinavian Irish Studies association, NISN, and the Spanish national association, AEDEI, were established in 2001, and both joined the larger network of EFACIS. All associations were alert to the lack of publication venues for research, and took care to establish affiliated high-quality journals: the *Irish University Review* (founded in 1970), *Études irlandaises* (here the journal actually preceded the foundation of the association, as it was set up in 1976), *Nordic Irish Studies Journal* (2002), *Estudios irlandeses* (2005), and finally *Review of Irish Studies in Europe* (2016) instigated by EFACIS; a vibrant Italian journal, *Studi irlandesi*, was established from the University of Florence in 2009.[6]

The solicitation of external funding for Irish Studies has been rather problematic, however. Despite the size of Ireland and its economy, the Irish government has always been exemplary in promoting its culture abroad, and a little of its funding has been provided even to a few university-based Irish Studies centres and to EFACIS; a case for extended, streamlined support for Irish Studies in Europe has recently been made in a white paper issued by EFACIS.[7] National and

EU-funded grants agencies may seem an obvious source to approach; however, projects that propose research exclusively in Irish culture tend to be swiftly disqualified, as such focus is deemed irrelevant by national funding bodies,[8] and too narrow for EU-funded schemes, which require research to be strictly comparative across a number of national contexts. This may be perceived as limiting the extent of scholarly analysis that may be done in the national culture; but on the positive side, the attitude of funding bodies makes a comparative approach to Irish culture a necessity, protecting Irish Studies – inadvertently as this mostly might be – from the dangers of insularity. As a matter of fact, much of the most exciting contemporary research in Irish culture has already been happening in comparative contexts, which have moreover unravelled some of the culture's neglected aspects to European students; for example, the flourishing of interest in the minority-language cultures of Europe over the last few decades has helped to facilitate the first translations of literature in Modern Irish into a number of European vernaculars and its coverage at least in some Irish Studies courses at universities.

Despite the obstacles that Irish Studies scholars in Europe have been facing as regards their position within universities and research institutes, together with the ubiquitous lack of resources, Irish Studies is a lively area with a great, multifaceted potential. To exemplify albeit briefly, the study of Irish culture and history may serve as a useful starting point for comparative research in colonialism and nationalism, and their relentless resonance, currently evidenced in the disastrous negotiations of Brexit, and the rise of populist neo-nationalism generally across the continent, in Russia and in the USA. An examination of how Irish literature and culture have been received in European countries will unravel the variegated strategies of domestication employed in the transfer, necessitated by the need for translation into a foreign language, and combined with the relative absence of an Irish diaspora. The resulting perceptions of Ireland in mainland Europe may ultimately complicate the ideas of canonicity or 'Irishness' established in the Anglophone world, and thus contribute to a reinvigoration of the critical discussion. Irish Studies experts abroad have a vital practical role to play in these processes: as a rule, it is they who promote Ireland and its culture in their countries most effectively, be it as organisers of events, translators, or commentators for and advisors to the media; as educators, it is they who train students to become further ambassadors of Irish culture.

NOTES

1. A detailed survey of the cultural construction of 'Celtic literatures', the development of Celtic philology, early travel to Ireland, and much more is to be found in

Joep Leerssen's two book-length studies, *Mere Irish and Fíor-Ghael: Studies in the Idea of Irish Nationality, Its Development and Literary Expression Prior to the Nineteenth Century*, 2nd edn (Cork: Cork University Press / Field Day, 1996) and *Remembrance and Imagination: Patterns in the Historical and Literary Representation of Ireland in the Nineteenth Century* (Cork: Cork University Press / Field Day, 1996).

2. The original four volumes were published in an abbreviated form in English as *Tour of a German Prince*, trans. by Sarah Austin (London: Wilson, 1831–2); the first complete English translation was brought out in an opulent edition only very recently: see Prince Hermann von Pückler-Muskau, *Letters of a Dead Man*, trans. by Linda B. Parshall (Washington, D.C.: Dumbarton Oaks Research Library and Collection, 2016). The assertion was made by literary historian Günter J. Vaupel; see *'Poor Green Erin'. German Travel Writers' Narratives on Ireland from before the 1798 Rising to after the Great Famine*, ed. and trans. by Eoin Bourke, 2nd rev. edn (Frankfurt a.M.: Peter Lang, 2013), p.112.

3. Eoin Bourke's anthology (referred to above) provides a representative sample from the German-speaking lands.

4. For a comprehensive survey, see *European English Studies: Contributions towards the History of a Discipline*, Vol. I, ed. by Balz Engler and Renate Haas (Leicester: The English Association, for ESSE, 2000), Vol. II, ed. by Renate Haas and Balz Engler (Leicester: The English Association, for ESSE, 2008).

5. [Andrew Carpenter], 'International Association for the Study of Anglo-Irish Literature: Report', *Irish University Review* 1.2 (Spring 1971), p.289.

6. The establishment of the British Association for Irish Studies (1985), the UK-based *Irish Studies Review* (1992) and their context are outside the remit of the present essay, as its task was to focus on mainland Europe only.

7. See *Irish Studies in Continental Europe Today and Its Potential* (Leuven: EFACIS, 2018).

8. The grant awarded in 2017 to the Gate Theatre Research Network by the Dutch national grants agency NWO has been a rare recent exception.

Beatriz Kopschitz Bastos

Irish Studies in South America

Although the Irish diaspora often conjures up images and issues related to the English-speaking world (the United Kingdom, the United States and Canada, Australia, and New Zealand), it has a remarkable presence in South America, where it is a strong and growing field of research. This brief overview gives an insight into some of the major advances, and principal themes, of Irish Studies in this region, and the contribution of this particular field to the larger domain of transnational and comparative cultural analysis.

HISTORY AND LEGACY

According to Edmundo Murray, 'the number of Irish who decided on Latin America as their temporary or permanent home is still a matter of debate among scholars. Argentina and Uruguay alone received approximately 50,000 Irish-born immigrants. Thousands more were scattered in the Caribbean, Brazil, Venezuela and Mexico as a result of military operations, trade and colonisation schemes'.[1] Murray explains that migration to Latin America was initially an extension of the Iberian dimension of the Irish diaspora. The early Irish presence in Latin America was connected to traditional links between the Irish in Britain, Spain, and Portugal, and even Italy. Among the migrants – permanent or temporary – who, with time, also came directly from Ireland, or through the United States, from the sixteenth to the nineteenth century, there were plantation owners, settlers, missionaries, merchants, adventurers, soldiers, workers, and people moved by personal motivations. Irish people and their descendants, like Admiral William Brown and Bernardo O'Higgins, played important roles in the history of Argentina and Chile, for example. Likewise, Roger Casement, in the history of Brazil and the Amazon region; and Eliza Lynch, in the history of Paraguay.[2] More recent arrivals, in the twentieth and twenty-first centuries, include business people, professionals, artists, journalists, intellectuals, and writers, as well as missionaries, who, in their anonymity, have been described as 'the most efficient Irish representatives in Latin America'.[3] In 2019, Fr Patrick Clarke was

Irish University Review 50.1 (2020): 221–228
DOI: 10.3366/iur.2020.0449
© Edinburgh University Press
www.euppublishing.com/iur

honoured by President Michael D. Higgins with the Presidential Distinguished Service Award for his forty years of charitable works in Vila Prudente in São Paulo.

When Roger Casement served as consul and consul general for the British crown in Brazil, in the early twentieth century, Ireland was, of course, still part of the United Kingdom, and Brazil had been an independent country for less than a century. Diplomatic relations with South America, however, are among the earliest in the history of the Irish Foreign Service. In 1919, Argentinean-born Eamon Bulfin, son of an Irish immigrant to Argentina, William Bulfin, was appointed by Eamon de Valera as representative to the government of Argentina. This, the first-ever mission of the Irish diplomatic service, was inaugurated even before the establishment of the Irish Free State. In 1921 two of Ireland's eight representatives were based in Latin America, as pointed out by Edmundo Murray: Bulfin in Argentina and Frank W. Eagan in Chile. Formal diplomatic relations with the region started in 1947, with the opening of a mission in Buenos Aires; the mission was upgraded to the status of Embassy in 1964. Diplomatic relations were established with Brazil in 1975 (with a resident Ambassador only since 2001, and the establishment of a Consulate General in São Paulo in 2014), and with Mexico in 1977.[4] In 2019, new Irish embassies were established in Chile and Colombia.

The history of academic relations between South American universities and cultural institutions and those in Ireland is also a longstanding one. With the support of numerous bodies – the Department of Foreign Affairs, the Cultural Relations Committee, Irish embassies and consulates, the British Council, Culture Ireland, and universities and cultural institutions – South America has welcomed dozens of academics, writers, and artists for academic exchange programmes, conferences, seminars, courses, and literary, theatre, and film festivals over the decades. Likewise, it has exported its own scholars and students in the field of Irish Studies to academic exchange programmes, courses, conferences, and cultural events in Ireland and in the international context.

While the history of this collaboration and exchange has of course been fostered by the efforts and funding of embassies, universities, and institutions – that is, by infrastructural support – it is also a product of individual personalities and motivations, and of the pioneering work of scholars, such as, for example, Professor Munira Mutran, from the University of São Paulo (USP), and Professor Maria Helena Kopschitz, from Fluminense Federal University, in Niterói, Rio de Janeiro. With Professor Laura Izarra, also from the University of São Paulo, they founded *Associação Brasileira de Estudos Irlandeses* – ABEI – in 1989, an organisation dedicated to the study of Irish culture, literature, art, and history, which has been one of the driving forces of Irish Studies in South America for thirty years.

In recognition of the exchange between these countries, University College Dublin honours and celebrates the work of Professor Maria Helena Kopschitz with an annual scholarship – the Maria Helena Kopschitz Scholarship – for a Brazilian student to undertake the UCD MA in Irish Literature and Culture. The associated annual Kopschitz lecture aims to provide a forum to examine Irish-South American links and connections.[5] Similarly, ABEI supports an annual scholarship for a Brazilian student in the MFA or MPhil programmes at Trinity College Dublin: the ABEI/Haddad Fellowship. It is noteworthy that Professor Munira Mutran received the title of Honorary Doctor from the National University of Ireland Maynooth in 2008, and in 2019 was granted the Presidential Distinguished Service Award, from President Michael D. Higgins, celebrating her achievements in the field of Irish Studies in Brazil and abroad.

ABEI has been publishing the *ABEI Journal*, gathering articles on Irish literature, history, culture, and diaspora, as well as literary texts and translations, since 1999. Other journals and periodicals in Brazil, such as *Ilha do Desterro*, at the Federal University of Santa Catarina, published since 1979, have devoted thematic issues to the field of Irish Studies. ABEI organises two annual events in the field of Irish Studies. The *Symposium of Irish Studies in South America* is an itinerant event that has taken place in various cities of Brazil, Argentina, and Chile, since 2006, and the *Forum of Irish Studies*, which is also itinerant, but located only in Brazil, has recently been held for the eighth time. Likewise, the W.B. Yeats Chair of Irish Studies at USP holds annual events, and the more recently founded NEI (*Núcleo de Estudos Irlandeses*), at the Federal University of Santa Catarina in Florianópolis, is celebrating its fourth year of foundation, with four annual *Fora of Irish Studies*. Other academic events, not necessarily focused solely on Irish Studies, have featured panels and lectures in the area.

In 2003, SILAS, the Society for Irish Latin American Studies, was founded to promote the study of relations between Ireland and Latin American countries. As its website states, 'Our range of interests includes the settlement, lives, and achievements of Irish emigrants to Latin America and their descendants, as well as the contemporary presence of Ireland in the life and culture of Latin America and the presence of Latin Americans in Ireland'.[6] The activity of the Society is distinguished by its interest in relationships, past and present, between Ireland and the Irish not only within South America but also beyond, including Iberia, the Caribbean, and Spanish-speaking North America.

SILAS publishes an online journal – *Irish Migration Studies in Latin America* – with original research about relations between Ireland and

Latin America, Spanish-speaking North America, the Caribbean and Iberia, from all academic disciplines within the humanities and social sciences, and also holds annual conferences in Ireland and Latin America, in places as distinct – for example – as Dublin and Havana.

AEIS – Asociación de Estudos Irlandeses del Sur – founded recently (in 2018), has also contributed to the continuing vibrancy of Irish Studies in South America, particularly in the southern part of the continent, organising or co-organising events in Argentina, Chile, and other countries, and fomenting research and publications.[7]

The voices of academic and cultural ambassadors for Irish Studies in South America are so many now, that it would be difficult to name with fairness all the participants in this wonderful and rich enterprise.

THEMES AND SINGULARITY

But what are the current issues and themes in the field of Irish Studies in South America? How is it distinctive? How is it cross-cultural? How is it shaped by having emerged in a non-Anglophone culture? How has it been forged by colonial and post-colonial contexts?

Among the variety of perspectives and activities that constitute Irish Studies in South America, including a still somewhat predominant focus on Irish literature and culture in the Irish and European contexts, some areas are worth exploring in order to answer those few questions satisfactorily: translation and translation studies; performance and film; diaspora and migration studies; and comparative studies.

Translation

Translation is perhaps one of the most intriguing elements in the current presence of Irish literature in South America. The catalogue of Irish literature and non-fiction translated into Brazilian Portuguese and Spanish includes classics such as Joyce, Shaw, Yeats, and Beckett; stars of the contemporary period, such as Seamus Heaney, Brian Friel, Tom Murphy, Marina Carr, Colm Tóibín, John Banville, and Anne Enright; and a few collections of short stories, with the work of some of the most renowned Irish short-fiction writers. More unexpected translations of Roger Casement's *Amazon Journal*, and of the poetry of Eiléan Ní Chuilleanáin, Canadian-Belfast resident Kathleen MacCracken, Moyna Canon, and Jessica Traynor, add new voices to this vibrant catalogue of contemporary translation in South America.

Likewise, translation and reflection on the role of Irish criticism have been part of this transpositional approach. The W.B. Yeats Chair of Irish Studies at the University of São Paulo, for instance, led a project entitled 'From Ireland to Brazil: Critical Texts', including academics from other universities in Brazil, and comprising research on, translation of, and publication of Irish critical texts, with a vast range of perspectives and voices. The aim of the project was to examine different critical trends in fiction, drama, and poetry developed by important Irish writers and critics, and those trends present in the cultural diaspora, in order to select aesthetic elements that could renew the literary critical debate in Brazil.

The theoretical and aesthetic discussion of literary translation and translation of criticism as a meeting, an approximation, of different cultures is one of the unique traits of the treatment and reading of Irish literature and criticism in South America. Translation is regarded as an analytical exercise in learning about oneself, that is to say, the local culture, through the lens of the other party, the 'other' (the foreign) culture. In this model, translation goes beyond linguistic questions in its concern for the local readership, or audience. How is translation in itself a literary and critical work? What adjustments need to be made to the text in terms of local practices and culture? What are the adjustments necessary for the rhythms and sounds of the target language? The filmmaker Pat Murphy stated in a lecture at the Huston School of Film and Digital Media, at the National University of Ireland Galway, in 2012, that 'influence can propose the notion of a fixed position, of one separate entity affecting another, but from [her] experience [she]'d rather speak of the porousness of influence, of border crossings, the non-recognition of boundaries'.[8] This is perhaps how the influence and legacy of Irish literature and criticism can be perceived in translation projects and studies: exercises of transatlantic and interculturally porous border crossings.

Stage

The same porousness is embodied by the field of performance and performance studies – perhaps even more so. Productions of canonical texts by Shaw, Beckett, and Wilde are part of the history of South American theatre. Also featured is the work of more contemporary dramatists such as Marina Carr, Brian Friel, Tom Murphy, Conor McPherson, Martin McDonagh, Marie Jones, Patricia Bourke Kennedy, Owen McCafferty, and Colin Murphy – to name just a few. Recent academic attention has focused on the ways in which these theatre translations and productions reach South American audiences and critics, and are, therefore, reshaped, re-appreciated, and reworked.

The work of Cia Ludens,[9] a theatre company based in São Paulo, is worth mentioning in this regard. The company has been contributing creatively to an approach in the contemporary scene that might be described as half artistic, half academic. Cia Ludens has been research-ing, translating, publishing, and staging Irish drama and Irish-related material in Portuguese for over fifteen years now, with plays by

Shaw, Friel, Tom Murphy, Jones, Vincent Woods, Colin Murphy, Mary Raftery, Hugo Hamilton, and McCafferty, for example, in productions, public readings, discussions, and publications. They provide a way of playing with and bridging gaps of space and culture between Ireland and Brazil. The company's method integrates Irish texts and Irish material with elements of Brazilian stage culture – a process of intercultural creation and cross-cultural exchanges, on stage and page, which culminated in Domingos Nunez's rendition of the life of Roger Casement in the theatre docudrama *The Two Deaths of Roger Casement* (2016), a South American response to the centenary of the Easter Rising and of Casement's execution.

Screen

Irish film also has a strong presence in South America, and in more than one way. Film festivals at several venues in South America such as Cinemateca Brasileira in São Paulo, Cine Teatro Guarany in Manaus, Instituto Nacional de Cine y Artes Visuales in Buenos Aires, and others in Chile and Uruguay, as well as commercial theatres, have consistently featured a wide range of subtitled Irish films. Buenos Aires, São Paulo, Florianópolis, and Manaus have held Irish film festivals, and other cities in South America exhibit Irish films as part of the European Film Festival every year, with the support of Irish embassies and consulates, Culture Ireland, and the Irish Film Institute.

A bilingual English-Portuguese series of publications, entitled *Ireland into Film: Screenplays and Critical Contexts*, featuring the scripts of renowned filmmakers such as John T. Davis, Thaddeus O'Sullivan, Alan Gilsenan, and Pat Murphy, and critical and contextual articles, and DVDs subtitled in Portuguese (and, in the case of O'Sullivan, also in Spanish), has been published, initially by the W.B. Yeats Chair of Irish Studies at the University of São Paulo, and now by the Federal University of Santa Catarina.

How these films travel, and what it means to have them exposed to South American audiences in other languages, dubbed or subtitled, has been the focus of not just film festival organisers, but also of their audiences and critics. Moreover, how the Irish in South America have been represented in both Irish and South American film is also a fascinating topic of ongoing research and appreciation.

Migration

Migration continues to be a fraught topic. Irish diaspora and migration studies in South America seek to establish the history of the Irish in the region, their legacy, their motivations, and the journeys that brought them to the South American region. They also pursue issues such as, for example, theoretical patterns of migration, adaptation, cross-cultural and cross-linguistic encounters, hybridism, hyphenated identities, and the colonial and post-colonial historical nets of relationship, mutual influence, and collaboration.

One particular space where migration is approached with empathy is in literary studies, perhaps none more so than Irish studies. Academics in this field study the literature and journalism of Irish migrants and their descendants, as well as the representation of such migrants in Irish literature and in that of their descendants.

Comparative studies

One particular angle of Irish Studies in South America that marks its uniqueness, is the prevalence of comparative research: using method-ologies to compare history, society, culture, and literature across different countries in South America and Ireland, with both quantitative and qualitative analysis, both geographically and over time, in trans-national comparisons and varying time frames. Comparative literary studies, in particular, aim to deal with Irish works in both English and Irish, and works in Portuguese, Spanish, and South American native languages, exploring movements, themes, forms, ideas, and relations between authors on both sides of the Atlantic. Like other fields of criticism in Irish Studies, these comparative studies are often informed by broader issues of class, gender, race, trauma and climate, for example, to cite just a few approaches.

Teaching

And last, but certainly not least, it should be emphasised that it is, perhaps above all, the teaching dimension, in the various undergradu-ate and post-graduate programmes, small or large, in big cities or smaller ones, scattered over South America, which most significantly confers the uniqueness of Irish Studies in the region: here the field is exposed to, and filtered by, communities of students with diverse cultural backgrounds, who, in many cases, have never been to Ireland but who nevertheless explore and enrich Irish Studies.

NOTES

1. Edmundo Murray, 'Secret Diasporas: the Irish in Latin America and the Caribbean', in *History Ireland – Ireland's History Magazine*. Available at: https://www.historyireland.com/20th-century-contemporary-history/secret-diasporas-the-irish-in-latin-america-and-the-caribbean/

2. In 2016, the Department of Foreign Affairs and Trade launched the exhibition, 'The Irish in Latin America', in Mexico. The exhibition later toured other countries in Latin America, and is available at: https://www.dfa.ie/irish-embassy/mexico/news-and-events/2017/irish-latin-america-exhibition/

3. Edmundo Murray, 'Secret Diasporas: the Irish in Latin America and the Caribbean'.

4. See: Edmundo Murray, 'Diplomatic Relations, Irish-Latin American", in *Ireland and the Americas – Culture, Politics and History, Vol 1*, ed. by J. P. Byrne, Philip Coleman and Jason King (Santa Barbara, CA, Denver, Oxford: ABC-CLIO, 2008), pp.256–257.

5. See all lectures at: https://www.youtube.com/playlist?list=PLtlNNPNOafm9e FMJzcmHseTzbKR1gUlsf

6. See: https://irlandeses.org/

7. See: https://asociaciondeestudiosirlandesesdelsur.wordpress.com/

8. Pat Murphy, 'Pat Murphy, filmmaker – my influences'. Available at: http:// podacademy.org/podcasts/pat-murphy-filmmaker-my-influences/

9. See: http://cialudens.com.br/

List of Books Reviewed

Faith Binckes and Kathryn Laing, *Hannah Lynch (1859–1904): Irish writer, cosmopolitan, New Woman*. Cork: Cork University Press, 2019. 248 pages. (Jane Mahony)

Noreen Doody, *The Influence of Oscar Wilde on W.B. Yeats: 'An Echo of Someone Else's Music'*. London: Palgrave Macmillan, 2018. 340 pages. (Jerusha McCormack)

Alan Graham and Scott Eric Hamilton (editors), *Samuel Beckett and the 'State' of Ireland*. Newcastle-upon-Tyne: Cambridge Scholars Publishing, 2017. 201 pages. (José Francisco Fernández)

Patrick Lonergan, *Irish Drama and Theatre Since 1950*. London: Methuen Drama, 2019. 263 pages. (Marie Kelly)

James McNaughton, *Samuel Beckett and the Politics of Aftermath*. Oxford: Oxford University Press, 2018. 226 pages; Derval Tubridy, *Samuel Beckett and the Language of Subjectivity*. Cambridge: Cambridge University Press, 2018. 221 pages. (James Little)

Christina Morin, *The Gothic Novel in Ireland, c. 1760–1829*. Manchester: Manchester University Press, 2018. 235 pages. (Nicky Lloyd)

Philip O'Leary, *An Underground Theatre: Major Playwrights in the Irish Language, 1930–80*. Dublin: University College Dublin Press, 2017. 383 pages. (Éadaoin Ní Mhuircheartaigh)

Irish University Review 50.1 (2020): 229
DOI: 10.3366/iur.2020.0450
© Edinburgh University Press
www.euppublishing.com/iur

Book Reviews

Faith Binckes and Kathryn Laing, *Hannah Lynch (1859–1904): Irish writer, cosmopolitan, New Woman*. Cork: Cork University Press, 2019. 248 pages.

In their introduction to this meticulously-researched and richly-detailed critical study of the author, critic, and translator Hannah Lynch, Faith Binckes, and Kathryn Laing observe that sources and accounts of Lynch's life and work were hitherto not only incomplete but inaccurate. Hers was a life and work only 'glimpsed' by scholars of late nineteenth-century Irish literary and political history as they worked through archives and periodicals. This volume presents a comprehensive and vivid critical appraisal of a provocative, fearless, and important writer who was active in the Ladies Land League in the early 1880s, engaged with the wider feminist political and literary networks which emerged from that political activity, a cosmopolitan 'vagabond' who travelled widely in Europe, and a key figure in female-oriented interconnecting literary spheres in Dublin, London, and Paris.

The first of six themed chapters explores the political and literary networks of Dublin in the 1880s. It builds on recent studies on the significance of the Ladies Land League, neglected both in the aftermath of its demise as well as in subsequent histories of the period, arguing that it was 'a crucial first line in a chain of political agency which stretches forward into the early twentieth century to connect with other feminist nationalist and suffragist organisations such as *Inghinidhe na hÉireann* and *Cumann na mBan*'. The account of the inaugural dinner of the Literary Ladies Dinner in London in May 1889, where a contemporary report seats Lynch with Katharine Tynan, Harriet Taylor, and Alice Corkran – a substantial representation of the short-lived Irish feminist and political movement at a foundational event for women writers – 'demonstrates and extends Tina O'Toole's contention that the Ladies Land League was intimately connected to the rise of the "Irish New Woman"'.

In the second chapter, a comparative critical reading of Lynch's *Through Troubled Waters* (1885) and George Moore's *A Drama in Muslin* (1886) illuminates the mutual preoccupations of two authors who

Irish University Review 50.1 (2020): 230–248
© Edinburgh University Press
www.euppublishing.com/iur

rejected the idealisation of the west of Ireland, critiqued the grip of the Catholic church, and drew attention to the lack of emancipation and opportunity for education for women and girls in Ireland. Lynch, like her contemporary Jane Barlow, drew the ire of Irish nationalists who accused her of perpetuating Irish stereotypes for the entertainment of a British audience. Lynch's retort to a reviewer in *United Ireland* that *Through Troubled Waters* was 'not written for an English market as the critic must well know. He cannot be so ignorant that I first wrote it for an Irish paper, through which it would more easily reach those so greatly in need of correction', anticipates Joyce's defence of *Dubliners* as a 'moral history' which provided a 'nicely-polished looking-glass' for Irish self-reflection.

Binckes and Laing argue that rather than writing against the nascent cultural revival of the 1880s and early 1890s, Lynch was writing for a different kind of renaissance, 'one that was woman-centred and required an awakening to certain realities in Ireland before cultural transformation could take place'. Such a position, they suggest, aligns her with Emily Lawless and Jane Barlow, as well as with James Joyce and George Moore, all of whom were ambivalent about the direction of the literary revival, but whose writing 'contributed to and embodied that revival'.

A third chapter on the literary coteries of London and Paris delivers a lively account of the women-centred networks which provided Lynch with the intellectual and emotional sustenance that allowed her to build a life and career in Paris and to write with authority about French literature and culture, in particular in her Paris Letters for the *Academy* in the 1890s, in which she reflected on the key issues and topics of the day including Irish national identity, imperialism, feminism, women's writing, and the state of modern literature.

There is a fascinating account of the Dreyfus affair which convulsed *fin de siècle* France. Lynch, a passionate defender of Dreyfus by virtue of her deep opposition to militarism, imperialism, and ideas of racial superiority, found herself at odds with Michael Davitt and other prominent Irish nationalists who she believed had been led into a 'moral blind spot' when their reflexive opposition to the consensus of the pro-Dreyfus British press led them to oppose a figure who in any other circumstances, she argued, they would have vigorously defended. The daughter of a Catholic, Fenian and Young Ireland household declared herself '*anti-Catholique, anti-militariste, anti-nationaliste... je suis très republicaine.*'

A fourth chapter examines Lynch's fertile output of feminist satires from 1896, whose explicitly cosmopolitan and transnational themes and settings interrogate the impact of social status on women's behaviour and the expression and representation of female identity and sexuality. Lynch appropriated and positively glossed the figure of the Irish vagabond to create heroines who crossed geographical and sometimes class barriers, as well as boundaries of acceptable female behaviour. While much of her work in this period was typical of emergent New Women fiction in its treatment of marriage, Binckes and Laing explore Lynch's ambivalence with the position of the Anglo-American New Woman, especially in regard to 'free love', suggesting that she was closer to the more conservative French feminism of the day.

A fifth chapter examines Lynch's substantial corpus of non-fiction travel writing in which architectural and cultural history from Spain to Greece merge. She herself maintained that her work was more than mere journalism, and in 'astutely [bridging] the gap ... between the literary and the popular [she] could and did insert political and social commentary within apparently apolitical pieces'. It is striking, for example, to read today her 1902 essay 'Rebel Catalonia' with the knowledge of the last few years of political turmoil in that region.

The final chapter is a study of Lynch's best-known work, *Autobiography of a Child* (1898), which perplexed contemporary readers with its blurring of the lines between fiction and autobiography and shocked with its account of institutional brutality. Lynch's provocative text – which drew a complaint from the Catholic hierarchy – drew on a wide range of cognate discourses including autobiography and child study, biography, memoir, fiction, *Bildungsroman*, *Künstlerroman*, rebel tale, Gothic thriller, Victorian classic, and fairy tale. In its exploration of childhood and memory, nature and nurture, and gender and nation, Lynch returns to the critique of Catholicism and British imperialism which recurs through her work. It is a valuable contribution to the growing field of Irish childhood studies.

The text of *Hannah Lynch (1859–1904): Irish writer, cosmopolitan, New Woman* is augmented by a comprehensive timeline of her life and works and detailed notes and references which provide a wealth of biographical and bibliographical detail. In short, this rich volume succeeds absolutely in its authors' aspiration that it will take its place in the ongoing reappraisal of the 'centrality and diversity of women's involvement in the literature of a hundred years before' as well as the growing body of scholarship that foregrounds a more complex narrative of the Irish Literary Revival.

Jane Mahony
Trinity College Dublin
DOI: 10.3366/iur.2020.0451

Noreen Doody, *The Influence of Oscar Wilde on W.B. Yeats: 'An Echo of Someone Else's Music'*. London: Palgrave Macmillan, 2018. 340 pages.

At last, here is a book that takes Oscar Wilde seriously: not as an artist, a gay martyr, nor even as a cultural icon, but as a thinker of endlessly generative ideas. How generative may be surmised by this accomplished book by Noreen Doody who, in meticulous detail, traces how Wilde's conceptual images enabled W.B. Yeats to create his own distinctive intellectual vision.

Intelligently organized, each chapter enables the reader to trace in detail the complicated flow of idea-images from Wilde to Yeats. Doody begins with the most concrete grounding of influence: the personal impact of the tall, urbane, successful Wilde on the young and insecure Yeats. They first met (on Wilde's invitation) at the older man's elegant house in London for Christmas dinner in 1888. On that occasion, Wilde read a draft of his essay, 'The Decay of Lying', to the young poet, its words striking a lasting impression.

But why was Yeats able to grasp the importance of Wilde's essay – revolutionary in inverting traditional notions of life and art – when others were not? As Doody explains, Yeats was natively receptive to Wilde's thinking because, as Anglo-Irish Protestant writers in an alien London, each implicitly understood the other's perspective. Whether on the current issues of Irish nationalism or the exceptional nature of the Celtic 'race', both authors were at that time battling English colonial contempt for the Irish – and countering it by subverting and recreating British stereotypes according to their own terms. The ease of their friendship flowed (typically for Dublin) from a similarly warm relationship between their parents: William Wilde being especially fond of 'the Yeatses' – both father and sons. In establishing such a context for mutual trust, both social and political, this chapter is eloquent, extensively researched, and completely convincing.

Once it moves away from the biographical, however, the argument for Wilde's influence is based largely on detailed textual analysis. Three key texts are involved: the essay 'The Decay of Lying'; the long prose letter written from prison (published as *De Profundis*); and Wilde's avant-garde play, *Salome*. In each case, the focus is on the evolution of Yeats's thinking on two key concepts: the mask and the image of the dancer. In procedure, the analysis seems at times relentless and overly forensic: designed to collect, cite, and analyse evidence with a view to an almost legal judgment as to how Yeats would put these idea-images to further use.

Reading these chapters in this way, however, destroys the spirit of these investigations. The method, which seems at first merely repetitious, might more fruitfully be compared to Yeats's own procedure of 'perning': spinning into a kind of vortex, gaining heft at each turn. According to this method, once a source in Wilde is discerned, its appropriation is recorded as spinning out in a circular motion: apparently redundant, but carefully marking how it takes on a new resonance at each turn.

This tracking of Yeats's use of the Wildean mask takes place in two chapters. For the reader, its evolution through the twelve or so versions of his early drama, *The Player Queen*, appears the most daunting. One must have the patience of an embryologist to trace the gradual transformation of Wilde's image into Yeats's potent concept. But such patience is amply repaid. For what these two chapters make clear is, firstly, that for Yeats, Wilde's thinking engenders an almost ceaseless stream of idea-images. And, secondly, they reveal how Yeats, as poet and thinker, exercised a sensibility on which nothing was lost, but, once used, was ultimately transformed. His sheer persistence in making multiple revisions of this (apparently hopeless) drama over nine years (from 1908 to 1917), alone demonstrates a heroic commitment to developing a philosophy by which he could remake himself, both as man and poet. In the end, what Yeats makes of Wilde, both the personality and the work, reveals just how Wilde's presentation of his identity as a performing self – self-made and ultimately, self-unmade – endowed Yeats with a crucial catalyst for generating his own poetic voice.

But 'influence' is a tricky word. While the author makes extensive use of Harold Bloom's theories of how one master shapes another, these are not always convincing. In these first chapters on the mask, where the textual evidence of the impact of Wilde on Yeats is incontrovertible, Doody makes her most compelling case. In the following chapters on *Salome*, her arguments appear less well founded. Even while a chapter is devoted to distinguishing Wilde's *Salome* from its many competitors for Yeats's attention, there are too many other examples to single it out as an exception.

There is also the fatal flaw in the argument: how can 'influence' be attributed when the writer formally rejects it? Or transforms it into its antithesis? As Doody notes, on at least two occasions, Yeats explicitly denied the influence of Wilde – specifically of *Salome*, which he saw twice (once at its first performance in 1905, the second time in 1906) – saying he disliked the play intensely. Are the denials simply a ploy by Yeats, enabling him to claim his idea-images as *sui generis*? Or, as Doody claims, are these denials in fact compelling evidence of Yeats's resistance to Wilde's power as a precursor, both as man and writer? Can it still count as 'influence' if one upends an imaginative concept into its opposite?

It is to the book's credit that it raises such large questions; this is only appropriate, as it is the outcome of a large project, representing the work of a scholarly lifetime. Starting as a doctoral thesis, the book occasionally betrays its origins. But for all such vestiges, there is the immense satisfaction of reading a study with the depth and the breadth of a lifetime's vision and revision – of wide reading, scrupulous research, and equally sustained reflection on the significant issues involved. Any scholar of Wilde or Yeats would be the poorer for not reading this book.

Jerusha McCormack
Beijing Foreign Studies University
DOI: 10.3366/iur.2020.0452

Alan Graham and Scott Eric Hamilton (editors), *Samuel Beckett and the 'State' of Ireland*. Newcastle: Cambridge Scholars Publishing, 2017. 201 pages.

A series of annual conferences under the title of 'Beckett and the State of Ireland' were held at UCD between 2011 and 2013. The much-awaited book with a selection of papers from those gatherings has been published, edited by two of the three organizers of the event, Alan Graham and Scott Eric Hamilton. Feargal Whelan was the third co-organizer.

The most interesting aspect of the volume's structure is that the nine papers of the collection are sandwiched between an introduction by Eoin O'Brien and an afterword by Seán Kennedy. This is very significant in that these two experts represent tradition (O'Brien) and modernity (Kennedy) in Beckett studies. O'Brien was a personal friend of Beckett and his book of photographs, with explanations, comments, and excerpts from Beckett's work, *The Beckett Country* (1986), initiated a new line of inquiry that grounded the author's writing in a particular geography, notably Foxrock, the wealthy Dublin suburb where he grew up, but also the city of Dublin and the nearby Wicklow mountains. It is equally apt that the book closes with a text by Seán Kennedy. He is one of the most respected second-generation scholars working on Beckett: several of his articles are in fact quoted in chapters in this collection, and his *Beckett and Ireland* (2010) has been highly influential in exploring dark aspects of the relationship between the 1969 Nobel Prize winner and his native country. Beckett famously erased most direct references to Ireland in his work, but research by academics such as Kennedy has shown that behind the ethereal background of his plays and novels lies an obsessive concern for Ireland.

The collection opens with Benjamin Keatinge's 'Rethinking Beckettian Displacement: Landscape, Ecology and Spatial Experience'. Keatinge addresses the issue of Beckett as a landscape painter, which demands a close focus on nuances, given the barren and empty landscapes associated with the author. Beckett was particularly sensitive to any tinge of nostalgia in his descriptions of the land of his youth, and this awareness can be appreciated in the taut and terse prose dealing with nature. At the same time, he was keen on the idea of infusing his geographic descriptions with references to the troubled history of Ireland, leading to a dream-like fictional territory, the 'site of historical repression and effacement of unspoken traumas'. The second chapter considers Beckett's misogyny, an aspect of his work that has attracted a great deal of controversy and discussion in the extensive critical literature. However, in '"Like fucking a quag": Exile, Sex and Ireland', Paul Stewart is able to observe the issue from an original perspective: that of Irish male Protestants who felt a decline in their influence within the newly-created State after Partition, and who also saw their masculinity come under pressure. Following this, Stewart explores the psychological trauma related to the abhorrence of women in the early phase of Beckett's literary production, as well as the historical circumstances that surrounded his coming of age as an author.

The third chapter, 'Torture and Trauma in Translation: Beckett's Theatre of Abuse', by Rodney Sharkey, deals with silence, ghosts, and secrets in Beckett's drama. In his plays, Beckett had no intention of offering a catharsis for traumatic events. Rather, according to Sharkey, he pays attention to the performance itself, making the spectator question 'the received notion of theatre as a fundamentally ethical project'. *Catastrophe* and *Not I* are the clearest examples of drama that reflects on torture and abuse, while at the same time rendering the audience complicit in the process by which actors are 'coerced' into interpreting their roles.

In Damien Lennon's *'Ni Trêve à Rien*: Beckett's Poetry of Self-Determination – The mirlitonnades' a convincing attempt is made to draw Beckett's minimalist short poems away from the marginal position they currently occupy in Beckettian criticism. The Mirlitonnades, 'rooted in exile', according to Lennon, also provide a vantage point from which to examine the author's later style. Scott Eric Hamilton, for his part, offers a comprehensive analysis of Beckett's first post-war novel in *'Mercier and Camier*: Narrative, Exile, Myth'. The enigmatic beginning of that novel, in which the narrator makes himself visible for the only time, allows Hamilton to study Beckett's complex prose style after the Second World War: 'The story Beckett creates through the narrator simultaneously creates the narrator through which the story is told.'

Rina Kim explores Beckett's representation of women in 'Psychoanalysis and Ireland in Beckett's Early Fiction' and rightly argues that Beckett's early heroines deviate from the stereotypical characterization of Irish women as suffering individuals longing to be saved. Beckett made ample use of psychological concepts, taken from notes collected through his reading of specialized books, in order to explore in his fiction conflicting aspects of his relationship with women and with Ireland. Following this is Amanda Dennis's chapter, 'On Roaming in *The Lost Ones*: Embodiment and Virtual Space', an erudite study of one of Beckett's most phantasmagorical narratives. Dennis establishes a comparison between the uses of virtual reality and the power of fiction to enhance the interpretation of our surroundings. In this sense, she proposes a reading of Beckett's *The Lost Ones* 'as a dynamic space that *interacts* with the real and, by doing so, destabilizes hierarchies between fictional and actual space'.

Siobhán Purcell presents an equally complex reading of one of Beckett's novels in 'The Defamiliarised Familial: Reading Anomalies, Heredity and Disability in *Watt*'. Here Beckett is shown to be an author who offered representations of disability that were in advance of his time. Writing against the climate of racial purity that had erupted in Europe in the 1930s, in *Watt* Beckett subverted the fear and hidden anxieties concerning degeneration by making dysfunctionality explicitly present, not only in the story, but also in the textual fabric of the novel. In the final essay of the collection, Alan Graham provides a revision of the allusions to the west of Ireland and to Gaelic found in Beckett's oeuvre. The chapter is appropriately entitled '"The skull in Connemara": Beckett, Joyce and the Gaelic West', and through an analysis of examples taken from *Watt*, 'First Love', and *Waiting for Godot*, among others, Graham portrays an author recoiling from the political nationalism of the 'antiquarians'. Meanwhile, Joyce's treatment of the West, notably in *A Portrait*, 'The Dead', and *Ulysses*, is offered as a point of reference from which to consider Beckett's own position on official attempts in his day towards a Gaelic racialization of the country. Contrary to the image of Beckett as a writer inhabiting an ahistorical realm, these chapters testify to the soundness of the historical approach in Beckett studies. The more ground that is covered in tracing the connections between Beckett and Ireland, the more complex a picture emerges, and the current volume is a significant step in this direction.

José Francisco Fernández
University of Almería
DOI: 10.3366/iur.2020.0453

Patrick Lonergan, *Irish Drama and Theatre Since 1950*. London: Methuen Drama, 2019. 263 pages.

At the centre of Patrick Lonergan's valuable new book on Irish drama and theatre since 1950 lies the premise that Irish dramatists over the last seventy years have presented 'their society as something that happens in cycles rather than in linear fashion'. Tying together 'disparate strands' and bringing heretofore 'neglected or unnoticed patterns' into view, Lonergan's aim is 'to reveal traditions and continuities that might not have been sufficiently visible before' and to show how theatre 'form has developed in cycles or waves.'

In his distinctively direct writing style, Lonergan brings these new insights into focus and cogently argues his case by sharing close observations on practices and theatre productions as well as drawing on a broad range of available literature, including his own significant contributions to the discourse – *Theatre and Globalization: Irish Drama in the Celtic Tiger Era* (2009) and *The Theatre and Films of Martin McDonagh* (2012) – as well as an exciting range of archival source material from The Abbey Theatre Digital Archive, the Gate Theatre Digital Archive, and the Taibhdhearc na Gaillimhe archive. Enlivened by evidence from these original sources, Lonergan's study offers a refreshing and revealing new look at the story of modern and contemporary Irish theatre which highlights the important presence and role of women in the shaping of the canon as well as the role of theatre practice (writing, directing, designing, and acting) in the development of form and in initiating 'acts of resistance.'

Chapters delve into the dynamic conversation between distinctively Irish performance practices and an international tradition which consistently fed new modes of exchange between the theatre and its audiences on issues of pressing concern in Ireland. Specific case studies show how international influences opened up new approaches to form and presented alternative possibilities for dramatists to explore prevalent themes and to instigate change. Described in the context of absurdist drama, for example, cyclical violence and narrative repetition in Brendan Behan's *The Hostage* offered a means of breaking a cycle, with identity treated as 'performative' and 'arbitrary' rather than essential. Thus, Lonergan concludes, 'the second renaissance' in Irish drama that began in the 1960s (as proposed by Fintan O'Toole) could not have happened without such developments occurring in the preceding decades.

Elsewhere, Lonergan takes a retrospective look at Irish theatre with new understandings following events such as #WakingTheFeminists and the theatre's responses to the abuses of the Catholic Church (the X Case, the Tuam babies, the Magdalene Laundries). In the chapter on

'Secularization and the "Post-Catholic" in Irish Theatre', examples such as the controversial staging of Tennessee Williams' *The Rose Tattoo* at the Pike Theatre and plays such as *Cock A Doodle Dandy* and *The Bishop's Bonfire* (Sean O'Casey), *An Triail* (Máiréad Ní Ghráda), *The Sanctuary Lamp* (Tom Murphy), *Eclipsed* (Patricia Burke Brogan), and *Pentecost* (Stewart Parker) demonstrate that Irish theatre-makers were not afraid to dismantle and reinvent form, to challenge the authority of the Catholic Church, nor to evade issues surrounding the sectarian divide. Rather, as Lonergan suggests, they exemplified 'how the Irish theatre – or, more frequently, individuals working within the Irish theatre (often in relative isolation) – led the way in exposing truths that would only later be acknowledged, first by the media and then by the state.' Returning to these topics in a later chapter in the book, Lonergan deals more specifically with the issue of difference and shows how various dramatists and theatre makers have manipulated the relationship between form and content to their own advantage to offer multiple meanings to political points of view on sectarianism, sexuality, and migration.

In a chapter on 'Internationalizing Irish Theatre' there is an illuminating overview of the influences of Bertolt Brecht on the director Tomás Mac Anna and writers such as Brian Friel and Tom Murphy as well as the legacies of modern European playwrights (particularly Anton Chekhov) on the work of Marina Carr and Lucy Caldwell. Moving on to explore a gendered perspective on the recycling of familiar Irish images, narratives, and tropes in Irish theatre, Lonergan insists on 'the centrality of feminist theatre-making to the development of the Irish tradition since 1950' and highlights the challenges and barriers faced by women dramatists in adapting work by prominent male authors. In her recycling of Synge's plays and her work with Martin McDonagh, Garry Hynes's oeuvre 'needs to be seen as a form of authorship in its own right', asserts Lonergan. Hynes 'cleared space for the production and reception' of McDonagh's work, and '[h]is success in turn demonstrates how the feminist strategy of rewriting can be appropriated and redeployed in other contexts.'

The literature on Irish theatre has been building steadily since the late 1990s/early 2000s and we now have an excellent body of monographs and collections on the work of individual theatre artists, strands of form, and theatre practice, thematic issues, and theoretical perspectives. Books that provide overviews of specific periods in history are crucial to the discourse in that they not only bring their own findings to the table but they expose avenues for further exploration. *Irish Drama and Theatre Since 1950* is a rich resource in all of these respects. Lonergan's concluding chapter brings the reader up to speed with the impact of the crash on Irish theatre since the 2000s but here, as elsewhere in the book, he identifies gaps that exist in the literature and points towards other potential approaches. At the rear of the book he then makes room for three of these in a carefully selected set of essays on John B. Keane and the art of the amateur (Finian O'Gorman), the history of performance art in Ireland (Áine Phillips), and stage design since the 1950s (Siobhán O'Gorman). As Lonergan himself explains in the introduction to the book, '[t]hese essays are included as having value in their own right but also aim to demonstrate that the history of Irish drama and theatre since 1950 is multifaceted and must continue to be explored'.

Marie Kelly
University College Cork
DOI: 10.3366/iur.2020.0454

James McNaughton, *Samuel Beckett and the Politics of Aftermath*. Oxford: Oxford University Press, 2018. 226 pages.

Derval Tubridy, *Samuel Beckett and the Language of Subjectivity*. Cambridge: Cambridge University Press, 2018. 221 pages.

When Beckett was lecturing on the theatre of Jean Racine in Trinity College Dublin, he repeatedly told his students that politics were irrelevant to the French playwright's plays: 'Politics ... hardly mentioned', one of his students duly noted down. For many years, the same attitude has been taken towards Beckett's own work, but James McNaughton's *Samuel Beckett and the Politics of Aftermath* successfully challenges the critical commonplace that Beckett's oeuvre is apolitical. McNaughton is convincing in his central claim that Beckett's work has a 'political intelligence' that deserves our critical attention. Key to this is Beckett's irony: McNaughton contends that the erasures of Beckett's work are not a retreat from history, but instead confront the reader with his protagonists' own evasions of historical calamity.

Precisely which histories are in question here? The archival backbone to McNaughton's study is provided by Beckett's 'German Diaries', taken in 1936–7 as Beckett toured Nazi Germany. The critical concept of 'aftermath' – developed in the introduction as a way of addressing how Beckett refigures Irish political history in *More Pricks than Kicks*, later expanded to address the idea that all of Beckett's work is locked into a version of the 'said before' – allows McNaughton to thread this archival source through the book, notably providing the backdrop to his readings of *Watt* and *Malone Dies*.

It also allows McNaughton to pose important questions about the political interpretation of art. How do allusions, archival material, and the relation between form and (often erased) political content function in an oeuvre like Beckett's? Adorno here comes into play as a key part of the argument. McNaughton uses newly available archival material to hone Adorno's sometimes 'vague' readings of Beckett's politics, making hay out of Beckett's draft reference to the German *'Eintopf'* (a one-pot stew promoted by the Nazis and reluctantly swallowed by Beckett during his time there), a precursor of Watt's famous 'pot'. Yet, even allowing for Adorno's claim that '[t]he unsolved antagonisms of reality return in artworks as immanent problems of form', some of the interpretations here feel strained. Following a compelling reading of the abattoir in Beckett's prose, and claiming that *The Unnamable* addresses the logic of the abattoir in the Second World War concentration camps, McNaughton opens up his argument to alternative interpretations: '[w]e should feel some resistance to this reading'. Certainly, he is right that Beckett's critique of specific instances of cruelty (and our ignorance of them) goes beyond universal, existentialist statements of the human condition. But interpretations which seek to reconnect Beckett's works to history always run the risk of closing the gap between work and world too suddenly. So for instance, the presence of house fires and state executions in Beckett's early story 'Dante and the Lobster' does not, for this reader, provide enough evidence that the story is rehearsing the atrocities of the Irish Civil War. At the same time, McNaughton is surely right that 'Beckett's work is radically sensitive and deeply attuned to the ethical stakes of universalizing, fictionalizing, or aestheticizing specific history'. His compelling readings of Beckett's early and mid-career writing will stimulate further important debates regarding the precise contours of Beckett's political aesthetic.

Though his book concludes with a reading of famine politics in *Endgame*, McNaughton elsewhere promises an investigation into the politics of Beckett's later work, mentioning specifically the theme of torture. It would be valuable to see how the concept of 'aftermath' works within the later limits of Beckettian subtraction.

Derval Tubridy's *Samuel Beckett and the Language of Subjectivity* takes up these very themes of torture and violence in Beckett's later works. Using as her philosophical lynchpin the centrality of aporia to Beckett's work, Tubridy starts with *Watt* and delineates the ethical implications of the construction and dissolution of subjectivity in Beckett's postwar theatre and prose. As Tubridy notes, subjectivity is particularly complex in more than one tongue, a fact which 'further complicates the already uncertain status of the voice that speaks in Beckett's writing'. This comes from Tubridy's analysis of *The Unnamable*, a novel which sets the stage for the later play *Not I*, as Tubridy strikingly demonstrates in her comparative analysis of the linguistic rhythm of the English versions of both texts.

While McNaughton reminds us of the material consequences of political rhetoric, Tubridy focusses on the materiality of language as it is spoken in Beckett's texts. She shows how in works like *How It Is* and *What Where*, the body is subjected to violence in vain attempts to speak a subject into being, reminding us of the always embodied nature of language. But this subject is very often disembodied in Beckett's drama. Analysing *Not I*, Tubridy astutely asks: 'Why is this disembodied voice who refuses, or is unable, to say "I" a female voice?' Tubridy's question calls to mind the fact that Beckett's performed voices come to be spoken by women as the embodiment of his protagonists simultaneously became less visible: the invisible Maddy Rooney in his first radio play *All That Fall*; Nell, confined to a bin, in *Endgame*; the mound-bound Winnie in *Happy Days*; W1 stuck in an urn in *Play*. As Tubridy argues, it is crucial the subject is female in works like *Rockaby, Footfalls*, and *Ill Seen Ill Said*. Surely Beckett's minimalism holds part of the answer: Tubridy points out that in *Not I*, attention is drawn to gender 'even when that gender is elided'. Yet this does not account for works such as *All Strange Away* or *Catastrophe* in which the body remains stubbornly gendered.

Tubridy's chapters begin with in-depth theorizations or historicizations of the topic at hand – frequently challenging the reader with the sheer number of critics rolled out to mark the critical field – before diving into close textual analyses of Beckett's works. The book is at its strongest when these historicizing and theorizing strands overlap, as when she roots her comparative analysis of Beckett and the Marquis de Sade in Beckett's engagement with the work of Maurice Blanchot. Blanchot provides the philosophical underpinning as Tubridy sets up her concluding argument that the origin of Beckett's writing comes from an embodied void. Can such a reading have political purchase? In her conclusion, having shown convincingly how the impurity of utterance shadows Beckett's work (a running theme is the persistent infiltration of any self by its other), Tubridy turns to Badiou's 'pure point of enunciation' as a means of opening up her argument to future development. But in following Badiou's shift from epistemology to ontology, one risks passing over the very materiality of subjectivity which Tubridy so successfully foregrounds elsewhere in the book.

For example, Tubridy rightly points out that '[t]he distinctly Irish connotations of Molloy and Malone and the linguistic punning of Watt and Knott give way to the austere simplicity of the single sound of Pim and Bom, Krim and Kram'. Yet it is not true that these latter names contain 'no referential connections'. Instead, they bear resonances from within and beyond the Beckettian oeuvre. Beckett refers to the Stalinist clowns Bim and Bom in drafts of *Fin de partie* and *Godot*, also using them in his early short prose and *Murphy*, where they are nicknames for sadistic asylum nurses. Far from refuting Tubridy's analysis, these intertextual and historical connections seem to support her assertion of the violence of language in *How It Is* and its interrelatedness with particular kinds of subjects, gendered, material, in various states of (dis)embodiment. In drawing our attention to the self as a linguistically, materially constituted entity in Beckett's writing, Tubridy's book deepens our appreciation of the ethics and politics of his work.

James Little
Charles University, Prague
DOI: 10.3366/iur.2020.0455

Christina Morin, *The Gothic Novel in Ireland, c. 1760–1829*. Manchester: Manchester University Press, 2018. 235 pages.

The Gothic Novel in Ireland, c. 1760–1829 aims to 'widen and broaden the boundaries of Irish gothic literature within the remit of both Irish and gothic studies'. Morin's introduction aligns her methodology with Franco Moretti's quantitative approach to nineteenth-century literary production and its goal of overturning traditional emphasis on individual canonical texts at the expense of their overlooked contemporary counterparts. In doing so, the introduction makes a compelling case for a combined quantitative and qualitative methodology that balances detailed close readings of individual works with a broader bibliographic overview of Irish gothic fiction in the Romantic period. The innovative approach of the work – which includes tables, charts, and maps alongside a valuable 'working bibliography' of 114 works of Irish gothic fiction published between 1762 and 1829 – serves to 'evidence the cultural amnesia that continues to shape and inform our interpretations of Irish literary production' in the period, revealing the literary gothic as a category perceived by both contemporary writers and readers as 'broad, formally and generically porous'.

This consideration of generic permeability forms the basis of the first two chapters of the book, in which Morin successfully undertakes a dismantling of the 'restrictive, largely artificial, formal, and generic categorisations that have hindered a full comprehension of Irish and gothic literature of this period'. Chapter 1 challenges critical perceptions of Thomas Leland's *Longsword, Earl of Salisbury* (1762) and Horace Walpole's *The Castle of Otranto* (1764) as the respective pioneers of the historical and gothic novel. Morin follows an established line of argument in the assertion that these modes cannot be read as inherently distinct fictional forms before moving on to the more illuminating contention that there is a 'continuity between the historical gothic fictions of the latter half of the eighteenth century and those of [Walter] Scott and his Irish contemporaries'. Chapter 2 extends this reassessment of generic categories with an engaging account of the contemporary terminology employed to indicate fictional works that we, as twenty-first century readers, have come to think of as gothic. Morin's account of the ubiquity of the term 'romance' as a generic indicator for Irish gothic novels presents a nuanced reading of these works as a self-conscious formal antithesis to eighteenth-century realism. This analysis offers both a suggestive account of the generic origins of the gothic supernatural and a valuable insight into the disparity between Romantic-period perceptions of genre and the artificial practice of modern generic labelling.

Morin's disruption of these 'defined formal, generic, stylistic, and narratological boundaries' extends to the 'deceptively smooth account' that defines Romantic-period gothic writing as 'a largely Anglo-centric phenomenon'. The final section of chapter 2 mounts a challenge to scholarly conceptions of 'Irish Romanticism as dominated by regional, national, and historical literary forms that rose to prominence in the years surrounding Anglo-Irish Union'. Morin argues that these forms – among them the canonical national tales of Maria Edgeworth, Sydney Owenson, and Charles Maturin – find their genesis in an earlier tradition of gothic fiction, making a persuasive case for the intersection of historical, national, and gothic modes and proposing a fertile tradition of Irish gothic Romanticism stretching back to the mid-eighteenth century. The analysis of gothic geographies in the third chapter provides new readings of a range of Irish gothic novels, including a compelling account of the Irish landscapes and 'English geography of terror' in the fiction of Elizabeth Griffith. These readings overturn assumptions that gothic fiction is characterised by the medieval Catholic continental settings of its canonical figureheads, revealing a hitherto unacknowledged phenomenon of Irish gothic novels that transplant the 'geographical otherness of exotic locations' to modern-day Ireland and England. These geographical and temporal shifts appear to 'exonerate Ireland from contemporary accusations of savagery linked to the "Celtic Fringe"', instead 'symbolically re-locating barbarism and savagery from Ireland and the Continent' to a violent and irrational gothic England. This engaging of new material reveals a tradition of gothic novels participating in a process of Irish cultural self-fashioning commonly identified with the national tale.

The final section of chapter three reads depictions of travel in Irish gothic fiction as a form of transnational cultural encounter. This is a somewhat brief but rich section of the book that makes an excellent case for future research that might build on Morin's analysis and the earlier work of scholars of the national tale including Miranda Burgess, Claire Connolly, and Julia M. Wright. The focus on the transnational range of Irish gothic fiction finds its fullest expression in the fourth and final chapter, which describes the material and 'textual placement' of the fiction of Regina Maria Roche as 'indicative of the geographical and ideological reach and impact of Irish gothic literary production' in the Romantic period. This chapter makes a series of original and engaging points that significantly expand our current understanding of Romantic-period print culture. Through the case study of Roche, Morin presents new insights into the 'imaginative and physical migration' of Irish authors following the devastating impact of the Act of Union on the Irish print industry and into the 'transcontinental and transatlantic connections' that enabled dissemination and reprinting of Minerva Press works across Europe, the Americas, and the British colonies. This fascinating account serves to underpin a wider argument about the bibliographic spread of Irish gothic fiction as part of a process of cultural transfer facilitated by emergent international networks of literary production.

Morin's revisionist study successfully dismantles long-held critical assumptions about both gothic and Irish fiction in the Romantic period. The close analysis of a range of Irish gothic novels uncovers the cultural and aesthetic significance of works hitherto denied scholarly attention on account of their status as disreputable minor literary productions, thus broadening and extending a body of recent work by critics such as Elizabeth Neiman and Franz Potter that contests existing models of gothic canonicity. This book also suggest new lines of enquiry into the workings of Romantic fiction in its uncovering of a self-conscious experimental approach to genre so often assumed to be the exclusive province of Romantic poetry. *The Gothic Novel in Ireland, c. 1760–1829* is an original and innovative intervention in the study of the novel that widens and deepens our understanding of fiction in the Romantic period, making it essential reading for scholars in the fields of Irish literature, gothic studies, and Romantic-era print culture.

Nicky Lloyd
Bath Spa University
DOI: 10.3366/iur.2020.0456

Philip O'Leary, *An Underground Theatre: Major Playwrights in the Irish Language, 1930–80*. Dublin: University College Dublin Press, 2017. 383 pages.

Philip O'Leary's most recent book, *An Underground Theatre*, examines the work of five major playwrights in the Irish language and their contribution to the Irish stage. Adding to his series on the Irish prose of the Revival and post-Revival years, this study gives centre stage to Irish drama, an oft-neglected branch of the Irish literary arts. While Irish poetry and prose fiction have developed at a steady pace since the Revival, drama has had more difficulty in successfully choreographing all the moving parts necessary for theatre – playwrights, a dedicated theatre space, directors and producers, competent actors, and, crucially, a dependable audience. These difficulties have restricted the growth of Irish drama and O'Leary contends that theatre in Irish was for much of the twentieth century an 'underground' art. The introduction to this book gives an overview of the history of Irish drama and the many challenges it faced, highlighting the 'marginal and frequently ignored role of theatre in Irish in the cultural life of the nation'. Pádraig Ó Siadhail made a similar observation in the opening lines of his pioneering study on the history of Irish language drama, *Stair Dhrámaíocht na Gaeilge 1930–80* (1993):

> Is í an drámaíocht an ghné is laige de ealaíona na Gaeilge. Tosaíodh ar an drámaíocht Ghaeilge a shaothrú den chéad uair ag tús na haoise seo mar chuid d'Athbheochan na Gaeilge, ach tar éis breis is nócha bliain, tá drámaíocht na Gaeilge ar fhorimeall shaol na Gaeilge go fóill.

> Drama is the weakest of the Irish arts. Irish drama first began to be developed at the beginning of the century as part of the Irish revival, but more than ninety years later, drama in Irish remains on the periphery of Irish-language life. (My translation)

Aside from Ó Siadail's history, there have been few full-length studies on Irish drama or dramatists. This new research by O'Leary aims to redress that imbalance and 'pay overdue attention to the work created for the stage by the most significant and influential Gaelic playwrights' in the fifty year period of the study. The five playwrights in question are Máiréad Ní Ghráda (1896–1971); Séamus Ó Néill (1910–81); Eoghan Ó Tuairisc (1919–82); Seán Ó Tuama (1926–2006); and Críostóir Ó Floinn (b. 1927). With a chapter dedicated to each playwright, O'Leary discusses their plays in chronological order and gives a summary of their critical reception, drawing extensively on contemporary reviews. He also gives details of the initial production and any revivals, along with an analysis of the plot. O'Leary's meticulous research and dedication to archival work help to flesh out the study and to contextualise the plays. He is to be especially commended on this attempt to capture something of the performances, rather than relying solely on the scripts.

The chapter on Máiréad Ní Ghráda, perhaps the most famous of the chosen playwrights, gives an insightful and comprehensive account of her contribution to Irish theatre. *An Triail*'s importance in the history of Irish plays cannot be in any doubt, and it is still frequently produced (most recently by Fibín and Aisling Ghéar). It was wonderful, however, to see her early one-act-plays and the sharp and witty political drama *Breithiúnas* receive long over-due recognition. Séamus Ó Néill's substantial and ambitious body of work is given careful consideration in the next chapter. Plays based on early Irish literature, on Irish and European history, and even a thriller of sorts are in the mix here and the sheer variety is impressive. Eoghan Ó Tuairisc's path from panto to tragedy is charted in Chapter 3, and it is interesting to note that O'Leary rates the Civil War based tragedy *Lá Fhéile Míchíl* as 'one of the finest plays in the Gaelic repertoire'. He makes a similar case for the masterful *Gunna Cam agus Slabhra Óir*'s status in the canon of Irish drama, though it doesn't appear to have been on stage since 1968. Finally, the prolific bilingual playwright Críostóir Ó Floinn is discussed, in a chapter that challenges previous critical commentary on his plays.

Though each chapter deals with a different playwright, we also get an insight into the context in which the work was written, and the institutions and producers who encouraged and in some cases collaborated with them in staging their work. Thus, the remarkable contribution and formative influence of Tomás Mac Anna is a recurring feature of the history of these playwrights. We see the central role he played in shaping Ní Ghráda's early one-act-plays and directing her groundbreaking *An Triail* (1964):

> Her interest in blending experimentation with a tested practical approach to crafting effective plays was only confirmed by her work with Tomás Mac Anna, another theatrical innovator willing to try anything he knew or thought would work on stage ... It was this commonsensical commitment to putting on a good show that made soulmates of Ní Ghráda and Mac Anna and kept their collaboration so successful for nearly two decades.

Mac Anna's understanding of stagecraft also shows in the chapter on Ó Tuairisc and there are interesting insights into the apprenticeship

Ó Tuairisc served writing bilingual pantomimes in the Abbey and the skills he gained from these shows:

> Tomás directed the whole thing. He sitting at a table at the side of the stage, his secretary beside him taking notes, some scene being rehearsed, people here and there rehearsing dances, or at the piano with Seán Ó Riada rehearsing songs, a man in one corner learning how to walk on stilts, two in another corner learning Irish ... myself in a separate nook on the stage writing hurriedly whatever was needed for the scene that was being put together. A call from Tomás: Ó Tuairisc, six lines for the giant Polyphemus. Verse please. And make it funny.

Mac Anna appears in a less positive role in the chapter on Críostóir Ó Floinn, as artistic director of the Abbey. Ó Floinn's fraught relationship with the national theatre and the resentment caused by the rejection of several of his plays highlight the difficulties sometimes experienced by playwrights in getting their work staged. Indeed, five plays published by Ó Floinn are discussed in this chapter, though they have never been produced. In one regard, it is difficult to defend their inclusion, yet in another way these scripts – with dialogue never once uttered on stage – speak volumes of a faltering and dysfunctional theatrical tradition. Those who did succeed in getting their work staged some-times faced other challenges – actors without the necessary competence in the Irish language to speak fluently, and poor audience numbers. The inclusion of a Gaeltacht-based playwright, might have offered a different perspective on these challenges, as although there may not have been a purpose-built professional theatre in rural Gaeltacht areas, there were native Irish-speaking actors and enthusiastic audiences. Some of the more recent Connemara Gaeltacht playwrights are mentioned in the thought-provoking Afterword – including Antaine Ó Flatharta, Joe Steve Ó Neachtain, Micheál Ó Conghaile, Breandán Ó hEaghra, and Darach Ó Scolaí – though I was somewhat surprised at the omission of Johnny Chóil Mhaidhc (Seán Ó Coisdealbha).

An Underground Theatre is an important publication – a fitting tribute to the chosen playwrights and many others in the theatre community. It will be an invaluable resource for academics but I would also hope that theatre practitioners might find something of interest in it. Perhaps then it might encourage a revival of some of the works cited and a resurrection of some of these buried scripts from the subterranean world described in O'Leary's study.

Éadaoin Ní Mhuircheartaigh
Dublin City University
DOI: 10.3366/iur.2020.0457